PROGRAMMING
USING
TURBO
PASCAL

THE PWS-KENT SERIES IN COMPUTER SCIENCE

Advanced Structured BASIC: File Processing with the IBM PC, Payne

Assembly Language for the PDP-11: RT-RSX-UNIX, Second Edition, Kapps and Stafford

Data Structures, Algorithms, and Program Style, Korsh

Data Structures, Algorithms, and Program Style Using C, Korsh and Garrett

FORTRAN 77 for Engineers, Borse

FORTRAN 77 and Numerical Methods for Engineers, Borse

Logic and Structured Design for Computer Programmers, Rood

Microprocessor Systems Design: 68000 Hardware, Software, and Interfacing, Clements

Modula-2, Beidler and Jackowitz

Problem Solving with Pascal, Brand

Problem Solving Using Pascal: Algorithm Development and Programming Concepts, Skvarcius

Programming Using Turbo Pascal, Riley

Structured BASIC for the IBM PC with Business Applications, Payne

Structured Programming in Assembly Language for the IBM PC, Runnion

Turbo Pascal for the IBM PC, Radford and Haigh

Using BASIC: An Introduction to Computer Programming, Third Edition, Hennefeld

Using Microsoft and IBM BASIC: An Introduction to Computer Programming, Hennefeld

VAX Assembly Language and Architecture, Kapps and Stafford

John H. Riley, Jr.
**Bloomsburg University
of Pennsylvania**

*PROGRAMMING
USING
TURBO
PASCAL*

PWS-KENT Publishing Company
Boston

PWS-KENT
Publishing Company

20 Park Plaza
Boston, Massachusetts 02116

PWS-Kent Publishing Company is a division of Wadsworth, Inc.

Library of Congress Cataloging-in-Publication Data

Riley, John H.
    Programming using Turbo Pascal.

    Bibliography: p.
    Includes index.
    1. PASCAL (Computer program language)   2. Turbo
Pascal (Computer program)   I. Title.
QA76.73.P2R53   1987   005.26   86-21239
ISBN 0-87150-088-4

Printed in the United States of America

    88   89   90   91 — 10 9 8 7 6 5 4 3 2

Sponsoring Editor: Bob Prior
Editorial Assistant: Kathleen Tibbetts
Production Coordinator: Jean Coulombre
Production: Carnes Publication Services, Inc./Edward C. Huddleston
Interior and Cover Design: Jean Coulombre
Cover Photo: Courtesy of French Railways—Lamber
Typesetting: Maryland Composition
Cover Printing: New England Book Components
Printing and Binding: R. R. Donnelley & Sons Company

To my family,
Joyce, John and Paul

PROGRAMMING USING TURBO PASCAL was designed to support a course similar to CS1 of the ACM Curriculum '78 guidelines and, as such, provides the student with a solid foundation in programming. This means the ability to write clear, understandable, and correct programs. Working with programs (creating new programs and modifying and maintaining old ones) is at the center of computing and any student in this discipline must learn to program well.

At the same time, I did not want a book that was merely a "how to use TURBO Pascal" book. I wanted a book that taught programming and served as an introduction to computer science. There are many places in this book where my experiences teaching upper-level courses (for example, data structures, file processing, programming languages) influenced the presentation of topics, and I have tried to anticipate the needs of other courses and topics in computer science. With these goals in mind this book has both a practical and an academic flavor.

This book is based on the implementation of Pascal for microcomputers called TURBO Pascal (produced by Borland International, Inc.). While no programming environment is perfect, TURBO is a very good one for learning Pascal and programming with a minimum of headaches.

TURBO Pascal provides almost all of the features of standard Pascal, plus a great many more. However, with the exception of strings, this book adheres to the features of standard Pascal. The string facilities of TURBO make it possible to work with non-numeric data early without struggling through the details of working with strings (packed arrays of characters) of standard Pascal. I have given detailed expla-

PREFACE

nations of all the elements of the language used and have provided many examples for clarification.

No mathematical training beyond high school algebra and a little geometry is assumed. Good writing habits may be more helpful than extensive mathematical training. Programming is hard, intellectual work that requires thinking, analysis, and synthesis. I hope that these skills will be amplified by using this text. Learning to program well is difficult yet the satisfaction gained can be great.

There are a number of features included in *PROGRAMMING USING TURBO PASCAL* that I consider outstanding and that distinguish this book from others:

- ○ The importance of careful program development is emphasized throughout the book. In particular, the two case studies, Chapters 9 and 13, detail how larger programs are slowly and methodically built.

- ○ A considerable number of carefully chosen working programs are included. All the programs in the book have been run, and output is given for most of them.

- ○ I have provided a large number of exercises. In addition to programming assignments, a variety of exercises enhances understanding of the concepts that underlie programming.

- ○ The appendices provide concise summaries of useful information such as TURBO system commands, operating system commands, editing commands, and so on.

The following conventions are used in the text. References are enclosed in square brackets ([ ]). All program file names are of the form CHmEXn.PAS, which stands for CHapter m, EXample program n. After the concept of the reserved word has been introduced all reserved words in the programs are capitalized. I have written the programs in a consistent style and a discussion of alternatives is contained in Appendix H.

ACKNOWLEDGMENTS

It would be impossible to acknowledge all the people who have taught me enough to be able to write this book. I have learned a great deal from my colleagues and I thank them all. I want to thank all of my students; they have educated me as much as I have educated them. The reviewers who read preliminary versions of the book made many valuable comments. They pointed out problems that I might not otherwise have noticed. My thanks go to: Randolph Forsstrom, Bergen Community College; Robert M. Holloway, University of Wisconsin–Madison; Joseph Hyman, El Camino College; William Jones, California State University–Dominguez Hills; J. Mailen Kootsey, Duke University; Connie Lightfoot, Taylor

University; Michael G. Main, University of Colorado–Boulder; J. Richard Rinewalt, Texas Christian University; R. Waldo Roth, Taylor University; and Phyllis Ann Williams, East Stroudsburg University. Their work is greatly appreciated.

My thanks also go to PWS Publishers, especially Bob Prior, for making this book a reality. Above all, I wish to thank my wife, Joyce. She read the first (and worst!) version of the book and made many suggestions in light of her own teaching experience. She also proofread later versions. Finally, she bore with me throughout the writing period. I am most grateful for her support.

All of these people have helped to prevent and eliminate mistakes in the book. Whatever errors remain are my responsibility. After all, I put them there in the first place. ❏

J.H.R., Jr.

CONTENTS

INTRODUCTION

In this chapter we attempt to provide an overview of the notions we will encounter in the course of this book, what we hope to accomplish, and our perspective on programming. This is done at a fairly general level. We consider programming to be very important and an interesting task. As a consequence, programming can be very rewarding. We hope that this book will assist you in becoming a good programmer and that you will learn to enjoy programming.

Programming is at the heart of many activities in the field of computing. Thus it is necessary to learn to program as the first step into the realm of computing. Although Pascal is the language used throughout this book, we believe that the techniques presented will be useful in doing all types of programming.

This chapter also discusses the task of problem solving in the context of programming. Problem solving is central to programming. It is impossible to give precise rules for solving problems. We will give some guidelines. Doing problems and seeing how others solve problems is probably the best way to become a good problem solver. The book by George Polya ([Po]) is a good reference for problem-solving techniques. ☐

CHAPTER 1

ON PROGRAMMING, LANGUAGES, AND PASCAL

1.1 WHAT IS PROGRAMMING?

Roughly speaking, programming is the activity which produces instructions for accomplishing some task. A program is the set of instructions produced as a result of this activity. In the latter half of the twentieth century, programming and programs in this sense usually imply the use of a computer (an electronic digital device). In particular, programming has come to mean programming or instructing a computer—i.e., providing the computer with a description of the steps to be taken to accomplish a given task. Before giving the computer a program it is necessary to describe how to accomplish the task. We shall use the word *algorithm* when our attention is focused more on describing the means of accomplishing some task than on instructing a computer. Sometimes, we will begin programming by fashioning an algorithm which will become the basis for our program.

DEFINITION

> An *algorithm* is a set of instructions for accomplishing some task. An algorithm is unambiguous, effective, and terminating (finite).

The words *unambiguous* and *terminating* are crucial in this definition. For example, the instruction "Add a little salt" in a recipe is ambiguous ("No, not that much salt!"). Similarly, instructions must lead to completion. There is a big difference between "Keep making left turns around the block" and "Keep making left turns around the block until you come to the bakery." Following the first instruction will make you very tired and hungry. Following the second will get you to a place where you can appease your hunger.

DEFINITION

> A (computer) *program* is an algorithm suitable for execution by a computer.

The aim of this book is to instruct the reader in the process of producing programs. Our goal is to enable you to produce programs for getting something done (by a computer). In fact, we are a little more ambitious than that. We want you to become a good programmer and a productive programmer. A good programmer writes good programs. The characteristics of a good program are discussed below. A productive programmer is one who makes good use of his or her time. In the long run, these two issues are not separate. In fact, together they constitute one aspect of what is known as structured programming. The old saw "haste makes waste" applies here. Programmers need to be patient and take the long view. Not doing so leads to long-term inefficiency. Unfortunately, the types of programs one must write as a student as part of the learning process do not possess many of the characteristics of production programs—i.e., programs which are actually used (and which people are paid to write). The differences between programs written by a student and by a professional are enormous. Some of these differences are listed in *FIGURE 1.1*. The techniques that are developed are meant to aid the latter type of programmer. We will always have the latter type of program in mind and be striving to address the issues that are listed in the far right-hand column of *FIGURE 1.1*.

Several things are implied in our discussion of programs and algorithms above.

The first is that there is a task to be accomplished. This task is usually not one of the programmer's choosing. Students are given assignments by instructors, and professionals program to meet users' needs. In both cases, successful accomplishment of the task begins with understanding the question. This is usually harder for the professional than for the student. In either case, not understanding the problem can have disastrous results. It follows that the programmer has a responsibility to find out exactly what is desired. This may require some persistence on the part of the programmer. A particular problem is that the program requestor may overestimate your understanding of his or her problem. It may be quite difficult to get the problem stated explicitly enough for you to program. It is also the case that many people don't understand how difficult it can be to program a computer to accomplish something. Perhaps this will change, but until it does you will be spending time answering "Why can't you just . . . ?" In any case, don't underestimate the importance of finding out exactly what you are supposed to do. (We hope

Differences Between Student and Production Programs		**FIGURE 1.1**

	Student Program	**Production Program**
Development time	Days to weeks	Months to years
People involved	Usually solo, sometimes two or three people	Usually a team (sometimes large), very rarely solo
Problem	Well-defined, explicit, small	Vague, complex, large
Input	Usually limited, correct	Unpredictable
Program life	Week	Years
Maintained, modified	Rarely	Almost always

the programming assignments in this book are explicit enough, but experience tells us not to be too optimistic.)

The second implication is that a program must accomplish the task—or, more precisely, that a computer executing the program must accomplish the task. This means that the program must produce the correct results and that it must be evident that it will produce the correct results. Briefly, a program must work and must be able to be seen to work. Although this seems obvious, many students attempt to program by guessing or by trial and error. This is unacceptable. First of all, arriving at a program in this manner takes longer and hence is counterproductive. Secondly, programs are too important to leave to chance. Programmers must know what their programs are doing. Although this may take the suspense out of programming ("Let's run it and see what happens"), it should give rise to some semblance of quality assurance, a characteristic often ignored by programmers.

To achieve these ends it is necessary that the program model, as faithfully as possible, the process that is being automated. If this is done, the program is more likely to produce the desired results. In case of discrepancies between the program and reality, it will also be possible to find where these discrepancies arise. Finally, doing this will enable the programmer to modify the program to reflect changes in the process with ease. A programmer ignores this guideline at great peril.

1.2   WHAT IS A PROGRAMMING LANGUAGE?

This book is about programming and the programming language Pascal. It is expected that you will program in other languages as well. (You may in fact have already programmed in another language.) You should be able to use some of the ideas and techniques you learn here when using these other languages. Part of one's appreciation for exactly what Pascal is and does stems from studying other languages. All programming languages fit the following definition.

DEFINITION

> A *programming language* is a set of notations and rules for combining the notations which are used to communicate algorithms.

Two words in this definition are especially worth noting. The first is *algorithm*, which we have discussed above. The second is *communicate*.

Communication implies that there is a sender and a receiver. In the case of programs there are two different classes of "intelligences" which must receive and understand the program. The first class consists of people who work with the program. The second class consists of computers which must actually carry out the program. Unfortunately, the two classes are radically different in the ways in which they operate. Humans are very good at seeing the overall picture and making inferences about the general nature of what is to be done. However, we are terrible with details and very slow in dealing with them. For example, we understand the ideas of arithmetic much better than we deal with long addition. Computers, on the other hand, are very good and incredibly fast in handling details ("high-speed idiots"), but they are completely unable to deal with new situations. All programming languages are designed so that both humans and computers can "understand" the programs written using them. Necessarily, this involves a great deal of compromise. The first programming languages were oriented almost entirely toward the computer. Later languages moved toward human comprehension (these are called high-level languages). It is interesting to speculate whether it will ever be possible to use a computer with a natural language.

1.3 ON SYNTAX AND SEMANTICS

All languages have two aspects: syntax and semantics.

> The *syntax* of a language is the set of formal rules determining the valid constructions of that language.

DEFINITION

> The *semantics* of a language are the rules determining the meanings (effects) of valid constructions of that language.

DEFINITION

It would be very difficult to specify the entire syntax of the English language (although there is general agreement on whether a specific sentence is syntactically correct). It would be impossible to give the semantics of English. Many sentences cannot be given unambiguous meanings. For example, does the sentence "The chicken is ready to eat" refer to a hungry fowl or a cooked fowl? Programming languages differ from natural languages in these regards. First, they tend to be small and can actually have their syntax entirely specified. Second, their semantics are totally unambiguous, the computer being a perfect (and final) arbiter of meaning. However, it may not be apparent what the meaning of a particular (legal) construct is from a book or a manual. For this reason it is sometimes necessary to "ask" the computer what the meaning of some statement is by using it in a small test program. It is infinitely better to do this as an experiment in an isolated and safe way than in a program in which the effect of the statement may be disguised or, worse yet, disastrous. Good programmers learn to write small programs to uncover meaning, to assure themselves of their own understanding, and to double-check manuals. Some of the exercises in this book are designed to get you into this habit.

A variety of means will be used to convey the syntax and semantics of Pascal. English prose and examples will always be present. Occasionally, flowcharts will be used for purposes of illustration. A very effective means of conveying syntax is the syntax diagram. A syntax diagram is a diagram which illustrates the way in which a valid construct may be formed. It consists of arrows which indicate the direction through the diagram and words or symbols. These are used to form the construct or refer to other syntax diagrams.

FIGURE 1.2 gives the syntax diagrams necessary to form a few English sentences. The first diagram indicates that a Sentence consists of a subject and a predicate followed by a period. A Subject is defined in the second diagram as being either a noun phrase or a pronoun. The two paths through the diagram indicate a choice. Similarly, a Noun phrase is defined as the word THE followed by an adjective followed by either the word BOY or the word GIRL. An Adjective can be a number of things. The straight line across the top indicates that it may consist of nothing. The diagram also indicates that either BIG or GOOD may be used as an Adjective. The loop below BIG signifies that either GOOD or BIG may be followed by a comma and then either GOOD or BIG. This looping may be done repeatedly. Thus an Adjective may be nothing, or "GOOD", or "BIG", or "GOOD, BIG", or "BIG, GOOD", or "GOOD, GOOD", or "BIG, BIG", or "GOOD, GOOD, BIG", and so on. It is understood that the looping cannot go on indefinitely. Finally we see that a Predicate consists of the word RAN or the word ATE followed by nothing or by the word SLOWLY or by the word QUICKLY. It would have been possible to define Predicate using Verb and Adverb and then defining Verb and Adverb appropriately. This is typical. It is usually possible to give rise to the same syntax with different syntax diagrams. The sentence "HE RAN QUICKLY" is derived as follows:

```
                       Sentence

          Subject    Predicate    .

          Pronoun    RAN QUICKLY .

               HE    RAN QUICKLY .
```

It should be noted that syntax diagrams usually need to be supplemented by other qualifications. For example, the syntax diagrams of *FIGURE 1.2* generate sentences of almost any length (by looping through the definition of Adjective). This could be resolved easily by stating that no sentence can contain more than eight words. Expressing this in a syntax diagram would be very difficult.

We will use syntax diagrams to define the syntax of Pascal. Appendix E contains syntax diagrams for TURBO Pascal. We urge you to get into the habit of referring to these diagrams to resolve questions of syntax. They frequently are all that is needed to answer simple questions.

Syntax Diagrams for Some Simple Sentences

FIGURE 1.2

Sentence

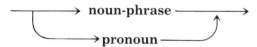

Subject

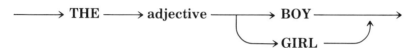

Noun phrase

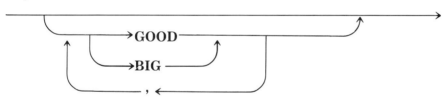

Adjective

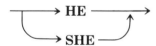

Pronoun

Predicate

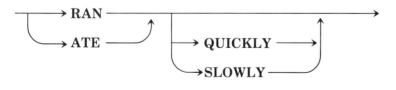

For example, the syntax diagrams of *FIGURE 1.2* can be used to see that "GIRL ATE SLOWLY" is incorrect because the word GIRL must be preceded by the word THE. However, if the sentences of *FIGURE 1.2* are limited by requiring them to have no more than eight words, the syntax diagrams will not indicate the error in "THE GOOD, GOOD, GOOD, BIG, BIG BOY ATE SLOWLY."

1.4   ON PASCAL

Pascal is a programming language which was invented by Niklaus Wirth in 1968. The book by Kathleen Jensen and Wirth [J-W] gives the original definition of the language as well as some insights as to its motivations. Wirth named his new language after the French mathematician Blaise Pascal (1623-1662), who invented a machine for doing arithmetic in 1642. Pascal is considered to be a high-level language—that is, it is oriented toward human comprehension. You will find, however, that it is certainly not a natural language. *FIGURE 1.3* is an example of a Pascal program.

If you examine the program in *FIGURE 1.3* you will probably conclude that it has something to do with a circle and its area, circumference, and radius. In fact, this is correct. The program gets (inputs or reads) the radius of a circle, calculates its area and circumference, and then displays (outputs or writes) the results.

Wirth designed Pascal to be a language for teaching computer science. We believe that it provides a solid foundation for serious programming and the study of computer science. Pascal has the additional virtue of being a relatively small language and at the same time a very expressive

FIGURE 1.3 | **A Simple Pascal Program**

```
PROGRAM Circle ( Input, Output );

{  This is a short program illustrating Pascal.

       Author    : John Riley
       Date      : March 2, 1986
       File name : CH1EX1.PAS
}

CONST
       Pi = 3.14159;

VAR
       Area,
       Circumference,
       Radius          : Real;


BEGIN { Circle }
  Writeln('Enter the radius of a circle');
  Readln(Radius);
  Area := Pi * Sqr(Radius);
  Circumference := 2 * Pi * Radius;
  Writeln('Area of circle : ', Area : 8 : 2);
  Writeln('Circumference  : ', Circumference : 8 : 2)
END. { Circle }
```

and powerful language. An excellent reference for the definition of Pascal is the book by Cooper [Co], which deals with ISO (International Standards Organization) Pascal. A reference for ANSI (American National Standards Institute) Pascal is [IEEE] or [Le].

Unlike many other academic languages, Pascal grew in popularity and began to be used in nonacademic settings. However, it will be a long time before it rivals COBOL or FORTRAN in use. Pascal also provided a basis for the design of Ada, the new language developed by the United States Department of Defense. For all of these reasons, the study of Pascal is advocated.

Pascal, like any other language, becomes useful only when it is implemented—that is, when it can actually be used on a computer. Part of the success of Pascal is due to several excellent implementations. Perhaps the excellence of the implementation can be attributed to the elegance of the language.

We have chosen to concentrate on the implementation of Pascal called TURBO Pascal. TURBO Pascal is produced by Borland International of Scotts Valley, California. Beyond the reasons mentioned above for studying Pascal, TURBO Pascal provides an environment in which the programmer can work productively. This book is intended to be a mixture of theoretical and practical considerations. There are also the advantages of working on microcomputers. TURBO Pascal is available on a wide range of microcomputers. Pascal is a good language for programming these remarkable machines. It is possible that Pascal will come to rival BASIC as a language for microcomputers.

1.5 ON DEVELOPING PROGRAMS

This chapter began with a discussion of algorithms and programs. The process by which these come into being was not indicated. It is possible to break this process into two phases. The first phase can be thought of as the problem-solving stage. The goal of the problem-solving stage is an algorithm. The second stage can be entitled the implementation stage. This stage should produce the program. *FIGURE 1.4* is a diagram of the entire process. As the diagram indicates, these processes are not independent.

When one first begins to program it is very easy to ignore the problem-solving stage, because the problems that are posed are exercises which are designed to familiarize the student with the features of the language. This is unfortunate, because eventually the problem-solving phase becomes the more important phase, and programmers who ignore it lead themselves astray.

> *Problem definition* is the process of specifying the exact requirements of the task at hand, clearly and unambiguously.

DEFINITION

FIGURE 1.4   The Program Development Process

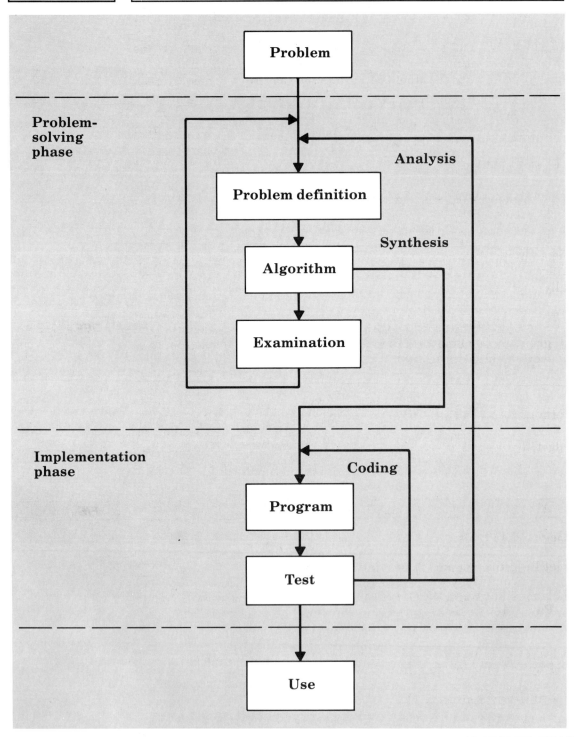

The first part of the problem-solving process is understanding the problem. This consists of determining the input (what is given), the output (what is to be produced), and the relationship between the two. For example, if the task is to produce a payroll, it is necessary to know the employees' identifications; means of determining wages (hourly pay or salary); deductions and other factors (overtime pay rates, bonuses, taxes); what is to be produced (checks, year-to-date summaries, etc.); and finally how the givens are used to produce the results. This is a matter of analysis. At this stage it is essential that the person asking for a program and the person who will be writing the program understand each other. The problems that can arise at this stage are similar to that of a driver and a passenger giving directions.

Driver: "Should I turn left here?"
Passenger: "Right."

From this example, the need for understanding is obvious. It is also necessary for programmers to communicate with each other. In the early stages of a program's development, this is not done with a program. Usually some less formal means are used for communication.

Pseudocode (structured English, algorithmic language, program design language or PDL) is an adaptation of English to express algorithms.

DEFINITION

After the programmer understands the problem, he or she begins to formulate an algorithm for the solution of the problem. This is a matter of synthesis. English is generally inadequate for the expression of the algorithm, so pseudocode is used. An example of an algorithm in pseudocode is given in *FIGURE 1.5*. This algorithm is designed to compute

Algorithm for Computing Weekly Pay for Hourly Employee

FIGURE 1.5

Begin Weekly Pay

Get EmployeeName, HoursWorked, HourlyRate

If HoursWorked > 40 Then   { Overtime, bonus 1.5 }
    Pay ← HourlyRate * 40 +
        1.5 * HourlyRate * (HoursWorked − 40)

Else   { Regular Pay }
    Pay ← HourlyRate * HoursWorked

Print EmployeeName, Pay

End Weekly Pay

an employee's pay. A leftward arrow indicates that the quantity computed to the right of the arrow is given to the quantity on the left. Since any hours worked over 40 hours are considered overtime, it is necessary to test whether this has happened and compute the pay accordingly. As the algorithm is developed it is necessary to examine what is emerging. It may become evident that some necessary pieces of information are missing. Then the programmer returns to the problem-definition step and may ask for more instructions from the program requestor. It is much, much easier and less costly to do this now rather than later on. Frequent consultation with the program requestor, although time-consuming, works to everyone's advantage.

When the programmer is convinced that the algorithm is complete, it is time to translate the algorithm into a program.

DEFINITION

> *Coding* **is the process of transforming an algorithm into a program in a specific computer language.**

DEFINITION

> **A** *bug* **(in a computer program) is an error, usually one that is difficult to correct.**

It is sometimes claimed that if the algorithm is constructed well enough, coding should be a relatively easy matter. Experience seems to suggest that although coding without a well-developed algorithm is impossible, even excellent algorithms may be difficult to code. For example, an algorithm may assume that absolutely precise arithmetic is possible, but a computer has limitations in this regard. For this reason, it is necessary to carefully test the program to ensure that it is doing what the programmer designed it to do. Testing may reveal mistakes in coding or, even worse, mistakes in the algorithm. In any case, no program should ever be used without thorough testing. On the other hand, testing is not infallible. The following quote (which can be attributed to the computer scientist Edsger W. Dijkstra) indicates this. "Testing shows the presence, not the absence of bugs." This means that it is impossible to test a program so thoroughly that the program is guaranteed not to have any errors. For most programs, there is a very large number of possible inputs and a correspondingly large number of ways that the program might execute. Anticipating all of these is virtually impossible.

However, by testing a program, bugs frequently come to light and are eliminated. For example, we might mistakenly have typed or written 400 instead of 40 in the algorithm above in the line computing Pay (as in *FIGURE 1.6*). Some test data probably would have shown that there was an error in the algorithm. (If this error was not caught the firm would issue some very large paychecks.) This might seem to be an unlikely and obvious error, but many rather minor typing errors cause major problems with programs and sometimes are not very easily uncovered.

| Algorithm for Computing Weekly Pay for Hourly Employee | **FIGURE 1.6** |

Begin Weekly Pay

Get EmployeeName, HoursWorked, HourlyRate

If HoursWorked > 40 Then   { Overtime, bonus 1.5 }
  Pay ← HourlyRate * 400 +
        1.5 * HourlyRate * (HoursWorked − 40)

Else   { Regular Pay }
  Pay ← HourlyRate * HoursWorked

Print EmployeeName, Pay

End Weekly Pay

1.6 AN ALGORITHM

In this section we illustrate the process of algorithm development with an example. The problem is to pick up a hand of playing cards and put them into order. Like many problems that need algorithms to be made into programs, this problem is one which seems simple and whose process is relatively familiar. In fact, the process is not difficult to envision. Essentially, the task is to give a description of this process.

We start by defining the problem. This means explicitly stating what is given and what is to be achieved. We have a pile of cards and they are to be put in order. A question arises as to what "order" means. For example, bridge cards and pinochle cards are not ordered in the same way. Let us use the bridge ordering in which clubs precede diamonds which precede hearts which precede spades. Within a given suit the cards are ordered from two through ten, jack, queen, king, ace. With this information we seem ready to begin. At any given stage of an algorithm's development it may be necessary to fill in gaps in the problem's definition.

Very simply, the process of gathering a hand may be described as picking up one card and inserting it into the correct place in the hand. Our first version of the algorithm follows.

```
While there are more cards
    Pick up a card
    Insert it in the hand in order
```

The indentation of the last two instructions indicates that they are to be done (in order) repeatedly while there are more cards. The instruction "Pick up a card" does not seem to need elaboration. But the process of insertion does seem to need further explanation. This process can be described as finding the correct position for the card and then placing it in that position.

```
While there are more cards
     Pick up a card
     Find the card's position
     Place the card into its position
```

To find the card's position we must perform two steps. First we pass over the cards in suits preceding the suit of the new card. Then we must find the card's place within its suit by passing over cards of the same suit which it outranks. To distinguish the card picked up from the card being examined, we call it the new card. We now have the following algorithm.

```
While there are more cards
     Pick up a new card
     While the new card's suit follows the current card's
          The current card is the next card in the hand
     While the new card's value exceeds the current card's
          The current card is the next card in the hand
     Place the card into its position
```

We notice two problems with the algorithm at this stage. The first problem is that after the instruction "Pick up a new card" the current card has not been specified. Of course it is the first card in the hand, and so we modify the algorithm.

```
While there are more cards
     Pick up a new card
     The current card is the first card in the hand
     While the new card's suit follows the current card's
          The current card is the next card in the hand
     While the new card's value exceeds the current card's
          The current card is the next card in the hand
     Place the card into its position
```

The second problem is that when the first card is picked up there are no cards in the hand. This causes a problem in doing the instruction "The current card is the first card in the hand." To take care of this we start by picking up a card before starting the loop.

```
Pick up a card
While there are more cards
     Pick up a new card
     The current card is the first card in the hand
     While the new card's suit follows the current card's
          The current card is the next card in the hand
     While the new card's value exceeds the current card's
          The current card is the next card in the hand
     Place the new card into its position
```

To finish we note that placing the new card in position consists of moving the cards beyond the current card and then inserting the new card into the position which is now vacant.

```
Pick up a card
While there are more cards
     Pick up a new card
     The current card is the first card in the hand
     While the new card's suit follows the current card's
          The current card is the next card in the hand
     While the new card's value exceeds the current card's
          The current card is the next card in the hand
     Move the cards beyond and including the current card
     Insert the new card into the hand
```

A version of this algorithm which uses some pseudocode conventions follows.

```
Get Card
While CardsLeft > 0
     Get NewCard
     CurrentCard ← FirstCard
     While NewCard.Suit > CurrentCard.Suit
          CurrentCard ← NextCard
     While NewCard.Value > CurrentCard.Value
          CurrentCard ← NextCard
     Move the cards beyond and including the current card
     Insert the new card into the hand
```

To make this algorithm more precise we need to refine the notion of a hand. If CardsInHand denotes the number of cards in the hand at any time, consider the hand to consist of Hand[1], Hand[2], ..., Hand[CardsInHand]. That is, Hand[1] denotes the first card in the hand, Hand[2] denotes the second card in the hand, and so on. To keep track of the card being compared we introduce another entity, Place, which must be set to 1 each time a comparison is done. With these considerations we have the revised algorithm

```
Get Hand[1]
CardsInHand ← 1
While CardsLeft > 0
     Get NewCard
     CurrentCard ← Hand[1]
     Place ← 1
     While NewCard.Suit > CurrentCard.Suit
          Increase Place by 1
          CurrentCard ← Hand[Place]
     While NewCard.Value > CurrentCard.Value
          Increase Place by 1
          CurrentCard ← Hand[Place]
     Move Hand[Place] through Hand[CardsInHand]
     Hand[Place] ← NewCard
     Increase CardsInHand by 1
```

The process of moving the cards to make room for the card to be inserted really means that Hand[Place] through Hand[CardsInHand] must become Hand[Place + 1] through Hand[CardsInHand + 1]. If this is done one card at a time, the last card must be moved first. To do this we introduce an entity I which takes on the values CardsInHand through Place (so I decreases in value).

```
Get Hand[1]
CardsInHand ← 1
While CardsLeft > 0
      Get NewCard
      CurrentCard ← Hand[1]
      Place ← 1
      While NewCard.Suit > CurrentCard.Suit
            Increase Place by 1
            CurrentCard ← Hand[Place]
      While NewCard.Value > CurrentCard.Value
            Increase Place by 1
            CurrentCard ← Hand[Place]
      For I starting at CardsInHand going down to Place
            Hand[I + 1] ← Hand[I]
      Hand[Place] ← NewCard
      Increase CardsInHand by 1
```

A final revision consists of noting that increasing a quantity by 1 implies adding 1 to the quantity and saving it. This last change gives the final algorithm. It would not be difficult to make this algorithm into a computer program.

```
Get Hand[1]
CardsInHand ← 1
While CardsLeft > 0
      Get NewCard
      CurrentCard ← Hand[1]
      Place ← 1
      While NewCard.Suit > CurrentCard.Suit
            Place ← Place + 1
            CurrentCard ← Hand[Place]
      While NewCard.Value > CurrentCard.Value
            Place ← Place + 1
            CurrentCard ← Hand[Place]
      For I starting at CardsInHand going down to Place
            Hand[I + 1] ← Hand[I]
      Hand[Place] ← NewCard
      CardsInHand ← CardsInHand + 1
```

Sometimes it is useful to emphasize the end of the statements which are to be done after the While by the notation EndWhile. If this is done for the Whiles (and the For) in the algorithm above, the following is obtained.

```
Get Hand[1]
CardsInHand  ←  1
While CardsLeft > 0
     Get NewCard
     CurrentCard  ←  Hand[1]
     Place  ←  1
     While NewCard.Suit > CurrentCard.Suit
           Place  ←  Place + 1
           CurrentCard  ←  Hand[Place]
     EndWhile
     While NewCard.Value > CurrentCard.Value
           Place  ←  Place + 1
           CurrentCard  ←  Hand[Place]
     EndWhile
     For I starting at CardsInHand going down to Place
           Hand[I + 1]  ←  Hand[I]
     EndFor
     Hand[Place]  ←  NewCard
     CardsInHand  ←  CardsInHand + 1
EndWhile
```

Although this algorithm seems complete to a person, it is not adequate for a machine. This is because a person would see how to take care of some problem situations in the obvious way. For example, in both of the inner While loops (While NewCard.Suit > CurrentCard.Suit and While NewCard.Value > CurrentCard.Value) it would be necessary to stop the loop when the last card in the hand is reached—that is, when Place = CardsInHand. Similarly, the second inner While loop also should only execute when the suit of the card to be inserted matches the suit of the cards being examined. This modification would be necessary for a computer implementation.

It may seem that the development of the algorithm above proceeded extremely slowly. This was done on purpose. The reader is urged to do likewise when developing algorithms. It is very difficult to write down a detailed algorithm. Programmers who attempt to write down a great deal at once almost always make mistakes by omitting something or assuming too much. This causes them to spend more time developing a correct algorithm than if they had proceeded in small steps.

The development of the card-sorting algorithm progressed from a very general description to a very detailed one. It is best to produce an algorithm in this way. Getting the overall picture first is essential to solving problems and writing algorithms. It is futile to attempt to master the details of the algorithm without an understanding of how they are to form the algorithm.

The card-sorting algorithm is extremely detailed. This is because an algorithm should be able to be executed by a machine. This amount of detail would not be necessary to instruct a human. Furthermore, the algorithm must be expressed in a language suitable for a machine and then communicated to the machine. This book deals with the language Pascal. In Chapter 2, the means of giving the computer instructions in this language are discussed.

1.7 SUMMARY

In order to produce a good computer program, it is necessary to devise an algorithm. An algorithm is a specification of the steps needed to accomplish a particular task. When this has been done, it is possible to write a program. A program is written in a programming language.

A programming language is used by a programmer to communicate an algorithm to a computer. All programming languages have two aspects, syntax and semantics. The syntax of a language is the set of rules for the language. The semantics of a language specify the meanings of the statements of the language.

This book uses the language Pascal, which was devised by Niklaus Wirth. More particularly, the version of Pascal known as TURBO Pascal is used. Pascal has many features which make it a good language for learning how to program.

It is important to remember that the good programmer starts by understanding the problem and then writing an algorithm to solve the problem. The algorithm becomes the basis of the program. ☐

EXERCISES

1. List ten of the three-, four-, and five-word sentences that can be constructed using the syntax diagrams of *FIGURE 1.2*. What is the minimum number of words that must appear in a sentence constructed using the rules of *FIGURE 1.2*?

2. Devise syntax diagrams which give all the two- and three-letter sequences made from the letters A, B, C, and D (for example, AA, AB, BA, BB, AAA, ABC, . . .).

3. Devise syntax diagrams which give all the ways you write your name. For example, you probably don't use your middle name all of the time and when you do you may just use your middle initial. If you use a nickname, include this possibility.

4. Try to predict what the program in *FIGURE 1.3* does when it is run on a computer.

5. Give a detailed explanation of how to get from a room on one floor to a room on another. Remember to open doors and turn on staircases if need be.

6. Give an algorithm for multiplying two binomials which have only one variable, x. That is, describe how to do the multiplication $(2x + 7)(5x - 4)$.

7. Write an algorithm which produces all the two- and three-letter sequences made from the letters A, B, C, and D (for example, AA, AB, BA, BB, AAA, ABC, . . .).

8. Put a pile of cards in front of you and use the algorithm of Section 6 to put them into your hand in order.

9. It is a good idea to examine what an algorithm does in "extreme" situations. Describe what the card-sorting algorithm does when only one card is given. Describe what happens when the new card precedes all the cards currently in the hand. Describe what happens when the new card follows all the cards in the hand.

10. Revise the algorithm in Section 1.6 by adding the conditions in the inner While loops that were mentioned.

11. Develop an algorithm which describes how to put cards into a hand in order as follows. The highest card in the hand is examined. If it is higher, than the new card, it is moved. Otherwise, the new card is inserted at the end of the hand. Then the next-highest card is examined. If it is higher than the new card, it is moved. If the new card is higher, it is inserted. The process of examining a card and comparing it with the new card continues until the place for the new card is found. Since the cards have been moved, the new card may be inserted at this time. This repeats until all the cards have been put into the hand.

12. Develop an algorithm for finding a person's name in a telephone book. Assume that the names in the telephone book are in alphabetical order. The pages of the book are numbered 1 to 200, and each page contains a list of 50 names. A person's name has been found if its page and place on the page are known. For example, given the name Wirth, your algorithm should report something like 184, 23 to indicate that Wirth is found on page 184 as the twenty-third entry on the page. Do not search the book in order!

13. This book uses the programming language Pascal. Find out what other programming languages are available to you.

14. Discuss the difficulties in attempting to use English (or any other natural language) as a programming language. Refer to the definition of a programming language.

INTRODUCTION

In the preceding chapter a general description of the programming process was given. One of the steps in that process is to communicate or give the program to the computer. To do this it is necessary to describe how to enter a program into the computer. To do this effectively, a discussion of the computer environment is necessary.

We will be working in the programming environment provided by TURBO Pascal and an operating system (MS-DOS or CP/M). This chapter is a discussion of these systems. Knowledge of these is necessary because both programmers and their programs must communicate with the "bare" or "raw" machine and its attached devices (known as peripherals) through intermediary software. It is this intervening software which enables us to use computers effectively. ☐

CHAPTER 2

OPERATING SYSTEMS AND THE TURBO ENVIRONMENT

2.1   OPERATING SYSTEMS AND COMPUTERS

By itself, a computer is very difficult to work with. A computer is an electronic device. This means that it manipulates electrical signals. Almost all people who use computers are not interested in manipulating these signals but have other, more practical matters in mind. For instance, a firm may want a computer to do its payroll calculations. The computer is made useful by disguising it so that it performs certain tasks in response to commands entered by the user. This disguising is done by placing various types of software between the user and the computer. A diagram of this appears in *FIGURE 2.1*. We may regard the ubiquity of computers as an indication of the successfulness of this effort. Very few people who use computers worry about the electronics of a computer.

DEFINITION

> *Hardware* **is the group of physical components comprising a computer system.**

FIGURE 2.1   **A Paradigm for Computing**

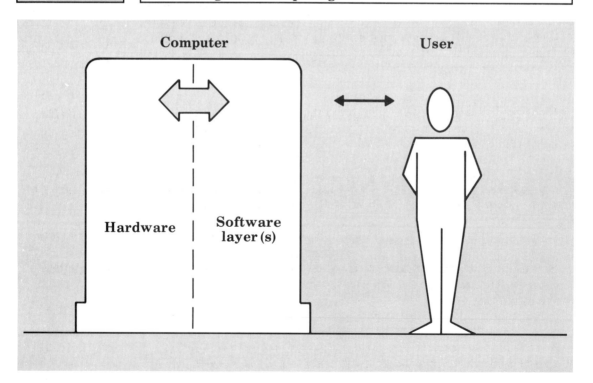

Software is a program or collection of programs.

DEFINITION

An *operating system* is a collection of programs which manages the resources of the computer and enables a user to utilize these resources.

DEFINITION

The first level of software that most computer users see is an operating system. Popular operating systems for microcomputers are CP/M, MS-DOS, and their relatives (CP/M-86 and PC-DOS). Another well-known operating system is UNIX (for minicomputers). There are many operating systems for mainframes. Because the operating system being used determines the characteristics of the computer, computers are often classified by the operating systems they run. So one hears of "CP/M machines" and "MS-DOS based machines," even though this is not entirely accurate.

The operating system for a microcomputer is stored on a floppy disk or on an internal or external hard disk. Each time the computer is turned on, the operating system must be loaded from the disk into memory. Exactly how this is accomplished varies from machine to machine. Some computers are designed to immediately start reading from a disk when turned on. Others wait for a disk to be inserted and a key pressed before the operating system is read from the disk. Find out the exact procedure for doing this on the machine you use. At this time, part of the operating system is put into the computer's memory for use. The rest of the operating system programs are kept on the disk.

Memory (core memory or core, random access memory or RAM) is the component of the computer used to hold data and instructions for use by the computer.

DEFINITION

Booting the system is the process of reading the operating system into memory (derived from pulling yourself up by the bootstraps).

DEFINITION

A *resident program* is an operating system program which is always present in memory after booting. A resident program executes immediately.

DEFINITION

A *transient program* is a (system) program which is stored on a disk and must be read from the disk into memory before being run.

DEFINITION

The parts of the operating system which are always present in the computer serve to direct the flow of data and control among the various components of the computer. For example, one of the functions of the operating system is to respond to a key of the keyboard being pressed. Under the direction of the operating system, the computer interprets the electronic signal and displays the appropriate character on the screen. When the return key is pressed, the sequence of characters that have been typed is interpreted by the operating system and the specified action takes place. If the command typed specified that something was to be printed on the printer, the operating system would direct that something to the printer. It is possible to attach a number of useful devices to a microcomputer. The video screen, keyboard, and disk drives should be considered as being attached to the computer. In addition to these, one may have a printer connected to the computer. We will assume that you are working with a system that includes a video screen, a keyboard, and two disk drives (probably built into the computer's case). Occasionally, we refer to a printing device that is attached to the computer. A diagram of this basic configuration is presented in *FIGURE 2.2*.

DEFINITION

> A *peripheral device* (or *peripheral*) is any device attached to the computer.

In the diagram in *FIGURE 2.2*, the arrows indicate the directions in which signals or information can be transmitted. The keyboard is strictly an input device, whereas the screen and the printer are only able to output or display information. The disk drives, on the other hand, function as both input and output devices. The diagram also indicates that the computer consists of two parts. The first is the memory, which will always contain some operating system programs and usually other things as well. The second component is able to manipulate and interpret the contents of the memory. This component has two parts. The arithmetic/logic unit (ALU) does the actual manipulation of data. For example, it performs addition. The other part is the control unit, which keeps track of instructions. The memory, the arithmetic/logic unit, and the control unit work together.

DEFINITION

> The *central processing unit* (*CPU*) consists of a memory, a control unit, and an arithmetic/logic unit.

DEFINITION

> A *system* (computer system) consists of a central processing unit along with peripheral devices.

Any program uses the resources of the computer mentioned above to accomplish the task at hand. Before a program can be executed or run,

Computer System   FIGURE 2.2

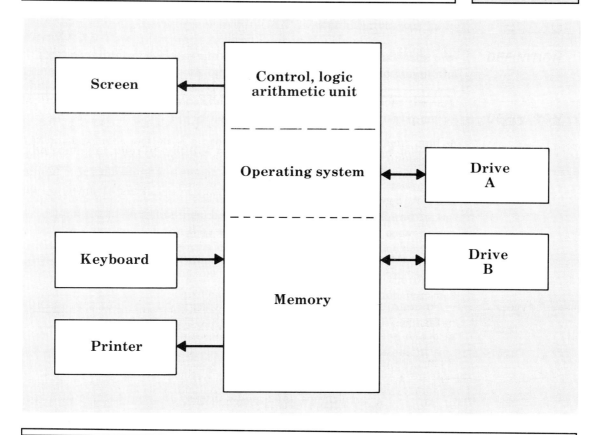

it must be stored in the memory of the computer. When a program is in the memory of the computer it is possible for the computer to follow the instructions of the program.

> **Running** or **executing** a program means to cause the computer to follow the instructions of the program.

DEFINITION

2.2 FILES

In general, operating systems have many functions. But on a microcomputer an operating system's most important function is the management of files. A microcomputer operating system also controls keyboard input, printing, and video display (all of which can be thought of as specialized files) and enables programs to be run. We will concentrate on how MS-DOS (PC-DOS) performs file management. (Almost everything stated here applies to CP/M as well.) A summary of the more frequently used commands of MS-DOS and CP/M is contained in Appendix A.

DEFINITION

A *floppy* (flexible diskette) is a thin, square envelope containing a magnetic recording surface for use with a computer.

A floppy can be damaged if you aren't a little careful. If it is damaged, the data that had been stored on it probably cannot be recovered. Never touch the magnetic recording surface of the floppy. Floppy disks are also sensitive to magnetism. Keep them away from motors, televisions, and other devices that are sources of magnetism. This includes some of the security devices in libraries. Pass your floppies to the attendant as you go through the device. A floppy may contain many hours of work, so protect it accordingly. Making a copy of your work on another disk (known as backing up the disk) will eliminate losses.

DEFINITION

A *floppy drive* is an electromechanical device (which may be part of a computer or attached to a computer) which is able to store or record (write) data on a floppy and retrieve (read) data from a floppy.

To use a floppy drive, a disk is inserted into the slot of the drive and then some sort of door or latch is closed. When the floppy is actually in use, a light will usually be on to indicate that the drive is active. Never open the drive while it is active. Remove the floppy when the drive is inactive. To remove the floppy, open the door of the drive and pull the disk out.

At the heart of many computer operations is the notion of *file*. To start, we give the following oversimplified definition.

DEFINITION

A *file* is a collection of data items which are related.

A file may contain a variety of different things. For example, most operating system programs are stored in files. Pascal programs that are created will be stored in files as well. Other uses for files are possible, but a file always contains items which have been lumped together. Except when a file is actually being worked on, it may be regarded as being stored on a floppy. In some ways a file is analogous to a big sheet of paper on which something has been written. For example, a list of names and telephone numbers could be stored in a file. However, one big difference is that a file on a floppy is written magnetically.

Another big difference between a file and a sheet of paper is that whereas we are able to search through a stack of papers and find the one we want just by looking at them, it is not possible for a computer to look at a collection of files and determine the needed one. For this reason every file must be given a name by which the computer can recognize it for purposes of storage and retrieval.

As an illustration, the Pascal programs in this book could be kept in a filing cabinet on pieces of paper or on a disk encoded magnetically. In the filing cabinet, the pieces of paper for each program would be put in a separate folder and labeled appropriately. The fourth example program of Chapter 3 might be labeled Chapter 3, Example 4. If this were done it would be easy to find the pieces of paper containing a particular program. Similarly, the file on the disk containing the program would be labeled CH3EX4.PAS.

Microcomputers frequently have two drives named A and B. When the operating system attempts to find a file it can only search the floppy in one of these drives. If the drive to be used is not specified, the operating system will use one drive. This is called the *logged drive*. Generally, when the computer is started the logged drive will be drive A. Its physical location varies from machine to machine. Specifying the drive is comparable to stating which drawer of a filing cabinet contains a particular file.

The *logged drive* is the drive which the computer will search to find a file if no drive is specified.

DEFINITION

The operating system has a convention for naming files. Each file is designated by a file name and extension or type. The file name and extension are separated by a period. A file name consists of one to eight characters. The legal characters consist of the letters A through Z, digits 0 through 9, and some (but not all) punctuation marks. Lower-case letters are automatically converted to upper case when used in file designators. Of the permitted punctuation symbols only the hyphen is frequently used. The file extension consists of zero to three characters. The file extension of zero characters is called the null extension. If the extension is null the period may be omitted. The file name and extension form the file designator.

The file name should be descriptive of the contents of the file. The file extension is used to denote the type of file. For example, the extension PAS will be used for files which contain Pascal programs. *FIGURE 2.3* contains some common extensions and their meanings. It is a good idea to adhere to these. Here are some examples of file designators and what we would expect to find in them.

GRADES.PAS   A Pascal program to do grades
FINAL.TXT   Text of a final

MARCH23.DAT   Data for March 23
GRADES.BAS   A BASIC program to do grades

It is possible to specify the drive on which the file is to be found by preceding the file name with the letter of the drive followed by a colon— e.g., B:GRADES.PAS, A:FINAL.TXT. This is necessary whenever the file is not on the logged drive, but is otherwise optional.

DEFINITION

> A *file designator* consists of an optional drive designator, a file name, and an optional file extension.

Whenever it is necessary to store or retrieve a file, its file designator must be used. A file designator is a bit more than a name for a file. It is the means of finding the file. It is also important to note the distinction between a file and a file designator. The former is a collection of data, the latter is the way to get to that collection. This distinction is frequently blurred, just as we usually do not distinguish between a person and his or her name. When we say "Paul went to bed" we mean that "The person named Paul went to bed." However, it is occasionally necessary to make this distinction explicit when working with files, and it should never be entirely forgotten.

Many of the operating system programs deal with files. These programs also act as commands. Some of the more useful commands are given in the table in *FIGURE 2.4*. See Appendix A for more information on MS-DOS and CP/M.

FIGURE 2.3   **Common File Extensions**

Extension	Meaning
.BAK	BAcKup file, usually created by an editor
.BAS	BASic program
.CMD	CoMmanD file, directly executable (CP/M-86)
.COM	COMmand file, directly executable (CP/M-80, MS-DOS)
.DAT	DATa file
.IN	INput file
.PAS	PAScal program
.OUT	OUTput file
.TMP	TeMPorary file
.TXT	TeXT file

| Operating System Commands | FIGURE 2.4 |

Command		Purpose	Example
MS-DOS	DIR	Display the names of the files on a disk	DIR
CP/M	DIR		
MS-DOS	COPY	Create a copy of a file	COPY OLDFILE NEWFILE
CP/M	PIP		PIP NEWFILE = OLDFILE
MS-DOS	DEL	Delete or erase a file	DEL JUNK.TXT
CP/M	ERA		ERA JUNK.TXT
MS-DOS	TYPE	View the contents of a file on the screen	TYPE READ.ME
CP/M	TYPE		TYPE READ.ME
MS-DOS	PRINT	Print a file on the printer	PRINT LETTER.TXT
CP/M	PIP		PIP LST: = LETTER.TXT

2.3   THE TURBO SYSTEM

Most of the work we will be doing will not be done at the operating system (MS-DOS or CP/M) level. We will use the TURBO system, which provides an environment for developing Pascal programs (as a matter of convenience we use "TURBO" instead of "the TURBO system"). TURBO does not entirely displace the operating system but rather works with the operating system (or, more accurately, with part of the operating system). One can think of using the TURBO system within the operating system, or that TURBO is another layer of software between the user and the computer. TURBO provides the user with some of the operating system functions. This section is a discussion of some of these features.

To start using TURBO you will need a disk with the file TURBO.COM on it. The disk will also need to have enough of the operating system on it to boot the system. TURBO.COM contains the TURBO system. The file TURBO.MSG will also be needed. These should not be the original files. Use copies of the originals! If you are starting to use TURBO on your own, make copies of these files. You should then use TINSNT.COM to adapt TURBO to your particular computer by following the instructions in the TURBO manual.

When the operating system has successfully booted itself, the system prompt (A>) will appear. At this point the operating system is waiting for a command (i.e., the name of a program to be run) to be typed at the keyboard. Type TURBO (not necessarily capitalized) followed by a RE-TURN. This starts TURBO running. The first thing you will see is a message followed by a question. *FIGURE 2.5* is an example of this. The error messages are useful, so type Y (or y). No RETURN is needed.

FIGURE 2.5

```
TURBO Pascal version 1.00 [CP/M, Z80]-Serial #$$$$$$$$$
Copyright (C) 1983 by BORLAND International, Inc.
Osborne 1


Include error messages (Y/N)?
```

TURBO will finish being loaded into memory. At this point the computer's memory will contain the operating system and the TURBO system. The remaining memory is available for use by the programmer. *FIGURE 2.6* illustrates how memory is used at this point. Initially, there is no program.

FIGURE 2.6   Microcomputer Configuration

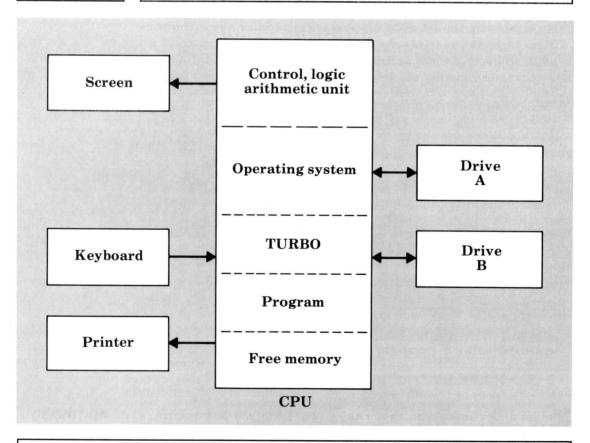

A menu of the TURBO commands is displayed at this point. *FIGURE 2.7* is a picture of the menu (MS-DOS version; others differ in details). In this section the commands needed to get started are discussed. The editor is described in detail in the following section.

The letters in the menu which are highlighted denote commands that can be entered in response to the prompt (>). TURBO responds immediately to the letter that is typed: no RETURN is needed. This can be a little disconcerting until you get used to it. The menu is not automatically displayed or updated in certain situations. To display the current menu, enter RETURN.

The first line of the menu gives the letter of the logged drive (A or B). Unless specified, any file will be assumed to be on this drive. To change the logged drive, type L (or l). The system will respond with

```
New drive:_
```

Enter the new drive followed by a colon (e.g., B:) and press RETURN. If you decide not to change the drive, just press RETURN. The new drive is not immediately shown on the menu. Type RETURN to have the menu show the new logged drive.

It is possible to have two files under consideration when using TURBO. These are known as the *work file* and the *main file*. We will only need a work file. Usually the work file will contain a Pascal program to be created, modified, or run. When TURBO is first started no work file has been designated, so there is no entry following Work file in the menu. To designate a work file, press W. TURBO will then print the message

```
Work file name:_
```

At this point any legal file designator (as discussed in Section 2.2 above) may be entered. The file designated will become the work file. If the

TURBO Menu

FIGURE 2.7

```
Logged drive: A
Active directory:\

Work file :
Main file :

Edit   Compile   Run    Save
Dir    Quit      compiler Options

Text :     0 bytes
Free : 62635 bytes

>_
```

designated file already exists on the disk, its contents will be placed in memory. If the designated file is not present, the message New File will be issued. This may happen unexpectedly. If you get the New File message when you want an existing file, check your spelling.

When you type W for a new work file, you may have a program in memory which is to be stored on the disk (with the appropriate file designator). If you haven't saved this file after you enter the new work file, the message

```
Workfile X:OLDFILE.TYP not saved. Save (Y/N)?_
```

will appear (X:OLDFILE.TYP being the old work file). Enter Y or N depending on what you want. If you type N, the old work file will not be saved.

Because the work file will be a Pascal program most of the time, it is possible to omit the period and the file extension or type when designating the work file. When the extension is omitted, TURBO will use the file extension .PAS.

Finally, don't use .BAK, .CHN, .COM, or .CMD as the extension for a work file. TURBO needs these for its own use.

The commands that have been discussed pertain to locating the file that is to be used to hold a program. The remaining commands are used after this file has been designated.

The command E is for invoking the editor. An editor (in general) is a program which enables you to create a file (by typing at the keyboard) or modify a file (by deleting or adding to the file). Typing E starts an editing session using the work file. How to use the editor is discussed in the following section.

The "native" language of the computer is not Pascal. Before a program can be run it must be translated into another program in the computer's own language. This process is known as *compiling* the program. The compile command (C) will cause the program that is in memory to be compiled. The resulting (compiled) program may either be in memory or be stored in a file, depending on the compiler option chosen. Since a program is automatically compiled when the run command is used, we will just use the run command.

DEFINITION

A *compiler* is a program for translating a program into another machine executable version.

DEFINITION

Compilation is the process of compiling a program.

Typing R (for run) in response to the TURBO prompt causes the program in the work file to be compiled and run. Either of these actions may be unsuccessful. If the program in the work file is not syntactically correct, compilation will not be completed. An error message will appear indicating the nature of the error and its location in the program. A similar response will result if an error occurs when the program is run. If there is an error in the program, TURBO assumes that it is to be corrected. Pressing the escape key (ESC) invokes the editor, placing the cursor where it detected the error (the cause of the error is at or before this point).

The save command (S) causes the contents of the work file to be saved on the disk, using the file designator of the work file. Because it is possible to lose a program when it is run, it is a good idea to save the work file before you run it. Get in the habit of doing this.

The directory command (D) performs the same function as the DIR command of the operating system. After D is typed the message

```
Dir mask:
```

appears. To have the files on a disk listed, type the letter for the drive, a colon (e.g., A:), and RETURN. Pressing RETURN causes the files on the logged drive to be displayed.

The quit command (Q) exits TURBO and returns you to the operating system. If you have not saved the work file since it was edited, you will be asked whether or not you want the work file saved. In response to the Y or N answer, TURBO saves or does not save the work file and then returns to the operating system.

The compiler options command (O) enables you to specify where the compiled program is to be stored. Unless otherwise specified, the compiled program is stored in memory. This is what we will be doing, so we won't use the O command.

FIGURE 2.8 is a table of the TURBO commands that are most often used. A summary of all the TURBO commands is included in the appendices.

TURBO Commands   **FIGURE 2.8**

Command	Use
L	Change the Logged drive
W	Start a new Work file
E	Invoke the Editor (using the current work file)
R	Run the program in the work file (includes compiling)
S	Save the work file on disk
Q	Quit TURBO, exit to operating system

A session using TURBO to create, save, and run a program would be something like the following, where a line signifies a new screen. We start at the operating system level and in response to the operating system prompt (A> or B>) we cause TURBO to be run by typing TURBO[RETURN] ([RETURN] denotes pressing the RETURN key).

```
A>TURBO
```

The operating system would cause TURBO to be read from the disk. TURBO would clear the screen and a message would appear as below:

```
TURBO Pascal version 1.00 [CP/M, Z80]-Serial #$$$$$$$$$
Copyright (C) 1983 by BORLAND International, Inc.
Osborne 1


Include error messages (Y/N)?_
```

The first three lines above describe the system being used. For example, the first line contains the information that version 1.00 is being used, the operating system is CP/M, and the computer is based on the chip designated Z80. The third line refers to the computer being used.

We always include error messages, so we type Y (no [RETURN] is needed). TURBO then loads the error messages into memory. While this is happening, the screen will look like the following (the line under the Y designates that the user typed it):

```
TURBO Pascal version 1.00 [CP/M, Z80]-Serial #$$$$$$$$$
Copyright (C) 1983 by BORLAND International, Inc.
Osborne 1


Include error messages (Y/N)?Y


Loading A:TURBOMSG.OVR
```

After a short while, the screen will clear and the TURBO menu will appear. This is depicted below. The symbol > is the TURBO prompt.

```
Logged drive: A
Active directory:\

Work file :
Main file :

Edit  Compile  Run    Save
Dir   Quit        compiler Options

Text :      0 bytes
Free : 62635 bytes

>
```

It is common practice to put the disk containing the operating system and TURBO ("the system disk") in drive A and the disk which contains Pascal programs ("the program disk") in drive B. If you follow this practice, change the logged drive to drive B so that all your programs will be stored on the disk in drive B. This is done by typing L and then B: (or b:) in response to the message "New drive :". After this is done the work file is usually named. This is done by typing W and then giving the file name in response to the prompt. These two steps are depicted below. Notice that only the name of the work file is given. The logged drive and the extension PAS are used. (Commands entered by the user are underlined.)

```
Logged drive: A
Active directory:\

Work file :
Main file :

Edit   Compile   Run     Save
Dir    Quit      compiler Options

Text :      0 bytes
Free : 62635 bytes

>L

New drive : b:

>W

Work file name : program1

Loading B:PROGRAM1.PAS
New File

>
```

The menu does not reflect the new logged drive or work file immediately. Pressing [RETURN] will clear the screen and show these changes.

```
Logged drive: B
Active directory:\

Work file : PROGRAM1.PAS
Main file :

Edit   Compile   Run     Save
Dir    Quit      compiler Options

Text :      1 bytes
Free : 62634 bytes

>
```

The next step would be to type E to invoke the editor and enter a program. Using the editor will be discussed in the next section. After finishing editing, always save your program on disk by typing S in response to the TURBO prompt. After the program has been saved it might be run by typing R. The following shows what would happen during these two steps.

```
>S

Saving B: PROGRAM1.PAS

>R

Compiling
    5 lines
Code :    48 bytes (7756-7786)
Free : 23420 bytes (7786-D302)
Data :     4 bytes (D302-D306)

Running
```

Two steps are involved in running the program. The first step is compiling. In this step the Pascal program is translated into a program which the computer can execute. The second step is running or executing the program. At this time the computer executes the instructions in the program produced by compiling.

The results of the program would appear at this point. After the program has finished running, TURBO resumes control and puts a prompt (>) on the screen. If it were time to quit, a Q would be entered. Doing this would return to the operating system level, which would issue its prompt (A> or B>). This would appear as follows.

```
>Q

A>
```

At this point, if a directory drive B disk were done, a file named PROGRAM1.PAS would be found. This file would contain the program created in the session with TURBO. The steps above are typical of those used in a session to write and run a program.

Two actions described above are very important if you don't want to lose programs. The first is to switch the logged drive to the program disk (normally in drive B:). This ensures that the program you create is stored on the program disk and not someplace else. The second thing to do is always save your program before running it. It is very easy to lose your program at this point. When you develop programs, get into the habit of changing the logged drive to the drive containing the program disk and always, always, always save your program before running it. There is nothing quite so disheartening as losing the fruits of an hour or more of work. If you are not convinced of this, wait until it happens to you! It will if you don't take these precautions.

A few comments need to be made about using TURBO as we have illustrated. First, the commands entered (L, W, E, S, R, Q) do not actually appear on the screen. It is not necessary to use capital letters. For example, we entered the work file name as program1. Typing R will cause the program in the work file to be compiled as well as run. The numbers that appear on the screen (in the lines Text and Free and after the word Compiling) indicate how much space the program is occupying in memory. We won't be concerned with them. Finally, the program written above had no errors, so that compiling and execution were completed. This is not always the case.

To review, a working session using TURBO starts by invoking TURBO from the operating system (A>TURBO). At this point it is a good idea to include error messages. Once in TURBO the first thing that should be done is to switch logged drives (L). Next the work file is named (W). The work file is then created or modified using the editor (E). After editing is finished, the work file should be saved (S). Then the program in the work file may be run (R). Most of the time it is necessary to repeat the last three steps (E, S, R) in order to get the program to run correctly. During the editing session the program is modified to eliminate (hopefully!) errors that were found when the program was run. At the end of the session, control is returned to the operating system (Q).

2.4   THE TURBO EDITOR

As we mentioned above, an editor is a program for creating or modifying a file. In many ways an editor performs the same function as a word processor. The primary difference is that an editor is designed with programs in mind whereas a word processing program is designed for the production of documents such as letters. The TURBO editor is modeled after the popular word processing program WordStar.

When you type the editing command (E) you begin editing the work file. If you haven't named a work file, TURBO will ask you for one. (Once again, the E doesn't actually appear on the screen.)

For example, to create the Pascal program of Chapter 1, let's suppose that we have named a work file (using the command W) with the name CH2EX1.PAS. Then typing E would start an editing session with the file named CH2EX1.PAS. This sequence would appear as below, where the line across the page indicates that the screen has been cleared and that output starts at the top of the page.

```
>E
```

```
    ------------------------------------------------
    Line 1  Col 1   Insert    Indent   B:CH2EX1.PAS
    —
```

The line across the top of the screen is called the status line. It provides information about the file being edited. The underline is called the cursor. It denotes exactly where an editing operation will occur. (Other symbols, such as a rectangle, are sometimes used, instead of the underline, as a cursor.) The first two entries of the status line give the current position of the cursor. When you first start, the cursor is in the first line (at the top) of the file and in the first column (to the left) of the file. Insert and Indent refer to certain features of the editor which we will disregard for the moment. The last item in the status line is the complete file designator of the work file, in this case B:CH2EX1.PAS.

Text can now be entered into the work file simply by typing letters (and other characters: punctuation and numbers) using the keyboard. As you do this the cursor will keep moving to the right. The cursor denotes where the next character that you type will be placed. In this context, pressing the space bar counts as a character. Entering a space causes the cursor to move to the right. The RETURN key causes the cursor to move to a new line down the page. Because the conventions for indentation in programs differ from those of ordinary writing, the cursor is moved under the first character of the line above. The Indent in the status line refers to this characteristic of the editor. Finally, notice that the line and column in the status line change as characters are entered.

If the program of Chapter 1 were typed, this is what might be seen after we were finished:

```
   Line 26    Col 1    Insert    Indent    B:PROGRAM1.PAS
PROGRAM Circle (Input, Output);

{ This is a short program ilustrating Pascal.

            Author    : John Riley
            Date      : March 2, 1986
            Fule name : CH2EX1.PAS
}

CONST
     Pi = 3.14159;

VAR
     Area,
     Circumference,
     Radius        : Real;

BEGIN { Circle }
  Writeln('Enter the radius of a circle');
  Readln(Raduis);
  Area := Pi *Sqr(Radius);
  Circumference := 2 * Pi * Radius;
  Writeln('Area o f circle : ', Area : 8 : 2);
  Writeln('Circumference   : ', Circumference : 8 : 2)
END.  { Circle }
  —
```

When we finish, the cursor is in the first column of the line after the end of the program (line 26, column 1). This is because we pressed the RETURN key after completing the last line. It is a good idea to put this extra (blank) line in to ensure that the last line of the program gets printed. Also notice that blank or empty lines count as lines (there are six of these in the program). At this point we notice some mistakes in the program. For example, an l is missing from the word "illustrating" in the third line. This is where an editor begins to shine. To correct this mistake we can move the cursor by using either the arrow keys (up, down, left, right) or the control key (CTRL) together with E (up), X (down), S (left), or D (right). (The control key always works with another key, the way the shift key does. That is, both the control key and the other key are pressed together.) So we move the cursor up and then to the left to the mistake, positioning the cursor where the l is to be placed. Typing l at this time will insert an l and move the remaining letters to the right. This is the meaning of Insert in the status line. Characters are inserted into the file where they are typed, and any characters on the same line are shifted to the right.

The next mistake is that the word "Radius" is misspelled in the second line following Begin. We move the cursor to the mistake. This time some letters need to be deleted. The DELETE key or CTRL/G deletes the character above the cursor. So we delete the offending characters and type in the correct ones. Similarly, we move the cursor under the u in the seventh line, delete it, and insert an i to get "File."

Spaces can be added and deleted like any other character. For example, in the twenty-first line we might want to put a space between the asterisk (*) and Sqr. Positioning the cursor under the S and pressing the space bar (at the bottom of the keyboard) inserts a space. The extra space between o and f in the twenty-third line can be deleted. The finished product is given below.

```
   Line 23   Col 18    Insert    Indent    B:PROGRAM1.PAS
PROGRAM Circle (Input, Output);

{ This is a short program illustrating Pascal.
         Author    : John Riley
         Date      : March 2, 1986
         File name : CH2EX1.PAS
}

CONST
     Pi = 3.14159;

VAR
     Area,
     Circumference,
     Radius           : Real;
```

```
BEGIN { Circle }
  Writeln('Enter the radius of a circle');
  Readln(Radius);
  Area := Pi * Sqr(Radius);
  Circumference := 2 * Pi * Radius;
  Writeln('Area of circle : ', Area : 8 : 2);
  Writeln('Circumference   : ', Circumference : 8 : 2)
END.  { Circle }
```

To return to the TURBO menu we type CTRL/KD. This exits the editor and resumes TURBO. The TURBO prompt will then appear. At this point you should save your work with the save command (S).

Using the editor it is easy to type and correct a program. In fact, the editor may be used to prepare any sort of typing. It takes a little practice to get the knack of using the editor. But once you do you'll find that your typewriter will be gathering dust.

Explanations of the most frequently used editing commands follow. These are enough to be able to work reasonably efficiently. A complete list of editing commands is given in Appendix C.

Typing any (noncontrol) character enters (inserts) the character at the position of the cursor. The characters to the right of the inserted character are shifted to the right. [RETURN] starts a new line.

The commands for moving the cursor are centered about an imaginary dot between the S and D keys of the keyboard. In *FIGURE 2.9* this dot is symbolized by an asterisk (*). Keys used for moving the cursor to the right are to the right of this dot, keys to move the cursor up are located above it. The relationships between the keys and movements are illustrated in *FIGURE 2.9*.

The combination CTRL/S moves the cursor one character to the left;

FIGURE 2.9   **TURBO Editing Keys (all used with the CTRL key)**

$$
\begin{array}{cccc}
Q & E\ R & T & \\
A & S*D & F\ G & \\
 & X\ C & & \\
\end{array}
$$

R Up a page
↑
E Up a line
↑

QS ← A ← S ← * → D → F → QD
Left of   Left a   Left a   ↓   Right a   Right   Right
line   word   character   character   a word   of line

X Down a line
↓
C Down a page

the combination CTRL/D moves it one character to the right. CTRL/A and CTRL/F move the cursor one word to the left or right, respectively. Roughly, a word is defined by blank spaces. The combinations CTRL/QS (meaning the CTRL key in combination with the Q and then S) and CTRL/QD move the cursor to the beginning (left) or end (right) of the current line. CTRL/E and CTRL/X move the cursor directly up or down (respectively) one line. CTRL/R and CTRL/C move the cursor up or down a page. A page is a certain number of lines, about the number that are on the screen at any time. On many microcomputers the up and down arrow keys move the cursor up and down a line and the right and left arrow keys move the cursor right and left a character. There may also be keys for moving up and down a page or to the right or left end of a line. For example, the HOME key moves the cursor to the beginning of the current line and the END key moves the cursor to the right end of the current line.

It is possible to delete various combinations of characters while using the editor. The DELETE key or the CTRL/G combination deletes the character above the cursor. The BACKSPACE key or the CTRL/- (hyphen) combination deletes the character immediately to the left of the cursor. This is particularly convenient for correcting mistakes as you type. Both CTRL/G and CTRL/- cause the characters to the right of the deleted character to be shifted to the left. The DELETE and BACKSPACE keys will also perform these deletions. CTRL/T deletes the word to the right of the cursor. CTRL/Y deletes the line in which the cursor is positioned. CTRL/Y causes all remaining lines to be moved up one.

To exit the editor and return to TURBO, type CTRL/KD (CTRL with K and then D). The TURBO prompt will appear at the bottom of the screen.

To add a whole new line, go to the end of the line preceding the line you want to insert and type a RETURN.

It takes a little time before you will be skilled and entirely comfortable when using the editor. However, if you practice you will become familiar with it.

2.5   THE IMPLEMENTATION PHASE

This chapter concludes with a more detailed look at the implementation phase. This is depicted in *FIGURE 2.10.*

In the problem-solving phase the programmer develops an algorithm to accomplish the task at hand. He or she then translates this into a computer program in some language. Using an editor, a program known as the *source program* is created.

> A *source program* is a computer program which is written in a language which cannot be run directly by the computer.   *DEFINITION*

FIGURE 2.10

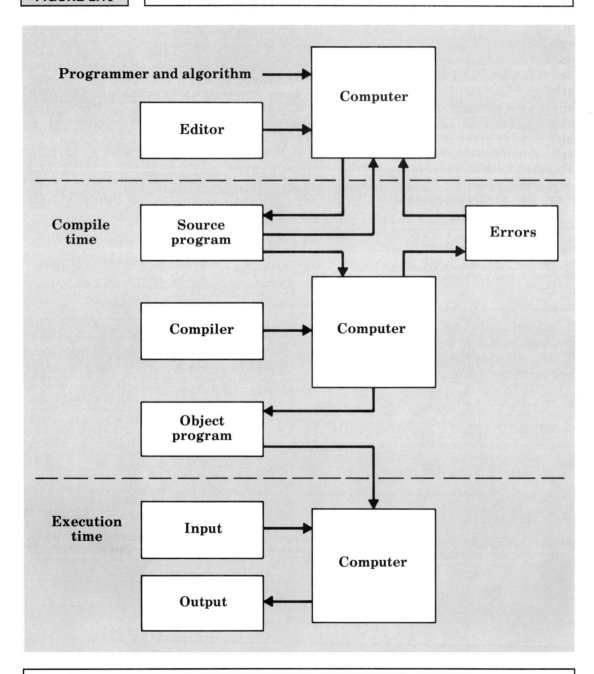

The source program is translated by the compiler into a program which can be run by a computer. In TURBO, the source program will be a Pascal program and will have the file extension PAS. During compilation, syntax errors (if any) are detected. These must be corrected using the editor to modify the source program. The process of compiling and correction may need to be repeated several times to obtain a syntactically correct source program. When the compiler is given a correct program it translates the program into another program which can then be executed. This program is known as an *object program*. Using TURBO as we have described above, this program would be placed in memory. Object programs have the file type COM (or CMD, CP/M-86).

> **An *object program* is a program in machine language which can be directly executed by a computer.**

DEFINITION

The language that the computer is able to execute directly is known as *machine language* or *machine code*. Machine language consists of sequences of electronic 0s and 1s (called bits) which instruct the computer to do certain tasks. It is not easy to learn and is very difficult to use for solving the types of problems we are interested in solving. Machine language is intimately related to assembly language. If you are interested in learning more about how the computer actually works, you should investigate these topics.

In practice it is possible that the three computers in *FIGURE 2.10* may be three different computers. This will not be the case for us. Furthermore, even a syntactically correct program may not run and produce correct (in terms of the problem) output. For example, if the addition symbol (+) appeared where a multiplication symbol (*) should have been in the program Circle, the program would have run. However, the program would not give the correct results. This sort of error is (alas!) not uncommon and can be very difficult to uncover.

2.6 SUMMARY

In order to program, it is necessary to be able to use the computer to create and execute programs. The operating system and TURBO are the means of doing this. Both manipulate files. A file contains a group of related items. In this chapter, files have been used to hold programs.

Both TURBO and the operating system provide commands to work with files. These are used by the programmer to enter, run, and save programs as well as to make copies and print programs.

An editor is used to create programs. Using an editor, the programmers enter their programs. A program is based on an algorithm which has been devised to solve the problem at hand. After the program has been entered, it may be run and used to accomplish the user's needs. ❏

EXERCISES

1. Find out how the computer you use boots the system.

2. Find out the names of the operating system programs on your computer which do the following (these are known as commands because they command the computer to do something):
   a. List the names of files on a logged drive.
   b. Erase a file.
   c. Display the contents of a file on the screen.
   d. Print a file on the printer.
   e. Make a copy of a file.
   f. Rename a file.
   g. Designate the logged drive.
   h. Stop (or break) a program which is running.
   i. Prepare a disk for use. (This is known as formatting the disk.)

3. Write the commands needed on the computer you use to do the following (in practice it is necessary to follow these with a RETURN):
   a. List the names of files on drive B.
   b. Erase a file named JUNK.TXT.
   c. Display the contents of the file named NEW.TXT.
   d. Change the logged drive to B.
   e. Print the file named PROGRAM1.PAS.
   f. Make a copy of the file named OLDFILE.TXT. The new copy is to be named NEWFILE.TXT. (Both are to be on drive B; assume that the logged drive is A.)
   g. Print the file on the disk in drive B which is named OUTPUT.DAT.
   h. Rename a file on drive B from NEW.TXT to NEWEST.TXT.

   Sometimes it is useful to be able to specify a group of files. This can be done using "wild-card" or "match-all" symbols. An asterisk (*) may be used in place of either a file name or a file extension. It specifies that any file name (or file extension) satisfies the file needed in a command. A question mark (?) is used to match any character in a file name or extension. For example, ERA B:JUNK.* or DEL B:JUNK.* means that all files in drive B named JUNK are to be erased, regardless of their extensions. The command DIR *.PAS causes all the names of files on the logged drive which have a PAS extension to be listed. DIR PROG????.BAS displays the names of all the files on the logged drive whose names start with PROG and whose extensions are BAS. (Wild-card symbols may also be used to respond to the D command of TURBO: e.g., Dir mask B:*.PAS produces a list of the Pascal programs on drive B.)

4. Write commands (using wild cards) to do the following.
   a. List the names of the files which (presumably) contain BASIC programs (BASIC programs usually have the extension .BAS).

b. Delete all the backup files on drive B (a backup file has the extension .BAK).

c. List the names of the files on the logged drive which start with PROG.

d. Delete all the files from the logged drive whose names are GARBAGE (and have any extension).

5. This exercise is designed to familiarize you with the TURBO environment. Although we have used capitals for the commands, you may use lower-case letters instead. In all other matters follow the instructions very carefully. Remember that operating system commands are entered with a RETURN; these may be corrected by backspacing (or left arrow). TURBO commands are not followed by a RETURN.

a. Obtain a disk with enough of the operating system to run the computer you are using as well as the TURBO files TURBO.COM and TURBO.MSG. Put this disk in drive A and boot the system.

b. Put a blank disk in drive B and, using the appropriate program, prepare the disk for use. This is known as formatting the disk.

c. Type DIR A: You should get a list of programs, almost all having the extension .COM .

d. Type DIR B: You should get some indication that there are no files on disk B: .

e. Type TURBO to load the TURBO system. In response to the question concerning error messages, type Y.

f. Type L and enter B:⟨RETURN⟩ as the new logged drive.

g. Type W and enter PROGRAM1⟨RETURN⟩ as the work-file name.

h. Type RETURN and observe the changes in the TURBO menu.

i. Type E and enter the program below. Use the editor to correct any errors you make. Use your name and the date in the appropriate place. (Remember: to exit the editor, type CTRL/KD.)

```
PROGRAM Greeting (Output);

{ A first program
     Author    : YOUR NAME
     Date      : THE DATE
     File name : PROGRAM1.PAS
}

BEGIN  { Greeting }
  Writeln('Hello');
  Writeln('Goodbye')
END.   { Greeting }
```

j. After exiting the editor (using CTRL/KD), type S to save this program.

k. Type D and then RETURN to see that the program has been saved.

l. Type R to run this program. If you have any errors, return to the editor and correct them and then repeat steps i, j, k, and l.

m. Type E to change the program above to look like the following.

```
PROGRAM Greeting (Input, Output);

{ A first program revisited

      Author    : YOUR NAME
      Date      : THE DATE
      File name : PROGRAM1.PAS
}

VAR
    Name : String[20];

BEGIN   { Greeting }
  Writeln('Hello');
  Write('What is your name? ');
  Readln(Name);
  Writeln('Hello ', Name);
  Writeln('It is nice talking to you!');
  Writeln;
  Writeln('Goodbye')
END.    { Greeting }
```

n. When you have finished modifying the program so that it looks like the one above, run it and enter your name at the appropriate place.

o. Type Q to quit TURBO. In response to the question, answer Y or N, depending on which version of the program you want saved.

p. Type DIR B:[RETURN] and notice that B now has a file. What is its name?

q. Display the contents of the program you wrote by entering TYPE B:PROGRAM1.PAS[RETURN].

6. This exercise is similar to exercise 5, and so the steps are not quite as detailed.

a. Boot the system (if you need to) and load TURBO (including the error messages).

b. Change the logged drive to B and start a work file named PROGRAM2.PAS.

c. Use the editor to enter the program that follows.

```
PROGRAM ManyHellos (Output);

{  A short program to write some hellos.

      Author    : YOUR NAME
      Date      : DATE
      File name : PROGRAM2.PAS
}

VAR
    I : Integer;
```

```
BEGIN { ManyHellos }
   For I := 1 to 20 Do
      Writeln('Hello')
END.  { ManyHellos }
```

d. Save and then run this program.
e. Use the editor to change the program to the one below.

```
PROGRAM ManyHellos (Output);

{  A short program to write some hellos.

      Author    : YOUR NAME
      Date      : DATE
      File name : PROGRAM2.PAS
}

CONST
      ManyTimes = 20;
VAR
      I : Integer;

BEGIN { ManyHellos }
   For I := 1 to ManyTimes Do
      Writeln('Hello')
END.  { ManyHellos }
```

f. Save and then run this program.
g. Change this program by replacing the 20 with 2000, so that it looks like this.

```
PROGRAM ManyHellos (Output);

{  A short program to write some hellos.

      Author    : YOUR NAME
      Date      : DATE
      File name : PROGRAM2.PAS
}

CONST
      ManyTimes = 2000;

VAR
      I : Integer;

BEGIN { ManyHellos }
   For I := 1 to ManyTimes Do
      Writeln('Hello')
END.  { ManyHellos }
```

h. Run this program. Try to use the BREAK or CTRL/C to stop this program after a few seconds. If this does not stop the program, you must let the program run to completion (2000 Hellos) or press the reset button (if your computer has one) or turn the computer off. If you press the reset button or turn the computer off you will need to reboot the system and start TURBO again. See what is in the file named PROGRAM2.PAS or B:PROGRAM2.PAS.

i. If you did exercise 5, type W and enter B:PROGRAM1.PAS. Run the program.

j. Quit TURBO and see what is stored on the disk in drive B.

7. Use the editor to write a letter telling how easy it is to use a computer to write a letter. (Suggestions: to your parents, spouse, boy or girl friend.) When you have finished, save the letter and then print it. (Don't forget to mail the letter.)

Chapter 1 contained an introduction to problem solving and algorithm development with the intent of producing an algorithm which would be the basis of a computer program. All programs must be written in some programming language. In this chapter enough of the language Pascal is introduced to write complete programs. Chapter 2 presented the environment in which this programming will be done. The environment provides the means of entering and correcting programs (using the editor), running programs, storing programs, and printing programs. All the programs presented have been created in this way. ☐

CHAPTER 3

PROGRAMS, CHARACTERS, AND STRINGS

3.1 IDENTIFIERS

Just as many objects encountered in daily life need labels, the items that are used in programming need some means of identification. This is more of a problem for the programmer than for a person who can describe one thing rather easily. For example, when used appropriately, any of the following would mean my means of transportation : "my car," "a small yellow car," "Pennsylvania license JMJ 923," "serial number JXJ98237-7254." There is a significant difference between the first two and the last two phrases. The first two are much more descriptive and natural whereas the last two are much more specific and identify the car exactly. Because a programmer is working with a machine, it is necessary to uniquely identify an item much as a serial number uniquely identifies an automobile. On the other hand, programs are read by people. This means that it is desirable to use identifiers which are mnemonic or descriptive. Pascal enables us to do both. Devising good labels requires effort by the programmer. A label in Pascal is formally known as an *identifier*.

DEFINITION

> An *identifier* is a sequence of characters which serves to name a programming entity.

The syntax of a Pascal identifier is quite simple. An identifier is comprised of a letter followed by zero or more letters or digits. A letter is one of the 26 from A through Z or a through z, and a digit is one of the ten from 0 through 9. A syntax diagram of this is contained in *FIGURE 3-1*. Most implementations of Pascal have both upper- and lower-case letters, and we use both. Exactly how many characters can be used to form an identifier varies from implementation to implementation, but it is generally fairly large. A limitation on identifiers is that they may not be split between lines. TURBO permits up to 127 characters in an identifier, but this is more than one should ever use. TURBO also extends the definition of an identifier to allow the underscore (__) to be used wherever a letter could be. In this text the underscore isn't used so that we conform to standard Pascal.

Since it is impossible to use a phrase (as in English) for an identifier, identifiers are frequently made of several words. We adopt the stylistic

FIGURE 3.1   Identifier

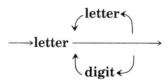

convention that the start of a word within an identifier is a capital letter and the remaining letters are small letters. Here are some legal and illegal identifiers.

Legal Identifiers

A

X

a

x

Down

YardsToGo

AVeryLongButNonethelessLegalIdentifier

Test3

Illegal Identifiers

2ndDown   { Starts with digit }

John'sBook   { ' not permitted }

Up And Down { Spaces not permitted }

There are also two lists of identifiers which Pascal uses itself. Those in the first group are known as *reserved words* and cannot be used as identifiers. Those in the second group are known as *standard identifiers* and may be redefined but thereby lose their original Pascal definitions. It is recommended that you don't use the standard identifiers unless you really have a good reason to do so. These two groups of identifiers are listed in *FIGURE 3.2* and also in Appendix F. Note that some of these are nonstandard—i.e., they are defined for TURBO Pascal but may not be in other implementations. (By standard Pascal we mean as defined in [Co] or [IEEE] or [Le].) Also be aware that other implementations add to the standard Pascal lists as well. Not every reserved word and standard identifier that is listed will be covered. Some of them involve techniques beyond the scope of this book. However, it is possible to cause an error by using a reserved word or standard identifier inadvertently, and so a complete list is useful. We will emphasize the reserved words in programs by capitalizing them.

A *reserved word* is an identifier which is used as a basic symbol of the language and cannot be redefined by the programmer.	**DEFINITION**

A *standard identifier* is an identifier which denotes an entity defined by the language itself. A standard identifier may be used by the programmer. In this case the original meaning of the standard identifier is lost.	**DEFINITION**

FIGURE 3.2

Reserved Words				
ABSOLUTE*	ELSE	IN	PACKED	THEN
AND	END	INLINE*	PROCEDURE	TO
ARRAY	EXTERNAL*	LABEL	PROGRAM	TYPE
BEGIN	FILE	MOD	RECORD	UNTIL
CASE	FOR	NIL	REPEAT	VAR
CONST	FORWARD	NOT	SET	WHILE
DIV	FUNCTION	OF	SHL*	WITH
DO	GOTO	OR	SHR*	XOR*
DOWNTO	IF	OVERLAY*	STRING*	

Standard Identifiers			
Abs	DelLine*	Kbd*	Real
Addr*	Delay*	KeyPressed*	Release*
Arctan	Dispose*	Length*	Rename*
Assign*	Delete	Ln	Reset
Aux*	EOF	Lo*	Rewrite
AuxInPtr*	EOLn	Lst*	Round
AuxOutPtr*	Erase*	LstOutPtr*	Seek*
BlockRead*	Execute*	Mark*	Sin
BlockWrite*	Exp	MaxAvail*	SizeOf*
Boolean	False	MaxInt	Sqr
BufLen*	FilePos*	Mem*	Sqrt
Byte*	FileSize*	MemAvail*	Str*
Chain*	FillChar*	Move*	Succ
Char	Flush*	New	Swap*
Chr	Frac*	NormVideo*	Text
Close*	FreeMem*	Odd	Trm*
ClrEOL*	GetMem*	Ord	True
ClrScr*	GoToXY*	Output	Trunc
Con*	HeapPtr*	Pi*	UpCase*
ConInPtr*	Hi*	Port*	Usr*
ConOutPtr*	HighVideo*	Pos*	UsrInPtr*
Concat*	IOResult*	Pred	UsrOutPtr*
ConstPtr*	Input	Ptr*	Val*
Copy*	InsLine*	Random*	Write
Cos	Insert*	Randomize*	Writeln
CrtExit*	Int*	Read	
CrtInit*	Integer	Readln	

* Nonstandard Pascal (TURBO only)

[Standard Pascal also includes the standard identifiers Get, Pack, Page, Put, Unpack.]

[When TURBO runs under MS-DOS or CP/M-86 the following are also standard identifiers: CSeg, DSeg, MemW, Ofs, PortW, Seg, SSeg.

When TURBO runs under CP/M the following are also standard identifiers: Bios, BiosHL, Bdos, BdosHL, RecurPtr, StackPtr.]

3.2 THE FORM OF A PASCAL PROGRAM

Before discussing the details of Pascal let's look at the general layout of a Pascal program. This will enable us to put the details in their proper place.

A Pascal program consists of a heading, a declaration section, a statement section, and a period (.). The declaration section and statement section together are known as a *block*. A very simple example of a Pascal program is given in *FIGURE 3.3*. The first line is the heading. The two lines starting with VAR form the declaration section. The lines starting with BEGIN and finishing with END are the statement section.

The first line of a program is the program heading. The program heading gives the name of the program and specifies how the program communicates with its environment. A program always uses files of one sort or another to communicate with its environment, and so describing the means of communication becomes a matter of naming the files used. For the time being we will just use the standard files Input (for the keyboard) and Output (for the screen). In this situation the program heading consists of the reserved word PROGRAM, an identifier (which is the name of the program), a left parenthesis, the key words INPUT and OUTPUT (separated by a comma), a right parenthesis, and finally a semicolon (;). The following is an example of a program heading.

```
PROGRAM Circle (Input, Output);
```

In general, the identifiers in the parentheses in the program heading refer to the files the program uses. It is possible, although not likely, that the program uses no files. *FIGURE 3.4* is a syntax diagram of the program heading. (In this syntax diagram, as in others, the abbreviation "ident." is used to denote an identifier.)

The program heading is followed by a block. A block consists of two sections. The first is a declaration section. The declaration section specifies (declares) the objects that will be used in the program. In this chap-

---

FIGURE 3.3

```
PROGRAM Add(Input, Output);

VAR
     I, J : Integer;

BEGIN
  Writeln('Enter two integers, separated by a space.');
  Readln(I, J);
  Writeln('Their sum is ', I + J)
END.
```

FIGURE 3.4

Program Heading

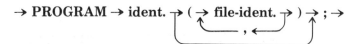

ter, one kind of object that may be declared in the declaration section will be discussed: variables. The second part of a block is the statement section. The statement section specifies the instructions of the program. *FIGURE 3.5* is a collection of syntax diagrams that define a block as we have just discussed. (These will need to be augmented as more features of the language are introduced.)

The definition of a program may now be given. A program consists of a program heading followed by a block followed by a period (syntax diagram in *FIGURE 3.6*). This is a general definition. This definition will be expanded by adding more to the declaration section and by introducing a variety of statements. (Notice that "statement" is not defined in *FIGURE 3.5*.) An example of a Pascal program using the above is given in

FIGURE 3.5

Block

Block

→ declaration-section → statement-section →

Declaration section

↱→ variable-declarations →↗

Variable declarations

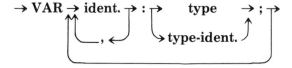

Statement section

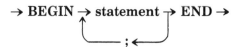

FIGURE 3.6

Program

→ program-heading → block → . →

FIGURE 3.7. This program asks the user for his or her name and age and then prints a message using this information. The 10 in STRING[10] limits the length of the name entered to 10 letters.

Notice that all the key words we mentioned (PROGRAM, Input, Output, VAR, BEGIN, END) are present as well as the necessary punctuation (; ( ) : .). On the other hand, the layout of the program on the page is free form. Pascal requires that certain things be present in a certain order, but exactly where they are on a page (or screen) is up to the programmer. In fact, the program in *FIGURE 3.8* is exactly the same program as far as the compiler is concerned. But the program in *FIGURE 3.7* is much more readable. You can actually pick out the parts of the program we defined above. You should strive to arrange your programs to be as readable as possible. Ways of making your program more readable will be pointed out as we progress.

Referring again to the program in *FIGURE 3.7* you can see examples of some of the items that were not defined. For example, the five lines between BEGIN and END are statements. The syntax diagram for a statement section indicates that there is a semicolon between statements. It is customary to put the semicolon at the end of a line. However, the semicolon serves to separate statements.

Another means of making a program more easily understood is comments. Comments may be inserted in a program to provide information that the program itself does not. For example, there is no place in a program to give the programmer's name. Comments have no effect on how the program works.

FIGURE 3.7

```
PROGRAM NextYear(Input, Output);

VAR
     Age  : Integer;
     Name : STRING[10];

BEGIN
  Writeln('What is your name?');
  Readln(Name);
  Writeln('How old are you, ', Name, '?');
  Readln(Age);
  Writeln('Next year you will be ', Age + 1)
END.
```

FIGURE 3.8

```
PROGRAM NextYear(Input, Output); VAR Age : Integer; Name :
STRING[10]; BEGIN Writeln('What is your name?'); Readln(Name);
Writeln('How old are you, ', Name, '?'); Readln(Age);
Writeln('Next year you will be ', Age+1) END.
```

Any place a blank may appear in a program, a comment may appear. A comment starts with a left brace ({) and ends with a right brace (}). It is also possible to start a comment with a left parenthesis asterisk ((*) and end it with an asterisk right parenthesis (*)). Here are some samples of comments.

```
{ This is a comment }
(* So is this. *)
{   A comment may extend over more
    than one line. }
```

Comments should provide useful information and explanations to the reader of the program. This includes the person who wrote the program. It is suggested that, after the program heading in a program, a brief description of the program (what it does), the programmer's name, the date the program was written, and the file name under which the program is stored be included in a comment. Sometimes it is helpful to explain

FIGURE 3.9

```
PROGRAM NextYear(Input, Output);

{ A simple illustrative program

      Author : John Riley
      Date   : December 7, 1986
      File name : CH3EX4.PAS
}

VAR
      Age  : Integer;
      Name : STRING[10];

BEGIN { NextYear }
  Writeln('What is your name?');
  Readln(Name);
  Writeln('How old are you, ', Name, '?');
  Readln(Age);
  Writeln('Next year you will be ', Age + 1)
END. { NextYear }
```

the purposes of variables and constants with a comment. We also label the BEGIN and END of our program with the program's name. With these conventions, the program in *FIGURE 3.7* would be written as in *FIGURE 3.9*.

Occasionally it is necessary to make comments on portions of the program whose purpose or working may be unclear. Never comment the obvious. For example, we would not write the following.

```
Age := Age + 1; { Add 1 to Age }
```

The comment merely restates the program statement and serves no purpose.

The use of comments is part of programming style. We will make some suggestions about style and the use of comments as we proceed. A set of programming style guidelines, based on our experience, is found in Appendix H. Opinions vary on the issue of style, but all stylistic conventions are designed to make programs more comprehensible. The book by Ledgard *et al.* [L-N-H] is an extensive discussion of these matters.

3.3 CHARACTERS AND STRINGS

Although computers were originally developed for doing large-scale arithmetic ("number crunching"), much of their modern use is for manipulating nonnumerical data. An example of this sort of task is putting a list of names in alphabetical order. TURBO Pascal allows these manipulations to be done by providing appropriate data types.

The first of these types is the standard Pascal type known as *characters*. Exactly what values are included in this type are *implementation dependent*. This means that the particular computer determines the exact characteristics of this type. It is understood that every implementation provides some set of characters.

A feature which is *implementation dependent* has its characteristics defined by the particular combination of software and hardware used to implement the language.

DEFINITION

About all that can be said with certainty about the characters in any implementation is that the characters include some punctuation symbols, the capital letters A through Z, and the digits 0 through 9. It can also be assumed that the capital letters and digits are in their usual orders. Many microcomputers use a character set known as the ASCII (American Standard Code for Information Interchange) characters. Throughout this book we will assume that this is the character set being used. *FIGURE*

3.10 contains the ASCII characters. This table is also included in Appendix G.

In Pascal, characters are always given in (single) quotes—e.g., 'A', 'B', 'C', 'a', 'b', 'c', '0', '1', '2', '3', ';'. This enables alphabetic characters to be distinguished from single-letter identifiers and numeric characters to be distinguished from integers.

The order of characters given in *FIGURE 3.10* is the order of the characters in TURBO Pascal. To the computer, any upper-case letter precedes any lower-case letter. Thus 'Q' precedes 'b'. Also, the numeric characters precede the alphabetic ones. The punctuation symbols are interspersed among the letters and digits.

The first column in *FIGURE 3.10* contains nonprinting or control characters. These are used to control the layout of items on a page and other things. For example, CTRL/M roughly corresponds to the character entered when the RETURN key is pressed. These won't be needed very often.

One character in *FIGURE 3.10* deserves special mention. This is the character numbered 32. SPC is an abbreviation for SPaCe. This is the character entered when the space bar is pressed. It has the effect of moving the cursor (on a video screen) or print head (in a printer) one space to the right without any character appearing.

Strings are built using characters. A *string constant* is a sequence of characters enclosed in single quotes. Here are some examples of strings.

```
'Hello'
'How are you?'
'Bloomsburg, Pennsylvania 17815'
'9934'
'This is a very long string which is still legal!'
```

As you can see, almost any printing character can be used in a string. The only character which causes a problem is the apostrophe or single quote (') because this character is used at the beginning and end of a string. To place an apostrophe in a string, we use two adjacent apostrophes which then count as one character, an apostrophe. This causes one apostrophe to appear. Here are two examples of strings with apostrophes.

```
'It''s not difficult to put an apostrophe in a string.'
'Richards''s car'
```

String constants are part of standard Pascal. TURBO Pascal (like some other implementations of Pascal) has more facilities for handling strings than are specified in standard Pascal. These will be used as needed.

Incidentally, strings are considered to be in the usual alphabetic order (roughly speaking). We will return to the exact means of comparison later on.

ASCII Table | **FIGURE 3.10**

Number	Character		No.	Char.	No.	Char.	No.	Char.
0	CTRL/@	NUL	32	SPC	64	@	96	`
1	CTRL/A	SOH	33	!	65	A	97	a
2	CTRL/B	STX	34	"	66	B	98	b
3	CTRL/C	ETX	35	#	67	C	99	c
4	CTRL/D	EOT	36	$	68	D	100	d
5	CTRL/E	ENQ	37	%	69	E	101	e
6	CTRL/F	ACK	38	&	70	F	102	f
7	CTRL/G	BEL	39	'	71	G	103	g
8	CTRL/H	BS	40	(	72	H	104	h
9	CTRL/I	HT	41	)	73	I	105	i
10	CTRL/J	LF	42	*	74	J	106	j
11	CTRL/K	VT	43	+	75	K	107	k
12	CTRL/L	FF	44	,	76	L	108	l
13	CTRL/M	CR	45	-	77	M	109	m
14	CTRL/N	SO	46	.	78	N	110	n
15	CTRL/O	SI	47	/	79	O	111	o
16	CTRL/P	DLE	48	0	80	P	112	p
17	CTRL/Q	DC1	49	1	81	Q	113	q
18	CTRL/R	DC2	50	2	82	R	114	r
19	CTRL/S	DC3	51	3	83	S	115	s
20	CTRL/T	DC4	52	4	84	T	116	t
21	CTRL/U	NAK	53	5	85	U	117	u
22	CTRL/V	SYN	54	6	86	V	118	v
23	CTRL/W	ETB	55	7	87	W	119	w
24	CTRL/X	CAN	56	8	88	X	120	x
25	CTRL/Y	EM	57	9	89	Y	121	y
26	CTRL/Z	SUB	58	:	90	Z	122	z
27	CTRL/[	ESC	59	;	91	[	123	{
28	CTRL/\	FS	60	<	92	\	124	|
29	CTRL/]	GS	61	=	93	]	125	}
30	CTRL/^	RS	62	>	94	^	126	~
31	CTRL/__	US	63	?	95	__	127	DEL

FIGURE 3.11

String

String

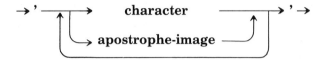

Apostrophe image

→ " →

FIGURE 3.11 contains the syntax diagrams for a string. Notice that the apostrophe or single quote requires a special case. What "character" refers to in this diagram is defined by the implementation and excludes the apostrophe.

A very important use of strings is as output to the users of a program. A string may be used as a message to the users either informing them that the program is in progress or telling them what they must be doing. Another important use of strings is to label other output, particularly numeric data. Examples of these uses will occur as we progress. A program which outputs a sequence of messages appears in *FIGURE 3.12*. This program prints three lines of messages on the screen. Each line consists of the string within a set of parentheses.

FIGURE 3.12

```
PROGRAM WakeUp(Output);

{  A program printing wake up messages.

     Author    : John Riley
     Date      : December 7, 1986
     File name : CH3EX5.PAS

}

BEGIN { WakeUp }
  Writeln('Please wake up.');
  Writeln('Wake up!');
  Writeln('GET OUT OF BED, LAZYBONES !')
END. { WakeUp }
```

3.4 VARIABLE DECLARATIONS

A computer (like a human) needs places to store items for future reference. For example, when you go shopping you make up a list of items you want to buy so that you don't forget anything. Of course, if you only need one or two items you don't make up a list. Pascal demands that all items that it uses be specified in the declaration section of a block. In this section, variable declarations are discussed.

A *variable declaration* has the effect of setting aside, naming, and organizing a certain portion of the computer's memory for use by the program. In the variable declarations, identifiers become names for specific locations in the computer's memory which are known as *variables*. By using a variable's name it is possible to use the value stored in the variable. It is also possible to place a new value in the variable by using the variable's name. We usually do not distinguish between the variable and the variable's name. This is similar to blurring the distinction between a person and the person's name ("Sue went to the store" is short for "The person named Sue went to the store").

In addition to providing the names of the variables in the variable declarations it is also necessary to specify the type or types of the variables. The type of a variable determines what values may be stored in that variable. For example, it is not possible to store characters in a variable which is not declared to be of character type. The type of a variable also determines what can be done with that variable. It makes sense to multiply variables which contain numbers, but it does not make sense to multiply variables containing strings. Pascal is very good at enforcing this sort of rule, which prevents programmers from doing things they shouldn't.

The variable declarations consist of the key word VAR followed by sequences of identifiers (separated by commas), a colon, a type or type identifier, and a semicolon. The syntax diagram for this is given in *FIGURE 3.13*.

The program in *FIGURE 3.14* has two variables declared: Age and Name. These are used to store the age and name of the person using the program. Since the age of a person is a number, Age is declared to be of integer type. The name of a person is a string, and so Name is declared

| Variable Declarations | FIGURE 3.13 |

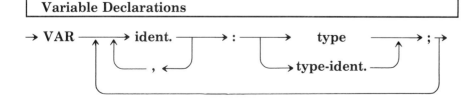

FIGURE 3.14

```
PROGRAM NextYear(Input, Output);

{    A short "conversational" program.

     Author    : John Riley
     Date      : December 1, 1986
     File name : CH3EX6.PAS
}

VAR
     Age  : Integer;
     Name : STRING[10];

BEGIN { NextYear }
  Writeln('What is your name?');
  Readln(Name);
  Writeln('How old are you, ', Name, '?');
  Readln(Age);
  Writeln('Next year you will be ', Age + 1)
END.  { NextYear }
```

to be of string type. The 10 in STRING[10] limits Name to holding ten letters. Extra letters would be ignored.

As the syntax diagrams indicate, it is possible to have several identifiers declared to be variables of the same type by listing them (separated by commas) before the colon type. When this is done, it is helpful to put each variable on a separate line. Indenting the variable names also seems to improve the readability of the program. For example, to declare variables to hold a first, middle, and last name (and an age), the following declarations would be made.

```
VAR
     Age         : Integer;
     FirstName,
     MiddleName,
     LastName    : STRING[10];
```

It is possible to use the same type or type identifier in more than one place in the variable declaration section, as in the following declarations.

```
VAR
     Age         : Integer;
     FirstName,
     MiddleName,
     LastName    : STRING[10];
     Year        : Integer;
```

However, an identifier may be declared only once in the declaration section. Thus the following is illegal because N is declared twice.

```
VAR
     M,
     N      : Integer;
     N      : STRING[10];
```

It is good programming practice to make variable names mnemonic—that is, the name of the variable should suggest what it contains. It is sometimes a good idea to add comments in the variable declarations to elaborate on the use of the variable. The following example illustrates this.

```
VAR
     Age           : Integer;      { Of employee }
     FirstName,
     MiddleName,
     LastName      : STRING[10];   { Of employee }
     Year          : Integer;      { Of birth    }
```

Of course, laying out the declarations and comments neatly can greatly improve the appearance and readability of your program. Because Pascal is free form, you can devise your own way of presenting the declarations. It should be neat and easy to read.

In order to declare that a variable is to contain a single character value, the key word CHAR (short for CHARacter) is used as the type in the variable declaration section. A variable of character type may contain any of the characters defined by the implementation. TURBO Pascal uses the ASCII character set (refer to *FIGURE 3.10*). Here is an example of using character variables to store three initials.

```
VAR
     FirstInit,         { First,                  }
     MidInit,           { Middle,                 }
     LastInit  : Char;  { Last Initial of a name  }
```

Notice that the identifiers for the variables used are suggestive of what the variables will contain. Comments are used to further clarify the intent of the programmer.

TURBO Pascal also provides *string variables*. A string variable is used to hold a sequence of characters. A string variable is declared using the key word STRING followed by the maximum length of the string that may be stored in the variable. This maximum length is enclosed in square brackets ([ ]). The maximum length specified must be an integer between 1 and 255. The syntax diagram for this is given in *FIGURE 3.15*.

| String Type | FIGURE 3.15 |

→ **STRING** → [→ **length** →] →

The program in *FIGURE 3.16* illustrates the use of character and string variables. This program asks the user for his or her first name, middle initial, and last name and then prints a message using this information. It should be noted that the name will not be centered using this program. Centering the name requires features of Pascal that have not been covered yet.

One of the questions that a programmer must resolve is what types of variables are needed to solve the problem. In the program in *FIGURE 3.16* it was fairly obvious that string variables were needed. But it was still necessary to estimate the length of these. Ten was chosen for the first name and twenty for the last name because last names tend to be longer than first names. In this situation, as in many others, it is much better to err in having more than enough room than too little room.

The variable declarations specify what identifiers are going to be used as variable names in the program. To promote correctness and understanding, all identifiers used in a program must be declared. Further-

FIGURE 3.16

```
PROGRAM EgoBoost(Input, Output);

{ A short program to personally encourage the user.


        Author    : John Riley
        Date      : December 7, 1986
        File name : CH3EX7.PAS
}

VAR
        FirstName : STRING[10];   { First name,     }
        MidInit   : Char;         { Middle initial, }
        LastName  : STRING[20];   { Last name       }

BEGIN { EgoBoost }
  Writeln('What is your first name?');
  Readln(FirstName);
  Writeln('What is your middle initial?');
  Readln(MidInit);
  Writeln('What is your last name?');
  Readln(LastName);
  Writeln;
  Writeln('**********************************************');
  Writeln('*                                            *');
  Writeln('    ', FirstName, ' ', MidInit, '. ', LastName, );
  Writeln('*                                            *');
  Writeln('*            IS A CERTIFIED STAR             *');
  Writeln('*                                            *');
  Writeln('**********************************************')
END.  { EgoBoost }
```

more, within the declaration section of a block, an identifier can be used for only one thing. An error will result if you attempt to use an identifier twice. An error will also occur if an identifier is used that has not been declared. The latter situation commonly arises from a typing mistake— e.g., FisrtName for FirstName. The error is reported as "Unknown identifier." The first thing to check when you get this error is your spelling.

The variable declarations set up variables for the program. These are locations in memory where values may be stored. Statements for storing and retrieving values are discussed in the next two sections.

3.5 THE ASSIGNMENT STATEMENT

In Section 3.4 we commented that the value stored in a variable may be changed as the program executes. We did not state how this was to be accomplished. The simplest way to change the value stored in a variable location is to use the *assignment statement*. The assignment statement has the effect of changing the value of a variable. When this is done, the old value of the variable is lost. The syntax diagram for the assignment statement is given in *FIGURE 3.17*.

The assignment statement consists of a variable (or, more precisely, a variable identifier) followed by the colon-equals combination followed by an expression. The variable (which must be declared in the variable declaration section) receives a value derived from the expression following the colon-equals combination. For now we will use characters, strings, and variables for expressions in our examples. Chapter 4 deals with numeric variables and with expressions. The colon-equals combination (:=) is known as the *assignment operator*. It is read "becomes," "is assigned," or "is set equal to."

The effect (or semantics) of the assignment statement is that the value to the right of the assignment operator is stored in the variable to the left of the assignment statement. In the program in *FIGURE 3.18*, two string variables, FirstPart and SecondPart, are declared. The first assignment statement (after BEGIN { Greeting }) stored the string 'Hello,' in FirstPart. The second assignment statement stored 'have a nice day.' in SecondPart. These values are then used to print a message. The effects of the variable declarations and these assignment statements on memory are depicted in *FIGURE 3.19*. This sort of diagram is sometimes referred to as a memory diagram or map. A question mark in a variable location indicates that the variable has not been given a value and that its value should be considered unknown.

| Assignment Statement | FIGURE 3.17 |

```
→  variable  →  :=  →  expression  →
```

FIGURE 3.18

```
PROGRAM Greeting(Output);

{ This program prints a simple message.

     Author    : John Riley
     Date      : December 7, 1986
     File name : CH3EX8.PAS
}

VAR
     FirstPart,                 { First,                      }
     SecondPart : STRING[20]; { Second part of message }

BEGIN { Greeting }
  FirstPart := 'Hello, ';
  SecondPart := 'have a nice day.';
  Writeln(FirstPart, SecondPart)
END.   { Greeting }



Output :

Hello, have a nice day.
```

The right side of an assignment statement may be a variable. In this situation, the value of the variable on the right is copied into the variable on the left of the assignment statement. This is illustrated in the program in *FIGURE 3.20*, which is a variation on the preceding program in which 'Hello,' is printed twice. In the second statement of this program the value of FirstPart is stored in SecondPart. So SecondPart is assigned the value 'Hello, '.

The value of the expression on the right side of an assignment statement must be of the same type as the variable on the left. For example, if a numeric variable is on the left side of an assignment statement a numeric value must be on the right side of the assignment statement. An error would occur if a string were on the right of an assignment statement and a numeric variable on the left. This property is known as *assignment compatibility*. Roughly speaking, a variable and a value are assignment compatible if they are of the same type. (An exception to this will be encountered in the next chapter.)

DEFINITION

> **A variable is *assignment compatible* with a value if the value may be stored in the variable.**

FIGURE 3.19

VAR

FirstPart,   {First,   }
SecondPart : STRING [20]; {Second part of message}

MS-DOS
TURBO
Program

FirstPart	?
SecondPart	?

Memory after declarations

FirstPart : = 'Hello, ';

FirstPart	Hello,
SecondPart	?

Memory after first assignment

SecondPart : = 'have a nice day.';

FirstPart	Hello,
SecondPart	have a nice day.

Memory after second assignment

Pascal checks assignment compatibility. An error will occur in compiling if assignment compatibility has been violated.

Whenever a variable appears on the right of an assignment statement, a value is obtained from its storage location in memory. If the variable has not been given a value (e.g., an assignment statement), the value

---

FIGURE 3.20   **Effect of SecondPart := FirstPart Upon Memory**

```
PROGRAM GreetingAgain(Output);

{ This program prints a simple message.

        Author    : John Riley
        Date      : December 7, 1986
        File name : CH3EX9.PAS
}

VAR
      FirstPart,               { First,                  }
      SecondPart,              { Second,                 }
      ThirdPart  : STRING[20]; { Third part of message  }

BEGIN  { GreetingAgain }
   FirstPart := 'Hello, ';
   SecondPart := FirstPart;
   ThirdPart := 'have a nice day.';
   Writeln(FirstPart, SecondPart, ThirdPart)
END.   { GreetingAgain }


Output:

Hello, Hello, have a nice day.
```

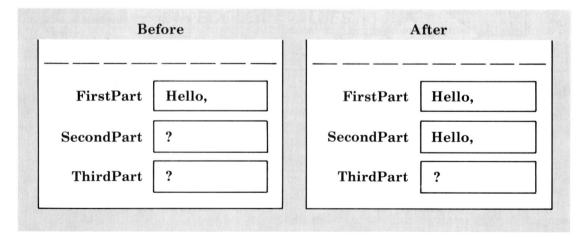

that is in the storage location is unknown to the programmer. This error is called an uninitialized variable. Some versions of Pascal detect this error. TURBO Pascal does not. This forces programmers to rely on their own planning. If strange results appear when you run a program, make sure that every variable used for a value has been given a value.

In algorithms, assignment is frequently denoted by a left arrow, as in

```
Distance ← Rate * Time
```

We use this notation for two reasons. First, algorithms often are hand-written, and the arrow is easy to draw. Second, the arrow indicates the direction in which values are being moved.

3.6 INPUT AND OUTPUT

Most programs have three aspects: input (getting data), processing (manipulating data, producing information), and output (transmitting data or information). In this section the two aspects input and output are covered.

In some ways, getting data and information into and out of the computer (or, more precisely, into and out of the computer's memory) is one of the trickier facets of programming. Here we begin this task for the keyboard and video screen. Incidentally, input and output are sometimes put together under the heading I/O (for Input/Output).

To get information from the keyboard we use the read or readln (pronounced "read line") statement. The TURBO Pascal implementations of these do not work like those of standard Pascal. The form of each of these is the key word READ or READLN followed by a list of variables. The list of variables is enclosed in parentheses and separated by commas. The effect of both of these statements is to get values for the variables from the keyboard. The exact syntax diagram is given in *FIGURE 3.21*.

FIGURE 3.21

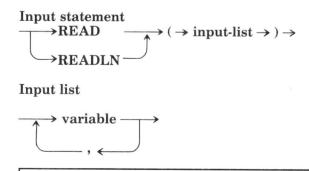

Input statement

```
  ┌──→ READ ────┐
  │             ├──→ ( → input-list → ) →
  └──→ READLN ──┘
```

Input list

```
  ┌──→ variable ──┐
  │               ├──→
  └──── , ←────────┘
```

For example, if Name is a string variable then either of the statements

```
Read(Name)
Readln(Name)
```

will cause the program to pause while a string is typed at the keyboard. The string typed will be stored in Name. The string must be followed by a [RETURN] (which is not stored in the string). The difference between read and readln is that if read is used the cursor will remain on the same line, whereas if readln is used the cursor will be advanced to the next line. This difference is used in the programs in *FIGURES 3.22* and *3.23*.

When the program in *FIGURE 3.22* is run, the word Running will appear. Nothing will happen until something is entered using the keyboard, because the read statement has caused the program to pause. If at this point we type JOE (followed by a [RETURN]), JOE will be stored in the variable Name. Following this the asterisk is printed on the same line and then the program ends.

The program in *FIGURE 3.23* differs from the program in *FIGURE 3.22* only in that it has a readln statement instead of a read statement. It runs exactly the same except that the asterisk is printed on a separate line as depicted. This is because the readln statement advances the cursor to the next line.

FIGURE 3.22

```
PROGRAM ReadExample (Input);

{ Program to illustrate the read statement.

     Author    : John Riley
     Date      : December 8, 1986
     File name : CH3EX10.PAS
}

VAR
     Name : STRING[20];

BEGIN { ReadExample }
  Read(Name);
  Writeln('*')
END.   { ReadExample }



Running
JOE*

>_
```

FIGURE 3.23

```
PROGRAM ReadlnExample (Input);

{ Program to illustrate the readln statement.

     Author    : John Riley
     Date      : December 8, 1986
     File name : CH3EX11.PAS
}

VAR
     Name : STRING[20];

BEGIN { ReadlnExample }
  Readln(Name);
  Writeln('*')
END.  { ReadlnExample }

¦
¦
¦
Running
JOE
*


>_
```

When a read or readln statement is executed, nothing appears on the screen to indicate that the program needs something typed. This means that whenever a read or readln is used, the person running the program has nothing telling him or her what to do. This can be corrected by outputting a message telling what is expected. A more reasonable version of the previous program is contained in *FIGURE 3.24*. This program prints a message to inform the user that a name is expected.

It is better to use readln instead of read so that the output is on distinct lines.

When the variable in a read or readln statement is a character variable, the first character on the line typed becomes the value of the character variable. If the RETURN is pressed, the character variable is set to CTRL/ Z.

If the variable to be input is a string variable, the characters typed are used to fill the string. If more characters are typed than the string has room for (i.e., the number of characters typed exceeds the maximum length of the string), the extra characters are ignored (or used to fill the next input item). If the number of characters entered is less than the maximum string length, the end of the string is empty. In this case, the length of the string is the number of characters entered. If there are no characters entered, the string variable is empty and has length zero. For example, if Name were a string variable of length 5 (that is, declared

FIGURE 3.24

```
PROGRAM ReadlnExample (Input);

{ Program to illustrate the readln statement.

     Author    : John Riley
     Date      : December 8, 1986
     File name : CH3EX12.PAS
}

VAR
     Name : STRING[20];

BEGIN { ReadlnExample }
  Writeln('Enter a name');
  Readln(Name);
  Writeln('*')
END.  { ReadlnExample }

│
│
│
Running
Enter a name
JOE
*


>_
```

using STRING[5]), then an input of JOE for Name would use only three of the five spaces of Name. However, if JOSEPHINE were entered, only JOSEP would be stored in Name. The characters after the fifth character would not be stored.

It is possible for an input statement to have more than one variable listed. If the variables are string or character variables, then the variables are filled in order. That is, the first variable in the list is filled from the keyboard input, then the second, and so on. In particular, if string variables are used, the first variable is filled to its maximum length before the next variable is filled.

How this works is shown in *FIGURE 3.25*. Assume that S1 and S2 have been declared as string variables of length 4. That is, the following declaration has been made.

```
VAR
   S1,
   S2 : STRING[4];
```

In the figure, EMPTY means that the string variable is empty, and a question mark means that the value of the variable is unknown. [RET] denotes the RETURN key.

FIGURE 3.25

Input Statement	Typed	Values	
		S1	**S2**
		?	?
Readln(S1, S2);	abc[RET]	'abc'	EMPTY
Readln(S1, S2);	abcdef[RET]	'abcd'	'ef'
Readln(S1, S2);	12 34 5[RET]	'12 3'	'4 5'
Readln(S1, S2);	xx[RET]	'xx'	EMPTY
Readln(S1, S2);	a b c d [RET]	'a b '	'c d '
Readln(S1, S2);	abcdefghi[RET]	'abcd'	'efgh'
Readln(S1, S2);	1 2[RET]	' '	' '

In these statements, all the places of S1 are filled before S2 receives any characters. Blanks (or spaces) count as characters when filling S1 or S2 (as in the third, fifth, and seventh lines). In the third line, 1, 2, 3, 4, and 5 are considered to be characters and are used to fill S1 and S2. Notice in the first and fourth lines that S2 becomes empty because there are no characters to fill it. In the last three lines, the ninth and ensuing characters are not used, because S1 and S2 each hold only four characters. So, at most, eight characters can be used by Readln(S1, S2). This means that the i in the sixth line of input is ignored and ' 1 2' is ignored in the last line. In the last line, this has the effect of filling both S1 and S2 with blanks.

Corresponding to the input statements read and readln are the output statements write and writeln (pronounced "write line"). These statements serve to communicate values to the programmer or user. The syntax for these is similar to that of the input statements. The key word WRITE or WRITELN is followed by a list of items to be output. The list of output items is enclosed in parentheses and the output items are separated by commas. Usually, the output list consists of strings and variables. The writeln statement is able to have an empty output list. The syntax diagrams for the output statement are given in *FIGURE 3.26*.

The effect of the output statement is to cause information to appear on the screen. A string or character (surrounded by single quotes) in the output list causes the string or character to appear on the screen. For example, the statement

```
Writeln('HELP! GET ME OUT OF HERE!');
```

would print HELP! GET ME OUT OF HERE! on the screen. If a string or character variable appeared in the output list, its value would be

FIGURE 3.26 | **Output Statement**

Output statement

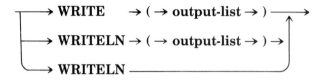

Output list

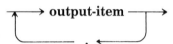

[Output-item is character, string, numeric, or Boolean value.]

printed. If S were a string variable of appropriate length, these two statements would do the same thing as the preceding statement.

```
S := 'HELP! GET ME OUT OF HERE!';
Writeln(S);
```

The difference between the write statement and the writeln statement is that the writeln statement causes the cursor to be placed at the beginning (far left) of the next line, whereas the write statement leaves the cursor immediately following (to the right of) the output. It is also possible to omit the output list in a writeln statement. (This is indicated by the third line of the syntax diagram.) A writeln by itself causes no output but causes the cursor to advance to the beginning of the next line. Usually this is used to cause a blank line to appear. These ideas are illustrated in the program in *FIGURE 3.27*, which contains only write and writeln statements. *FIGURE 3.27* also contains the output of this program. (Note that there is no variable section.)

Because the first three statements of the program in *FIGURE 3.27* are write statements, the output that follows each of them continues on the same line. The next three statements are writeln statements, and so the cursor is advanced to the next line after they are executed and the output which follows is on a new line. The two writeln statements without an output list cause two blank lines. Finally, a message indicating the program's completion is output.

As we noted when discussing the input statement (read or readln statement), no prompt is issued. This means that you should put a message (using a write or writeln statement) before the input statement. If a write statement is used, the cursor will be left on the same line after the message is put on the screen. We have found this to be a convenient way of prompting for input from a video screen. For example, if Name is a string variable, the lines

```
Write('Enter your name>');
Readln(Name);
```

would cause the message

```
Enter your name>_
```

to appear (the underline denotes the cursor). At this point the user would enter his or her name (or goof around) as follows.

```
Enter your name>MARY BAKER
```

Of course the input must be followed by a RETURN. This would place

FIGURE 3.27

```
PROGRAM WriteWriteln(Output);

{  A short program illustrating write and writeln.

     Author :     John Riley
     Date :       December 11, 1986
     File name : CH3EX13.PAS
}

BEGIN { WriteWriteln }
  Write('ABC');
  Write('123');
  Write('XYZ', '789');
  Writeln('ABC');
  Writeln('123');
  Writeln('XYZ', '789');
  Writeln;
  Writeln;
  Writeln('THAT''S ALL!')
END. { WriteWriteln }

Output:

ABC123XYZ789ABC
123
XYZ789


THAT'S ALL!
```

the input in the variable Name. Unfortunately, this technique will not work if the output device is a printer. If a printer is being used, stick to writeln statements for output.

Providing users with messages indicating what is expected of them is one aspect of making the program "user friendly." This is very important. A program which is otherwise very good will not be successful if users find it difficult to work with. You should never forget that the persons using the program may have little knowledge about computers and no knowledge about how the program works and what it expects as input. Good programmers program to meet users' needs.

3.7 DOCUMENTATION

The programs in this chapter have focused on characters and strings. This has been done because it is necessary to use strings to communicate, in both input and output. In the next chapter, numeric data is discussed and used in input and output but will still need to be labeled. This provides documentation to the user as to the meaning of the input. For example, the number 1,000,000 itself is meaningless, whereas most of us are impressed by $1,000,000. On the other hand, a million atoms constitute less matter than is contained in a speck of dust. Labeling output and prompting input for the user are very important.

Similarly, it is necessary to assist the reader of a program. Pascal, when used well, is largely what is known as self-documenting. This means that the language helps, and to some extent forces, the programmer to be explicit about what he or she is doing. The object of the programmer should be to write an algorithm which correctly and "cleanly" solves the problem and to write a program which communicates the algorithm.

Comments are a means of providing useful information to the reader of a program. The two uses of comments are to provide information not contained in the code of a program and to elaborate or explain something within the code. An example of the first type of comment is a comment immediately following the program heading. We always put the purpose of the program, the author, the date, and the file name in this comment. You probably have noticed that this has been done in a consistent manner. Consistency is a great virtue in writing programs as well as in writing prose.

An example of a comment which elaborates the code is a comment beside a variable declaration, as in

```
VAR
        FirstName : STRING[10];   { First name,          }
        MidInit   : Char;         { Middle initial,      }
        LastName  : STRING[20];   { Last name of employee }
```

Occasionally, a comment beside a piece of code explains the reason for the code. The following is an example of this.

```
If P^.Next = Nil Then { End of list has been reached }
```

The comment explains the significance of the statement (which may not be obvious) and prepares the reader for what follows.

Comments are not an afterthought; they are an integral part of the programming process. You should put appropriate comments in your program as you write it. For the same reason, as additional features of Pascal are introduced, comments that are appropriate are discussed.

3.8 SUMMARY

All Pascal programs consist of a program heading followed by a declaration section and a statement section.

Variable declarations are found in the declaration section. A variable declaration names a portion of memory for the purpose of storing values, such as characters or strings. Characters are defined using a standard code, such as ASCII. A character variable serves to store a single character, such as a letter. Strings or string constants consist of a sequence of characters. A string variable contains a string constant. The maximum number of characters that may be stored in a string variable is given in its declaration.

The statement section of a program begins with the key word BEGIN and ends with END followed by a period. Read and readln statements are used to obtain values for variables from the keyboard. Write and writeln statements are used to display information on the video screen. The assignment statement is used within the program to store values in variables.

A program should also contain comments which serve to assist the reader of the program. ❏

EXERCISES

1. Mark the following as legal or illegal identifiers.

HorseRadish

Mommy'sBoy

NinetyEight.Six

321BlastOff

ThreeTwoOneBlastOff

BlastOff123

BlastOff1:2:3

2. Find and correct the errors in the following program pieces and programs.

a.
```
VAR
      S1;
      S2 : STRING[20];
```

b.
```
VAR
      S1, S2 : STRING(20);
```

c.
```
VAR
      S10,
      S10 : STRING[10];
```

d.
```
PROGRAM Ch3Num3d(Input, Output);

VAR
      S1,
      S2  : STRING[10];

BEGIN { Ch3Num3d }
     Writeln('Enter two strings);
     Readln(S1; S2),
     Writeln(S1)
END.   { Ch3Num3d }
```

e.
```
PROGRAM Ch3Num3e(Input, Output);

VAR
      S1,
      S2 : STRING[10];

BEGIN  { Ch3Num3e }
     Writeln('Enter a string');
     Readln(S1);
     Writeln(S2)
END.    { Ch3Num3e }
```

3. Give the output of the following programs.

a.
```
PROGRAM Ch3Num4a(Output);

BEGIN { Ch3Num4a }
  Write('Hello ?');
  Writeln('Hello !');
  Writeln('HELLO !!!')
END.
```

b.
```
PROGRAM Ch3Num4b(Output);

VAR
      S : STRING[20];

BEGIN { Ch3Num4b }
  S := 'Four score and';
```

```
            Write(S);
            S := ' seven years ago,';
            Writeln(S);
            S := ' our fathers';
            Writeln(S)
         END.  { Ch3Num4b }
```

c.   ```
     PROGRAM Ch3Num4c(Output);

     VAR
          S : STRING[5];

     BEGIN { Ch3Num4c }
        S := 'ABC';
        Writeln(S, '*', S);
        S := 'A B C D E';
        Writeln(S)
     END. { Ch3Num4c }
     ```

4.  Change the comments and variable names in the following program
    so that it is easier to understand. This program works. Do not change
    what it does.

```
PROGRAM Ch3Num5(Input, Output);

{ A short program

Author : Yours truly
}

VAR
      C1,
      C2 : Char;        { Two character variables }
      S1,
      S2 : STRING[20]; { Two string variables     }

BEGIN
   C1 := '.';   { Store a period in C1 }
   Writeln('Enter your first name please');
   Readln(S1);
   Writeln('Enter your middle initial');
   Readln(C2);
   Writeln('Enter your last name');
   Readln(S2);
   Writeln;
   Writeln(S1,' ', C2, C1, ' ', S2)
END.
```

5. Write a program which asks the user his or her name and then uses
    the name in a greeting to the user.

6. Write a program which asks the user for his or her first and last
    names (separately) and then prints the name twice. On one line, the
    name is to appear, first name then last name. On another line, the
    name is to be printed last name first, and a comma is to appear
    between the last and first names.
```

7. Write a program which prints a large version of your initials on the screen using asterisks. For example,

```
*********        *   *          *  *
*          *     *   *          *  *
*          *     *     *     *     *
*          *     *       * *        *
*********        *          *       *
*                *                  *
*                *                  *
*                *                  *
*                *                  *
*                *                  *
```

8. Write a program which makes a rectangle on the screen made of asterisks. Make the rectangle seven asterisks wide and four high, as below.

```
*******
*     *
*     *
*******
```

9. Write a program which asks the user for a character and then uses that character to form a triangle which is five lines high and is nine characters wide at the base. For example, if x were entered the following would appear.

```
    x
   x x
  x   x
 x     x
xxxxxxxxx
```

10. Write a program which asks the user for his or her first and last names and then prints the user's initials in a message. The names are to be entered on separate lines. A run might look like this:

```
Enter your first name >PAUL
Enter your last name >SMITH

Hello, P. S. !
```

Hint: Read the names into character variables.

In the preceding chapter, programs in Pascal were introduced. All of the programs in Chapter 3 dealt with strings and characters. In this chapter, numeric and Boolean values and variables are discussed.

Many programming problems involve the processing of numeric data. In fact, all of the first computers (circa 1945 to 1950) were designed to do numeric calculations. This gave these computers the label "number crunchers." There are still many computing problems which are numeric in nature. Even those problems which are not oriented toward numbers use numeric data types.

Boolean (or logical) values consist of True and False. They are used extensively in controlling the order of statement execution. It is hard to conceive of a major program which does not use Boolean values.

Both Boolean and numeric values may be combined to yield other values. For numeric values, one way of combining numeric values is by doing arithmetic. A good portion of this chapter is devoted to discussing how to combine numeric and Boolean values.

This chapter closes with a discussion of another sort of declaration section—the constant declarations. Most of the programs in later chapters will have both constant and variable declarations. ☐

CHAPTER 4

NUMERIC
AND BOOLEAN
DATA TYPES

4.1 NUMERIC VALUES AND VARIABLES

Every program manipulates data objects. Pascal forces programmers to be careful in their use of these. For example, although it makes sense to talk about the next whole number, it does not make sense to talk about the next decimal number. (What number follows 4.56? Is it 4.561? 4.5601? 4.560001?) In this section, the numeric types of objects Pascal programs manipulate are introduced.

Integers are numbers without a fractional or decimal part. These are sometimes called whole numbers. In mathematics there is an infinite number of integers, but any computer is limited in the number of integers it can use. In Pascal, an integer is a sequence of digits optionally preceded by a plus (+) or minus (−) sign. Here are some examples of legal and illegal integers.

Legal

7

− 10

0

01

234

+ 89

− 909

Illegal

56. (Decimal point not allowed)

2,574 (Comma not allowed)

34.0 (Decimal point not allowed)

The syntax diagram for constructing an integer is given in *FIGURE 4.1*. In this diagram we explicitly enumerate the digits. (This wasn't done for letters or characters, because, in general, they are limited by the implementation.)

Pascal documents the limitation on integers explicitly. There is a constant denoted MaxInt which is the maximum integer that a particular implementation allows. The range of integers is then defined to be the integers between − MaxInt and MaxInt (inclusive). The restriction on the size of MaxInt is usually a consequence of the underlying computer architecture and varies among implementations of Pascal. On a microcomputer it may not be very large. The operations (such as addition and multiplication) that are defined for integers are discussed in depth later on in this chapter.

Integer variables are declared in the variable section by using the key word INTEGER. Integer variables may be used in input (read, readln),

FIGURE 4.1

Integer

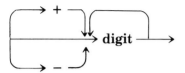

Digit

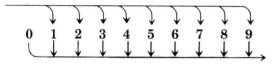

output (write, writeln), and assignment (using :=) statements much as string and character variables are used. The program in *FIGURE 4.2* illustrates these ideas. This program adds and multiplies two integers obtained from the keyboard and displays their sum and product. Notice that the program prompts the user with a message indicating the necessary input and labels the output (using strings). Programs continue to be written in the same style as in Chapter 3. The results of running the program are also shown in *FIGURE 4.2*. The numbers 12 and 13 are entered by the user (and followed by [RETURN]).

The second type of numbers that Pascal implements are known as *reals*. Real numbers are numbers which have a decimal part. Reals and integers have different representations within the computer. Furthermore, arithmetic operations are done on reals and integers in different ways. Thus, although both can be considered to be numbers, they are distinct types. Usually an integer may be used wherever a real may be used. However, there are many places where an integer (and not a real) must be used.

A real number may be represented in two forms. The first is a *decimal number*. In this case, a real number is a sequence of digits followed by a decimal point (period) followed by a sequence of one or more digits. This number may be preceded by an optional plus or minus sign. There must be at least one digit both to the left and right of the decimal point. The second form for a real number is *scientific notation*. In this case the real consists of a decimal number (as just described) followed by the letter E followed by a signed or unsigned integer or an integer followed by E and a signed or unsigned integer. The integer following the E signifies that the preceding number is to be multiplied by that power of ten (as in the

FIGURE 4.2

```
PROGRAM AddAndMultiply(Input, Output);

{  A simple program to add and multiply two numbers.

     Author  :   John Riley
     Date :      December 14, 1986
     File name : CH4EX1.PAS
}

VAR
     FirstNum,                 { Entered from the keyboard }
     SecondNum,                { Entered from the keyboard }
     Product,
     Sum       : Integer;

BEGIN { AddAndMultiply }
  Write('Enter an integer >');
  Readln(FirstNum);
  Write('Enter an integer >');
  Readln(SecondNum);
  Sum := FirstNum + SecondNum;
  Product := FirstNum * SecondNum;
  Writeln;
  Writeln('The sum of ', FirstNum, ' and ', SecondNum, ' is ',
          Sum);
  Writeln('Their product is ', Product)
END. { AddAndMultiply }


Enter an integer >12
Enter an integer >13

The sum of 12 and 13 is 25
Their product is 156
```

usual scientific notation). Here are some examples of legal and illegal reals.

Legal

1.2

1.0

−2.3

+9.8

0.0

−34.567

0.000583

−7739000.0

35.67E3   { = 35670.0 }
− 45.8E − 4   { = -0.00458 }
67.89E + 11   { = 6789000000000.0 }
+ 59.5222E − 9 { = 0.0000000595222 }
36E5   { = 3600000.0 }

Illegal

1.   {No digit to the right of the decimal point}

− .9   {No digit to the left of the decimal point }

1,234.0 {No commas allowed}

3.4E9.0 {No decimal point allowed in the exponent}

The syntax diagram for the form of a real number is given in *FIGURE 4.3*. Because of the various possibilities for a real number, it is somewhat more complicated than syntax diagrams we have previously encountered.

As with integers, there is a limit to which real numbers can be represented in the computer. TURBO Pascal permits positive reals to be no smaller than about $1E − 38$ and no larger than about $1E + 38$. Thus a number such as $1E − 40$ will be regarded as zero, whereas a number such as $1E42$ will cause an error. It is advisable not to use the extreme ends of the reals (near $1E − 38$ and $1E + 38$). A tenth of a number near zero may be regarded as zero, and ten times a very large number may cause what is known as an overflow error. Using appropriate units of measurement can help in this regard. Astronomical distances are better measured in light-years than in feet, and internal times in a computer should be expressed in microseconds (millionths of a second), nanoseconds (billionths of a second), or picoseconds (trillionths of a second) rather than in hours or years.

Real numbers have 11-digit accuracy in TURBO Pascal. As a consequence, arithmetic combinations of reals of greatly different magnitudes will probably not be accurate. Adding a tenth $(1E − 1)$ to a trillion $(1E12)$ will yield a trillion, not a trillion and a tenth.

Real variables are declared using the key word REAL. Real variables may be used in input, output, and assignment statements. As an illus-

FIGURE 4.3

Real

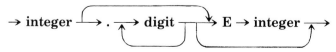

tration, *FIGURE 4.4* contains the adding and multiplying program (of *FIGURE 4.2*) revised to use real variables. The results of running this program with input data 1.01 and 2.002 are also given in *FIGURE 4.4*. Notice that the output is in scientific notation. We will shortly see how to obtain real output in decimal notation.

It is possible to have more than one integer variable or real variable in a read or readln statement. In fact, it is possible to mix integer and real variables along with string and character variables in an input statement. However, we strongly advise that you don't have string variables and numeric variables in the same input statement, because the exact spacing of the input may be critical and difficult for the user to supply.

When an integer or real variable is used in an input statement, the

FIGURE 4.4

```
PROGRAM RealAddAndMultiply(Input, Output);

{  A simple program to add and multiply two numbers.

      Author :    John Riley
      Date :      December 14, 1986
      File name : CH4EX2.PAS
}

VAR
      FirstNum,               { Entered from the keyboard }
      SecondNum,              { Entered from the keyboard }
      Product,
      Sum        : Real;

BEGIN { AddAndMultiply }
  Write('Enter an integer >');
  Readln(FirstNum);
  Write('Enter an integer >');
  Readln(SecondNum);
  Sum := FirstNum + SecondNum;
  Product := FirstNum * SecondNum;
  Writeln;
  Writeln('The sum of ', FirstNum, ' and ', SecondNum, ' is ',
          Sum);
  Writeln('Their product is ', Product)
END. { AddAndMultiply }


Enter a number >1.01
Enter a number >2.002

The sum of   1.0100000000E+00 and   2.0020000000E+00   is
  3.0120000000E+00
Their product is 2.0220202000E+00
```

FIGURE 4.5

```
PROGRAM RealAddAndMultiplyRevised(Input, Output);

{  A simple program to add and multiply two numbers.

     Author :     John Riley
     Date :       December 14, 1986
     File name : CH4EX3.PAS
}

VAR
     FirstNum,                { Entered from the keyboard }
     SecondNum,               { Entered from the keyboard }
     Product,
     Sum        : Real;

BEGIN { AddAndMultiplyRevised }
  Write('Enter two numbers (separated by space) >');
  Readln(FirstNum, SecondNum);
  Sum := FirstNum + SecondNum;
  Product := FirstNum * SecondNum;
  Writeln;
  Writeln('The sum of ', FirstNum, ' and ', SecondNum, ' is ',
          Sum);
  Writeln('Their product is ', Product)
END. { AddAndMultiplyRevised }


Enter two numbers (separated by space) >1.3 2.4

The sum of  1.3000000000E+00 and 2.4000000000E+00   is
 3.7000000000E+00
Their product is  3.1200000000E+00
```

values input (what the user types) must be in the format of the variable. For example, a comma may not be used in inputting 1000. The values input for numeric variables must be separated from other input by at least one space. An integer may be input to a real variable. We could have written the adding program as shown above in *FIGURE 4.5* in order to have the two numbers input at once.

The syntax of input statements is given in *FIGURE 4.6*. Notice that the only items that may be input are integer, real, character, and string variables. It is also possible to use a readln without any input items. A readln without variables simply causes the program to pause until the [RETURN] is pressed. This is usually preceded by a message, as in the following.

```
  Writeln('Press RETURN to continue');
  Readln;
```

FIGURE 4.6

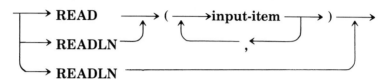

Input statement

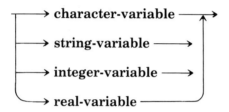

Input item

Just as important as the input statement is the output statement. The key words WRITE and WRITELN designate the output statement. Using an output statement, character, string, numeric, and Boolean values may be printed on the screen. The value to be output may be given by a variable or be given explicitly or be the result of a calculation (known as an expression). The program in *FIGURE 4.7* illustrates this idea. When run, the program prints 4 on three consecutive lines.

As in the input statement, more than one item may appear in the list of items to be output. It is also possible to use a writeln without an output list. This causes a new line to be started.

It is important to present the results of a program as intelligibly as possible. The programmer bears the responsibility for putting the output in a form which is as comprehensible as possible. For example, whenever a large amount of numeric data is to be output, it is arranged in a table. This is known as *formatting*.

DEFINITION

> To *format* output means to specify the appearance or layout of data being output.

For any output item in a write or writeln statement it is possible to specify the number of spaces the output item is to occupy on the page or screen. This is done by following the item with a colon and the number of characters it is to occupy. This number is known as the *field width*.

FIGURE 4.7

```
PROGRAM OutputExample(Output);

{ A program to illustrate variables, values, and expressions
  in the writeln statement.

     Author :        John Riley
     Date :          December 16, 1986
     File name :     CH4EX4.PAS                  }

VAR
     I,
     J   : Integer;

BEGIN { OutputExample }
  I := 4;
  Writeln(I);
  Writeln(4);
  J := 8;
  Writeln(J - I)
END.   { OutputExample }


Output :

4
4
4
```

The output is placed in the column as far to the right as possible. This is known as *right-justified output*. If the output item is smaller than the field specified, it is preceded by blanks. If the output item requires more space than is specified, then more space will be used. The program in *FIGURE 4.8* illustrates this. The output produced by this program is to the right of the statement that caused it. The vertical line indicates the left of the screen or page. Notice that by specifying the field width it is possible to align columns of output.

To output real values in decimal form, it is necessary to supply two numbers. The first number is the field width, as discussed above. The second number is known as the *decimal places parameter*. It specifies the number of digits that are to appear to the right of the decimal point. Here are some examples (X and Y are real variables).

```
                                     Output
X := 123.456;
Y := 654.321;
Writeln(X:8:3, Y:8:3);        | 123.456 654.321
Writeln(X:9:2, Y:9:2);        |  123.46    654.32
```

FIGURE 4.8

```
PROGRAM FormatExample(Output);

{ A program to illustrate field width.

      Author :        John Riley
      Date :          December 16, 1986
      File name :     CH4EX5S
}

VAR
      I : Integer;
      S : STRING[10];

BEGIN { FormatExample }                     OUTPUT
   I := 123;
   S := 'ABCDE';
   Writeln(I : 8);                              123
   Writeln(S : 8);                            ABCDE
   Writeln(I : 8, S : 8);                       123    ABCDE
   Writeln(S : 8, I : 8);                     ABCDE      123
   Writeln(I : 2);                            123
   Writeln(S : 2)                             ABCDE
END. { FormatExample }
```

Notice that rounding will occur. To produce dollars and cents, 2 is used as the decimal places parameter as in the following example (Cost is a real variable).

```
Writeln('Total cost :  $', Cost:7:2);
```

Always be careful to make the field width wide enough to hold the digits to the right and left of the decimal point as well as the decimal point itself.

The syntax diagrams for the write and writeln statements are contained in *FIGURE 4.9*. The diagrams indicate that an output item may be a character, string, integer, real, or Boolean value. Unlike the input statements (read and readln), the items in the output list do not have to be variables. This means that if I and J are integer variables which have been assigned values, the following statement will output their sum.

```
Writeln(I + J);
```

In practice this does not occur very often. Usually the output items are variables whose values are to be output and strings which serve to label the output.

The syntax diagrams also show that writeln (but not write) may be used without any output items. Writeln without any output items simply starts a new line. Blank lines are used to separate groups of output. Skipping three lines helps the reader. Three writeln statements will do this. Although each statement usually occurs on a separate line, some programmers find it convenient and readable to put the three writelns on one line of the program like this:

```
Writeln; Writeln; Writeln;
```

Of course, this is a matter of personal preference.

FIGURE 4.9

Output statement

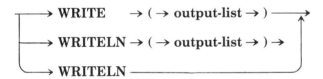

Output list

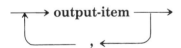

Output item

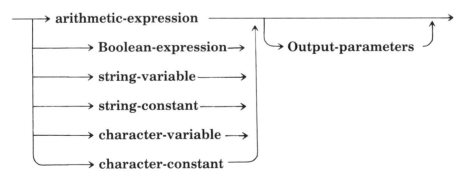

Output parameters

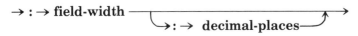

4.2 CONSTANTS

A variable's value may be changed during the execution of a program. Indeed, this is what makes variables useful. However, there may be values which should be labeled with an identifier but which do not change when the program runs. Pascal provides a means of doing this by using *constant declarations*. Constant declarations enable the programmer to label values and ensure that they aren't changed.

Constant declarations appear in the declaration section of a program preceding variable declarations. The constant declaration section starts with the reserved word CONST. Then each constant is given by an identifier, an equals sign, the value of the constant, and a semicolon. For example, in a program used to find the circumference of a circle given its radius, the number 6.2832 (twice pi) is needed. This constant would be declared:

```
CONST
     TwoPi = 6.2832;
```

A program using this declaration is given in *FIGURE 4.10*.

A constant declaration sets aside a location in memory under a certain name and stores a value in it. This value may not be changed by the

FIGURE 4.10

```
PROGRAM CircumferenceFromRadius(Input, Output);

{    Program to find the circumference of a circle, given its
     radius.

     Author :      John Riley
     Date :        December 23, 1986
     File name :   CH4EX6.PAS
}

CONST
     TwoPi = 6.2832;

VAR
     Radius,
     Circumference : Real;

BEGIN { CircumferenceFromRadius }
  Write('Enter the radius of a circle >');
  Readln(Radius);
  Circumference := TwoPi * Radius;
  Writeln('Circumference of circle > ', Circumference:8:4)
END. { CircumferenceFromRadius }
```

| **Constant Declarations** | | **FIGURE 4.11** |

$\rightarrow$ **CONST** $\longrightarrow$ **identifier** $\rightarrow$ = $\rightarrow$ **constant** $\rightarrow$; $\longrightarrow$

program. The syntax diagram for the constant declarations is given above in *FIGURE 4.11*. Many constants may be named in the constant declarations. The constant that follows the equals sign may be a number (integer or real), a string or character value, or the name of a constant which has already been defined.

The following is an example of a constant declaration section which declares several constants.

```
CONST
     TwoPi                  = 6.2832
     RadiusToCircumference  = TwoPi;
     Big                    = MaxInt;
     DaysInWeek             = 7;
     WondersOfTheWorld      = 7;
     NumberOfDwarves        = 7;
     Blank                  = ' ';
     Period                 = '.';
     Warning                = 'Violators will be prosecuted';
```

The first line (consisting of the word CONST) tells the computer that what follows is the declaration of constants. The second line (TwoPi = 6.2832) associates the identifier TwoPi with the real value 6.2832. The next line makes RadiusToCircumference equal to TwoPi, or 6.2832. Then either of these constants could be used to compute the circumference of a circle given its radius. The fourth line sets Big equal to the predefined constant MaxInt. The next three lines associate the identifiers DaysInWeek, WondersOfTheWorld, and NumberOfDwarves with the integer 7. The next two lines define two character constants which might be useful in manipulating text. The last line establishes Warning as the string 'Violators will be prosecuted'.

Using constants can greatly enhance a program's readability and modifiability. For example, if a program dealt with the number of days in a week, the seven dwarves, and the ancient wonders of the world, the number 7 would arise in three different contexts. A given occurrence of 7 might refer to any one of these. Understanding exactly to what 7 referred might be difficult. Using the identifiers above would eliminate this problem. Furthermore, if an eighth wonder of the world were discovered, changing the program to reflect this would be easy given the declarations above. This would be accomplished by changing the 7 in the sixth line to 8. If the number 7 had been used throughout the program, this would be quite a chore, because we would have to look at every occurrence of 7 and decide whether it referred to days in the week, dwarves, or wonders. Similarly, TwoPi is easier to understand than 6.2832. Constants will be used whenever possible. This is a good programming practice.

A constant may be used anywhere its value may be used. For example, a string constant (such as Warning in the above) may be used in an output statement and a numeric constant may be used in calculations. But a constant may never appear on the left side of an assignment statement, because the value of a constant may not be changed during a program's execution.

Constants make a program more readable and easier to modify. It is a good idea to use constants and not literals (explicitly written constants, such as 6.2832).

4.3 CALCULATIONS

In Chapter 3 we discovered that the right side of an assignment statement produces a value which is to be stored in the variable to the left of the assignment operator (:=). For numeric variables, the right side frequently consists of an arithmetic or algebraic expression whose value is to be computed. This value is then stored in the variable. The expression may combine values obtained from variables and constants.

Because it makes sense to consider arithmetic expressions containing integers, reals, and combinations of both, Pascal allows us to do this. On the other hand, because we can assign only integer values to integer variables, we need to know what the type of the result is.

For example, adding the two integers 3 and 4 in the expression 3 + 4 produces the integer 7. This is not the same as adding the two real numbers 3.0 and 4.0, which produces the real number 7.0. The plus symbols in these two expressions signify two different operations. In the first expression (3 + 4), the addition is integer addition. In the second expression (3.0 + 4.0), the plus sign means real addition. These additions are not done in the same way by the computer. *FIGURE 4.12* gives the symbols for the arithmetic operators and the types of their results (which depend on the types of the values used in the expression).

DEFINITION

An *operator* is a function which produces a value from another value or values.

DEFINITION

An *operand* is a value used by an operator (possibly with other operands) to produce a value.

Arithmetic Operators

FIGURE 4.12

Operator and Meaning	Types of Operands		
	Integer Integer	Integer Real	Real Real
	Type of Result		
+ Addition	Integer	Real	Real
− Subtraction	Integer	Real	Real
* Multiplication	Integer	Real	Real
/ Division (real)	Real	Real	Real
DIV Division (integer)	Integer	Error	Error
MOD Remainder (integer)	Integer	Error	Error

For example, in the expression $3 + 5$, the numbers 3 and 5 are operands and the plus symbol (+) is the operator. Most operators have two operands; some have only one.

A *binary operator* has two operands.

A *unary operator* has one operand.

The addition operator (+, as in X + Y) is an example of a binary operator. Negation (−, as in −X) is a unary operator. The minus symbol (−) also denotes the subtraction operator (as in X − Y). Subtraction is a binary operation.

An *arithmetic operator* has numerical operands and a numerical result.

DEFINITION

> To *evaluate* an expression means to produce a value from the
> expression (by applying operators and using the current val-
> ues of the variables and constants).

Like most other computer languages, Pascal uses + for addition, −
for subtraction, and * for multiplication. For all three of these operators,
if both operands are integer valued the result is an integer, whereas
otherwise the result is real. Integer results are always exact (if they don't
exceed MaxInt). Real arithmetic frequently is not exact. This can lead to
surprises. An old programming adage is that 10.0 * 0.1 doesn't always
equal 1.0 .

Pascal provides three division operators. Two are used for doing integer
division and one real division. The operator / denotes real division and
always results in a real result. It is an error to divide by zero. The DIV
and MOD operators may have only integer operands, and both have integer results. DIV produces the quotient of the first operand divided by
the second (e.g., 17 DIV 5 is 3 and 29 DIV 6 is 4). MOD produces the
remainder of such a division (e.g., 17 MOD 5 is 2 and 29 MOD 6 is 5).
The second operand may not be 0 in either division.

An exponentiation operator is not present in *FIGURE 4.12*. That is,
there is no provision for general powers—e.g., three to the fourth power
(81). However, squares (where the power is 2) and square roots (where
the exponent or power is 1/2) are provided. Later on, we will see how to
build our own exponentiation function.

In an expression, multiplications and divisions (*, /, DIV, and MOD)
are performed before additions and subtractions (+ and −). This means
that 9 + 3 * 4 is evaluated by first doing the multiplication, giving 9 +
12, and then adding to give 21 (instead of doing the addition first, which
would produce 12 * 4, and then multiplying, giving 48). This is called
precedence of operators. For the same reason, 15 + 6 DIV 3 gives 17 (=
15 + 2) and not 7 (= 21 DIV 3). If two operators of equal precedence are
present in an expression, the operations are performed left to right. Thus
9 − 4 + 3 is evaluated as 5 + 3, or 8, and not 9 − 7, or 2. Similarly, 4
* 3 DIV 12 is 12 DIV 12, not 4 * 0.

DEFINITION

> The *precedence* (or *priority*) of operators is the specification
> of which operators are to be applied first.

As in algebra, the usual order of evaluation can be overridden by the
use of parentheses. An expression in parentheses is evaluated before any
other operation is applied. For example, 3 * (5 + 7) is evaluated as 3 *
12 (36). We will also use parentheses to improve the readability of
expressions. For example, we prefer (6 − 2) + 4 to 6 − 2 + 4 even though
the two expressions have the same meaning.

It is a good idea to surround the operators (+, −, *, /)in expressions
by spaces to increase legibility. DIV and MOD must be surrounded by
spaces to distinguish them from identifiers.

Pascal has some predefined functions, and it is possible for programmers to define their own functions as well. When a function is used in an expression, its value is found by using the value (or values) supplied to the function, which may be an expression (or expressions). Function evaluation has precedence over any other operation.

Expressing all of these possibilities in a syntax diagram takes some care and we do not do so here. The syntax diagrams defining an expression are contained in the appendices.

An item which we have not made explicit is supplying a constant directly. Such a constant is known as a *literal constant* or *literal*—e.g., 3.4 or 7.99 . In actual programs, literals are to be avoided. For example, in a program which computes pay, it is better to use a constant, BonusFactor (declared in the constant declaration section), rather than the literal 1.5. Most numbers that occur in a program have meanings, and these meanings should be documented.

> A *literal constant* (or *literal*) is a constant which is given explicitly in a program.

DEFINITION

Here are some examples of arithmetic expressions, their values, and the types of their values.

Arithmetic Expressions

Expression	Value	Type	Notes
J / 2	3.0	Real	(/ is always real)
R DIV 3	Error		(R is real, DIV is for integers)
3.0 * 5	15.0	Real	
R + J	17.0	Real	
2R	Error		(* to multiply)
4 * (R + 3)	56.0	Real	(R is real)
J MOD 4	2	Integer	
37 DIV 2 * J	108	Integer	(18 * 6)
36 / (R + 1)	3.0	Real	
5 DIV (J MOD J)	Error		(Division by 0)
5 DIV J	0	Integer	
− 3 * R	− 33.0	Real	
4.0 − (3 + J)	− 5.0	Real	
R * J	66.0	Real	

[J = 6 (an integer variable); R = 11.0 (a real variable)]

Pascal has a small number of predefined or built-in arithmetic functions and constants of which you should be aware. They are useful in doing numeric calculations. These functions and constants are listed in *FIGURE 4.13*. Note that some of the functions listed are not standard. It is important to note the type of the argument (i.e., value supplied to the function) and of the result of the function.

DEFINITION

> **The *argument* of a function is the value supplied to the function when it is evaluated.**

FIGURE 4.13   **Arithmetic Functions and Constants**

Name	Argument Type	Result Type	Notes
MaxInt	None	I	Largest integer implemented
Pi	None	R	3.1415926536 **NS**
Abs(X)	I or R	Same	Absolute value of X
ArcTan(X)	I or R	R	ArcTangent of X
Cos(X)	I or R	R	Cosine of X, X in radians
Exp(X)	I or R	R	Exponential of X
Frac(X)	I or R	R	Fractional part of X **NS**
Int(X)	I or R	R	Integer part of X **NS**
Ln(X)	I or R	R	Natural logarithm (log base e) of X, X positive
Sin(X)	I or R	R	Sine of X, X in radians
Sqr(X)	I or R	Same	Square of X
Sqrt(X)	I or R	R	Square root of X, X nonnegative
Odd(X)	I	Boolean	True if X is odd, false if X is even
Round(X)	R	I	X rounded off
Trunc(X)	R	I	X truncated
Random	None	R	Random real greater than or equal to 0 & less than 1 **NS**
Random(X)	I	I	Random integer greater than or equal to 0 & less than X **NS**

(I stands for Integer, R stands for Real. Same means result is of same type as argument. NS stands for NonStandard implemented by TURBO).

The predefined functions of Pascal each use only one argument. It is enclosed in parentheses. For example, to obtain the square root of four we would write Sqrt(4) (2.0).

As has been mentioned, there are places where an integer value may be used but not a real value. The functions Round and Trunc enable the programmer to convert a real value to an integer value. Of course, some loss of accuracy occurs when this is done. Pascal forces the programmer to state how this accuracy is being lost. The programmer is either rounding off the result (rounding) or dropping the digits after the decimal point (truncation).

Here are some examples of functions used in expressions. Again let's assume that J is an integer variable with the value 6 and that R is a real variable with the value 11.0.

Expression	Value	Type	Notes
Odd(J)	False	Boolean	
2*Sqr(J)	72	Integer	
Round(4.6)	5	Integer	
Trunc(4.6)	4	Integer	
Round(5.2)	5		
Cos(R * Pi)	1.0	Real	
Ln(Exp(R))	11.0	Real	Functions may be nested or composed

This section concludes with a short program (*FIGURE 4.14*) which illustrates the use of functions. This program computes the roots of a quadratic equation. The use of a, b, and c is traditional in mathematics. They have no mnemonic value, but it is usually wise to be consistent with tradition.

FIGURE 4.14

```
PROGRAM QuadraticRoots(Input, Output);

{ Program implementing the quadratic formula.

    Author  :    John Riley
    Date :       December 24, 1986
    File name :  CH4EX7.PAS
}

VAR
    a,                  { Coefficient of square term }
    b,                  { Coefficient of linear term }
    c,                  { Constant term              }
    Disc,               { Discriminant               }
    Root1,              { First root                 }
    Root2 : Real;       { Second root                }
```

(continued)

```
BEGIN { QuadraticRoots }
  Writeln('This program solves the quadratic equation.');
  Write('Enter the coefficient of square term >');
  Readln(a);
  Write('Enter the coefficient of linear term >');
  Readln(b);
  Write('Enter constant term >');
  Readln(c);
  Disc := Sqr(b) - 4 * a * c;
  Root1 := (-b + Sqrt(Disc))/(2 * a);
  Root2 := (-b - Sqrt(Disc))/(2 * a);
  Writeln('The roots of the equation : ', Root1:8:2, ' ',
          Root2:8:2)
END. { QuadraticRoots }


Output:

This program solves the quadratic equation.
Enter the coefficient of square term >2
Enter the coefficient of linear term >8
Enter constant term >6
The roots of the equation :     3.00     1.00
```

It should be noted that the program in *FIGURE 4.14* will result in a run-time error in two situations. If the user enters 0 for a, a division-by-zero error occurs. An error also occurs if the discriminant (Disc) is negative, because it is not possible to take the square root (Sqrt) of a negative number. Guarding against these kinds of errors is important if software is to be useful. We will discuss Pascal statements which programmers use to do this guarding in ensuing chapters.

4.4 BOOLEAN VALUES

The last of the predefined types of Pascal is the *Boolean* type. This type is named in honor of George Boole (1815–1860), an English mathematician who formulated rules for working with these values. This data type is sometimes called the logical data type.

The Boolean data type has only two values: True and False. This may seem to limit the usefulness of this data type, but the Boolean type turns out to be very handy. Boolean variables may be declared in the variable section using the standard identifier BOOLEAN. For example, we might want to denote whether or not a quadratic equation has real roots. This could be done by declaring a Boolean variable HasRealRoots.

```
VAR
  HasRealRoots : Boolean;    { Is True when equation has real
                               roots }
```

Boolean values may not be input. This means that a Boolean variable may not appear in a read or readln statement. However, they may be output, as in the following.

```
Writeln('The equation has real roots : ', HasRealRoots);
```

When a Boolean value is used in an output statement, TRUE or FALSE appears.

In practice, the values True and False are rarely used explicitly. Usually a Boolean value is produced as the result of a comparison. To continue with our example, whether or not a quadratic equation has real roots depends on whether or not the discriminant is positive. Thus, if Disc is a real variable containing the value of the discriminant, the assignment statement

```
HasRealRoots := Disc >= 0.0;
```

stores True or False in HasRealRoots as appropriate.

The program in *FIGURE 4.15* is a modification of the quadratic roots program (*FIGURE 4.14*) to indicate whether or not the equation has real roots.

An expression such as Disc $>= 0.0$ is called a Boolean expression. In their own way, Boolean expressions are just as useful as arithmetic expressions. Boolean values often arise as the result of comparing two expressions. For the time being we will use arithmetic expressions and strings in comparisons. Later on we will see that other sorts of values may be compared. It only makes sense to compare expressions of the same type. For instance, a string cannot be compared to a numerical value. However, integers and reals may be compared (the integer is considered to be real).

FIGURE 4.15

```
PROGRAM RealRoots(Input, Output);

{ Program to indicate the presence of real roots for a quadratic
  equation.

     Author :     John Riley
     Date :       December 26, 1986
     File name : CH4EX8.PAS
}

VAR
     a,                { Coefficient of square term }
     b,                { Coefficient of linear term }
     c,                { Constant term              }
     Disc : Real;      { Discriminant               }
     HasRealRoots : Boolean; { Indicates presence of real roots }
```

(continued)

```
BEGIN { RealRoots }
  Writeln('This program indicates whether a quadratic equation');
  Writeln('has real roots or not.');
  Write('Enter the coefficient of square term >');
  Readln(a);
  Write('Enter the coefficient of linear term >');
  Readln(b);
  Write('Enter constant term >');
  Readln(c);
  Disc := Sqr(b) - 4 * a * c;
  HasRealRoots := Disc >= 0.0;
  Writeln('The equation has real roots : ', HasRealRoots)
END. { QuadraticRoots }


Output:

This program indicates whether a quadratic equation
has real roots or not.
Enter the coefficient of square term >3
Enter the coefficient of linear term >5
Enter constant term >2
The equation has real roots : TRUE
```

Pascal has six operators for comparison of expressions. These operators are known as *relational operators*. Their symbols, names, and meanings for numbers, characters, and strings are given in *FIGURE 4.16*.

DEFINITION

> **A *relational operator* is an operator which produces a Boolean value based on whether or not a relation between two quantities is true.**

Here are some examples of relational expressions and their values. Let's suppose that I and J are integer variables with the values 3 and 6 and that X is a real variable with the value 9.8.

Expression	Value
$I = J$	False
$I <> J$	True
$2 * I = J$	True
$I + 1 < J - 4$	False
$2 * X <= 20.0$	True
$X > I$	True

You are cautioned against comparing real numbers for equality, because two real values are rarely exactly the same. It is not a good idea to rely on $(1000 * 0.001) = 1.0$ being True.

Relational Operators

FIGURE 4.16

Symbol	Name	Meaning
=	Equality	True when the operands' values are equal
<>	Inequality	True when the operands' values are not equal
<	Less than	True when the first operand precedes the second operand
<=	Less than or equal	True when the first operand equals or precedes the second operand
>	Greater than	True when the second operand precedes the first operand
>=	Greater than or equal	True when the second operand equals or precedes the first operand

Strings are ordered by doing a comparison of their characters using the order of the characters defined by the implementation. The order of two strings is defined by the first character (going from left to right) at which they differ. This is the normal way in which words are put in order. For example, ACE precedes ACTOR because E comes first in the first character in which they differ (E versus T). However, the computer extends this ordering to include characters which are not alphabetic. Also, because all upper-case letters precede all lower-case letters (ASCII), unexpected results may arise. Finally, if two strings are of unequal length and the shorter string and the longer string agree for the length of the shorter string, the shorter string precedes the longer. Here are some comparisons of strings.

Expression	Value	Comment
'CAR' < 'CAT'	TRUE	'R' precedes 'T'
'CAT' > 'CAr'	FALSE	'T' precedes 'r'
' CAT' = 'CAT'	FALSE	' CAT' has a blank
'1 CAR' <= '1 CAT'	TRUE	'R' precedes 'T'
'CAR' < 'CART'	TRUE	Shorter string precedes longer when they start the same
'CAR' < 'CAR '	TRUE	Shorter precedes longer
'CAR 54' >= 'CAR 57'	FALSE	'4' precedes '7'
'HELP' <= 'help'	TRUE	'H' precedes 'h'
'HELP !' <= 'HELP ?'	TRUE	'!' precedes '?'

Like numeric values, Boolean values can be combined to yield other Boolean values. This is sometimes known as Boolean algebra. Not surprisingly, the operators used are called Boolean operators. Standard Pascal has three Boolean operators. TURBO Pascal has these three along with a fourth. The standard Pascal Boolean operators are NOT (negation), OR (disjunction), and AND (conjunction). The nonstandard Boolean operator is XOR (exclusive OR). The values that these operators produce are usually expressed in tables known as truth tables. Truth tables for these operators are given in *FIGURE 4.17*.

Below are listed some examples of Boolean expressions formed using these operators. I is an integer variable with the value 10, and J is an integer variable with the value 20.

Expression	Value
NOT(I = 10)	False
(I < J) AND (J < 15)	False
(I = 10) OR (J = 15)	True
(I < J) AND ((I = 10) OR (J = 15))	True
(I <> J) AND ('Cat' = 'CAT')	False

The Boolean operators may be summarized in this way. NOT P is the opposite (or reverse) of P. P AND Q is True only when both P and Q are

---

FIGURE 4.17   **Boolean Operators**

Negation (NOT)

P	Not P
True	False
False	True

Conjunction (AND)

P	Q	P And Q
True	True	True
True	False	False
False	True	False
False	False	False

Disjunction (OR)

P	Q	P Or Q
True	True	True
True	False	True
False	True	True
False	False	False

Exclusive Or (XOR)

P	Q	P Xor Q
True	True	False
True	False	True
False	True	True
False	False	False

True. P OR Q is True if either P or Q is True or if both are True. P XOR Q is True when either P or Q is True, but not both.

The syntax diagrams defining Boolean and relational expressions are deferred to the appendices.

The Boolean operators can be very useful. If we wanted to check that the integer variable Grade had been assigned a legal score (between 0 and 100), we could test to see whether or not the expression (0 <= Grade) AND (Grade <= 100) was True.

Like arithmetic operators, Boolean operators obey rules of precedence. Negation (NOT) is done before any other operation. Conjunction (AND) is done before disjunction (OR). Parentheses are used to override precedence. To illustrate these rules, suppose that P, Q, and R are Boolean variables with the values False, False, and True, respectively. Then we have the following results.

Expression	Value	Comment
NOT P AND Q	False	True AND False
NOT (P AND Q)	True	NOT False
NOT P OR Q	True	True OR False
NOT (P OR Q)	True	NOT False
P AND Q OR R	True	False OR True
P AND (Q OR R)	False	False AND True
P OR Q AND R	False	False OR False
(P OR Q) AND R	False	False AND True
P AND NOT Q OR R	True	False AND True OR True, so False OR True

All three logical operations (NOT, AND, OR) are done before any relational operator (=, <>, <, <=, >, >=) is used. For example, the expression I < 0 AND 1 <= J would be evaluated by ANDing 0 and 1, comparing I with this result, and so forth. This might not be considered an error by some compilers (including TURBO). This makes it necessary to parenthesize all comparisons. So the preceding expression would be written (I < 0) AND (1 <= J). Parentheses also increase readability.

If two ANDs or two ORs occur in an expression, they are evaluated from left to right. This means that the expression P AND Q AND R is evaluated as if it had been written (P AND Q) AND R.

The meaning of a long Boolean expression can be difficult to understand. For this reason, it is a good idea to keep Boolean expressions short. It is also wise to parenthesize to be explicit in meaning. Adding parentheses to a Boolean expression will sometimes eliminate a bug in a program.

4.5   A PROGRAM

In this section we give an example of a program which uses some of the features we have discussed in this chapter.

We are to write a program for computing landscaping costs. The cost of a landscaping job depends on the area to be landscaped and the number of shrubs planted. It costs $0.60 per square foot of landscaping and $7.50 for each shrub. The user is to enter the length and width of the area to be landscaped and then the number of shrubs. A message indicating whether or not the cost exceeds $1000 is to be printed as well.

To start solving this problem, we break it into three smaller problems.

```
Obtain the measurements and number of shrubs.
Calculate the cost.
Print the results.
```

Let us call the length and width Len and Width and the number of shrubs Shrubs. Using these we can refine the first of the steps above as follows.

```
Obtain the measurements and number of shrubs.
   Prompt user, get Len.
   Prompt user, get Width.
   Prompt user, get Shrubs.
Calculate the cost.
Print the results.
```

To find the total cost of the job we need to find the cost of the shrubs and the basic cost for the area landscaped. The cost of the shrubs is obtained by multiplying $7.50 by the number of shrubs. To find the other cost we first obtain the area landscaped by multiplying the length times the width and then multiply the area (square footage) by the cost per square foot ($0.60). Using our algorithmic notation, we now have the algorithm below.

```
Obtain the measurements and number of shrubs.
     Prompt user, get Len.
     Prompt user, get Width.
     Prompt user, get Shrubs.
Calculate the cost.
     Area ← Len * Width
     Cost ← Shrubs * ShrubCost + Area * SquareFootCost
Print the results.
```

To finish the algorithm we need to specify the details in the third step. It is a good idea to summarize the data used in making a calculation so that the user knows what data was used to obtain the results. Because a message concerning whether or not the cost exceeded the budget, we make a comparison and store its result. Including the details of the third step, we obtain our final algorithm. It is understood that printing a quantity also involves labeling the quantity with a message.

```
Obtain the measurements and number of shrubs.
     Prompt user, get Len.
     Prompt user, get Width.
     Prompt user, get Shrubs.
Calculate the cost.
     Area ← Len * Width
     Cost ← Shrubs * ShrubCost + Area * SquareFootCost
Print the results.
     Print Len, Width, Shrubs
     Print Cost
     InBudget ← (Cost <= Budget)
     Print InBudget
```

This algorithm becomes the basis of our program.

Because the square foot cost, shrub cost, and figure for excessive cost remain the same each time the program is to be used, these numbers are stored as constants. Because the other quantities change, they are stored in variables as they change. The finished program, which reflects these considerations, is given in *FIGURE 4.18*. A sample run is included as well.

Notice that the input is prompted carefully, telling the user exactly what is expected. The numbers that were entered are redisplayed as part of the final output. This lets the user know exactly what numbers were used to calculate the cost. Because it is easy to enter 500 instead of 50, causing a large increase in cost, this is very valuable. This practice is known as echoing the input and should be done wherever practical.

FIGURE 4.18

```
PROGRAM LandScape ( Input, Output );

{   This program calculates the cost of doing simple landscaping.
    The cost is based on the yard's size and the number of shrubs.

        Author    : John Riley
        Date      : December 26, 1986
        File name : CH4EX9.PAS
}

CONST
     SquareFootCost =  0.60;   { Basic fee of $0.60 per sq. ft  }
     ShrubCost      =  7.50;   { Cost for one shrub             }
     Budget         =  1000;   { Amount allocated for landscape }

VAR
     Area,                     { Area,                          }
```

(continued)

```
      Len,                   { Length,                 }
      Width      : Real;     { Width of Yard in feet   }
      Shrubs     : Integer;  { Number of shrubs        }
      Cost       : Real;     { Total cost              }
      InBudget   : Boolean;  { To indicate excess costs }
BEGIN { LandScape }
  Writeln('Landscaping costs');
  Write('Enter length of yard (in feet) >');
  Readln(Len);
  Write('Enter width of yard (in feet) >');
  Readln(Width);
  Area := Len * Width;
  Write('Enter number of shrubs >');
  Readln(Shrubs);
  Cost := Area * SquareFootCost + Shrubs * ShrubCost;
  Writeln;
  Writeln('Cost for ', Len:6:2, ' by ', Width:6:2, ' yard');
  Writeln('with ', Shrubs, ' shrubs is $', Cost:8:2);
  InBudget := Cost > Budget;
  Writeln;
  Writeln('Landscaping is within budget : ', InBudget)
END. { LandScape }


Landscaping costs
Enter length of yard (in feet) >50
Enter width of yard (in feet) >20
Enter number of shrubs >3

Cost for  50.00 by  20.00 yard
with 3 shrubs is $    82.50

Landscaping is within budget : TRUE
```

4.6 SUMMARY

Three data types have been discussed in this chapter: the two numeric types integer and real and the Boolean type. Integers are used to express whole numbers. Frequently they are used for counting. Reals are used to express numbers which may have a fractional or decimal part. The Boolean data type consists of the two logical values True and False.

Integer and real values and variables may be combined using the arithmetic operators (+, −, *, /). The integer data type also has two special operators related to division: DIV and MOD. In addition to these operators, there are predefined functions which are useful in working with these data types.

Boolean values are most often produced by comparisons. Relational operators ($=$, $<>$, $<$, $<=$, $>$, $>=$) are used to make comparisons. Boolean values are combined using logical operators (NOT, AND, OR).

Constant declarations are used to identify quantities which will remain fixed throughout the program. They are very useful for writing programs which are easy to read and maintain.

By using these features of Pascal it is possible to write programs whose execution proceeds from top to bottom. In the next chapter, ways of changing this are discussed. ◻

EXERCISES

1. Find out what MaxInt is on your computer. Is it big enough to store a Social Security Number (nine digits long) as an integer? Is it big enough to store all Zip Codes as integers? What about Zip + 4? If an integer variable cannot hold a Zip Code, what sort of variable should be used? Hint: Does it make sense to add Zip Codes?

2. Usually (maybe always) MaxInt is one less than two raised to a power. Find out what this power is for the implementation of Pascal you use.

3. Classify the following as legal integers, reals, and characters or as being illegal.

1.0	1.	1	29.8
'2'	.22E4	$-2,345$	2,55E9.0
0.99	$-45.45E-45$	.93E6	11.22
'5'	-890	88.E$+77$	-89.66

4. Find the value and type of each of the following arithmetic expressions. If there is an error, indicate this. Assume that J is an integer variable which has the value 7 and that X is a real variable which has the value 13.6.

9.0 + 12	17 MOD 5
2.0 * 3.0E2	12 / 5
2 * (J + X)	3 * Round(X / 2)
10 MOD J	X Div J
3 * Sqr(J)	Sqrt(7 * J)
Trunc(X) DIV 3	X $-$ Round(X)
X $-$ Trunc(X)	(45 DIV J) * J + (45 MOD J)
Sqrt(J $-$ X)	((J $-$ 2) * 3.0) $-$ X / 2

5. Put the following list of strings in order. That is, each string in the ordered list should precede the following. Use ASCII ordering.

   'DOG'

   'DOGGED'

   'dogs'

   'dog'

   ' DOG'

   ' DOg'

   '1 Dog'

   'No dogs'

   'a dog'

   '1 dog'

   '1 dog'

   ' Many dogs'

   ' 2 dogs'

   'DOG'

6. Evaluate the following Boolean expressions. Assume that X and Y are real variables with the values 3.3 and 4.4 and that C is a character variable with the value 'M'.

(X * Y) > 0	(X > 0) AND (Y <= 0)
NOT(X <> Y)	(3 * X > Y) OR (X <= 1.0)
(C <> 'M') OR (C <> 'm')	C <= 'a'
('0' <= C) AND (C <= '9')	'CAT' <= C
'Cat' = 'CAT'	'DOG' <= 'cow'

7. Give the exact output of the following statements. I and J are integer variables with the values 789 and −1234.

```
Writeln('Hello' : 10);
Writeln(I, ' -- ', J);
Writeln(I : 6, J : 12);
Writeln(I : 2, J : 3);
Writeln('Twice ', I, ' is ', 2 * I);
```

8. Find and correct the errors in the following constant and variable declaration sections.

```
a.   CONST
          OneThousand = 1,000
          Message      : 'Help I am trapped ;

     VAR
          23Skidoo : Integer;
          Name     : String[ StringLength ];
```

b. ```
    CONST
            BigNum   = 100;
            BiggerNum   = 200;
            BiggestNum = LargeInt;

    VAR
            Sum   = Integer;
            Average = String[-100]
    ```

c.  ```
    CONST
            HowMany : Integer;

    VAR
            Sum         : Integer;
            CourseNum : Integer;
            Average,
            Sum         : Real;
    ```

Exercises 9 through 22 are Pascal programming exercises. Begin to develop a style of programming which is readable. Refer to the programs in this chapter and to Appendix H for suggestions on style. Use appropriate spacing and commenting conventions. Prompt all input, and label all output.

9. Write a program which asks the user his or her name and then uses the name in a greeting to the user.

10. Write a program that has the user input two words and then prints TRUE or FALSE to indicate whether or not the words are in order. When run, the program should look something like (where CAT and DOG are the words entered):

```
Enter a word >CAT
Enter another word >DOG

The words are in order : TRUE
```

11. Write a program which takes the cost of an item and finds the sales tax due on that item. The sales tax is 7%. The output should contain the item's cost, the sales tax, and the total of the cost and sales tax. Format the output appropriately.

12. Change the program you wrote for Exercise 11 to reflect a decrease in sales tax to 6.5%. Do not write a new program.

13. A certain shirt takes four and a half yards of cloth, twelve buttons, and twenty yards of thread to manufacture. Write a program in which the user enters the number of shirts to be made. The output is the yards of cloth, number of buttons, and yards of thread that are needed to make the shirts.

14. Write a program which calculates how many gallons of paint are needed to paint the walls of a room. The user is to enter the length and width of the room as well as the number of windows and doors

(which are not to be painted). A gallon of paint will cover 450 square feet. A door is 18 square feet and a window 9 square feet. The height of the room is 7.5 feet.

15. Modify the program of Exercise 14 to accommodate a new brand of paint which covers 500 square feet. Do not write a new program.

16. Write a program which gives the user (presumably a runner) his or her pace in minutes and seconds per mile when he or she enters a time for a ten-kilometer race (in minutes and seconds). Prompt all input and label output. Ten kilometers is 6.2137 miles. Hint: Convert time to seconds before calculations. Use the DIV and MOD operators to convert seconds to minutes and seconds.

17. Write a program to compute taxicab fare on the basis of mileage as follows. The first fifth of a mile costs twenty-five cents and each ensuing fifth of a mile costs ten cents. Assume that the passenger rides at least a fifth of a mile. The input is to be a decimal number expressing the numbers of miles ridden.

18. Modify the program of Exercise 17 to reflect a fare increase to thirty cents for the first fifth of a mile and fifteen cents for each ensuing fifth of a mile. Do not write a new program.

19. Write a program which calculates the (simple) interest earned on a deposit for a user. The user is to input the rate (as a percentage) and the principal (the amount deposited). The formula for simple interest is given below, where Rate must be expressed as a decimal.

Interest is Rate times Principal

20. Write a program which calculates the continuous interest earned on an investment for a user. The user is to input the amount invested, the annual rate (as a percentage), and the time (in years) of the investment. The formula for continuous interest is given below, where Rate must be expressed as a decimal. (Use the exponential function.)

Interest is Principal times e to the product of the Rate and Time minus the Principal

21. Write a program which attempts to add two integers whose sum is greater than MaxInt and then output the result. Do you get an error?

22. Write a program which has for input three numbers. The product of the first two is to be compared with the third. If they are equal, this should be indicated. When run, the program should do something like this:

```
Enter two numbers (separated by a space) >2.0   3.0
Enter their product >6.0

The two numbers,   2.00    3.00 give the product    6.00 : TRUE
```

Try your program with pairs of numbers like 1.0 and 0.1, 1000.0 and 0.001, 16 and 0.0625 (which is 1/16).

23. Suppose that I and J are positive integers and that R is a real number. What are the values of the following expressions? If you can't think of the answer, substitute some specific values and see what you get.

((I DIV J) * J) + (I MOD J)
Sin(I * Pi)
Cos(2 * J * Pi)
Ln(Exp(R))
Sqrt(Sqr(R))

24. There are some rules which may be used to simplify Boolean expressions.

First, each of the relational operators has an opposite. Equality (=) and inequality (<>) are opposites, < and >= are opposites, and > and <= are opposites. When NOT precedes an expression containing a relational operator, NOT may be eliminated by replacing the relational operator by its opposite. Thus NOT(X = Y) is the same as X <> Y , NOT(X < Y) is the same as X >= Y, and so on. (Here X and Y are comparable expressions.)

The second way of simplifying Boolean expressions is through the use of *De Morgan's rules*, named after Augustus De Morgan (1806–1871). These rules state that NOT(P AND Q) is the same as (NOT P) OR (NOT Q) and that NOT(P OR Q) is the same as (NOT P) AND (NOT Q). (Here P and Q are Boolean valued expressions.) By using these rules we may sometimes make Boolean expressions somewhat simpler. For example, NOT((X < 0) AND (Y < 0)) is equal to (NOT (X < 0)) OR (NOT(Y < 0)), which is equal to (X >= 0) AND (Y >= 0). Finally, NOT(NOT P) is the same as P whenever P is Boolean valued.

Use opposite relational operators and De Morgan's rules to simplify the following Boolean expressions so that they do not contain NOT. Assume I and J to be integer variables. (You may need to use De Morgan's rules more than once to simplify some of these.)

NOT((I > 0) AND (J <= 0))
NOT((I >= J) OR (J < 0))
NOT(((I = J) AND (J > 0)) OR (J >= 0))
NOT((I > 100) AND (NOT((J = 0) OR (J = 100))))

25. We have mentioned that a variable is a location in memory used to store a value. Exactly where this is located is given by a quantity known as the variable's *address*. TURBO provides a means of determining the address of a variable. In versions of TURBO running under MS-DOS or CP/M-86, the address of a variable consists of two parts: the *offset* and the *segment* of the variable. The segment is a portion of memory and the offset is the position within the segment at which the variable is located. The offset of a variable is given by OFS(variable) and the segment by SEG(variable), where "variable" is

the identifier of the variable. When TURBO runs under CP/M, the address of the variable is given by ADDR(variable-ident). All of these quantities are integers. Addressing in memory is done by *bytes* (groups of eight bits).

Write a program which declares three integer variables and three real variables and then prints their addresses using the functions OFS and SEG or the function ADDR. How many bytes does an integer occupy? How many bytes does a real occupy? You might want to try these with Boolean, character, or string variables.

In Chapters 3 and 4 we saw how to make a simple program which executed a list of statements in order. In this chapter we introduce Pascal statements which serve to determine when other statements are executed. These statements enable the programmer to cause statements to be executed repeatedly and to allow us to cause different statements to be executed depending on a certain condition. This permits us to solve much more difficult problems. Mastering these statements is very important. ◻

CHAPTER 5

FUNDAMENTAL CONTROL STRUCTURES

5.1 THE THREE FUNDAMENTAL CONTROL STRUCTURES

Although setting up a list of statements to be executed (as we did in Chapters 3 and 4) allows us to exploit some of the computer's power, it would hardly make programming worthwhile. With a good calculator we would be able to obtain the same results without any programming. In order to fully utilize the computer's capabilities we need (at least) to be able to cause some statements to be done many times. It also turns out to be useful to be able to cause statements to be done or not done according to some criterion. Statements which specify the order of execution of statements are known as *control statements* or *control structures*. Over the years, many ways of implementing control statements have been used.

DEFINITION

A *control statement* or *control structure* is a statement which is used to specify (or control) which statements are executed.

FIGURE 5.1   Sequence

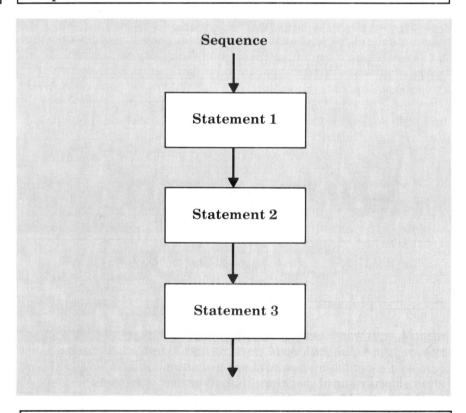

In 1966, it was proven by Bohm and Jacopini that exactly three control structures were sufficient to program any algorithm [B-J]. It has been argued since then that programmers should conceive of their algorithms in terms of these statements. Furthermore, programs written using these statements are more likely to be correct and easier to read. This is one aspect of what is known as "structured programming." Another aspect of this philosophy is the understanding that programming is a discipline which requires thought and planning before coding.

The first fundamental control structure is the *sequence*. This is the natural order we saw in Chapters 3 and 4. A sequence is a group of statements which are executed in order. *FIGURE 5.1* illustrates this structure. Each box in the diagram represents a statement which is either an action (input, output, calculation) or another control structure.

Repetition	*FIGURE 5.2*

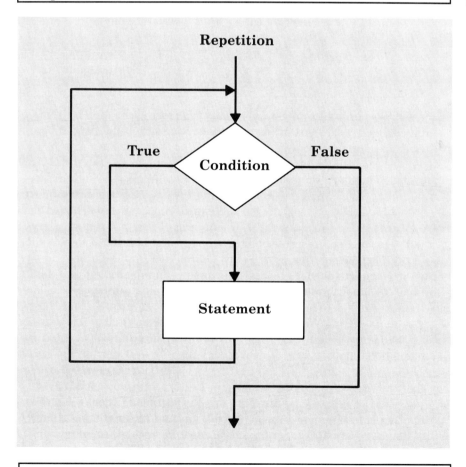

The second control structure is known as the *repetition* (or *iteration* or *loop*) structure. In this structure a statement is executed as long as some condition (a Boolean expression) is True. This structure is depicted in *FIGURE 5.2* on the previous page. In this diagram the diamond indicates that a condition is to be tested (found True or False). If the condition is True, the statement which follows (again an action or another control structure) is to be executed again. If the condition is False, execution passes to the statement following the repetition statement.

The third control structure that is necessary is known as the *decision* (or *selection*) structure. The decision structure causes one of two statements to be done depending on whether a condition is True or False. If the condition is True, one statement is done; if it is False, the other statement is done. The statement to be done may be the null or empty statement which causes nothing to be done. The decision structure is diagrammed in *FIGURE 5.3*.

By putting the control structures within each other it is possible to form complex patterns of control. An example of how these may be put together is given in *FIGURE 5.4*. This diagram consists of a sequence of three statements. The first and last of these are actions of some kind.

FIGURE 5.3   Selection

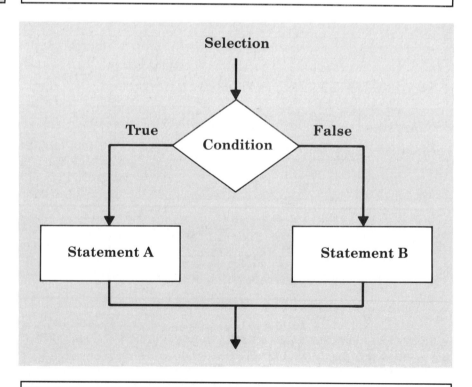

Composition of Control Structures   FIGURE 5.4

Composition of Control Structures

First statement of
sequence (action)

Second statement of
sequence (repetition)

Statement in
loop (sequence)

First statement in
sequence (decision)

Second statement
of sequence
(action)

Third statement of
sequence (action)

The second is a loop. Within the loop there is a sequence of two statements. The first statement within the loop is a selection statement. By putting control statements together in this way it is possible to accomplish any programming task.

The programmer should not aim to produce complex programs. The simplest solution is the best one, and introducing unnecessary complexity should be avoided. The use of these control structures should aid in this end. Unfortunately, programs seem to become complex with very little effort. Try to formulate simple solutions and programs. This requires great discipline on the programmer's part.

For each of the control structures that have been discussed, there is only a single entrance into the structure and a single exit from the structure. This is sometimes called "one entrance–one exit." This is a very useful characteristic. It aids in improving program readability by allowing the reader to determine exactly which statement preceded a particular statement and which statement will follow the current statement. This also helps in the construction of correct programs, because the conditions under which a statement must be executed are known. The programmer does not have to worry about a statement being executed under unanticipated circumstances. This is a very desirable quality in a program.

5.2 THE COMPOUND STATEMENT

Many Pascal control statements, like the repetition and selection statements discussed above, allow only one statement to follow the control structure and be executed. Yet we will often want to have a sequence of statements executed after a particular condition is found to be true. The Pascal statement for grouping statements together as one statement is known as the *compound statement*. It corresponds to the sequence structure discussed in Section 5.1.

The compound statement consists of the key word BEGIN followed by a sequence of statements which are separated by a semicolon and then followed by the key word END. Thus the statement part of a block is a compound statement. The syntax diagram for the compound statement is presented in *FIGURE 5.5*.

FIGURE 5.5   Compound Statement

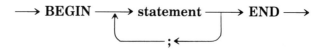

Null Statement   FIGURE 5.6

$$\longrightarrow$$

The statement section of a program is a compound statement, and so we have been using compound statements already. Here is another example of a compound statement (Name is a string variable and Age is an integer variable):

```
BEGIN
   Write('Enter your name >');
   Readln(Name);
   Write('Enter your age > ');
   Readln(Age)
END
```

Although the statements within the compound statement are separated by semicolons, the semicolons are usually placed at the end of a statement. This makes the semicolon look as if it were a statement terminator (in English, the period serves as a sentence terminator). Although an extra semicolon will not cause any problems in some situations, it will in many others. Be careful when using semicolons.

Sometimes an extra semicolon does not cause any problems because there is a statement in Pascal which consists of nothing. This is called the *null* or *empty statement*. Its syntax diagram (see *FIGURE 5.6*) contains nothing. Below is an example of a compound statement which contains three null statements. There is one between BEGIN and the first semicolon, one between the two semicolons, and one between the last semicolon and END.

```
BEGIN
   ;
   ;
END
```

Of course, it doesn't make much sense to do this.

When the compound statement is used in conjunction with a control structure, it is helpful to label the END of the compound statement with a comment. This lets the reader know which control structure is being ended. In simple situations, a key word may suffice to do this. In more complex cases, more than the key word may be needed. Additionally, the statements within the compound statement are usually indented. This makes it easier to see which statements are included between BEGIN and END. The BEGIN and END that follow a control structure will also be indented. Using these stylistic conventions and a control structure we will introduce in the next section, we would write program fragments as follows:

```
WHILE Sum < 100 DO            WHILE BigSum < 1000 DO
   BEGIN                         BEGIN
      Readln(Item);                 LittleSum := 0;
      Sum := Sum + Item             WHILE LittleSum < 100 DO
   END   { WHILE }                     BEGIN
                                          Readln(Item);
                                          LittleSum := LittleSum + Item
                                       END; { WHILE LittleSum < 100 }
                                    BigSum := BigSum + LittleSum
                               END { WHILE BigSum < 1000 }
```

5.3   THE WHILE STATEMENT

This section contains a discussion of the Pascal statement which implements the repetition control structure. This statement is known as the *while statement*. The while statement has the following form. Key words are capitalized for emphasis.

```
WHILE condition DO
   statement-to-be-repeated
```

Usually the statement to be executed within the while loop is a compound statement. For this reason, the while statement often looks something like this:

```
WHILE condition DO
   BEGIN
      statement;
      statement;
      ⋮
      statement;
      statement
   END; { WHILE }
```

The comment after the END of the compound statement informs the reader that the compound statement is within the while loop.

The program in *FIGURE 5.7* uses a while loop to accumulate a sum of numbers entered from the keyboard. When the sum exceeds 100 (NumberToExceed), the loop is exited.

The while statement consists of the key word WHILE followed by a Boolean expression, the key word DO, and any Pascal statement. *FIGURE 5.8* contains a syntax diagram for this statement. For the sake of convenience, a Boolean expression is called a condition. In the program

FIGURE 5.7

```pascal
PROGRAM ExceedTheNumber(Input, Output);

{  A program to add numbers until they exceed a given number.

       Author     : John Riley
       Date       : December 26, 1986
       File name  : CH5EX1.PAS
}

CONST
     NumberToExceed = 100;

VAR
    Item,                { Input item }
    Sum     : Integer;   { Accumulates sum }

BEGIN { ExceedTheNumber }
  Writeln('This program adds numbers until their sum is less');
  Writeln('than ', NumberToExceed, '.');
  Writeln;
  Sum := 0;
  Writeln('Enter integers to be added.');
  WHILE Sum < NumberToExceed DO
    BEGIN
      Write('Enter a positive integer >');
      Readln(Item);
      Sum := Sum + Item
    END; { WHILE }
  Writeln;
  Writeln('Sum is ', Sum)
END. { ExceedTheNumber }
```

in *FIGURE 5.7* the condition is Sum < NumberToExceed. When the while statement is executed in a program, the condition is evaluated. If the condition is True, the statement following the DO of the while statement (the statement within the while statement) is executed. In the preceding program the statement is a compound statement containing an output, an input, and an assignment statement. If the value of the condition is True, the statement following DO is executed and control is passed to the while statement. The condition is evaluated again, and if it is True the statement within the while statement is executed. If the condition is

While Statement

FIGURE 5.8

$\longrightarrow$ WHILE $\longrightarrow$ Boolean-expression $\longrightarrow$ DO $\longrightarrow$ statement $\longrightarrow$

False, control passes to the statement following the while statement. The cycle of evaluating the condition and executing the statement continues as long as the condition is True.

A programming task that is not uncommon is the forming of a sum of numbers. A while loop can be used to program the solution to this problem. The main idea of the algorithm can be expressed as follows:

```
While there are more numbers
     Get another number
     Add it to the sum
Print the sum
```

This version of the algorithm is not suitable as a basis for a program. We recognize that "number" and "sum" must be variables. Values for number are obtained as input. However, the initial value of sum is not specified in the algorithm above. What is the sum before the adding starts? 0. These considerations are reflected in the next version of the algorithm:

```
Sum ← 0
While there are more numbers
     Get(Number)
     Sum ← Sum + Number
Print(Sum)
```

The phrase "there are more numbers" needs further elaboration. Usually it is not known in advance how many numbers are to be added. Let us suppose that only positive numbers (or zero) are to be added. Then a negative number can be used to signal the end of the input. This gives the following version of the algorithm:

```
Sum ← 0
While Number ≥ 0
     Get(Number)
     Sum ← Sum + Number
Print(Sum)
```

Unfortunately, this is not correct. Once again, a value must be supplied to a variable (Number) before it is used. Number must be obtained before the loop. Of course, Number must also be obtained within the loop. Thus the algorithm must be modified:

```
Sum ← 0
Get(Number)
While Number ≥ 0
     Sum ← Sum + Number
     Get(Number)
Print(Sum)
```

Notice that within the loop the order of the assignment statement and the input statement have been reversed. This is so that when the negative number signifying the end of the input is entered, it is not added to the sum. A consequence of this is that the algorithm works correctly even if there are no numbers to be added. In this case, the only entry would be a negative number and the statements within the while loop would not be executed at all.

The program in *FIGURE 5.9* uses the while statement in a program based on our algorithm. A sample of what this looks like when it is run follows the program. The commands S (for save) and R (for run) do not actually appear on the screen. Notice that we save our program before we run it. This is very important whenever a program has a loop in it, because if the program is not correct the only way to stop it may be to turn the computer off. When the computer is turned off, the contents of memory, including the program, are lost.

Notice that we continue to use the conventions we have already discussed. As programs become more complex, this becomes more and more important. For example, notes, in the form of comments, about the purpose of the various variables are made. Comments also indicate the BEGIN and END of the program. Indentations indicate which statements are included within other statements. The first executable statement of the program sets the variable Sum to zero, which reflects that when the program starts, nothing has been added. The three output statements which follow tell the user what the program is doing and expects as input. The first input item is then read. (If it were negative, the statement within the while statement would be skipped.) The statement within the while statement is a compound statement which contains three statements. The END of the compound statement is marked with { WHILE } to signify that it is the end of the while loop or statement.

There is no semicolon after the Readln in the while loop, because it does not need to be separated from any other statement. Similarly, since the last Writeln is not followed by another statement, it does not need a semicolon after it.

The while loop terminates only when the Boolean expression which follows WHILE becomes False. Thus, if this condition never becomes False, the loop is nonterminating or infinite. An infinite loop always indicates a programming error. Unfortunately, it is not too difficult to inadvertently program an infinite loop. Most of the programs you will write as exercises will run to completion in at most a few minutes. If you have a program which is running for more than five minutes it probably has an infinite loop (unless there is a lot of input). In this situation you will have to stop the program. This can be accomplished with a BREAK or CTRL/C or by pushing the reset button. If all else fails, turn the machine off. This is a last resort. Some of these actions will cause your program to be lost. This is why it is important to save your program before running it (unless you are very fond of typing).

FIGURE 5.9

```
PROGRAM Summer ( Input, Output );

{ This is a simple program which tallies the positive numbers
  entered from the keyboard.  Input is terminated by entering
  a negative number.

        Author     : John Riley
        Date       : March 20, 1986
        File name  : CH5EX2.PAS
}

VAR
    Item,                   { Input item }
    Sum     : Integer;   { Accumulates sum }

BEGIN { Summer }
  Sum := 0;
  Writeln('Enter integers to be added, end with a negative');
  Writeln(' number.');
  Write('Number (negative to stop) >');
  Readln(Item);
  WHILE Item >= 0 DO
    Begin
      Sum := Sum + Item;
      Write('Number (negative to stop) >');
      Readln(Item)
    END; { WHILE }
  Writeln;
  Writeln('Sum is ', Sum)
END. { Summer }

>S

Saving B:CH5EX2.PAS
>R

Compiling
  30 lines
Code :   291 bytes (79FB - 7B1E)
Free : 22496 bytes (7B1E - D2FE)
Data :     8 bytes (D2FE - D306)

Running
Enter integers to be added, end with a negative
 number.
Number (negative to stop) >8
Number (negative to stop) >9
Number (negative to stop) >6
Number (negative to stop) >-9

Sum is 23
```

To make sure that a loop terminates, there must be something occurring in the loop which eventually causes the condition to be False. In the program in *FIGURE 5.9*, the condition governing the while loop became false when a negative number was input from the keyboard. A special value (or values) is often used to stop a loop. Below is a program fragment which counts the number of nonzero integers input. The special value which stops the loop is 0. (All variables are assumed to be integers.)

```
ItemCount := 0;
Write('Enter a positive number (0 to quit)>');
Readln(Item);
WHILE Item <> 0 DO
   BEGIN
      ItemCount := ItemCount + 1;
      Write('Enter a positive number (0 to quit)>');
      Readln(Item)
   END; { WHILE }
```

When special values are used to terminate a loop, it is imperative to let the user know how to terminate the loop. This was done in the program fragment above with a parenthetical remark within the prompt to the user.

The loops in the preceding fragment and in the program of *FIGURE 5.9* are examples of common programming tasks. The loop in the fragment above is a counting loop: it counts a number of items. The loop in *FIGURE 5.9* is a summing loop. If both the counting and summing are done in one loop, a division will give the average of the numbers entered. Of course, you should not attempt to average zero items. However, to take care of this we need an additional control structure.

5.4   THE IF-THEN-ELSE STATEMENT

The next control statement we cover in this chapter is the if-then-else statement, which is the Pascal statement for the decision structure that was mentioned in Section 1.

The if-then-else statement has two possible forms. The first consists of the key word IF followed by a Boolean expression, the key word THEN, and a statement. The second form is the same as the first except that it is followed by an else clause, which consists of the key word ELSE followed by a statement. The general form is one of the following:

```
IF condition THEN
   statement-for-true-condition


IF condition THEN
   statement-for-true-condition
ELSE
   statement-for-false-condition
```

If the Boolean expression following IF is True, the statement following THEN is executed. If the Boolean expression is False, the statement following ELSE is executed if the else clause is present. If the else clause is not present and the condition is False, nothing is executed. In either case, after the if-then-else statement control is passed to the statement which follows. *FIGURE 5.10* contains the syntax diagram for the if-then-else statement.

FIGURE 5.10		If-Then-Else Statement

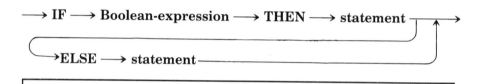

In many instances the statements that follow THEN and ELSE are compound statements, because only one statement can follow either. This happens whenever it is necessary to have a sequence of actions taken. But it must be noted that when these are grouped using a compound statement they form one statement within the if-then-else statement. A consequence of this is that a semicolon never precedes the ELSE of an if-then-else statement.

As an example of the use of the if-then-else statement, consider the following fragment of a program dealing with the quadratic equation. (All the variables have been declared to be real variables).

```
Discriminant := Sqr(b) - 4 * a * c;
IF Discriminant >= 0 THEN { There are real roots }
    BEGIN
        Root1 := (-b + Sqrt(Discriminant))/(2 * a);
        Root2 := (-b - Sqrt(Discriminant))/(2 * a);
        Writeln('Roots are ', Root1, ' , ', Root2)
    END { IF }
ELSE
    Writeln('No real roots');
```

This program fragment produces the real roots of a quadratic equation with coefficients a, b, and c if real roots exist. A compound statement is needed after THEN, because there are several actions to be performed. None is needed after ELSE since only one output statement is used. This fragment also illustrates our style of writing the if-then-else statement, particularly when a compound statement is used. The statements following THEN and ELSE are indented. This indicates that they are within

the if-then-else statement. The END of the compound statement is annotated (with { IF }) to show with which control structure it is associated.
Frequently a comment is put beside a BEGIN or after a THEN or ELSE
to clarify what is being done.

If-then-else statements (and while statements) may be nested—that
is, the statement following THEN or ELSE may be another if-then-else
statement. The following example is an elaboration of the preceding one
and illustrates this.

```
Discriminant := Sqr(b) - 4 * a * c;
IF a <> 0 THEN
   IF Discriminant >= 0 THEN { There are real roots }
      BEGIN
         Root1 := (-b + Sqrt(Discriminant))/(2 * a);
         Root2 := (-b - Sqrt(Discriminant))/(2 * a);
         Writeln('Roots are ', Root1, ' , ', Root2)
      END { IF }
   ELSE { The roots are imaginary }
      BEGIN
         RealPart := -b/(2 * a);
         ImagPart1 := Sqrt(-Discriminant)/(2 * a):
         ImagPart2 := -Sqrt(-Discriminant)/(2 * a):
         Writeln('Roots are complex');
         Writeln('First root, Real part : ', RealPart,
                 'Imaginary Part : ', ImagPart1);
         Writeln('Second root, Real part : ', RealPart,
                 'Imaginary Part : ', ImagPart2)
      END { ELSE }
ELSE { The equation is degenerate }
   Writeln('Equation is not quadratic.');
```

In this example the statement following the THEN of the first if-then-
else (IF a <> 0) extends from IF Discriminant > = 0 to END { ELSE }.
The statement following THEN or ELSE may be rather lengthy. This is
not uncommon for both the if-then-else and the while statements. Again,
indentation is used to indicate which statements are part of other statements. Experienced programmers rely on this sort of visual clue when
reading programs. There are variations on the indentation scheme we
are using, but all of them help the reader of the program. After a while
you will probably find a style of indentation you like. Once you have,
stick with it. We caution you that indentation is for people. The compiler
completely ignores indentation.

In the fragment above we have split a long output line across two lines.
This is permitted if the split is done where a blank space (not within a
string) may occur. Doing this can make working on your program easier,
because most computers can display only a limited width (length of line)
of program at one time. Also, many printers have a limited width that
they will print. If you want to be consistent with your indentation, split-

ting output lines becomes necessary. In this situation it is a good idea to continue the output items under the previous items as we have done.

One last comment needs to be made about the if-then-else statement. When if-then-else statements are nested, an else clause is always matched with the nearest if (above). This causes a problem whenever the nested if-then-else statement does not have an else clause and the outer if-then-else statement does. If this occurs the compiler will match the else with the inner if. Below is a diagram of the situation where the programmer wants statement2 done if condition1 is False and if condition1 is False then condition2 is to be tested before statement1 is executed. This is what the indentation indicates.

```
        Programmer's intent

   ┌──→ IF condition1 THEN
   │        IF condition2 THEN
   │            statement1
   └──→ ELSE
            statement2
```

However, the compiler will match the else with IF condition2, and if condition1 is False no action will occur.

```
        Compiler's interpretation

        IF condition1 THEN
   ┌──────→ IF condition2 THEN
   │            statement1
   └──────→ ELSE
                statement2
```

Probably the most straightforward way out of this dilemma is to put the inner if-then-else within a compound statement as follows:

```
        Solution

   IF condition1 THEN
        BEGIN
            IF condition2 THEN
                statement1
        END { IF condition1 }
   ELSE
        statement2
```

The compiler will then use the compound statement as the statement that follows the then, and because that contains the inner if-then statement, no problem arises.

5.5 THE REPEAT-UNTIL STATEMENT

There is a statement which is similar to the while statement and is sometimes convenient to use. This is the repeat-until statement. The essential difference between the while statement and the repeat-until statement is that the repeat-until statement does the testing of a condition at the end of the loop.

The syntax diagram of the repeat-until statement is given in *FIGURE 5.11*. The key word REPEAT is followed by a sequence of statements

Repeat-Until Statement

FIGURE 5.11

FIGURE 5.12

```
PROGRAM RepeatUntilEx ( Input, Output );

{
      Author    : John Riley
      Date      : February 19, 1986
      File name : CH5EX3.PAS
}

VAR  Answer : Char;

BEGIN { RepeatUntilEx }
  REPEAT
     Writeln('Hello');
     Writeln;
     Write('Do you want me to say hello again? (Y/N)');
     Readln( Answer );
     Writeln
  UNTIL Answer = 'N';
  Writeln('Goodbye')
END. { RepeatUntilEx }

Output :

Hello
Do you want me to say hello again? (Y/N)Y
Hello
Do you want me to say hello again? (Y/N)N
Goodbye
```

which are separated from one another by semicolons. This sequence is followed by the key word UNTIL and a condition (Boolean-valued expression).

The effect of the repeat-until statement is to execute the sequence of statements and then evaluate the condition following the key word UNTIL. If the condition is False, the sequence of statements is executed again. After the statements are executed the condition is evaluated. When the condition becomes True, control passes to the statement following the repeat-until statement. The program in *FIGURE 5.12* on the preceding page illustrates the use of the repeat-until statement.

The key words REPEAT and UNTIL mark the beginning and the end of the statements to be executed in the loop, so there is no need to use a compound statement as with the while loop. Sometimes the while statement is said to perform a pretest and the repeat-until statement to perform a posttest. It should also be noted that the while loop continues

FIGURE 5.13   **Loops**

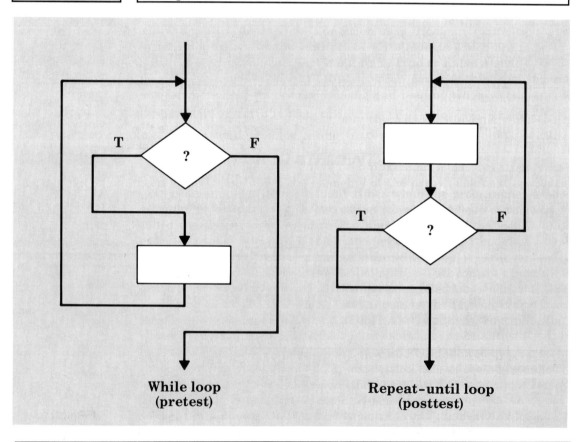

While loop
(pretest)

Repeat–until loop
(posttest)

when the condition is True, whereas the repeat-until loop continues when the condition is False. The flow diagrams in *FIGURE 5.13* illustrate these differences.

Sometimes a loop may be written using either the while statement or the repeat-until statement. In our experience the while loop is usually used. This is because there is almost always some circumstance in which the loop is not to be executed. Since the statements within a repeat-until loop are always executed once, it is inappropriate when the body of the loop may not be executed.

5.6 ON DEVELOPING PROGRAMS

Control statements allow the development of more complex programs. In fact, it is possible to write any flow of control using only the statements given so far. However, it would be extremely difficult to do so. Pascal provides other features to simplify programs.

Unhappily, it is also possible to create a large number of errors or bugs with these statements. As was indicated in *FIGURE 2.9*, errors can be detected when the program is compiled. The errors found at this time are generally *syntax errors*. A syntax error is an error in using the basic rules of formation of the language. Syntax errors can arise from any point in the program except within a comment. Generally these are relatively easy to correct. An example of a syntax error would be a missing semicolon. Consulting a syntax chart is often very helpful in correcting a syntax error. When TURBO discovers a syntax error, a message is given and then the editor is invoked with the cursor at the position where the compiler discovered the error. This may not be the actual position of the error. This would happen, for example, if a quotation mark were omitted at the end of a string. The next quotation mark (which was intended to start a string) will be taken as the end of the first string. The compiler would then take the first word of the second string (e.g., Hello) and attempt to interpret it as Pascal and probably not succeed. The program fragment below illustrates this.

```
                         ˘Missing quote
Writeln('Enter your name );
Readln(Name);
Writeln('How are you ', Name, ' ?');
         ˆError detected
```

The moral of this is that an error may not be at the position indicated by the compiler.

A *syntax error* is an error caused by violation of the rules of formation of a language.

DEFINITION

Errors may occur when the program is executed. These are known as *run-time errors*. (The run-time error message may be the output of the execution phase.) An example of a run-time error would be an attempted division by zero. A run-time error can be caused by very simple things or very complex things. Usually a run-time error happens when a programmer either does not understand the semantics of the language or commits an error in his or her logic. It may not be clear which of these is the underlying cause of the run-time error. An inadequate command of the language can be cured by study and work. Correcting an algorithm may be very difficult, and the entire programming process may need to be restarted from the beginning. Errors in the algorithm or in the coding of the algorithm will also be indicated by incorrect output. Testing the program with some special values for input may reveal the error.

DEFINITION

> A *run-time error* is an error that causes the program execution to terminate prematurely.

5.7 PROGRAMS USING THE WHILE AND IF-THEN-ELSE STATEMENTS

The control statements may be nested to perform a variety of tasks. Since many (possibly most) programs do some action repeatedly, loops are very common. In Section 5.3 we saw how to use loops to count and sum an input list.

It is also possible to find the high and low items in an input list using an if-then-else statement within a while loop. To do this, two variables— say High and Low—are needed to hold the high and low values. Each item we process in the loop is compared with High and Low using an if-then-else statement. If the item exceeds High or is less than Low, the item becomes the new High or Low. To start we must give High and Low values. The first item is used for High and Low. The pseudocode in *FIG-URE 5.14* does this.

This algorithm might be used in a program to find the high and low grades of a group of students as well as to find the average. As in many programs, a main part of such a program is a loop which is done until the user terminates it. Usually more than one thing is done within the loop. For example, in a program which finds the high, low, and average values of a list, it is necessary to check each new input to see if it is a new high or low. It is also necessary to count the number of items input and accumulate their sum in order to do the average. After the loop ends, a computation is done and the results are printed. A program which does this is presented in *FIGURE 5.15*. Examples of running the program are also included.

| Algorithm for Obtaining the High and Low Items in a List | **FIGURE 5.14** |

```
Get(Item)
High ⟵ Item
Low ⟵ Item
While there are more items
  Get(Item)
  If Item > High Then
    High ⟵ Item
  If Item < Low Then
    Low ⟵ Item
End While Loop
```

FIGURE 5.15

```pascal
PROGRAM ClassAnalysis ( Input, Output );

{ This is an example using the while loop.  The program reads
  names and grades of students and determines the high grade,
  the low grade, and the average of the class.

      Author    : John Riley
      Date      : February 3, 1986
      File name : CH5EX4.PAS
}

CONST
     Stop = -1;   { Indicates end of input }

VAR
     Grade,                  { Grade read }
     NumOfStudents,          { Number of students in the class }
     HighGrade,              { Highest grade found }
     LowGrade,               { Lowest grade found }
     SumOfScores   : Integer; { Accumulates the total of the grades }
     ClassAverage  : Real;   { Class Average }


BEGIN { ClassAnalysis }
  Writeln;
  Writeln('This performs a simple analysis of class grades.');
  Writeln('Enter the grades one per line.  End with ', Stop);
  Write('Enter grade > ');
  Readln( Grade );
  HighGrade := Grade;
  LowGrade := Grade;
```

(continued)

```pascal
      NumOfStudents := 0;
      SumOfScores   := 0;
      WHILE Grade <> Stop DO
         BEGIN { Process a grade }
            NumOfStudents := NumOfStudents + 1;
            SumOfScores   := SumOfScores + Grade;
            IF Grade > HighGrade THEN
                HighGrade := Grade;
            IF Grade < LowGrade THEN
               LowGrade := Grade;
            Write('Enter grade (', Stop, ' to quit) >');
            Readln( Grade )
         END; { WHILE }
      Writeln;
      IF NumOfStudents <> 0 THEN
         BEGIN
            ClassAverage := SumOfScores / NumOfStudents;
            Writeln('Class Summary');
            Writeln;
            Writeln('Number of Students :    ', NumOfStudents : 3 );
            Writeln('Highest Grade :         ', HighGrade : 3 );
            Writeln('Lowest Grade :          ', LowGrade : 3 );
            Writeln('Class Average :         ', ClassAverage : 6 : 2 )
         END { IF }
      ELSE
         Writeln('No students processed');
      Writeln
   END. { ClassAnalysis }
```

```
This performs a simple analysis of class grades.
Enter the grades one per line.  End with -1
Enter grade > 90
Enter grade (-1 to quit) >80
Enter grade (-1 to quit) >70
Enter grade (-1 to quit) >60
Enter grade (-1 to quit) >-1


Class Summary

Number of Students :    4
Highest Grade :        90
Lowest Grade :         60
Class Average :        75.0


This performs a simple analysis of class grades.
Enter the grades one per line.  End with -1
Enter grade > -1


No students processed
```

At this point you should be able to read this program with little difficulty. Notice that a check is made to ensure that a division by zero does not occur (If NumOfStudents <> 0 Then the division is done). Although we would expect the user of this program to run it when he or she actually has student grades to be processed, the user is allowed to enter no students (maybe the gradebook was forgotten). Anticipating all possibilities is known as *defensive programming*. The user does not expect the program to terminate with a run-time error. The user is provided with a message ('No students processed') in this situation. This is good programming psychology. Let the user know what has happened. In this same vein, we urge you to label all output clearly. Numbers out of context are usually meaningless.

> **Defensive programming** is programming to anticipate errors and taking appropriate programming steps to ensure that the program keeps running.

DEFINITION

5.8   SUMMARY

Control statements or structures are used to specify the order in which statements are executed. The three types of control structures are sequence, loop, and decision. Statements in a sequence are executed in order. The statements in a loop are executed repeatedly. The decision structure allows different statements to be executed on the basis of a condition.

The compound statement of Pascal groups statements into a sequence. The compound statement starts with BEGIN and finishes with END. Statements within the compound statement are separated by semicolons.

Two loop statements are the while loop and the repeat-until loop. The while loop tests the condition for continuing the loop before the loop is executed. The repeat-until loop tests the condition after the statements in the loop have been executed.

A decision statement of Pascal is the if-then-else statement. The if-then-else statement has two forms: with and without the else clause.

These statements may occur within one another. This is known as nesting the statements. Nested statements enable programmers to construct complex programs. Complex programs require more discipline in their design and construction.

In the next chapter we will introduce additional types of variables which make it easier to design and construct complex programs. A loop statement and decision statement for working with these will also be introduced.   ❑

EXERCISES

1. Describe what the following program does. You might want to confirm your description by running the program.

```
PROGRAM TooHighTooLow (Input, Output);

CONST
     JustRight = 64;

VAR
     Guess : Integer;

BEGIN { TooHighTooLow }
  Writeln('Guess the number.');
  Write('Enter an integer >');
  Readln(Guess);
  WHILE Guess <> JustRight DO
     BEGIN
       IF Guess > JustRight THEN
          Writeln('Too high, try again')
       ELSE
          Writeln('Too low, try again');
       Write('Enter an integer >');
       Readln(Guess)
     END; { WHILE }
  Writeln('You got it!')
END. { TooHighTooLow }
```

2. Give the output of the following program. How many times is the statement within the while loop executed? What would happen if I were initially −1 (instead of 3)?

```
PROGRAM Looper ( Output );

VAR
     I : Integer;

BEGIN { Loop }
  I := 3;
  WHILE I < 21 DO
     BEGIN
        Writeln( I );
        I := 2 * I - 1
     END; { WHILE }
  Writeln( I )
END. { Loop }
```

3. Give the output of the following program. What would happen if I were 16 instead of 13 to start? Give a condition for the initial value of I which would guarantee that the loop ends. To the best of our

knowledge it is not known that this program will terminate for every positive initial value of I.

```
PROGRAM UpAndDown ( Output );

VAR
   I : Integer;

BEGIN { UpAndDown }
   I := 13;
   WHILE I <> 1 DO
      BEGIN
         Writeln( I );
         IF Odd( I ) THEN
            I := 3 * I + 1
         ELSE
            I := I DIV 2
      END; { WHILE }
   Writeln('Done')
END. { UpAndDown }
```

4. Give the output of the following program. What would be the output if the values of I and K were interchanged? Describe what the statement following K := 14 does.

```
PROGRAM OneTwoThree ( Output );

VAR
   I, J, K : Integer;

BEGIN { OneTwoThree }
   I := 17;
   J := 12;
   K := 14;
   IF I < J THEN
      IF J < K THEN
         Writeln(I, ' ', J, ' ', K)
      ELSE
         IF I < K THEN
            Writeln(I, ' ', K, ' ', J)
         ELSE
            Writeln(K, ' ', I, ' ', J)
   ELSE
      IF J < K THEN
         IF K < I THEN
            Writeln(J, ' ', K, ' ', I)
         ELSE
            Writeln(J, ' ', I, ' ', K)
      ELSE
         IF K < I THEN
            Writeln(K, ' ', J, ' ', I)
END. { OneTwoThree }
```

5. Find the errors in the following Pascal program fragments.

a.
```
    { Assume all variables are integers. }

I := 0
WHILE I <= 10 DO
    BEGIN
        Writeln('Enter an integer');
        Readln(J)
    END; { WHILE }
```

b.
```
    { Assume X is an initialized real variable }

IF X >= 0 THEN
    Writeln(X, 'is positive');
ELSE
    Writeln(X, 'is negative');
```

c.
```
    { Assume all variables are real variables and initialized. }

IF X >= 0 THEN
    Y := Sqrt(X);
    Z := Sqrt(Y)
ELSE
    Y := 0;
    Z := 0;
```

6. Design and code a Pascal program which keeps count of the number of characters entered from the keyboard until a period is entered. A sample run should look like the following.

```
Enter a character (. to stop) > a
Enter a character (. to stop) > r
Enter a character (. to stop) > b
Enter a character (. to stop) > ?
Enter a character (. to stop) > .

4 characters entered
```

7. Design and code a Pascal program in which the user enters a list of words and the program returns the first and last words in the list in alphabetical order. Use a special value to terminate the input. A run would look like this:

```
Enter a word (Z to stop) > OBOE
Enter a word (Z to stop) > VIOLIN
Enter a word (Z to stop) > CLARINET
Enter a word (Z to stop) > TRUMPET
Enter a word (Z to stop) > Z

First word (alphabetically) : CLARINET
Last word (alphabetically)  : VIOLIN
```

8. Design and code a Pascal program which returns the first and last words entered in a list. Use a special value to terminate the list. A sample of a run of the program would look like this:

```
Enter a word (Z to stop) > OBOE
Enter a word (Z to stop) > VIOLIN
Enter a word (Z to stop) > CLARINET
Enter a word (Z to stop) > TRUMPET
Enter a word (Z to stop) > Z

First word entered : OBOE
Last word entered  : TRUMPET
```

9. Design and code a Pascal program which counts the number of integers in the input list which exceed the first integer in the list. Use a special value to terminate the list. For example,

```
Enter a number (-99 to stop) > 20
Enter a number (-99 to stop) > 15
Enter a number (-99 to stop) > 25
Enter a number (-99 to stop) > 30
Enter a number (-99 to stop) > 53
Enter a number (-99 to stop) > -99

   3 numbers in the list exceeded 20
```

10. Write a program which acts as a simple cash register. The price of items bought is entered, one per line. The input is ended by the value 0. The total of these items is to be output. A sales tax of 6% is to be computed, displayed, and then added to the total to give the final total due. For example,

```
Item price (0 to end) >2.99
Item price (0 to end) >1.79
Item price (0 to end) >3.45
Item price (0 to end) >0

Subtotal :   8.23
Tax      :   0.49
Total    : $ 8.72
```

11. Modify the program of Exercise 10 to reflect a change in sales tax to 7% and allow for an amount tendered to be entered and change owed to be output.

```
Item price (0 to end) >2.99
Item price (0 to end) >1.79
Item price (0 to end) >3.45
Item price (0 to end) >0

Subtotal :   8.23
Tax      :   0.58
Total    : $ 8.81

Amount tendered >10.00
Change   : $1.19
```

12. Design and code a Pascal program which finds the average of a list
of integers that are input from the keyboard. End the input with
−9999. A sample run should look like the following.

```
Enter an integer (-9999 to stop) > 4
Enter an integer (-9999 to stop) > 6
Enter an integer (-9999 to stop) > 12
Enter an integer (-9999 to stop) > 10
Enter an integer (-9999 to stop) > -9999

The average of 4 items is 8
```

13. Design and code a Pascal program which requests positive integers
from the user until their sum exceeds 100 and then outputs the number of integers that were input. A sample run should look like the
following.

```
Enter a positive integer > 29
Enter a positive integer > 58
Enter a positive integer > 9
Enter a positive integer > 67

4 numbers needed to exceed 100
```

14. Modify the program of Exercise 13 so that the user enters the number
to be exceeded as the first input of the program.

15. Design and code a program which computes employees' pay as follows.
An employee's hourly pay rate and hours worked for the week are
entered (as two decimal numbers—e.g., 6.80 40). The employee's pay
is pay rate times hours worked except for those hours worked over
40, which are paid at one and a half times the usual pay rate. The
end of the data is indicated by input of 0. The total pay is then to be
printed. Here is an example of a run.

```
This   program  computes employees' pay.   Enter
each  employee's hourly pay rate and hours worked
as decimal numbers separated by a blank space.
Enter two zeros (0 0) to end the program.

Enter pay rate, hours worked > 5.0   35
Pay is $175.00

Enter pay rate, hours worked > 4.0   45
Pay is $190.00

Enter pay rate, hours worked > 0   0

Total payroll is $365.00
```

How hard would it be to change your program to make the cutoff
for overtime 37.5 hours?

One of the attractive features of Pascal is its richness of data types. In addition to the built-in data types (Boolean, integer, character, real, and string), it is possible for the programmer to define his or her own data types. In this chapter we give a brief discussion of data types and then develop three user-defined data types. The chapter is finished by introducing some control structures which are very useful in working with these data types. ☐

CHAPTER 6

ENUMERATED TYPES, SUBRANGES, CASE AND FOR STATEMENTS

6.1   DATA TYPES

As part of the problem-analysis phase, the programmer should identify the entities that are to be manipulated in the program as well as how they are to be represented. For example, a name will almost certainly be a string, a salary a real number, and a grade one of the characters 'A', 'B', . . ., 'F'. These are examples of data types.

DEFINITION

> A *data type* is a specification of how memory is to be organized and used for storing variables.

Recall that memory is simply a place where a large quantity of 0s and 1s can be stored. A 0 or a 1 is known as a *bit* (for *bi*nary dig*it*). A single 0 or 1 is too small to be useful, and so bits are generally organized into groups of eight within the computer. Such a group is known as a *byte*. When an integer variable is declared, the compiler organizes a small part of memory (16 bits or two bytes) to be interpreted as an integer. Certain operations on this piece of memory then become available. The pattern of bits stored in the integer variable may be replicated in another part of memory which is organized in the same way. Arithmetic operations on this portion of memory also become available. In short, quite a lot is entailed by a variable being declared an integer.

In Chapters 3 and 4 the predefined data types Boolean, integer, character, real, and string were discussed. In addition to the nonstandard type string, TURBO provides a nonstandard type byte. A byte is an integer in the range from 0 to 255. We won't use this type, because its main use is in connection with the low-level facilities of TURBO. In addition to these predefined types, Pascal permits the creation of data types to meet varying needs. A hierarchy of the data types of this chapter and the preceding chapters is given in *FIGURE 6.1*. This includes all of the simple types. Pointer types and other structured types will be discussed in later chapters.

Data types can be grouped into three categories as shown in *FIGURE 6.1*. The *simple types* are types whose elements are atomic—i.e., not capable of being decomposed any further (at least for practical purposes). These are sometimes called scalar types. The simple types have the additional property that any two elements of a simple type may be compared. That is, if X and Y are elements of the same simple type, then one and only one of the following is true: X < Y or X = Y or X > Y. An *ordinal type* is a simple type which has the additional feature that each element of the ordinal type, except the first, is preceded by a unique element of the ordinal type and each element, except the last, is followed by a unique element. The only simple type which is not an ordinal type is REAL. This is because it is impossible to define the next real number.

Classification of Data Types

FIGURE 6.1

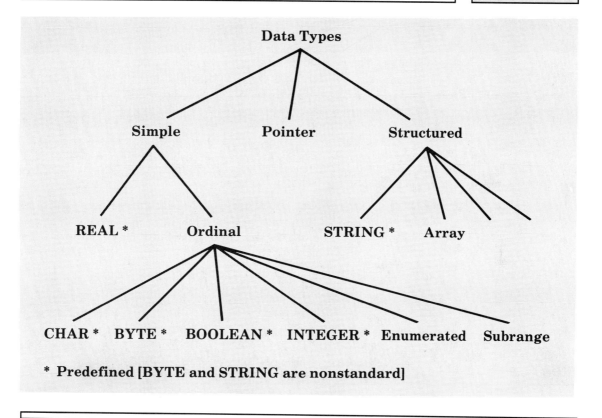

* Predefined [BYTE and STRING are nonstandard]

A *simple data type* is a data type which is not built from other data types and has a comparison operator defined on its elements.

DEFINITION

An *ordinal data type* is a simple data type for which the predecessor of every element (except the first) and the successor of every element (except the last) is defined.

DEFINITION

In Sections 3 and 4 of this chapter, the two user-defined ordinal data types are presented. These are the *enumerated data type* and the *subrange data type*. In combination with the predefined simple types, these form all the simple types.

The other two categories of data types that appear in *FIGURE 6.1* are *pointer data types* and *structured data types*. Pointer data types are discussed in Chapter 14. A structured data type is a data type which is built from other (presumably simpler) data types. The predefined data type string is an example of a structured data type. A string is built from the data type character. In the next chapter, arrays will be discussed. Later other structured data types (records, files, and sets) will be introduced. The variety of data types provided by Pascal is very useful.

DEFINITION

> A *structured data type* is a data type comprised of an organized collection of other data types.

6.2 TYPE DECLARATIONS

In addition to providing mechanisms for describing new types, Pascal also allows the programmer to give them names. This is done in the *type declaration section*. The type declaration section occurs between the constant declarations and the variable declarations of a block. After a type has been given a name, the name can be used as a data type for declaring variables and for defining other data types. This facility is useful in building data types and documenting the data structures that are being used in a program. It is good programming practice to declare data types (i.e., give a data type a name) and then use these in declaring variables rather than declaring variables directly in terms of data types. Examples will make these notions clearer as we go along.

The type declaration section consists of the key word TYPE followed by a sequence of type declarations. Each type declaration consists of an identifier (for the new data type), an equals sign (=), a type specification (of the new data type), and a semicolon. The syntax diagram for this is presented in *FIGURE 6.2*. With what we have learned so far, all we are able to do is rename the types we already know. In the next section we will see how to define our own types.

FIGURE 6.2   Type Declaration Section

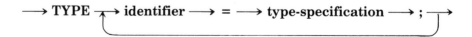

$\longrightarrow$ TYPE $\longrightarrow$ identifier $\longrightarrow$ = $\longrightarrow$ type-specification $\longrightarrow$; $\longrightarrow$

For example, if we wished, we could have the following declarations.

```
CONST
     LongStringSize  = 30;
```

```
TYPE
    WholeNumber = Integer;
    Decimal     = Real;
    LongString  = STRING[ LongStringSize ];
    ShortString = STRING[ 6 ];
    NameType    = LongString;

VAR
    I         : WholeNumber;   { Loop Index }
    Salary    : Decimal;       { Employee's Salary }
    Name      : NameType;      { Employee's Name }
    DeptAbbr  : ShortString;   { Department Abbreviation }
```

The first two declarations in the type declaration section simply illustrate
that new names may be given to old types. In this case there is no good
reason for doing so. There are, however, situations in which this capability is useful. The remaining declarations are illustrative of the way in
which constant, type, and variable declarations are used together. The
declarations above achieve the following, if written out directly.

```
VAR
    I         : Integer;       { Loop Index }
    Salary    : Real;          { Employee's Salary }
    Name      : STRING[ 30 ];  { Employee's Name }
    DeptAbbr  : STRING[ 6 ];   { Department Abbreviation }
```

From this example, it can be seen that the programmer is given the
power to create his or her own data types such as LongString, ShortString,
and NameType. This is convenient, because any time the programmer
needed to declare a variable which was to be a name, he or she could just
declare the variable using NameType, without needing to recall what the
length of a name was to be.

The program in *FIGURE 6.3* is an example of the use of type declarations. In this program it is obvious what the type of a name is. It is
also clear that the programmer decided that names would be no more
than 30 characters in length. Furthermore, changing this decision would
be easy.

FIGURE 6.3

```
PROGRAM Greeting(Input, Output);

{ A short program to issue a greeting to the user.

    Author :      John Riley
    Date :        December 29, 1986
    File name :   CH6EX1.PAS
}

CONST
    NameLen = 30;
```

(continued)

```
TYPE
     NameType = STRING[NameLen];

VAR
     Name : NameType;


BEGIN { Greeting }
  Writeln;
  Write('Hello. What''s your name? ');
  Readln(Name);
  Writeln('It''s nice to meet you, ', Name, '!')
END.  { Greeting }
```

Output:

```
Hello. What's your name? GEORGE
It's nice to meet you, GEORGE!
```

6.3 ENUMERATED TYPES

Pascal allows the programmer to devise his or her own simple, ordinal types by using *enumerated types*. An enumerated type is a type which is declared simply by listing the constants of the type within parentheses. The syntax diagram for an enumerated type is given in *FIGURE 6.4*. TURBO Pascal refers to these types as *user-defined scalar types* or *declared scalar types* (as in [J-W]). We will follow the standard terminology and call them enumerated types (as in [Co], [IEEE], and [Le]).

The identifiers listed between the parentheses become the constants of this type. These identifiers must be unique. The following program fragment illustrates the use of this type declaration.

```
TYPE
     Months =  (Jan, Feb, Mar, Apr, May, Jun, Jul, Aug, Sep,
                Oct, Nov, Dec);
     Cookies = (ChocChip, Sandwich, Butter, PNutButter);

VAR
     ThisMonth,
     NextMonth  : Months;
     Batch      : Cookies;
     Size       : (Small, Med, Large, XLarge);
```

The first declaration in the type section establishes a new type, Months, whose constants are Jan, Feb, Mar, Apr, May, Jun, Jul, Aug, Sep, Oct, Nov, Dec. The next declaration in the type section defines a new type, Cookies, which has the constants that are listed. In the variable declaration section we have declared two variables, ThisMonth and Next-Month, to be of type Months. The variable Batch is of type Cookies. In

Enumerated Type

FIGURE 6.4

the last line the variable Size has been declared to be of an unnamed type whose constants are Small, Med, Large, XLarge. It is usually not a good idea to use an unnamed type in this way. The documentation provided by using the type declaration section is worth the effort. With these declarations the following statements could appear in a program.

```
ThisMonth := Jan;
NextMonth := Feb;
Batch := Butter;
Size := Small;
ThisMonth := NextMonth;
NextMonth := Mar;
```

In the first four assignment statements above, constants are being assigned to variables of the appropriate type. In the fifth line, the value of NextMonth is assigned to ThisMonth. This is permitted, because ThisMonth and NextMonth are of the same type, Months.

An enumerated type is an ordinal type. The order of the constants of an enumerated type is that in which they are listed. For example, the Months, as listed, are in their usual order. In the type Cookies, ChocChip precedes Sandwich which precedes Butter which precedes PNutButter. (This, too, is a natural order, because chocolate chip cookies are the best type of cookie!) Using this order, the comparison operators apply, with $<$ meaning precedes and $>$ meaning succeeds. These are natural extensions of the operators as we have already been using them. For example, ChocChip $<$ Butter is True and Jan $>$ Mar is False. The comparison operators and their meanings are given in *FIGURE 6.5*. Each of these operators is a binary operator. It is illegal to compare variables or constants of different types—e.g., ThisMonth $<$ Size is illegal. This helps to ensure program correctness.

FIGURE 6.6 contains a small program which uses an enumerated type to control a loop. The output of the program is also given.

The constants of an enumerated type are numbered starting with 0. For example, in the type Months, Jan is number 0, Feb is number 1, and Dec is number 11. The function Ord is defined on any ordinal type (predefined or user defined) and returns the ordinal number of its argument.

FIGURE 6.5 **Comparison Operators for Ordinal Types**

Symbol	Meaning
=	Equals (Expression is true when both operands evaluate to the same constant)
<>	Does not equal (Expression is true when operands evaluate to different constants)
<	Precedes (Expression is true when the left operand precedes the right in the order of the type)
<=	Precedes or equals (in the order of the type)
>	Succeeds (Expression is true when the left operand follows the right operand in the order of the type)
>=	Succeeds or equals (in the order of the type)

FIGURE 6.6 **PROGRAM EnumeratedTypeEx(Output);**

```
{ A program to illustrate enumerated types.

      Author :          John Riley
      Date :            December 30, 1986
      File name :       CH6EX2.PAS
}

TYPE
      SizeType = (Small, Med, Large, Giant);

VAR
      Size : SizeType;

BEGIN { EnumeratedTypeEx }
  Size := Small;
  WHILE Size <> Giant DO
    BEGIN
      IF Size = Small THEN
          BEGIN
            Write('Small, getting larger ');
            Size := Med
          END; { Then }
      IF Size = Med THEN
          BEGIN
            Write('and larger ');
            Size := Large
          END;
      IF Size = Large THEN
```

(continued)

```
        BEGIN
          Writeln('and larger yet!');
          Size := Giant
        END { IF }
    END; { WHILE }
  Writeln('GIANT SIZE!')
END. { EnumeratedTypeEx }
```

Output:

```
Small, getting larger and larger and larger yet!
GIANT SIZE!
```

With the declarations above, Ord(Jan) is 0, Ord(Feb) is 1, Ord(ChocChip) is 0, and Ord(PNutButter) is 3. The ordinal number of a character is determined by the implementation. We will use the ASCII character set (see Appendix G) and thus have (for example) Ord('A') equal to 65, Ord('q') equal to 113, and Ord('7') equal to 55.

For the character type there is a function which is the opposite of Ord. This is the character function Chr. Chr has one argument, an integer between 0 and 127. The value of Chr is a character which corresponds to the integer. For example, Chr(66) is 'B'.

For any ordinal type there are two predefined functions which return the predecessor and successor of a given ordinal constant. These are PRED, the predecessor function, and SUCC, the successor function. These are defined for any ordinal type. In the type Months, Succ(Jan) is Feb and Pred(Feb) is Jan. For an integer I, Succ(I) is I + 1 and Pred(I) is I − 1. Pred and Succ are also defined for characters—e.g., Pred('X') is 'W' and Succ('8') is '9'. The ordering of characters is implementation dependent. We are using the ASCII ordering. Pred is undefined for the first constant of a type, and Succ is undefined for the last constant of a type.

Using the successor function we can rewrite the preceding program and make it shorter and neater. This revised program appears in *FIGURE 6.7*. The output remains the same.

FIGURE 6.7

```
PROGRAM EnumeratedTypeExRevised(Output);

{ Another program to illustrate enumerated types.

    Author :        John Riley
    Date :          December 30, 1986
    File name :     CH6EX3.PAS
}

TYPE
    SizeType = (Small, Med, Large, Giant);
```

(continued)

```
VAR
      Size : SizeType;

BEGIN { EnumeratedTypeExRevised }
   Size := Small;
   WHILE Size <> Giant DO
      BEGIN
         IF Size = Small THEN
            Write('Small, getting larger ');
         IF Size = Med THEN
            Write('and larger ');
         IF Size = Large THEN
            Writeln('and larger yet!');
         Size := Succ(Size)
      END; { WHILE }
   Writeln('GIANT SIZE!')
END. { EnumeratedTypeExRevised }

Output:

Small, getting larger and larger and larger yet!
GIANT SIZE!
```

Below is an outline of a program which contains a loop to go through the months of the year.

```
PROGRAM MonthLooper(Input, Output);

{ ... 
}



TYPE
      Months = (Jan, Feb, Mar, Apr, May, Jun,
                Jul, Aug, Sep, Oct, Nov, Dec);

VAR
      ThisMonth : Months;



ThisMonth = Jan;
WHILE ThisMonth < Dec DO
      BEGIN

            { Do this month's processing }

         ThisMonth := Succ(ThisMonth)
      END; { WHILE }
   { Do the processing for Dec }
```

The loop had to be terminated when ThisMonth became Dec, because Succ(Dec) is undefined. This necessitates treating Dec as a special case. There is another loop control structure in Pascal which does not have this problem. This structure is covered later in the chapter.

As another example, here is a loop which prints the alphabet on one line. C denotes a character variable.

```
C := 'A';
WHILE C <= 'Z' DO
   BEGIN
      Write(C);
      C := Succ(C)
   END; { WHILE }
Writeln;
```

In this loop we do not need a special case for 'Z', because the successor of 'Z' is defined.

Enumerated data types are very useful in documenting the flow of control in a program. If ThisYear is an integer variable then it is not hard to discern the purpose of the following.

```
IF ThisMonth = Dec THEN { New Year }
   BEGIN
      ThisMonth := Jan;
      ThisYear := ThisYear + 1
   END { IF }
ELSE
   ThisMonth := Succ(ThisMonth);
```

Enumerated types cannot be input by or output to a user, because there is no means of converting enumerated constants to sequences of characters. This means that both of the following statements are illegal.

```
Readln(ThisMonth);
Writeln(ThisMonth)
```

The judicious definition of types and their use can greatly improve the readability and correctness of a program. You may have observed that we could do without enumerated types and just use integers. For example, instead of the constants Jan to Dec above we could have used the numbers 1 to 12 . The danger here is that it would be very easy to use the number 14 for a month inadvertently. We believe that it is better for a program to terminate (with a run-time error) than to continue and produce incorrect results.

6.4 SUBRANGE TYPES

Very frequently we use variables for which the entire range of a data type is inappropriate. If our program involved test scores which were integers in the range 0 to 100, we would not want to assign the number 200 to the test score. Pascal provides a means of doing this via the *subrange type*. A subrange of any ordinal type (predefined or user defined) is declared by listing the first and last constants of the subrange separated by two periods. The first constant in the declaration must precede the second constant (in the order defined by the type). *FIGURE 6.8* gives the syntax diagram of this type. Notice that because Real is not an ordinal type we cannot have subranges of Real. Any operations on the type from which the subrange is extracted can be used on the values of the subrange. For example, on a subrange of integers the usual arithmetic operations are still defined.

DEFINITION

> The *host* or *underlying type* of a subrange is the type from which the subrange is extracted.

The following are some examples of subrange declarations.

```
TYPE
    SmallNumbers   = 0..10;
    CapitalLetters = 'A'..'Z';
    Months         = (Jan, Feb, Mar, Apr, May, Jun, Jul, Aug, Sep,
                      Oct, Nov, Dec);
    WarmMonths     = Jun..Aug;
    Cookies        = (ChocChip, Sandwich, Butter, PNutButter);
    GoodCookies    = ChocChip..Butter;
```

In the line following Type, SmallNumbers is declared to be a subrange of integer. Integer is the host or underlying type. The next line establishes CapitalLetters as a subrange of character. In the following two lines a type Months is declared along with a subrange of this type. The last two lines declare another type and subrange. It is also possible to use subranges directly in the declarations of variables, as in the following declarations.

```
VAR
    C : 'a'..'z';
    I : 1..100;
```

It is possible to use declarations to document the intended use of variables and other quantities. If we were writing a program to process test

| Subrange Type | *FIGURE 6.8* |

$\longrightarrow$ constant $\longrightarrow$ .. $\longrightarrow$ constant $\longrightarrow$

scores and assign grades we might have the declarations below. Not only would these declarations document the program, but we would also be able to use the items defined elsewhere in our program. For example, if we were finding the lowest and highest scores by using a while loop, as in Chapter 5, we could use the constants MaxTestScore and MinTestScore for the initial LowScore and HighScore. This idea is illustrated in the program in *FIGURE 6.9*.

These declarations would also make changing the program easier. If the user wanted to have the test scores range from 0 to 200, the change would be obvious and rather easy to accomplish. Because programs are often modified, designing them to accommodate change has significant benefits over the lifetime of the program.

There are other advantages of using subranges. Because a variable of a subrange type stores a smaller number of values, it may use less memory (and never uses more) than a variable of the original type. For example,

FIGURE 6.9

```
PROGRAM ClassAnalysis(Input, Output);

{ Program to find high, low and average of a set of grades.

    Author :       John Riley
    Date :         December 30, 1986
    File name :    CH6EX4.PAS
}

CONST
    MaxTestScore = 100;
    MinTestScore = 0;
    Stop = -99;          { Ends input }

TYPE
    TestRange = MinTestScore .. MaxTestScore;

VAR
    NumOfTests,
    SumOfTests,          { Used for average   }
    Test :     Integer;  { Test entered       }
    HighTest,            { Highest test score }
    LowTest :  TestRange;{ Lowest test score  }
    Average :  Real;     { Class average      }
```

(continued)

```
BEGIN { ClassAnalysis }
  Writeln('Class analysis');
  NumOfTests := 0;
  SumOfTests := 0;
  HighTest := MinTestScore;
  LowTest := MaxTestScore;
  Writeln('Enter test scores, one per line.');
  Writeln('Enter ', Stop, ' to end.');
  Write('Enter test >');
  Readln(Test);
  WHILE Test <> Stop DO
      BEGIN
        IF (MinTestScore <= Test) AND (Test <= MaxTestScore) THEN
          BEGIN { Process a valid score }
            NumOfTests := NumOfTests + 1;
            SumOfTests := SumOfTests + Test;
            IF Test > HighTest THEN  { Test is new high }
                HighTest := Test;
            IF Test < LowTest THEN   { Test is new low }
                LowTest := Test
          END { IF }
        ELSE
          BEGIN { Test entered was illegal }
            Writeln('Illegal score');
            Writeln('Tests must be between ', MinTestScore,
                ' and ', MaxTestScore)
          END; { ELSE }
        Write('Enter test (', Stop, ' to end) >');
        Readln(Test)
      END; { WHILE }
  IF NumOfTests <> 0 THEN
      BEGIN
        Average := SumOfTests=NumOfTests;
        Writeln;
        Writeln('High : ', HighTest, '   Low : ', LowTest,
            '   Average : ', Average:7:2)
      END { IF }
  ELSE
      Writeln('No students processed.')
END. {  ClassAnalysis }

Output:

Class analysis
Enter test scores, one per line.
Enter -99 to end.
Enter test >80
Enter test (-99 to end) >90
Enter test (-99 to end) >80
Enter test (-99 to end) >75
Enter test (-99 to end) >110
Illegal score
Tests must be between 0 and 100
Enter test (-99 to end) >100
Enter test (-99 to end) >-99
High : 100    Low : 75    Average :   85.00
```

a variable of the subrange type 0..255 requires half the storage of an integer variable.

More importantly, we can have the computer detect attempts to assign values which are not in the appropriate range. Such a value is called an *out-of-range* value. In the program in *FIGURE 6.9*, an attempt to assign 1000 to either HighTest or LowTest should be considered an error.

The detection of an out-of-range value during *range checking* usually is a run-time error. This means that the program terminates. Although this is not desirable, it is better than producing incorrect results. For example, suppose that three test scores were to be entered and then averaged. If the scores were supposed to be in the range 0 to 100 and the scores 80 80 110 were entered mistakenly for 80 80 10, an error should occur. Without range checking this might not be noticed, because the average of 80 80 110 is 90, which is in the correct range. Because the correct average (of 80 80 10) is 56.7, this is a significant error. Well-written programs are designed to catch as many of these errors as possible. In addition to programming to detect out-of-range assignments, it is possible to have the system perform range checking.

Range checking is the automatic detection of an attempt to assign an out-of-range value to a variable.   *DEFINITION*

Range checking is not normally present in TURBO Pascal. Range checking must be activated by using what is known as a *compiler switch*.

A compiler may have features that the programmer can turn on or off. Sometimes these are called compiler switches and the features are said to be *activated* or *deactivated*. The means of doing this in TURBO are known as *compiler directives*. A compiler directive appears in the program itself as a special comment. It consists of a left brace ({), followed by a dollar sign ($), a single letter which designates the compiler directive, a plus or minus (+ or −) indicating whether the feature is being activated or deactivated, and a right brace (}). As a consequence, you should not start a comment with {$. Compiler switches change the action of the compiler and affect the behavior of a program. They should be used with care. The *default* or *assumed values* of the compiler switches in TURBO have been chosen to make programs execute as quickly as possible.

A *default value* is a value which is used when no other value has been given to a quantity.   *DEFINITION*

To maximize the speed of execution, range checking in TURBO is normally deactivated. To activate range checking, the compiler directive {$R + } must be used within the program. It is possible to deactivate range checking by using {$R−} . Range checking can be turned on and off repeatedly within a program. Range checking is recommended.

An example of the effect of using range checking is presented in *FIGURE 6.10*. In the variable section, I is declared to have values in the integer subrange 0 through 10. When the program is run, I is first assigned the value 11. Although this is out of the range declared for I, no error occurs, because range checking is off at this point. Control passes to the writeln statement which follows, and the message "I is out of range but unchecked" appears. The next line contains the compiler directive which activates range checking. In the ensuing line the value 12 is attempted to be assigned to I, and this causes the run-time error. The

FIGURE 6.10

```
PROGRAM RangeExample ( Input, Output );

{  This is a small program illustrating the use of range
   checking in TURBO.

       Author :      John Riley
       Date :        March 31, 1986
       File name :   CH6EX5.PAS
}

VAR
    I : 0..10;  { A variable to check }

BEGIN { RangeExample }
  I := 11;
  Writeln('I is out of range but unchecked');
  {$R+}   { This compiler directive activates range checking }
  I := 12;
  Writeln('Now I is 12')
END. { RangeExample }

>R
Compiling
   20 lines
Code : .......
Free : .......
Data : .......

Running
I is out of range but unchecked

Run-time error 91, PC = 0054
Program aborted

Searching
  18 lines
Run-time error position found.  Press <ESC>_
```

TURBO Pascal Reference Manual [TP] informs us that run-time error 91 is "Scalar or subrange out of range." If we pressed the ESCAPE key to correct the error when the editor is invoked, we would find the cursor positioned under the semicolon following 12.

In practice, it is a good idea to turn range checking on at the beginning of a program. An appropriate place for the directive is before the constant declarations of the main program.

6.5   THE CASE STATEMENT

In this section and the next, the last two control statements of Pascal are presented. These will simplify our programming with ordinal data types.

The if-then-else statement is a *two-way branch*. This reflects the fact that the Boolean type is two-valued (True, False). For ordinal types with more than two constants it would be convenient to have a statement which selects a statement to be executed on the basis of the ordinal value of an expression. This is known as a *multiway branch* and is depicted in *FIGURE 6.11*. (E is an expression whose value is of some ordinal type which includes the values V1, V2, V3, . . . , Vn. S1, S2, S3, . . . , Sn are statements which are to be executed when E has the values V1, V2, V3, . . . , Vn, respectively.)

By testing E = V1, E = V2, etc., and using nested if-then-else statements it would be possible to program the control structure of *FIGURE 6.11*. However, it would be somewhat messy if there were a large number of possible values. This makes errors more likely. The Pascal *case statement* allows this to be done directly.

The form of the case statement is outlined below. The case statement starts with the key word CASE followed by an expression which has an ordinal value. If this value is found among the lists of values following OF, the corresponding statement is executed. If the value is not among the values in the list, the statements following ELSE are executed.

```
CASE ordinal-expression OF
    list-of-values-1 : statement-1 ;
    list-of-values-2 : statement-2 ;
    list-of-values-3 : statement-3 ;
         ⋮
    last-list-of-values : last-statement
ELSE
    else-statement-1 ;
    else-statement-2 ;
         ⋮
    last-else-statement
END
```

An example of a case statement which is used to describe integers follows. In this example the ordinal type is integer and I is an integer variable.

```
CASE I OF
    0 :                    Writeln('Zero');
    1, 3, 5, 7, 9, 11 :    Writeln('Small odd number');
    2, 4, 6, 8, 10, 12 :   Writeln('Small even number');
    13..19 :               Writeln('In the teens');
ELSE
    Writeln('Indescribable')
END;   { Case }
```

Each list of values consists of constants separated by commas (e.g., 1, 3, 5, 7, 9, 11) or a range of constants (e.g., 13..19). Individually named constants and ranges may appear in the same list. However, no value may occur more than once in all the lists. Standard Pascal does not permit subranges in the lists of a case statement. The else clause (ELSE and the

FIGURE 6.11

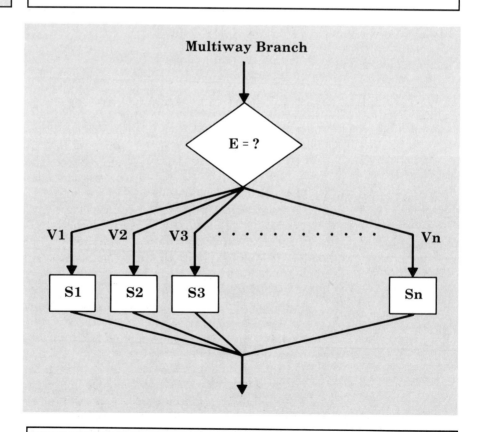

| Case Statement | **FIGURE 6.12** |

Case Statement

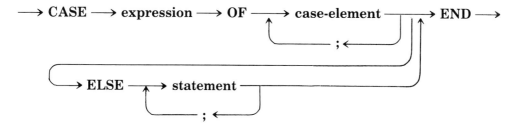

Case element

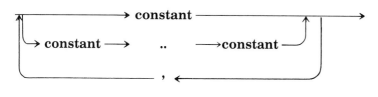

Case list

statements following ELSE) may be omitted. The else clause is not standard, but many implementations of Pascal have such a clause. Frequently the key word OTHERWISE is used. *FIGURE 6.12* contains the syntax diagram of the case statement.

In practice, the ordinal expression is almost always an ordinal variable. Only one statement may follow each list of constants in the case statement. If more than one action needs to be taken, the statements must be grouped using a compound statement. The END of the case statement should be labeled with a comment.

The expression that appears after the key word CASE and the constants which appear in the case list must all be of the same ordinal type. When the case statement is executed, the expression is evaluated. If the value of the expression is among the constants listed among the various case lists, the statement following the colon after the case list containing the expression's value is executed. If the expression's value is not among the constants in the case lists, then whenever the else clause is present the statements following it are executed. If the else clause is not present and the value of the expression is not present among the constants, then control passes to the statement following the case statement. A constant may appear in only one of the case lists, either explicitly or as an element of a subrange. The program in *FIGURE 6.13* clarifies these semantic issues. This is a simple program to tell the user what sort of character he or she has entered. Notice that blank lines have been placed between groups of constants. This has been done to make the program easier to read. Without the blank lines it might be difficult to distinguish the different groups of constants. Notice that the statement following the constant Stop is the null statement, because no action should be taken when the user wishes to stop. A sample run follows the program.

The constants in the case statement need not be in order. For example, in the program in *FIGURE 6.13* the small letters could have occurred first. However, any constant may appear only once. This means that ranges cannot overlap.

We have noted that only one statement can follow the colon after a list of constants and that if there are several statements to be executed in a given case they must be grouped together in a compound statement. The next program fragment is an example of this. The statements in this program are used to assign measurements to variables for shirt sizes.

```
TYPE
     Sizes = (Small, Med, Large, XLarge);

VAR
     Size   : Sizes;   { Size of shirt       }
     Sleeve,           { Sleeve length,      }
     Collar : Real;    { Collar, in inches   }



CASE Size OF
   Small  : BEGIN
               Sleeve := 33;
               Collar := 14.5
            END; { Small }
   Med      : BEGIN
               Sleeve := 34;
               Collar := 15
            END; { Med }
   Large  : BEGIN
               Sleeve := 35;
               Collar := 16
            END; { Large }
   XLarge : BEGIN
               Sleeve := 36;
               Collar := 17.5
            END   { XLarge }
END; { CASE }
```

This example also illustrates the use of enumerated constants (Small, Med, Large, XLarge) in the case statement. The use of constants makes

FIGURE 6.13

```
PROGRAM LetterClassifier(Input, Output);

{ A program to classify letters using the case statement.

     Author :        John Riley
     Date :          December 30, 1986
     File name :     CH6EX6.PAS
}

CONST
     Stop = '*';     { Character to end input }

VAR
     CharIn : Char;  { Character entered }

BEGIN { LetterClassifier }
  REPEAT
     Write('Enter a letter, ', Stop, ' to quit. >');
     Readln(CharIn);
     CASE CharIn OF
        'A', 'E', 'I',
        'O', 'U'            : Writeln('A vowel.');

        'B'..'D', 'F'..'H',
        'J'..'N', 'P'..'T',
        'V'..'X', 'Z'       : Writeln('A consonant');

        'Y'                 : Writeln('A vowel or consonant');

        'a'..'z'            : Writeln('A small letter.');

        Stop                :   { Do nothing, quit }

     ELSE
        Writeln('Not a letter')
     END { CASE }
  UNTIL CharIn = Stop
END.  { LetterClassifier }

Output:

Enter a letter, * to quit. >i
A small letter
Enter a letter, * to quit. >I
A vowel
Enter a letter, * to quit. >h
A small letter
Enter a letter, * to quit. >Y
A vowel or consonant
Enter a letter, * to quit. >8
Not a letter
Enter a letter, * to quit. >*
```

FIGURE 6.14   **Equivalent Constructs**

```
IF Condition THEN              CASE Condition OF
    StatementTrue                  True  : StatementTrue;
ELSE
    StatementFalse                 False : StatementFalse
                               END { CASE }
```

the program easily understood. (It is apparent that the Collar of a Large shirt is 16 inches.) Furthermore, this fragment does not have the else clause as part of the case statement. Finally, notice that each END of a compound statement is labeled with the constant which causes its execution.

To demonstrate the relation between the case statement and the if-then-else statement, we note that the two constructs in *FIGURE 6.14* are equivalent. In this figure Condition is a Boolean expression and StatementTrue and StatementFalse are statements which are to be executed depending on whether Condition is True or False. Usually the if-then-else statement is used in this situation, because this is what most programmers are accustomed to using and reading when working with Boolean expressions.

6.6 THE FOR STATEMENT

In programming there are many times when the programmer wishes a loop to be executed with a succession of values. A loop of this sort is called a *counter-controlled loop*. The number of times the loop is to be executed can be determined before the loop is begun. Although it is possible to implement this situation with the while loop, it is convenient to have a specific control structure for doing this. This control structure is called the *for statement* in Pascal. Counter-controlled loops (with integers) were present in the first high-level languages. In fact, in older (more primitive) versions of BASIC and FORTRAN the counter-controlled loop was the only loop available.

The for statement consists of the key word FOR followed by a variable, the assignment operator (:=), an expression, one of the key words TO or DOWNTO, another expression, the key word DO, and a statement. The general form of a for statement is shown below.

```
FOR variable := first-expression TO second-expression  DO
     statement-to-be-repeated
```

FIGURE 6.15 contains a syntax diagram of the for statement. The variable and two expressions of the for statement must be of the same ordinal type. The variable is known as the *loop-control variable* or *loop index*. The first expression is called the *initial value* and the second the *final value*.

A simple example of the for statement is written below. I is an integer variable.

```
FOR I := 1 TO 10 DO
    Writeln(I);
```

This statement outputs the first ten integers, one per line.

When the for statement is executed, the two expressions are evaluated. The statement following DO is executed once for each of the values between the initial value and the final value (including both the initial and final values). The loop-control variable is assigned increasing values if the key word TO is used and decreasing values if the key word DOWNTO is used. If TO is used and the final value precedes the initial value, the statement is not executed. Similarly, if DOWNTO is used and the final value succeeds the initial value, the statement is not excuted. Because only one statement can follow DO if more than one statement is to be executed, they must be grouped using the compound statement. For example, if I and N are integer variables the following program fragment prints a table of squares of the integers less than or equal to N if N is positive. If N is zero or negative the writeln statement is not executed.

```
FOR I := 1 TO N DO
    Writeln(I : 3, I * I : 6);
```

Since char is an ordinal type, the variable and expressions of the for statement may be character valued. The ordering is determined by the implementation, which for microcomputers is almost always determined by the ASCII standard. If C is a character variable, this program fragment

For Statement   **FIGURE 6.15**

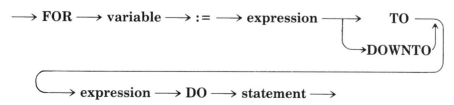

prints the capital letters and their ordinal numbers. Recall that Ord is the function which returns the ordinal number of an ordinal variable.

```
FOR C := 'A' TO 'Z' DO
   Writeln(C, ' ', Ord(C));
```

This example is dependent on the collating sequence defined by the implementation. If the capital letters were not contiguous in the collating sequence, this fragment would print the extra characters that were interspersed among the capital letters.

Because an enumerated type is an ordinal type it may be used in the for statement. Thus, the following is legal.

```
TYPE
     Colors = (Red, Yellow, Blue);

VAR
     C : Colors;



Write('Fading from ');
FOR C := Blue DOWNTO Red DO
   BEGIN
     CASE C OF
        Red     : Write('red');
        Yellow  : Write('yellow');
        Blue    : Write('blue')
     END; { CASE }
     Write(' to ')
   END; { FOR }
Writeln('nothing');
```

This would produce the message "Fading from blue to yellow to red to nothing." In this example we have used a compound statement within the for statement and have labeled the END with { FOR } as you would expect.

To illustrate the relationship between the for and while statements in *FIGURE 6.16*, we code (almost) equivalent control structures using both. Here V is a variable and E1 and E2 are expressions of some ordinal type.

We now make some comments on the use of the for statement.

The loop-control variable of the for statement should be handled with care. Never (intentionally or otherwise) alter the loop-control variable within the loop. In particular, this means that assigning a value to the loop-control variable should not occur. Standard Pascal considers such an assignment an error but does not specify the consequences (e.g., program termination, infinite loop) of such an assignment. TURBO Pascal is consistent with this. Although the reference manual states that an assignment to a loop-control variable is not to be made, it does not indicate the

| Equivalent Control Structures | FIGURE 6.16 |

```
FOR V := E1 to E2 DO              V := E1
   BEGIN                          WHILE V <= E2 DO
                                     BEGIN
      { Body of loop }
                                        { Body of loop }
   END;   { FOR }
                                        V := Succ(V)
                                     END; { WHILE }
```

result. In addition, standard Pascal leaves the value of the loop-control variable undefined after the loop terminates. TURBO leaves the loop-control variable with the final value if the loop is executed. If the loop is not executed, no assignment is made to the loop variable. It is good programming practice not to use the loop-control variable for other purposes. Furthermore, for integer loop-control variables, the identifiers I, J, and K are commonly used when there is no intrinsic meaning to the loop-control variable. Similarly, C is often used for a loop-control variable which is a character.

Because only ordinal types may be used in the for statement, real variables and expressions may not be used. If you need to loop in increments of a small amount (such as 0.1), use a while loop. The vagaries of real arithmetic make the while statement using an inequality safer.

If the initial value or the final value is given by a variable, an assignment to the variable within the for statement will not change the number of times the loop is executed. For example, if I, M, and N are integer variables, the following prints only the numbers 1, 2, 3, and 4.

```
M := 1;
N := 4;
FOR I := M TO N DO
   BEGIN
      Writeln(I);
      M := -2;
      N := 17
   END; { FOR }
```

As with other control statements, for statements may be nested. The program in *FIGURE 6.17* illustrates this idea. The for statement is very convenient in this situation. A large part of the program is concerned with making the output look as nice as possible. For example, five of the six constants are used to specify constants for the layout of the table. Notice that the for statement is used to draw a horizontal line of the appropriate length by repeatedly printing a hyphen. The table the program produced is at the bottom of the figure. Getting the output to look decent is hard work but is very important. It frequently involves explicit counting, and the for statement is very useful in doing this.

FIGURE 6.17

```pascal
PROGRAM MultiplicationTable(Output);

{ This program produces a table of products starting at 1
  and ending with the specified limit.

      Author :       John Riley
      Date :         December 30, 1986
      File name :    CH6EX7.PAS
}

{$R+}   { Turn on range checking }

CONST
   TableSize       = 5;    { Size of table to be printed  }
   LeftMargin      = 8;    { Spaces used on left of table }
   ColumnWidth     = 5;    { Spaces used for each column   }
   IntegerField    = 3;    { Field size for integers       }
   MarginLessField = 5;    { Left margin minus spaces for
                             integer,  MarginLessField =
                             LeftMargin – IntegerField      }
   ColumnLessField = 2;    { Column minus spaces for
                             integer, ColumnLessField =
                             ColumnWidth – IntegerField      }

TYPE
   Index = 1..TableSize;   { Range of numbers forming products }

VAR
   I, J    : Index;        { Loop indices  }
   K,                      { Loop index    }
   Product : Integer;      { Holds product }

BEGIN { MultiplicationTable }
  Writeln;
  Writeln('Multiplication Table');
  Writeln;
  Write('*  |':LeftMargin);
  FOR J := 1 TO TableSize DO
     Write(J:IntegerField, ' ':ColumnLessField);
  Writeln;
  FOR K := 1 TO LeftMargin + ColumnWidth*TableSize DO
     Write('-');
  Writeln;
  FOR I := 1 TO TableSize DO
     BEGIN
       Write(I:IntegerField, '|':MarginLessField);
       FOR J := 1 TO TableSize DO
          BEGIN
            Product := I * J;
            Write(Product:IntegerField, ' ':ColumnLessField)
          END; { FOR J }
```

(continued)

```
        Writeln
     END { FOR I }
END.  { MultiplicationTable }
```

Output:

Multiplication Table

```
     *  |  1    2    3    4    5
   -------------------------------
     1  |  1    2    3    4    5
     2  |  2    4    6    8   10
     3  |  3    6    9   12   15
     4  |  4    8   12   16   20
     5  |  5   10   15   20   25
```

6.7 EXAMPLE PROGRAM

In this section we solve a problem which, when programmed, involves some of the ideas discussed in this chapter.

An instructor wants a program which assigns grades to students at the end of the semester. A course average, which is the average of the four test scores, is used to determine the course grade, which is one of A..E. Averages of 90..100 are awarded an A, 80..89 a B, 70..79 a C, 60..69 a D, and 0..59 an E.

As usual, we begin with a very general outline of an algorithm and gradually fill in details. Our first algorithm is as follows.

```
While there are more students
     Calculate an average
     Award a grade
```

Our first refinement consists of deciding that the loop will continue by asking the user if there are more students.

```
Output Message('Are there more students? (Y/N)')
Get(Answer)
While Answer = 'Y'
     Calculate an average
     Award a grade
     Output Message('Are there more students? (Y/N)')
     Get(Answer)
```

We next consider the problem of calculating an average. This consists of two steps: forming the sum of the tests and dividing to obtain an average.

```
Output Message('Are there more students? (Y/N)')
Get(Answer)
While Answer = 'Y'
     Form TestSum
     TestAve ← TestSum / NumOfTests
     Award a grade
     Output Message('Are there more students? (Y/N)')
     Get(Answer)
```

To find TestSum we initialize it to 0 (within the loop, because it must start at 0 for each student). Then we obtain the test scores and add them to TestSum.

```
Output Message('Are there more students? (Y/N)')
Get(Answer)
While Answer = 'Y'
     TestSum ← 0
     For I ← 1 To NumOfTests
          Get(TestScore)
          TestSum ← TestSum + TestScore
     TestAve ← TestSum / NumOfTests
     Award a grade
     Output Message('Are there more students? (Y/N)')
     Get(Answer)
```

Awarding a letter grade consists of deciding on the letter grade and then outputting it. To implement the decision we use a case structure in our algorithm.

```
Output Message('Are there more students? (Y/N)')
Get(Answer)
While Answer = 'Y'
     TestSum ← 0
     For I ← 1 To NumOfTests
          Get(TestScore)
          TestSum ← TestSum + TestScore
     TestAve ← TestSum / NumOfTests
     Case TestAve Of
          90..100 : Grade ← 'A'
          80..89  : Grade ← 'B'
          70..79  : Grade ← 'C'
          60..69  : Grade ← 'D'
          0..59   : Grade ← 'E'
     Output(Grade)
     Output Message('Are there more students? (Y/N)')
     Get(Answer)
```

This algorithm is the basis for our program, which is shown in *FIGURE 6.18*. Notice the use of constants and subranges to clearly document the intended meanings. Of course, much more in the way of prompting and labeling is done in the program than in the algorithm. After all, the program is the finished product and not the blueprint. A minor detail is

FIGURE 6.18

```
PROGRAM Grader(Input, Output);

{    Program to award grades based on average of test scores.

     Author :       John Riley
     Date :         April 25, 1986
     File name :    CH6EX8.PAS
}

{$R+}    { Turn on range checking }

CONST
   NumOfTests = 4;
   TestMin    = 0;
   TestMax    = 100;
   AMax       = TestMax;
   AMin       = 90;
   BMax       = 89;
   BMin       = 80;
   CMax       = 79;
   CMin       = 70;
   DMax       = 69;
   DMin       = 60;
   EMax       = 59;
   EMin       = TestMin;

TYPE
   TestRange = TestMin..TestMax;
   LetterGrade = 'A'..'E';

VAR
   Answer    : Char;              { Holds Y (yes) or N (no) }
   TestScore,                     { One test score }
   TestAve   : TestRange;         { Average of tests }
   TestSum   : Integer;           { Sum of tests }
   Grade     : LetterGrade;       { Letter grade awarded }
   I         : 1..NumOfTests;     { Loop Index }

BEGIN { Grader }
  Writeln('Grader');
  Writeln;
  Write('Are there more students? (Y/N)');
  Readln(Answer);
  WHILE (Answer = 'Y') OR (Answer = 'y') DO
     BEGIN
        TestSum := 0;
        FOR I := 1 TO NumOfTests DO
           BEGIN
             Write('Enter test ', I, ' > ');
             Readln(TestScore);
             TestSum := TestSum + TestScore
           END; { FOR }
        TestAve := TestSum DIV NumOfTests;
```

(continued)

```
      CASE TestAve OF
         AMin..AMax : Grade := 'A';
         BMin..BMax : Grade := 'B';
         CMin..CMax : Grade := 'C';
         DMin..DMax : Grade := 'D';
         EMin..EMax : Grade := 'E'
      END; { CASE }
      Writeln('Grade awarded : ', Grade);
      Write('Are there more students? (Y/N)');
      Readln(Answer)
   END { WHILE }
END.  { Grader }
```

Output:

```
Grader

Are there more students? (Y/N)Y
Enter test 1 > 80
Enter test 2 > 90
Enter test 3 > 70
Enter test 4 > 80
Grade awarded : B
Are there more students? (Y/N)Y
Enter test 1 > 95
Enter test 2 > 90
Enter test 3 > 98
Enter test 4 > 87
Grade awarded : A
Are there more students? (Y/N)Y
Enter test 1 > 78
Enter test 2 > 67
Enter test 3 > 79
Enter test 4 > 61
Grade awarded : C
Are there more students? (Y/N)N
```

letting Answer be 'Y' or 'y' to continue the loop. Because a user may not know that there is a difference (to the computer) between these letters, we have programmed so that the program works correctly in this situation.

6.8 SUMMARY

In addition to the predefined simple types (Boolean, char, integer, and real), Pascal permits programmers to define their own types. Types are declared in the type declaration section, which occurs between the constant declarations and the variable declarations. A type declared in this way may be used to declare variables in the same way the predefined types may be used.

An enumerated type is declared by an explicit listing of the constants of the enumerated type. A variable of an enumerated type may only be assigned the constants of the enumerated type.

The ordinal types are Boolean, char, integer, and enumerated. Three functions are defined for the ordinal types: Pred, Succ, and Ord. For the character data type there is an additional function, Chr.

Subranges of ordinal types are used whenever a variable is not to take the full range of values provided by a type. Range checking is used to ensure that values in the correct range are assigned to variables.

The two control statements are convenient for working with ordinal data types. These are the case statement, which is a multiway branch or decision statement, and the for statement, which is a counter-controlled loop.

In the next chapter another data type, the array, will be developed. The data types and statements of this chapter are very useful in working with arrays. ❑

EXERCISES

1. Suppose that the following declarations are made.

```
TYPE
    Colors      = (Red, Orange, Yellow, Green, Blue, Violet);
    HotColors   = Red..Yellow;
    CoolColors = Green..Blue;

VAR
    RainbowColor : Colors;
    FireColor    : HotColors;
    WaterColor   : CoolColors;
```

Furthermore, suppose that the following assignments have been made.

```
RainbowColor := Yellow;
FireColor. := Orange;
WaterColor := Blue;
```

   a. Give the values of the following expressions. (If the value does not exist, consider it undefined.)

```
Pred(FireColor)              Pred(Pred(FireColor))
Succ(FireColor)              Succ(Pred(WaterColor))
Ord(RainbowColor)            FireColor = Red
Ord(FireColor)               WaterColor < Blue
Ord(WaterColor)              RainbowColor = WaterColor
Pred(RainbowColor)           Succ(RainbowColor) = FireColor
Succ(Succ(RainbowColor))     Red <= FireColor
Ord(Succ(WaterColor))        Succ(Yellow) >= Pred(Blue)
```

b. Is the comparison FireColor < WaterColor legal? If it is, give its value.

c. Is the assignment FireColor := WaterColor ever legal?

d. Find the errors in the following program fragments. (Continue to use the declarations made above.)

i.
```
RainbowColor := Red;
WHILE RainbowColor <= Violet DO
    BEGIN

        { Process the color }

        RainbowColor := Succ(RainbowColor)
    END;   { WHILE }
```

ii.
```
Writeln('The colors of the rainbow');
FOR RainbowColor := Red TO Violet DO
    Writeln(RainbowColor);
```

2. Use the ASCII table to find the values of the following expressions.

```
Ord('G')                    Succ('*')
Pred('?')                   Ord(Succ('a'))
Pred(Chr(75))               Chr(Ord('m') + 2))
Chr(Ord(Succ('P')))         Chr(5 + Ord('A') - 1)
Chr(3 + Ord('a') - 1)
```

3. Suppose that X and Y are variables of the same ordinal type. Mark each of the following expressions as True (if the expression is always True), False (if the expression is always false), or Undecidable (if the expression is sometimes True and sometimes False).

```
X < Pred(X) whenever Ord(X) <> 0    (Ord(X) < Ord(Y)) = (X < Y)
(X <= Y) OR (X > Y)                 (X = Y) AND (X <> Y)
X <= Succ(X)
Succ(Pred(X)) = X whenever Ord(X) <> 0
```

4. Find the errors in the following program fragments.

a.
```
VAR   QPA : Real;



CASE QPA OF
    0.00 .. 0.99 : Writeln('Consider for academic dismissal');
    1.00 .. 1.99 : Writeln('Put on probation.');
    2.00 .. 2.99 : Writeln('No action');
    3.00 .. 4.00 : Writeln('Put on dean's list.')
END; { CASE }
```

b.
```
VAR C : Char;


CASE C OF
    'A', 'E', 'I', 'O', 'U' : Writeln(C, ' is a vowel.');

    'B', 'C', 'D', 'F', 'G',
    'H', 'J' .. 'N', 'P' .. 'Z' : Writeln(C, ' is a consonant)
ELSE
    Writeln(C, ' is not an upper-case letter.')
END; { CASE }

```

c.
```
VAR I, Sum = Integer;


Sum := 0;
FOR I := 1 TO 10 DO
   BEGIN
      I := I + 1;
      Sum := Sum + I
   END; { FOR }

```

5. Suppose I is an integer variable. Rewrite the following using a case statement.

```
IF (1 <= I) and (I <=4) Then
   IF I <= 2 Then
      IF I = 1 Then
         Writeln(I, ' is the first number.')
      ELSE
         Writeln(I, ' is the first prime number.')
   ELSE
      IF I = 3 Then
         Writeln(I, ' is the first odd prime number.')
      ELSE
         Writeln(I, ' is the first even perfect square.')
ELSE
   Writeln(I, ' is not interesting.')
```

6. Use the while loop to construct a counter-controlled loop corresponding to the for statement with the key word DOWNTO (i.e., a loop in which the counter is decreasing). Refer to *FIGURE 6.16*.

7. In the text we mentioned that the two constructions in *FIGURE 6.16* are almost equivalent. In what way are they not equivalent?

8. Write a program which prints the lower-case letters and their ASCII codes.

9. Write a program which prints all the printing characters and their ASCII codes. Hint: These start with the blank ' ' and end with the tilde ' ˜ '.

10. Write a program which does a countdown from a specified positive integer which the user enters. That is, the integers from the given integer are printed in descending order to 0.

11. Write a program which prints a table of the first ten powers (1 to 10) of two. (Recall that Pascal does not provide exponentiation. To do this, accumulate a product by repeatedly multiplying by 2.)

12. Write a program which has as input characters read from the keyboard, one per line, and outputs the number of vowels, consonants, Ys, and nonletters that were entered. The input is to be terminated by entering an asterisk (*).

13. Write a program which generates all three-letter sequences of A, B, C, and D. Hint: Use three nested for statements and let the loop variable for each range from 'A' to 'D'. The statement within the innermost loop should output the three loop variables.

14. Write a program which produces a table of the sums of the integers between 1 and 10. Format the output to look as neat as possible.

15. Write a program which analyzes test grades. The user is to enter test scores in the range 0 to 100. The input is terminated by the special value −99. The output is to consist of the number of legal scores (in the range 0 to 100) and the number of scores in each of the intervals 90 to 100, 80 to 89, 70 to 79, 60 to 69, and 0 to 59. Entries which are not in the correct range should not be included.

16. Modify the program in Exercise 15 so that it produces the average score as well. Also divide the range 0 to 59 into two ranges, 0 to 49 and 50 to 59.

17. Modify the program in Exercise 15 or 16 so that the highest and lowest (legal) scores are output as well.

INTRODUCTION

The preceding chapters have concentrated on simple data types. In this chapter, the first of the structured data types, the *array*, is discussed. A structured data type is a data type which is constructed from simpler data types. Structured data types enable the programmer to organize the data that a program must manipulate.

The array is probably the easiest of the structured data types to handle. Arrays are present in most high-level programming languages, and so a programmer must learn how to use them. Arrays allow the programmer to declare a group of variables and access them easily.

Because strings are closely related to arrays and are so prevalent in computing, they are also discussed. (Recall that the string data type is nonstandard.)

Structured data types, such as the array, are very useful for organizing the data that a program will be manipulating. This permits solution of problems which cannot be solved using simple variables. ☐

CHAPTER 7

ARRAYS AND STRINGS

7.1 ARRAYS

All the data types discussed so far allocate memory for only one variable at a time. This would be very inconvenient if, for example, we wished to store the test scores for 30 students. We would have to declare the variables TestScore1, TestScore2, . . ., TestScore30. Furthermore, working with these 30 variables would be tedious at best. To input the values for these 30 variables, we would have to program something like the following.

```
Writeln('Enter test Score >');
Readln(TestScore1);
Writeln('Enter test Score >');
Readln(TestScore2);
Writeln('Enter test Score >');
Readln(TestScore3);
Writeln('Enter test Score >');
Readln(TestScore4);
Writeln('Enter test Score >');
Readln(TestScore5);
Writeln('Enter test Score >');
Readln(TestScore6);
Writeln('Enter test Score >');
Readln(TestScore7);
Writeln('Enter test Score >');
Readln(TestScore8);
Writeln('Enter test Score >');
Readln(TestScore9);


Writeln('Enter test Score >');
Readln(TestScore27);
Writeln('Enter test Score >');
Readln(TestScore28);
Writeln('Enter test Score >');
Readln(TestScore29);
Writeln('Enter test Score >');
Readln(TestScore30);
```

The array data type overcomes these limitations. By use of the array data type, a block of variables which are all of the same type may be allocated. It is also possible to access the individual components of the array rather easily using what is known as an *index*. The individual components of the array may be used in exactly the same ways that any other variable of that type may be used. For example, each element of a real array may be used as a real variable. It is possible to use array variables in an assignment statement, provided that the arrays on the left and right of the assignment operator have the same index and the same base type. The following fragment of a program has two real arrays declared in the VAR section and then some assignments to illustrate this.

```
VAR
     A, B : ARRAY[1..5] OF Real;   { Declares 2 array variables }

     A[1] := 2.0;      { First component of A assigned 2.0 }
     A[2] := 3.0;      { Second component of A assigned 3.0 }
     A[3] := A[1];     { Third component of A assigned value of
                         first component }
     A[4] := A[1] + A[2];   { Fourth component of A assigned sum of
                              first and second }
     A[5] := A[1] * A[4];   { Fifth component of A assigned product
                              of first and fourth }
     B := A;        { The components of A are assigned to the
                      components of B }
```

In this example, the declarations in the variable section have the effect
of declaring ten real variables: A[1], A[2], A[3], A[4], A[5], and B[1]..B[5].
In the first five assignment statements the components of A are used as
real variables. In the last assignment statement, the contents of A are
copied into B. This is equivalent to five assignment statements: B[1] : =
A[1]; B[2] : = A[2]; etc.

> **An *array* is a structured data type composed of a fixed number
> of data elements or components, all of the same type and such
> that each data element or component within the array may be
> referenced by use of the array's name and an index (or
> subscript).**

DEFINITION

> **The *index type* or *subscript type* defines the fixed number of
> data elements that can be stored in an array and the means
> of accessing them.**

DEFINITION

> **The *component type* or *base type* of an array is the type of
> the data elements within an array.**

DEFINITION

In a program, we might see declarations using arrays such as those
below. The index type for both arrays is a subrange of integers. The component type of the arrays is real.

```
TYPE
     BigRealArrayType = ARRAY[1..20] of Real;

VAR
     BigRealArray :    BigRealArrayType;
     LittleRealArray : ARRAY[1..5] of Real;
```

Any data type may be used as the component type of an array. The index type must be an ordinal type. In principle there is no limit to how large an array may be, but in practice there is. Because an array declaration declares many variables at once, memory is used up in large pieces. Because memory is used for a variety of purposes, there may not be as much memory available as the programmer would like to use for variables. For example, the programmer might want an array of 1000 strings of length 20. This would take about 20K of memory (20,000 bytes of memory). If the program was very large, this amount of memory might not be available.

An array type is declared by using the key word ARRAY followed by a left square bracket ([ ), the index type, a right square bracket ( ]), the key word OF, and then the base type. The index type can be given by an identifier or given directly. *FIGURE 7.1* presents the syntax diagrams for the array type.

The following is another example of the array type used in the variable declaration section which we wish to discuss. Suppose we needed to record the test averages of ten students. We might do this as follows.

```
VAR
      TestAve : ARRAY[1..10] OF Real;
```

This allocates ten real variables in memory grouped together under the

FIGURE 7.1 | **Array Type**

Array type

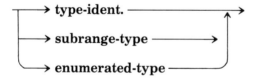

$\longrightarrow$ ARRAY $\longrightarrow$ [$\longrightarrow$ index-type $\longrightarrow$] $\longrightarrow$ OF $\longrightarrow$ base-type $\longrightarrow$

Index type

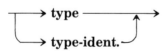

$\longrightarrow$ type-ident. $\longrightarrow$
$\longrightarrow$ subrange-type $\longrightarrow$
$\longrightarrow$ enumerated-type $\longrightarrow$

Base type

$\longrightarrow$ type $\longrightarrow$
$\longrightarrow$ type-ident. $\longrightarrow$

name TestAve. The index type of this array is the integer subrange 1..10. The base type of TestAve is real. The elements of an array are individually accessed by using the array's name, a left bracket, an expression with a value of the index type, and a right bracket. In the preceding example, the components of the array are TestAve[1], TestAve[2], . . ., TestAve[10]. You should think of the memory allocated to look something like the following.

TestAve

TestAve[1]	
TestAve[2]	
TestAve[3]	
TestAve[4]	
TestAve[5]	
TestAve[6]	
TestAve[7]	
TestAve[8]	
TestAve[9]	
TestAve[10]	

After this declaration we would be able to use the individual components of TestAve as below, where I is an integer variable.

```
TestAve[1] := 92.0;
TestAve[2] := 85.3;
I := 3;
TestAve[I] := 93.4;
I := 6;
TestAve[I] := 4.0 + TestAve[I - 3];
```

After this sequence of statements has been executed, we would see the following values stored in TestAve. A blank box indicates that no assignment was made to that location.

TestAve

	TestAve
TestAve[1]	92.0
TestAve[2]	85.3
TestAve[3]	93.4
TestAve[4]	
TestAve[5]	
TestAve[6]	97.4
TestAve[7]	
TestAve[8]	
TestAve[9]	
TestAve[10]	

Make sure you understand why these values are in the locations shown. If we had declared two variables to be of the same array type, e.g.,

```
VAR
      JrTestAve, SrTestAve : ARRAY[1..10] OF Real;
```

then it would be possible to assign the contents of B to A in an assignment statement.

```
JrTestAve := SrTestAve;
```

This would have the effect of copying all of SrTestAve into JrTestAve. This is an example of a general fact about variables in Pascal. If two variables are of the same type (which is not a file), then an assignment from one to the other is possible.

As mentioned, the base type of an array may be of any type. This includes another array. Thus we could have the following declaration.

```
VAR
      A : ARRAY[1..4] OF ARRAY['A'..'E'] OF Integer;
```

If you think of an array as a list, then this declares A to be a list of lists. In particular, A[1], A[2], A[3], A[4] are all arrays with index type 'A', . . ., 'E' and base type integer. The individual components of A are indexed by an integer and a character. This forms a table whose columns are labeled 1 to 4 and whose rows are labeled 'A' through 'E'. Memory could be depicted as being organized as in the following diagram.

A

A[1]	A[2]	A[3]	A[4]
A[1]['A']	A[2]['A']	A[3]['A']	A[4]['A']
A[1]['B']	A[2]['B']	A[3]['B']	A[4]['B']
A[1]['C']	A[2]['C']	A[3]['C']	A[4]['C']
A[1]['D']	A[2]['D']	A[3]['D']	A[4]['D']
A[1]['E']	A[2]['E']	A[3]['E']	A[4]['E']

The following assignments would then be possible. (I is an integer variable and C is a character variable.)

```
A[3]['C'] := 89;
A[2]['E'] := 12;
A[2]['A'] := 2 * A[2]['E'];
I := 1;
FOR C := 'A' TO 'E' DO
  BEGIN
     A[1][C] := I;
     I := 2 * I;
  END; { FOR }
A[4] := A[1];
```

The effect of the for loop in the above is to put the numbers 1, 2, 4, 8, 16 in the first column (A[1]) of the array A. Because A[1] and A[4] are of the same type (Array['A'..'E'] of Integer), they are assignment compatible and the last statement copies the contents of the first column of A into the fourth. After these statements have been executed, A would have the following contents.

A

	A[1]		A[2]		A[3]		A[4]
A[1]['A']	1	A[2]['A']	24	A[3]['A']		A[4]['A']	1
A[1]['B']	2	A[2]['B']		A[3]['B']		A[4]['B']	2
A[1]['C']	4	A[2]['C']		A[3]['C']	89	A[4]['C']	4
A[1]['D']	8	A[2]['D']		A[3]['D']		A[4]['D']	8
A[1]['E']	16	A[2]['E']	12	A[3]['E']		A[4]['E']	16

It is possible to carry the process of declaring an array of arrays further and talk about an array of arrays of arrays or even an array of arrays of arrays of arrays. These are known as *multidimensional arrays*. The example above is a two-dimensional array. As a matter of convenience, there is an alternative notation for declaring and using multidimensional arrays.

DEFINITION

> The *dimension* of an array is the number of index types used in declaring the array.

Instead of declaring ARRAY[ ] OF ARRAY[ ] OF we can accomplish the same end by writing the index types separated by commas within one set of brackets, thus dispensing with the need to declare ARRAY OF repeatedly. This is indicated in *FIGURE 7.2*. Similarly, we can reference individual elements within the array by writing all the necessary indices, separated by commas, within a set of brackets.

In the two-dimensional case, this means that ARRAY[index1, index2] OF base and ARRAY[index1] OF ARRAY[index2] OF base are equivalent. Also, the same variable is denoted by both A[I1][I2] and A[I1, I2]. Because of the mathematical heritage of computing, the second form is preferred. However, there are many situations when you should keep in mind that a two-dimensional array is an array of arrays.

Frequently, arrays are built from arrays and other data structures. This usually should be done in such a way as to reflect the underlying

FIGURE 7.2 | **Multidimensional Arrays**

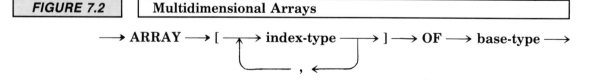

problem. If we were processing three test scores for each of 30 students, we would have declarations of the following sort.

```
CONST
     NumOfStudents = 30;
     NumOfTests    = 3;
     MaxScore      = 100;
     MinScore      = 0;

TYPE
     TestRange  = MinScore..MaxScore;
     TestScores = ARRAY[1..NumOfTests] OF TestRange;
     StuTests   = ARRAY[1..NumOfStudents] OF TestScores;

VAR
     Scores : StuTests;
```

Then Scores[15, 2] would refer to the fifteenth student's second test score. Scores[21] would denote the list of the three test scores of the twenty-first student. Notice that although we can obtain the test scores of any student as a unit (e.g., Scores[5]), it is not possible to refer to an array of the first test scores for the entire class. This is something of a limitation. If we consider a two-dimensional array as a table, we are only able to refer to the columns of the array as lists. It is not possible to use a row as a list. We have deliberately chosen the order above as being more natural. There are 30 students each with three test scores rather than three tests of 30 students. Furthermore, it is certain that a program to do grades would average the three test scores of each student, and thus having these accessible in one array is convenient. There may not be a computation involving all of the first test scores. Observe that our declarations facilitate some changes very easily. Changing the class size or number of tests would be trivial.

In the examples presented, subrange types have been used as the index types. The syntax diagram indicates that it is also possible to use an enumerated type for the index type. Here is an instance of an enumerated type being used as the index type for an array. Notice that it clarifies the meaning of the array's entries. It is assumed that the array Hours contains the hours worked each day and that PayRate contains an hourly wage before the statements involving them are executed.

```
CONST
     SundayBonusFactor   = 2;
     SaturdayBonusFactor = 1.5;

TYPE
     DaysOfWeek  = (Sun, Mon, Tues, Wed, Thurs, Fri, Sat);
     HoursWorked = ARRAY[DaysOfWeek] OF Real;
```

```
VAR
      Day        : DaysOfWeek;
      PayRate,
      Pay        : Real;
      Hours      : HoursWorked;


Pay := Hours[Sun] * PayRate * SundayBonusFactor;
FOR Day := Mon TO Fri DO  { Accumulate pay }
      Pay := Pay + Hours[Day] * PayRate;
Pay := Pay + Hours[Sat] * PayRate * SaturdayBonusFactor;
Writeln('Weekly Pay : $', Pay : 8 : 2);
```

Working with arrays almost always involves the use of loops to work with each component of the array. Many times, the exact number of elements to be manipulated is known and the for loop is appropriate. For multidimensional arrays, nested loops are used.

To conclude this section, we present a revision of the program in Chapter 6 which produced a multiplication table. This time the products are stored in an array, which is then used to output the table. The program appears in *FIGURE 7.3*. Its output is the same as that of the original program.

FIGURE 7.3

```
PROGRAM MultiplicationTable(Output);

{ This program produces a table of products starting at 1
  and ending with the specified limit.  An array is used to
  store the products formed.

      Author :        John Riley
      Date :          December 30, 1986
      Revised :       December 31, 1986
      File name :     CH7EX1.PAS
}

{$R+}   { Turn on range checking }

CONST
      TableSize     = 5;    { Size of table to be printed  }
      LeftMargin    = 8;    { Spaces used on left of table }
      ColumnWidth   = 5;    { Spaces used for each column   }
      IntegerField  = 3;    { Field size for integers       }
      MarginLessField = 5;  { Left margin minus spaces for
                              integer,  MarginLessField =
                              LeftMargin - IntegerField     }
      ColumnLessField = 2;  { Column minus spaces for
                              integer, ColumnLessField =
                              ColumnWidth - IntegerField    }
```
                                                    (continued)

```
TYPE
   Index = 1..TableSize;   { Range of numbers forming products }
   TableType = ARRAY[Index, Index] OF Integer;

VAR
   I, J    : Index;        { Loop indices   }
   K       : Integer;      { Loop index      }
   Product : TableType;    { Holds products }

BEGIN { MultiplicationTable }
   FOR I := 1 TO TableSize DO        { Form the products }
      FOR J := 1 TO TableSize DO
         Product[I, J] := I * J;

   Writeln;                          { Print the table    }
   Writeln('Multiplication Table');
   Writeln;
   Write('* |':LeftMargin);
   FOR J := 1 TO TableSize DO
      Write(J:IntegerField, ' ':ColumnLessField);
   Writeln;
   FOR K := 1 TO LeftMargin + ColumnWidth*TableSize DO
      Write('-');
   Writeln;
   FOR I := 1 TO TableSize DO
       BEGIN
          Write(I:IntegerField, '|':MarginLessField);
          FOR J := 1 TO TableSize DO
            Write(Product[I, J]:IntegerField, ' ':ColumnLessField);
          Writeln
       END { FOR I }
END.  { MultiplicationTable }
```

In this program, blank lines are used to separate the portions of code which fill the array with products and print the table. This is akin to grouping sentences in paragraphs. It makes the program easier to read. A short comment to the right of the code documents the purpose of the section of code.

Range checking is important when working with arrays, and the program in *FIGURE 7.3* has range checking turned on. If an array has components that are numbered 1 to 10, it doesn't make sense to refer to the eleventh component of an array. Be careful when working with arrays to make sure that the indices used are always in the correct range.

7.2 WORKING WITH ARRAYS

There are several common processes that a programmer encounters when working with arrays and some standard techniques for accomplishing them. Some of these techniques are presented in this section.

Very commonly it is necessary to enter items into a list and then process the list.

FIGURE 7.4 contains a program which processes a list of numbers using arrays. You should be able to read this program without difficulty. The use of an array to accomplish this task is unnecessary. It would be possible to find the maximum and average of a list of numbers entered from the keyboard simply by comparing the item just read with the previous maximum and keeping a running sum. However, there are situations in which it is necessary to store data in an array before processing it. A sample run of the program also appears in *FIGURE 7.4*.

For a more realistic example, suppose that an instructor wants a program to manage class records. For each student, a name and a test grade are to be recorded and then compared with the average of the test grades. Because the average will not be found until all the students' grades have been entered, the names and grades must be stored. Arrays are appropriate for doing this.

As in this situation, it frequently happens that we do not know ahead of time exactly how many items of a given data type will be needed. For example, at the beginning of the semester an instructor will not know the exact number of students in a class. However, he or she will know the maximum number of students that can be enrolled. If an array is needed to hold the students' names for a grade-processing program, the maximum number of places is used for the size of the array and a separate variable holds the actual number of students enrolled. If the maximum

FIGURE 7.4

```
PROGRAM MaxAndAverage ( Input, Output );

{  This is an example of the use of arrays. A group of
   positive integers is read from the keyboard into an array.
   The array is then processed to find the average of the
   numbers and the maximum number.

        Author    : John Riley
        Date      : April 12, 1986
        File name : CH7EX2.PAS
}

{$R+}   { Turn on range checking }

CONST
     ListSize = 50;
     Stop     = -1;

TYPE
     Index   = 1..ListSize;
     IntList = ARRAY[Index] OF Integer;
```

(continued)

```
VAR
     Avg    : Real;        { Average of list         }
     ItemIn,               { Number read             }
     Max,                  { Maximum number in list  }
     Sum    : Integer;     { Sum of entries          }
     I      : Index;       { Loop index              }
     Size   : 0..ListSize; { List size               }
     List   : IntList;     { List of integers read   }


BEGIN { MaxAndAverage }
  Size := 0;
  Writeln;
  Writeln('Enter positive integers, one per line.');
  Writeln('Enter ', Stop : 2, ' to end input.');
  Write('Enter integer >');
  Readln(ItemIn);
  WHILE ItemIn <> Stop DO
     BEGIN
        Size := Size + 1;
        List[Size] := ItemIn;
        Write('Enter integer >');
        Readln(ItemIn)
     END; { WHILE }
  IF Size <> 0 THEN
     BEGIN
        Max := List[1];
        Sum := List[1];
        FOR I := 2 TO Size DO
           BEGIN
              Sum := Sum + List[I];
              IF List[I] > Max THEN
                 Max := List[I]
           END; { FOR }
        Avg := Sum/Size;
        Writeln('Maximum of list : ', Max);
        Writeln('Average of list : ', Avg : 8 : 2)
     END { IF }
  ELSE
     Writeln('No numbers entered.')
END. { MaxAndAverage }


Output:

Enter positive integers, one per line.
Enter -1 to end input.
Enter integer >23
Enter integer >12
Enter integer >45
Enter integer >10
Enter integer >-1
Maximum of list : 45
Average of list : 22.50
```

number of students that could be enrolled was 35, we would probably have declarations as shown below. For the test scores we will need another array. Each entry in this array should be the test score of the corresponding student named in the array StuName. Arrays such as these are sometimes called *parallel arrays*. Pascal has another structure (the record) which simplifies this problem, but other languages do not, and so you should be aware of this technique. To accommodate the grades we would have the following declarations.

```
CONST
     MaxNumStudents = 35;
     NameLength     = 20;

TYPE
     NameType      = STRING[NameLength];
     StuNameArray  = ARRAY[1..MaxNumStudents] OF NameType;
     GradeArray    = ARRAY[1..MaxNumStudents] OF Integer;

VAR
     NumOfStudents : 0..MaxNumStudents;
     StuName       : StuNameArray;
     Grade         : GradeArray;
     Name          : NameType;
```

When this is done, we should think of the arrays as shown in *FIGURE 7.5*.

We interpret *FIGURE 7.5* as indicating that the first student's name is S. Black and that his or her grade is 100.

This problem can be broken into three parts. First, the names and grades must be obtained and stored in the arrays. The next part consists of calculating the average. Finally, the names and grades of students, along with a message indicating above or below average, must be printed.

A more detailed specification of the first part is that it must have the names and grades entered into the arrays StuName and Grade and keep count of how many students have been entered. If the names are being entered from the keyboard, the easiest way is to use a loop which is terminated by a special entry. An algorithm for doing this follows. Because initially there are no students, NumOfStudents is set to 0. Every time a name which is not 'Q' is entered, there is another student, so NumOfStudents is increased and the name is stored in the next component of the array. The grade for this student is then obtained and stored.

```
NumOfStudents ← 0
Get(Name)
While Name <> 'Q'
     NumOfStudents ← NumOfStudents + 1
     StuName[NumOfStudents] ← Name
     Get(StudentGrade)
     Grade[NumOfStudents] ← StudentGrade
     Get(Name)
```

	StuName		**Grade**
StuName[1]	BLACK S	Grade[1]	100
StuName[2]	BROWN K	Grade[2]	67
StuName[3]	GREEN P	Grade[3]	89
StuName[4]		Grade[4]	
StuName[5]		Grade[5]	
StuName[34]		Grade[34]	
StuName[35]		Grade[35]	

The Pascal statements below implement this algorithm, taking into consideration the additional fact that the size of the array should not be exceeded.

```
NumOfStudents := 0;
Writeln('Enter the students'' names, one per line.');
Writeln('Enter Q to stop.');
Write('Enter name >');
Readln(Name);
WHILE (Name <> 'Q') AND (NumOfStudents < MaxNumStudents) DO
   BEGIN
      NumOfStudents := NumOfStudents + 1;
      StuName[NumOfStudents] := Name;
      Writeln('Enter the student''s grade >');
      Readln(Grade[NumOfStudents]);
      Write('Enter name (Q to stop) >');
      Readln(Name)
   END; { WHILE }
```

Notice that we have allowed for the possibility of there being no students in the class (a very unpopular teacher). We have also made certain that the class's capacity cannot be exceeded. Be sure that you understand the program fragment above, because it solves a frequently occurring task.

The next part of the program finds the average of the grades. To do this it is necessary to go through the list of grades and sum the grades. The average is then computed by dividing this sum by the number of students. An algorithm for doing this is as follows.

```
GradeSum ← 0
For I ← 1 to NumOfStudents
      GradeSum ← GradeSum + Grade[I]
Average ← GradeSum/NumOfStudents
```

Notice that the loop index goes only from 1 to the number of students, not to the array size. This reflects that the entire array may not be in use.

Code based on this algorithm appears below. It includes a check so that a division by zero cannot take place.

```
  IF NumOfStudents <> 0 THEN
    BEGIN
      SumOfGrades := 0;
      FOR I := 1 TO NumOfStudents DO
          SumOfGrades := SumOfGrades + Grade[I];
      ClassAverage := SumOfGrades/NumOfStudents
    END; { IF }
```

The last part of the program consists of printing the names and grades of students along with the message indicating above or below average. To decide which message must be printed, a comparison of the student's grade with the average grade must be made. An algorithm accomplishing this is as follows.

```
For I ← 1 to NumOfStudents
      Output(StuName[I], Grade[I])
      If Grade[I] ≥ Then
            Output('Above Average')
      Else
            Output('Below Average')
```

Pascal statements for this appear below, enclosed in a test to make sure that there actually are some students to be processed.

```
  IF NumOfStudents <> 0 THEN
      BEGIN
        Writeln;
        Writeln('   NAME   ':NameLength, ' GRADE');
        FOR I := 1 TO NumOfStudents DO
            BEGIN
              Write(StuName[I]:NameLength, ' ', Grade[I]:3);
```

```
        IF Grade[I] >= ClassAverage THEN
            Writeln('     Above average')
        ELSE
            Writeln('     Below average')
      END { FOR }
   END  { IF }
```

These statements, along with some statements to produce summary information, are incorporated in the program in *FIGURE 7.6*. A sample run of the program is given as well. The program produces a list of student names, grades, and a message indicating whether a score was above or below average.

Another important aspect of using arrays is that of finding an element in an array. For example, if information were stored as in *FIGURE 7.5*, the user might want to know a particular student's grade. To do this the program would have to know the index of the grade, which is the same as the index of the student's name. This would be found by searching the array StuName. More specifically, each name in the array StuName must be compared with the name to be found. This means going down the list until the name is found or the list is exhausted. This basic idea is contained in the three-line algorithm below (which obviously needs refinement). Place is a variable to hold the index or location of NameToFind in the array StuName.

```
While NameToFind is not Found and List is not Exhausted
    If the next entry in StuName is NameToFind Then
          Assign Place
```

To refine this algorithm we introduce a Boolean variable, NameFound. Initially, NameFound is False (the NameToFind hasn't been found yet). When the name has been found, NameFound becomes True.

```
NameFound ← False
While  Not NameFound and List is not Exhausted
    If the next entry in StuName is NameToFind Then
          Assign Place
          NameFound ← True
```

We complete the algorithm by noting that to go through the list an index is needed. If NameToFind has been found, the current index is Place. This suggests that Place should be the index. Furthermore, by comparing Place with NumOfStudents we can tell whether the entire list has been searched.

```
NameFound ← False
Place ← 0
While  Not NameFound and Place < NumOfStudents
    Place ← Place + 1
    If StuName[Place] = NameToFind Then
          NameFound ← True
```

FIGURE 7.6

```pascal
PROGRAM ClassAnalysis(Input, Output);

{ A program to use student names and scores and print whether
  the score was above or below average.

      Author :        John Riley
      Date :          December 31, 1986
      File name :     CH7EX3.PAS
}

{$R+}    { Turn on range checking }

CONST
   MaxNumStudents = 35;
   NameLength    = 20;
   Stop          = 'Q';  { Ends input }

TYPE
   NameType      = STRING[NameLength];
   StuNameArray = ARRAY[1..MaxNumStudents] OF NameType;
   GradeArray    = ARRAY[1..MaxNumStudents] OF Integer;

VAR
   NumOfStudents : 0..MaxNumStudents;
   StuName       : StuNameArray;      { Holds students' names  }
   Grade         : GradeArray;        { Holds students' grades }
   Name          : NameType;          { Name input             }
   I,                                 { Loop index             }
   SumOfGrades   : Integer;           { To find average        }
   ClassAverage  : Real;              { Average of grades      }


BEGIN { ClassAnalysis }
                                          { Input section }
   NumOfStudents := 0;
   Writeln('Enter the students'' names, one per line.');
   Writeln('Enter ', Stop, ' to stop.');
   Write('Enter name >');
   Readln(Name);
   WHILE (Name <> Stop) AND (NumOfStudents < MaxNumStudents) DO
      BEGIN
         NumOfStudents := NumOfStudents + 1;
         StuName[NumOfStudents] := Name;
         Write('Enter the student''s grade >');
         Readln(Grade[NumOfStudents]);
         Write('Enter name (', Stop, ' to stop) >');
         Readln(Name)
      END; { WHILE }

   IF NumOfStudents <> 0 THEN                { Averaging section }
```

(continued)

```
      BEGIN
        SumOfGrades := 0;
        FOR I := 1 TO NumOfStudents DO
            SumOfGrades := SumOfGrades + Grade[I];
        ClassAverage := SumOfGrades/NumOfStudents
      END; { IF }

  IF NumOfStudents <> 0 THEN              { Output section }
      BEGIN
        Writeln;
        Writeln('   NAME   ':NameLength, ' GRADE');
        FOR I := 1 TO NumOfStudents DO
            BEGIN
              Write(StuName[I]:NameLength, ' ', Grade[I]:3);
              IF Grade[I] >= ClassAverage THEN
                  Writeln('    Above average')
              ELSE
                  Writeln('    Below average')
            END; { FOR }
        Writeln;
        Writeln('Students processed : ', NumOfStudents:6);
        Writeln('Average :          : ', ClassAverage:6:2)
      END   { IF }
  ELSE
      Writeln('No students processed.')
END.  { ClassAnalysis }


Output:

Enter the students' names, one per line.
Enter Q to stop.
Enter name >JONES, J
Enter the student's grade >78
Enter name (Q to stop) >SMITH, K
Enter the student's grade >89
Enter name (Q to stop) >GREEN, M
Enter the student's grade >90
Enter name (Q to stop) >BLACK, S
Enter the student's grade >82
Enter name (Q to stop) >REED, T
Enter the student's grade >83
Enter name (Q to stop) >Q


            NAME      GRADE
          JONES, J    78      Below average
          SMITH, K    89      Above average
          GREEN, M    90      Above average
          BLACK, S    82      Below average
           REED, T    83      Below average

Students processed :     5
Average            :  84.40
```

Using these ideas, Pascal statements which will perform the task of producing a given student's grade are as follows.

```
Write('Enter the student's name >');
Readln(NameToFind);
NameFound := False;
Place := 0;
WHILE (NOT NameFound) AND (Place < NumOfStudents) DO
    BEGIN
        Place := Place + 1;
        IF StuName[Place] = NameToFind THEN
            NameFound := True
    END; { WHILE }
IF Found THEN
    Writeln(NameToFind, ' received a grade of ', Grade[Place])
ELSE
    Writeln(NameToFind, ' not found in list.');
```

In order to locate NameToFind in StuName, an exact match must occur. This means that if upper-case letters are used in the array and the user enters lower-case letters the name will not be found. It also means that extra blanks will cause Name not to match StuName even if they agree otherwise. A user would not like this very much. Another way of stating this is that the above program is not "user friendly." Creating user-friendly software can be difficult and time-consuming because of the need to anticipate problems like this.

Care has been taken to check only the part of StuName which is in use. In particular, Place cannot exceed MaxNumStudents because NumOfStudents cannot.

In this section the arrays have been processed "as is." No attempt has been made to rearrange the elements of the array. The next section is devoted to doing this.

7.3 THE INSERTION SORT

One task which requires the use of storage is sorting. This is a very common problem in computing. Many algorithms have been devised for arranging a list in some prescribed order (usually alphabetic or numeric). The storage used may be internal (in memory) or external (using files). Internal sorts are faster and easier to write. On the other hand, the number of items which can be sorted by an internal sort is limited by memory and is not suited for very large lists. Frequently, arrays are used for the storage needed for an internal sort. *FIGURE 7.7* is a program which uses an algorithm known as the *insertion sort* to read items and put them in their correct order in an array.

FIGURE 7.7

```
PROGRAM GetArrayInOrder (Input, Output);

{ This program obtains a list of words from the keyboard and
  puts it into order.  An insertion  sort is used.

  Author    : John Riley
  Date      : April 12, 1986
  File name : CH7EX4.PAS
}

{$R+}   { Turn on range checking }

CONST
   ListMaxSize = 50;
   StopChar    = '*';
   StLen       = 15;    { Length of string }

TYPE
   Index    = 1..ListMaxSize;
   Word     = STRING[StLen];
   WordList = ARRAY[Index] OF Word;

VAR
    Size : 0..ListMaxSize;   { Number of list items    }
    Item : Word;             { Item read from keyboard }
    I,                       { Loop index              }
    Pos  : Index;            { Position to insert item }
    List : WordList;         { List of items           }


BEGIN { GetArrayInOrder }
  Writeln('Enter the words to be sorted, one per line.');
  Writeln('End with ', StopChar);
  Write('Enter a word >' );
  Readln(Item);
  IF Item <> StopChar THEN
     BEGIN
       List[1] := Item;
       Size := 1;
       Write('Enter a word >' );
       Readln(Item)
     END   { IF }
  ELSE
     Size := 0;
  WHILE Item <> StopChar DO
     BEGIN
       Pos := 1;
       WHILE (Item >= List[ Pos ]) AND          { Find item's place }
             (Pos < Size) DO                     { in list           }
          Pos := Pos + 1;
       IF Item < List[ Pos ] THEN   { Item is to be inserted }
```

(continued)

```
       BEGIN
         FOR I := Size DownTo Pos DO
            List[ I + 1 ] := List[ I ];
         List[ Pos ] := Item;
         Size := Size + 1
       END { IF }
    ELSE    { Item is at the end of the list }
       BEGIN
         Size := Size + 1;
         List[ Size ] := Item
       END; { ELSE }
    Write('Enter a word >');
    Readln( Item )
  END; { WHILE }
Writeln;
Writeln('List in order');
FOR I := 1 to Size DO
   Writeln(List[I]);
Writeln
END. { GetArrayInOrder }


Output:

Enter the words to be sorted, one per line.
End with *
Enter a word >MAUCHLY
Enter a word >HOPPER
Enter a word >TURING
Enter a word >BABBAGE
Enter a word >DIJKSTRA
Enter a word >KNUTH
Enter a word >*

List in order
BABBAGE
DIJKSTRA
HOPPER
KNUTH
MAUCHLY
TURING
```

The basic idea of the insertion sort is simple. It corresponds to the method some people use to pick up a hand of cards in order. One card at a time is picked up and placed in its correct place among the cards that have already been picked up. An algorithm to do the insertion sort was developed in the last section of Chapter 1. Some subtle problems occur when we try to implement this technique in a computer program while thinking of an entry as a card and an array as a hand.

To make this problem concrete, suppose that A is an array which is to be filled with its entries in order. To make the discussion clearer, we will also assume that duplicate entries never occur. At all times in the insertion sort, A is to have its items in order. There are two good reasons for requiring this. First, if at all times A is in order, it is in order when we finish. Second, if at any time in developing the algorithm we violate this condition, we will know that we have made a mistake. Furthermore, we can use the knowledge that A is in order at certain places when we develop the algorithm. To start, we write the following.

```
While there are more items
     Get(NewItem)
     Put NewItem into its position in A
```

We break the task of putting NewItem in place into two steps: finding its place and inserting it.

```
While there are more items
     Get(NewItem)
     Find Position of NewItem in A
     Insert NewItem into A[Position]
```

Finding the position of NewItem in A requires that we keep track of how many elements of A are currently being used. Let's call this the Size of the list. Each time an item is added to the list, Size is increased by 1. Initially, Size is 0.

```
Size ← 0
While there are more items
     Get(NewItem)
     Find Position of NewItem in A
     Insert NewItem into A[Position]
     Size ← Size + 1
```

NewItem gets inserted in A after all the entries that precede it. So to find the Position of NewItem it is necessary to use a while loop to compare NewItem with entries already in A. The loop terminates when A[Position] follows NewItem. Because the entries in A are in order, this gives the Position of NewItem. However, we must make sure that a comparison can be made in all cases. Because the list is empty when the first item is inserted, this cannot be done. To remedy this we simply insert the first item in A[1].

```
If there is an item
     Get(A[1])
     Size ← 1
Else
     Size ← 0
While there are more items
     Get(NewItem)
     Position ← 1
     While NewItem > A[Position]
          Position ← Position + 1
     Insert NewItem into A[Position]
     Size ← Size + 1
```

This is not quite correct, as you may have noticed. We have not taken into consideration that we should search only through A[Size]. Amending this we have the following version of our algorithm, which reflects that Position should be increased only when it is less than Size.

```
If there is an item
     Get(A[1])
     Size  ←  1
Else
     Size  ←  0
While there are more items
     Get(NewItem)
     Position  ←  1
     While NewItem > A[Position] and Position < Size
          Position  ←  Position + 1
     Insert NewItem into A[Position]
     Size  ←  Size + 1
```

Before NewItem is inserted into A[Position] it is necessary to move the entries of A following NewItem out of the way. (If you keep a hand of cards in order from left to right, insertion of a card requires that the cards to its right be shifted.) After this has been done it is possible to insert NewItem into A[Position]. These two steps are now included in our algorithm.

```
If there is an item
     Get(A[1])
     Size  ←  1
Else
     Size  ←  0
While there are more items
     Get(NewItem)
     Position  ←  1
     While NewItem > A[Position] and Position < Size
          Position  ←  Position + 1
     For I  ←  Size down to Position
          A[I + 1]  ←  A[I]
     A[Position]  ←  NewItem
     Size  ←  Size + 1
```

This is still not correct, however. Position is the correct location for NewItem whenever the loop ends and NewItem < A[Position]. But the loop may also be terminated when Position = Size. When the loop terminates with Position = Size, we may have either NewItem < A[Position] or NewItem > A[Position]. The first case is the one that has already been handled. The second case is handled by noting that if NewItem > A[Position] and Position = Size, then NewItem must be a new last item for the list. This is easy to take care of.

```
If there is an item
     Get(A[1])
     Size ← 1
Else
     Size ← 0
While there are more items
     Get(NewItem)
     Position ← 1
     While NewItem > A[Position] and Position < Size
          Position ← Position + 1
     If NewItem < A[Position] then
          For I ← Size down to Position
               A[I + 1] ← A[I]
          A[Position] ← NewItem
          Size ← Size + 1
     Else
          Size ← Size + 1
          A[Size] ← NewItem
```

The last algorithm above is the basis of the program which appears in *FIGURE 7.7*. This program puts a list of words in order.

Let us illustrate how this program works with an example. (For the sake of brevity we will assume that ListMaxSize is 15 and that the words being entered are all letters.) Suppose that List contains the nine letters 'A', 'C', 'E', 'G', 'J', 'K', 'N', 'P', 'R'. Size is then 9. Suppose that 'H' is read into Item. Because 'H' is not StopChar, the while loop is begun and I is set to 1. The values of the variables are depicted in *FIGURE 7.8*. A question mark denotes an unknown or unassigned value.

The while loop ends when I is assigned 5, because Item ('H') does not follow ($>=$) List[5] ('J'). Because Item < List[I] is True, Pos is assigned

---

FIGURE 7.8

Before   **WHILE (Item $>=$ List[I]) AND**   { **Find item's place** }
                    (I $<$ Size) DO   { **in list**   }

Item	**I**	**Pos**	**Size**
'H'	1	?	9

List

'A'	'C'	'E'	'G'	'J'	'K'	'N'	'P'	'R'	?	?	?	?	?	?
1	2	3	4	5	6	7	8	9	10	11	12	13	14	15

FIGURE 7.9

After   Pos := I;

Item	I	Pos	Size
'H'	5	5	9

List

'A'	'C'	'E'	'G'	'J'	'K'	'N'	'P'	'R'	?	?	?	?	?	?
1	2	3	4	5	6	7	8	9	10	11	12	13	14	15

the value contained in I. The diagram of variables now is as in *FIGURE 7.9*.

The for loop which follows then copies the letters in List between positions 9 and 5 one to the right. By copying from right to left we ensure that we are never copying over a letter that has yet to be copied. After the for loop is complete we have the situation depicted in *FIGURE 7.10*. Because I is used as a loop-control variable, we regard its value after the loop is executed as unknown.

At this point, all that remains is to insert Item and adjust Size. This is done in the next two lines and results in our diagram of variables being as shown in *FIGURE 7.11*.

FIGURE 7.10

After   FOR I := Size DownTo Pos DO
                 List[I + 1] := List[I];

Item	I	Pos	Size
'H'	?	5	9

List

'A'	'C'	'E'	'G'	'J'	'J'	'K'	'N'	'P'	'R'	?	?	?	?	?
1	2	3	4	5	6	7	8	9	10	11	12	13	14	15

FIGURE 7.11

After   List[Pos] := Item;
Size := Size + 1;

Item	I	Pos	Size
'H'	?	5	10

List

'A'	'C'	'E'	'G'	'H'	'J'	'K'	'N'	'P'	'R'	?	?	?	?	?
1	2	3	4	5	6	7	8	9	10	11	12	13	14	15

You should carefully examine the program in *FIGURE 7.7* to make sure you understand why it works in all cases. It is helpful to follow the program through, keeping track of the values of the variables as we have done in *FIGURES 7.8* through *7.11*. This technique is known as *hand tracing* a program and is valuable in understanding and debugging programs.

There are other ways of sorting an array. A competent programmer should learn at least one thoroughly and be familiar with several others. Different sorting algorithms are appropriate for arrays of different sizes. The insertion sort is suitable for smaller arrays (fewer than 50 elements).

The program in *FIGURE 7.7* illustrates how useful the for statement is in working with arrays. Any time the number of array elements to be processed is known, the for statement is the statement to be used. When the number is not known, a while (or repeat-until) loop should be used. An example of this is the search for the place to insert an item. You should learn to distinguish these situations to make good use of the control statements that Pascal provides.

The use of appropriate control statements in conjunction with appropriate data types can aid in program readability, maintainability, and efficiency. The case statement works well with ordinal types. The for statement is useful with arrays.

7.4 STRINGS AS ARRAYS

A great deal of computing involves the use of characters and strings. Standard Pascal provides a limited form of string variables (as packed arrays of characters indexed by a range of integers). Standard Pascal does not specify any functions that use strings except that two strings may be compared.

TURBO Pascal, like a number of other implementations of Pascal, has a predefined type String. Usually, an implementation of Pascal is more flexible with strings than standard Pascal demands. For example, standard Pascal requires that strings must be of exactly the same length to be compared. It also requires that the string on the right side of an assignment statement be exactly the same size as the string variable on the left. At best, this is cumbersome. In addition to eliminating the restrictions on length, most implementations of Pascal provide some string-handling routines.

One advantage of using strings instead of arrays of characters is that TURBO allows string variables to be input and output directly. Implementations of Pascal without a similar facility require more work to read in arrays of characters. TURBO regards strings of differing lengths to be compatible, and thus strings may be used easily in assignment statements. This eases the programmer's task.

This section is a brief discussion of strings and their processing. Keep in mind that exactly which characters may occur in a string is dependent on the character set implemented by the machine. TURBO Pascal uses the ASCII character set (Appendix G).

Recall that a string constant is a sequence of characters enclosed in single quotes (or apostrophes). A string variable is an array of character variables declared using STRING[StLen] where StLen denotes the maximum number of characters that may be stored in the string variable. The maximum number of characters that may appear in any string (variable or constant) is 255. The actual number of characters stored in a string variable S is given by Length(S).

Because a string is an array, the individual components of the string—that is, the characters in the string—may be individually accessed. If S is a string, S[1] through S[Length(S)] each contain one of the characters in S.

When a string value is to be stored in a string variable and the string value is longer than the maximum length of the string variable, the rightmost characters of the string are dropped. If the string value supplied is shorter than the length of the string variable, the rightmost characters of the string variable are undefined and the string variable's actual length is adjusted accordingly. These rules apply whether the string value is obtained from the right side of an assignment statement or as input from the keyboard.

To work effectively with strings, it is necessary to understand more precisely what storing a string in an array of characters entails.

Suppose that StLen is an integer constant which denotes the length of the string variables we wish to use. For the sake of definiteness let us suppose that StLen is 8. Then we would declare a string variable S as follows:

```
VAR
    S : STRING[StLen];
```

The effect of this declaration, in terms of memory allocation, is this:

```
VAR
     S : ARRAY[0..StLen] OF Char;
```

This means that we should think of the storage of S being nine character variables (S[0] through S[8]) as in this diagram:

S

S[0]   S[1]   S[2]   S[3]   S[4]   S[5]   S[6]   S[7]   S[8]

The characters comprising the string stored in S are stored in the locations S[1] through S[8]. S[0] contains a character whose ordinal number is the number of characters in the string stored in S. The first 32 characters in the ASCII table are control characters, and these will be needed to denote shorter strings. A control character will be denoted by prefixing it with a circumflex (ˆ). For example, to denote a string of length 2 we would store ˆB in S[0]. The null character (ASCII value 0) is used to signify a string of length 0. With these conventions, the effect of the statement

```
S := 'uvwxy';
```

on memory would be the following:

S

ˆE	u	v	w	x	y	?	?	?

S[0]   S[1]   S[2]   S[3]   S[4]   S[5]   S[6]   S[7]   S[8]

The character ˆE in S[0] denotes that S currently has five characters, because ˆE has ordinal number 5. These five characters are stored (in order) in locations S[1] through S[5]. The remaining characters of S (S[6], S[7], and S[8]) are undefined. If we were now to assign the string of characters representing the digits to S

```
S := '0123456789';
```

the memory locations for S would look like this:

S

ˆH	0	1	2	3	4	5	6	7

S[0]   S[1]   S[2]   S[3]   S[4]   S[5]   S[6]   S[7]   S[8]

^H denotes that eight characters are stored in S. Notice that the last two characters of the string '0123456789' (8 and 9) were not stored in S because only eight characters may be stored in S.

From the above we may deduce that the number of characters stored in S is given by Ord(S[0]). TURBO provides this as a predefined function, Length, which has one argument, a string constant or variable. For example, with S as above, Length(S) is 8. Since Length is also defined for string constants, Length('ABCD') is 4.

The individual characters within a string may be accessed as if they were in an array. After the assignment

```
S := 'HELLO';
```

S[1] is 'H' and S[2] is 'E'. S[6], S[7], and S[8] are all undefined. S[0] is ^E. Individual characters may be assigned as in

```
S[1] := 'G';
S[2] := 'o';
S[3] := 'o';
S[4] := 'd';
FOR I := 5 to 7 DO
    S[I] := '!';
```

(where I is an integer variable). These statements leave S[0] unchanged. As a consequence, S[0] may not have the correct value and Length(S) may not be 7. When the programmer works with the individual characters of a string, he or she bears the responsibility of changing S[0] to the correct length. If NewLen denotes the new length of the string S, this is done by the statement

```
S[0] := Chr(NewLen);
```

To illustrate these ideas we give a program fragment which has the effect of

```
St1 := St2;
```

where St1 and St2 are string variables. Assume that the maximum length of St1 is given by Len1 (i.e., St1 is of type String[Len1]). Let I and NewLen be integer variables. Then the assignment statement above is equivalent to the following code:

```
IF Length(St2) < Len1 THEN          { Find the new length for St1 }
    NewLen := Length(St2)
ELSE
    NewLen := Len1;

FOR I := 1 TO NewLen DO             { Assign characters from St2 }
    St1[I] := St2[I];               { to    St1                  }

St1[0] := Chr(NewLen);              { Adjust the length of St1   }
```

This points out an advantage of having an implementation which provides string manipulations. Although the code is not difficult, it would be inconvenient (and prone to error) to have to include it every time we wanted to assign string variables. Furthermore, we would also have to write routines to assign character input to string variables and to assign string constants to string variables. These routines would be more difficult to write.

When a string variable S is being output, the number Length(S) determines how many characters of S are output. In fact, the statement

```
Write(S);
```

is equivalent to

```
FOR I := 1 TO Length(S) DO
   Write(S[I]);
```

where I is an integer variable. Because of this, if a string variable does not have its length changed after an assignment to its characters, its output may not be correct. Thus the output of the program fragment which follows is 'ABCD', not 'ABCDXXX' as might be expected.

```
VAR
     S : STRING[10];

  S := 'ABCD';
  S[5] := 'X';
  S[6] := 'X';
  S[7] := 'X';
  Write(S);
```

It should be emphasized that the null character (which is ASCII character 0) is not the same as the space or blank (ASCII character 32). The null character has no effect on output. The space character causes the output mechanism to move forward the width of one character. On a video screen, this means that the cursor is moved one to the right. On a printer, the print head is moved one to the right. For both the printer and the video screen, the effect is to leave a blank space. The space character can be given literally as ' '. The notation SPC is sometimes used for the space character.

A consequence of the way in which string variables are output is that the number of spaces used when a string variable is output varies. This causes problems when the programmer is attempting to produce output which is aligned in columns, because the placement of information fol-

FIGURE 7.12

```
PROGRAM BlankFill(Input, Output);

{ This program replaces the unfilled characters in strings
  with blanks.

      Author    : John Riley
      Date      : December 31, 1986
      File name : CH7EX5.PAS
}

{$R+}  { Turn on range checking }

CONST
      Blank       = ' ';
      StringLen   = 20;
      MaxListSize = 10;
      Stop        = '*';     { Ends input }

TYPE
      StringType  = STRING[StringLen];
      StringArray = ARRAY[1..MaxListSize] OF StringType;

VAR
      NumOfStrings,               { Number of strings entered }
      I, J        : Integer;      { Loop indices              }
      StringIn    : StringType;   { String read in            }
      List        : StringArray;  { List of strings           }

BEGIN  { BlankFill }

  NumOfStrings := 0;
  Writeln('Enter strings, one per line. End with ', Stop);
  Write('Enter string >');
  Readln(StringIn);
  WHILE (StringIn <> Stop) AND (NumOfStrings < MaxListSize) DO
      BEGIN
         NumOfStrings := NumOfStrings + 1;
         List[NumOfStrings] := StringIn;
         Write('Enter string (', Stop, ' to end) >');
         Readln(StringIn)
      END;   { WHILE }

  Writeln;
  Writeln('Strings as input');
  Writeln;
  FOR I := 1 TO NumOfStrings DO
      Writeln('*', List[I], '*');

  Writeln;
  Writeln('Strings right justified');
  Writeln;
  FOR I := 1 TO NumOfStrings DO
      Writeln('*', List[I]:StringLen, '*');
```

(continued)

```
FOR I := 1 TO NumOfStrings DO    { Pad with blanks }
   BEGIN
     FOR J := Length(List[I]) + 1 TO StringLen DO
         List[I][J] := Blank;
     List[I][0] := Chr(StringLen)    { Adjust length }
   END; { FOR I }

   Writeln;
   Writeln('Padded with blanks');
   Writeln;
   FOR I := 1 TO NumOfStrings DO
      Writeln('*', List[I], '*');
   Writeln
END.   { BlankFill }
```

```
Enter strings, one per line. End with *
Enter string >ABC
Enter string (* to end) >X Y Z
Enter string (* to end) >1234567890
Enter string (* to end) >*

Strings as input

*ABC*
*X Y Z*
*1234567890*

Strings right justified

*              ABC*
*            X Y Z*
*       1234567890*

Padded with blanks

*ABC              *
*X Y Z            *
*1234567890       *
```

lowing the string variable on the same line will vary. A report of student
names and grades should have the grades in a column:

Name	Test 1	Test 2	Test 3
ADAMS, ANN	98	83	87
JOHNSON, SAMUEL	88	81	92

The grades should be aligned even if the names are not of the same length. This will not occur if the names differ in length and the statement

```
Writeln(StuName[I], Test1[I], Test2[I], Test3[I]);
```

is used (in a loop) where the variables indicate the obvious quantities. One might attempt to align the output by using a field-width specification following StuName[I]. However, this causes the names to be right justified, something like this:

```
Name                           Test 1    Test 2    Test 3

              ADAMS, ANN         98        83        87
         JOHNSON, SAMUEL         88        81        92
```

This is not what we would like. One way out of this dilemma is to replace the undefined characters in StuName with blanks and adjust the length of StuName. Then outputting StuName will always take the same number of characters.

A program which fills the ends of strings with blanks is presented in *FIGURE 7.12* on the preceding pages. Also shown are the results of running this program with the input consisting of ABC (three letters), X Y Z (three letters with a space between each pair of letters), and 1234567890 (the ten digits). To emphasize the exact placement of the output strings, they have been placed within pairs of asterisks.

7.5 SUMMARY

The array data type is a structured data type which is used when many variables of the same type are needed. A one-dimensional array serves as a list. A two-dimensional array may be used to represent a table. The components of an array variable may be accessed by using an index. The for statement is used to process a known number of components of an array.

Arrays occur frequently in computing. It may be necessary to have the entries in an array in order. A sorting algorithm is used to arrange the components of the array in order. One sorting algorithm is the insertion sort.

A string is used to hold sequences of characters (words, names, etc.). A string is a one-dimensional array of characters.

Because the processing of arrays can be somewhat complex, it is convenient to isolate the various stages of such processing. In the next chapter, a means of doing this will be developed. ❑

EXERCISES

1. Give the output of the following programs.

a.
```pascal
PROGRAM Ch7Num1a(Output);

{  Chapter 7, Number 1a, Give the output.

      Author :       John Riley
      Date :         April 28, 1986
      File name :    CH7NUM1A.PAS
}

CONST
   ArraySize = 8;

TYPE
   IntArray = ARRAY[1..ArraySize] OF Integer;

VAR
   A : IntArray;
   I : Integer;    { Loop index }

BEGIN   { Ch7Num1a }
   FOR I := 1 TO ArraySize DO
      A[I] := 2 * I;
   FOR I := 1 TO ArraySize DO
      Write(A[I]:4);
   Writeln
END.   { Ch7Num1a }
```

b.
```pascal
PROGRAM Ch7Num1b(Output);

{  Chapter 7, Number 1b, Give the output.

      Author :       John Riley
      Date :         April 28, 1986
      File name :    CH7NUM1B.PAS
}


TYPE
   IntArray = ARRAY['a'..'e'] OF Integer;

VAR
   A : IntArray;
   C : Char;          { Loop index }

BEGIN   { Ch7Num1b }
   FOR C := 'a' TO 'e' DO
      A[C] := Ord(C) - Ord('a');
   FOR C := 'a' TO 'e' DO
      Write(A[C]:4);
   Writeln
END.   { Ch7Num1b }
```

```
c.    PROGRAM Ch7Num1c(Output);

      {  Chapter 7, Number 1c, Give the output.

            Author :        John Riley
            Date :          April 28, 1986
            File name :     CH7NUM1C.PAS
      }

      CONST
         StLen = 8;

      TYPE
         StType = STRING[StLen];

      VAR
         S : StType;
         I : Integer;    { Loop index }

      BEGIN   { Ch7Num1c }
        S := 'ABCDE';
        FOR I := 1 TO Length(S) - 1 DO
           Write(S[I]:2);
        Writeln
      END.   { Ch7Num1c }
```

2. Suppose the following declarations are made.

```
CONST

      ArraySize = 10;

TYPE
      ArrayRange   = 1..ArraySize;
      ListType     = ARRAY[ArrayRange] OF Integer;
      TableType    =
   ARRAY[ArrayRange, ArrayRange] OF Integer;

VAR
      I, J, K        : Integer;
      List1, List2   : ListType;
      Table1, Table2 : TableType;
      Continue       : Boolean;
```

Find the errors in the following segments of programs.

```
a.    I := 3;
      List1[I] := List2[4*I];

b.    List1 := Table[1] + 3;

c.    { Assume List1 and List2 contain values }
      List1 := List1 + List2;
```

```
d.    I := 0;
      WHILE I <= ArraySize DO
          BEGIN
            I := I + 1;
            Table1[I, I] := I
          END; { WHILE }

e.    I := 0;
      WHILE I < ArraySize DO
          BEGIN
            Table1[I, ArraySize - 1] := 2 * I;
            I := I + 1
          END; { WHILE }
      Table2[2] := Table1[1];

f.    { Assume  List1 contains values and K has a value.}
      Continue := True;
      I := 1;
      WHILE Continue OR I <= ArraySize DO
          IF List1[I] = K THEN
              Continue := False
          ELSE
              I := I + 1;
```

3. Describe the effect of having attempted to copy over from left to right in the program of *FIGURE* 7.7 by using the following for loop.

```
    FOR I := Pos to Size DO
        List[I + 1] := List[I];
```

4. Write a Pascal program which reads a list of positive integers into an array and then outputs every other integer in the list (starting with the first). The end of the input list is indicated by an input of 0. You may assume that there are no more than 30 integers in the list.

5. Write a Pascal program which reads a list of positive and negative integers and puts the positive integers in one array and the negative integers in another. The program then outputs two columns of integers, the positives and negatives. The end of the list of integers is indicated by 0. There are no more than 40 integers (positive and negative). The numbers of positive and negative integers may be different. For example, the input

```
4
5
-9
6
-11
8
10
0
```

should give the output

```
4              -9
5              -11
6
8
10
```

6. Write a program which reads a number of strings from the keyboard and stores them in an array. This list is terminated by an input of Q (for quit). No more than 20 strings are to be entered. The user then enters strings to be found in the array. If a string is found, its position in the array is output. If a string is not found, an appropriate message is output. The user terminates this list with a Q. Your program should do something like this.

```
Enter a string (Q to Quit) > BAT
Enter a string (Q to Quit) > FAT
Enter a string (Q to Quit) > HAT
Enter a string (Q to Quit) > MAT
Enter a string (Q to Quit) > Q

Enter a string to find (Q to Quit) > FAT
FAT is in position 2
Enter a string to find (Q to Quit) > CAT
CAT not found
Enter a string to find (Q to Quit) > Q
```

7. Write a program which reads a string and then prints the characters of the string down the page one per line. The string will contain no more than 20 characters. For example,

```
Enter a string > HI THERE

H
I

T
H
E
R
E
```

8. Write a program which prints strings backwards. A string is to be entered by the user and then printed backwards. Use a special value to terminate the input.

9. Write a program which reads a sequence of integers (terminated by some special value) and then outputs the average of the numbers as well as the number of integers that were above the average and the number that were equal to or below the average. You will need to read the numbers into an array so that you can then compare them with the average.

10. The median of a list of numbers is the number in the list which is "halfway" down the list in the sense that as many numbers lie above this number as below it. More precisely, if there are N items in the list and N is odd, then the median is in the $(N + 1)/2$ place. If N is even, the median is the average of the $N/2$ and $N/2 + 1$ entries. It is not difficult to find the median of a list of numbers in an array which is in order. Use the insertion sort of the program in *FIGURE 7.7* (or another sort, if you know one) to put a sequence of numbers into an array in order and then find the median of the numbers.

11. The insertion sort program presented in this chapter puts entries in the array as they are read. Using the program of *FIGURE 7.7* as a guide, write a program which reads a sequence of integers into an array and then uses a modified version of the insertion sort to put the array (which is full) in order. Then print the ordered array. The modified insertion sort is analogous to picking up all the cards in a hand and then, moving from left to right, taking each card and inserting it in the correct place among the preceding cards. In terms of the program of *FIGURE 7.7*, this means that Item will be taken from the successive entries of List.

12. Write a program which eliminates the underscore (_ , ASCII character 95) from a string entered by a user. For example, Yards_To_Go should be changed to YardsToGo. This would be necessary to transfer a program from an implementation of Pascal (e.g., TURBO) which permits the underscore in an identifier to one which does not.

13. Write a program which centers the words in a string in a line of length 66. That is, there should be as many blank spaces to the left of the first nonblank character of the string as there are to the right of the last nonblank character of the string. (If there is an odd number of blanks to be put at the two ends, put an extra blank on the right.) From 1 to 15 lines are to be input and then output. For example, if a menu were entered, the following should be output.

```
                    TODAY'S MENU


                   Soup Du Jour

                      Salad

          Green Peas    Carrots

                       Ham

                    Apple Pie

           Coffee          Tea
```

14. Write a program which produces the transpose of a matrix. The transpose of a matrix is the matrix obtained by switching the rows and columns. The user is to enter the number of rows and columns and then the entries of the matrix one per line. Up to ten rows and ten columns are to be permitted. The original matrix and the transposed matrix should be displayed. Running the program should result in something like this.

```
Program to produce the transpose of a matrix

Enter the number of rows and columns > 2 3
Enter row 1 column 1 number >1
Enter row 1 column 2 number >2
Enter row 1 column 3 number >3
Enter row 2 column 1 number >4
Enter row 2 column 2 number >5
Enter row 2 column 3 number >6

Original Matrix
    1    2    3
    4    5    6

Transposed Matrix
    1    4
    2    5
    3    6
```

15. Write a program which prints the sum of two matrices. The sum of matrices is obtained by adding the corresponding entries of the matrices. For example,

```
Program to produce the sum of two matrices

Enter the number of rows and columns > 2 3

Enter first matrix
Enter row 1 column 1 number >1
Enter row 1 column 2 number >2
Enter row 1 column 3 number >3
Enter row 2 column 1 number >4
Enter row 2 column 2 number >5
Enter row 2 column 3 number >6

Enter second matrix
Enter row 1 column 1 number >11
Enter row 1 column 2 number >22
Enter row 1 column 3 number >33
Enter row 2 column 1 number >44
Enter row 2 column 2 number >55
Enter row 2 column 3 number >66

First matrix
    1    2    3
    4    5    6
```

```
Second matrix
  11   22   33
  44   55   66

Sum
  12   24   36
  48   60   72
```

16. Refer to the discussion of address functions which precedes the last exercise in Chapter 4. Use the appropriate functions or function to write a program which declares three arrays, each of ten elements, with base types char, integer, and real, and then prints the addresses of each array as well as the addresses of each of the components of the array. Do the same exercise with variables which you have declared to be of some enumerated type and with variables which are of subrange types.

INTRODUCTION

Early in the history of programming it was recognized that considerable benefits could be derived from isolating segments of code which were used over and over again. These pieces of programs were called *subroutines* or *subprograms*. One benefit was that less memory was needed to store the program, because the same piece of code only appeared once. This was very important when memory was at a premium. Another advantage was that if a subroutine was designed well it could be used in many different programs and thus save programmers' time. As a consequence, most (perhaps all) computer languages provided a mechanism for creating subprograms. In the era of structured programming, subroutines were recognized to have a third benefit. This was that using subroutines enabled programmers to break a large problem into smaller problems which would (hopefully) be easier to solve.

Pascal has two distinct kinds of subprograms: *procedures* and *functions*. Furthermore, both procedures and functions may be either predefined or user defined. We have already encountered a number of the predefined procedures (e.g., Read and Write) and functions (e.g., Trunc and Round). In this chapter, user-defined procedures and functions are introduced, and a number of aspects of using them are discussed. ❑

CHAPTER 8

SUBPROGRAMS

8.1 PROCEDURES

Roughly speaking, a Pascal *procedure* is a program within a program. The main difference between a program and a procedure is that a program runs within the operating system (or TURBO) environment, whereas a procedure must be run within the context of a program. Like a program, a procedure may contain declarations of constants, types, and variables as well as statements to be executed. In fact, a procedure may even contain procedures within itself. The declarations and statements within a procedure define the procedure. That is, the declarations and statements describe exactly what the procedure does when the program causes the procedure to be executed. This is known as *calling* or *invoking* the procedure.

It is also necessary to name the procedure. The name of the procedure is used within the program to invoke the procedure. For example, if we had defined a procedure to print ten blank lines and named it Put10BlankLines, we could have the following statement in our program.

```
    Put10BlankLines;
```

This procedure could be called more than once, as in the following few lines.

```
    Put10BlankLines;
    Writeln('TO ERR IS HUMAN');
    Put10BlankLines;
    Writeln('TO FORGIVE IS DIVINE');
    Put10BlankLines;
    Writeln(' - Alexander Pope ');
```

Usually it is necessary to supply some data to a procedure. A more useful procedure than Put10BlankLines would be one that printed a specified number of blank lines. If such a procedure were designed, the way to tell it how many blank lines to print would be to follow the procedure's name with the desired number enclosed in parentheses. We would then be able to modify the preceding example to have three blank lines between the lines of the quote and five after the quote in this way:

```
    PutBlankLines(10);
    Writeln('TO ERR IS HUMAN');
    PutBlankLines(3);
    Writeln('TO FORGIVE IS DIVINE');
    PutBlankLines(5);
    Writeln(' - Alexander Pope');
```

The 10 in the first call of PutBlankLines indicates that 10 is to be used in the procedure to control how many blank lines are to be printed. Similarly, the 5 in the third line is used to specify that five blank lines are to be printed. Of course, this presumes that PutBlankLines uses the number supplied to determine the number of blank lines to print.

We will later see that it is also possible for a procedure to return data to a program.

A *procedure call* or *invocation* forms another type of Pascal statement, the *procedure statement*. Thus Put10BlankLines and PutBlankLines(5) are both statements. When they appear in a sequence of statements, they must be separated from the next statement by a semicolon.

Before a procedure may be called, it must be defined. An example of a *procedure definition* (for PutBlankLines) appears in *FIGURE 8.1*. The first line is the procedure heading. In this line, the procedure is named (PutBlankLines) and the data that is to come from the invocation is named (NumOfBlankLines) along with its type (Integer). The remaining lines form the body of the procedure. A variable is declared (I), and some actions (statements) are specified.

> **A *procedure definition* is the block within the program (declarations and statements) which specifies the procedure's actions and a procedure heading. The procedure heading names the procedure and specifies how values are to be transmitted between the program and the procedure.**

DEFINITION

> **A *procedure call* or *invocation* occurs when a program causes the procedure to be executed or run.**

DEFINITION

A program may have any number of procedures and functions defined. The declarations of these occur after the variable declaration section of

FIGURE 8.1

```
PROCEDURE PutBlankLines(NumOfBlankLines : Integer);

{  This procedure prints a specifed number of blank lines. }

VAR
   I : Integer;  { Loop index }

BEGIN { PutBlankLines }
   FOR I := 1 TO NumOfBlankLines DO
      Writeln
END; { PutBlankLines }
```

the program and before the executable statements of the program. A *procedure declaration* consists of a procedure heading and a block. At this point, a relatively complete description of a program can be given, as well as its syntax diagram. A program consists of a program heading followed by a block and then a period. A block consists of declarations (constants, type, variables, and procedures and functions) and a statement section.

Because a procedure is very similar to a program, its description and syntax are similar to a program's. A procedure declaration consists of a procedure heading followed by a block and then a semicolon.

The syntax diagrams defining a program and procedure as described are presented in *FIGURE 8.2*. (These apply to both standard and TURBO Pascal.)

To place the use of a procedure in context, consider the program in *FIGURE 8.3*. This is a simple program which draws "squares" for the user. It includes one procedure, DrawASquare.

Within the procedure DrawASquare we have declared a constant (Symbol = ' * ') and a variable (I : Side). These declarations are available only within the procedure. This means that Symbol and I are not able to be used by the main program, SquareDrawer. The statements which actually draw the "square" follow these declarations. (When the "square" is printed it appears rectangular, because the space between the vertical characters is greater than that between the horizontal characters.)

The statements of the program itself are between Begin { SquareDrawer } and End. { SquareDrawer } . The user is asked for a size to be used in drawing the square. This number is read into the variable Size. After this is done the procedure DrawASquare is invoked.

When DrawASquare is invoked, the value contained in Size is transmitted to the variable N in the procedure heading. This is known as *passing a value*. DrawASquare then uses the value of N to draw the square. A variable (or value) supplied in a procedure call is known as a *parameter*. The variable or variables within the parentheses (if any) in

---

FIGURE 8.2   **Program and Procedure**

Program

$\longrightarrow$ **program-heading** $\longrightarrow$ **block** $\longrightarrow$. $\longrightarrow$

Program heading

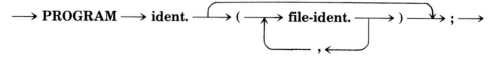

(continued)

Block

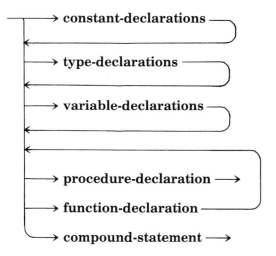

Procedure declaration

⟶ procedure-heading ⟶ block ⟶ ; ⟶

Procedure heading

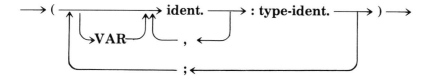

Parameter section

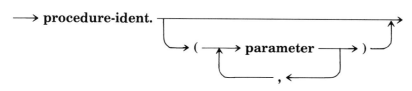

Procedure statement

the procedure heading are also known as parameters. There must be an exact correspondence between the parameters in the procedure call and the parameters in the procedure heading. Each parameter in the procedure call must match a parameter in the procedure heading of the same type. The parameters in the call and the heading are matched moving left to right. In *FIGURE 8.3* the procedure has only one parameter, N. Because the type of N is Side, the value passed to it must also be of type Side.

A sample of the result of running program SquareDrawer is also given in *FIGURE 8.3*. In this example the integers 5, 2, 1, 3, and 0 are read into Size and then passed to DrawASquare.

DEFINITION

> A *parameter* (or *argument*) is a variable or value used in performing a computation or executing a subprogram.

FIGURE 8.3

```
PROGRAM SquareDrawer ( Input, Output );

{   This is a program to illustrate the use of a procedure.   A
    user enters a number and a square of that size is drawn.

        Author    : John Riley
        Date      : April 15, 1986
        File name : CH8EX1.PAS
}

CONST
      MaxSide = 50;    { Side of largest square }

TYPE
      Side = 0..MaxSide;

VAR
      Size : Side;


PROCEDURE DrawASquare(N : Side);

{ This procedure draws a square of size N using a given symbol. }

CONST
      Symbol = '*';   { Character to form sides }

VAR
      I : Side;   { Loop index }

BEGIN { DrawASquare }
  Writeln;
```

(continued)

```
   FOR I := 1 TO N DO      { Form top side }
      Write(Symbol);
   Writeln;

   FOR I := 1 TO N - 2 DO                      { Form left & right }
      Writeln(Symbol, ' ' : N - 2, Symbol);   { sides             }

   FOR I := 1 TO N DO      { Form bottom side }
      Write(Symbol);
   Writeln;
   Writeln;
END; { DrawASquare }


BEGIN { SquareDrawer }
   Writeln('This program draws squares.');
   REPEAT
      Write('Enter the size of square, (0 to stop) >');
      Readln(Size);
      DrawASquare(Size)
   UNTIL Size = 0
END. { SquareDrawer }
```

Output:

```
This program draws squares.
Enter the size of square, (0 to stop) >5

*****
*   *
*   *
*   *
*****

Enter the size of square, (0 to stop) >2

**
**

Enter the size of square, (0 to stop) >1

*
*

Enter the size of square, (0 to stop) >3

***
* *
***

Enter the size of square, (0 to stop) >0
```

It is useful to be able to distinguish the parameters of the procedure call and those of the procedure itself. The following definitions do this.

DEFINITION

> An *actual* (or *calling*) *parameter* is a value or variable communicated to a subprogram when the subprogram is invoked. An actual parameter appears in the statement invoking a subprogram.

DEFINITION

> A *formal* (or *dummy*) *parameter* is a variable declared in a subprogram. A formal parameter is used in the execution of the subprogram and exists only while the subprogram is being executed. A formal parameter may receive a value from an actual parameter when the subprogram is invoked, or may transmit a value to an actual parameter when the subprogram terminates.

There are two distinct types of parameters that can be used to pass values between a procedure and a calling program. These are distinguished by the presence or absence of the key word VAR in the parameter section of the procedure heading. Any variables which are not preceded by VAR are known as *value parameters*. The parameter N in the program in *FIGURE 8.3* is a value parameter. Variables in the parameter section which are preceded by the key word VAR are known as *variable parameters*. As an example, consider the following procedure heading.

```
Procedure P (Var I, J : Integer; M, N : Integer;
             Var X, Y : Real; R1, R2, R3 : Real);
```

In this heading, I and J are variable parameters of type integer, and X and Y are variable parameters of type real. M and N are value parameters of type integer, whereas R1, R2, and R3 are value parameters of type real. Notice that VAR applies only to the list of parameters that immediately follow it. In the case above, VAR does not apply to M, N, R1, R2, or R3. There is a significant difference between using value and variable parameters.

When a value parameter is declared in a procedure heading, it denotes a new variable which can be used in the procedure. This variable receives its initial value from the value of the corresponding quantity in the procedure call. This is illustrated in *FIGURE 8.4*.

Because only a value is needed for a value parameter, any expression of the appropriate type may be used in the procedure call corresponding to a value parameter. For example, in the program in *FIGURE 8.3*, any of the following would be legal invocations of the procedure DrawASquare.

```
 |
 |
DrawASquare(7);
DrawASquare(7 + 2);
DrawASquare(2 * Size);
DrawASquare( (3 * Size) Mod 2 );
 |
 |
```

Parameters in the procedure heading which are preceded by VAR (variable parameters) become new names for the variables used in the procedure invocation. That is, within a procedure a variable parameter uses the same memory location as the corresponding variable in the procedure invocation. This implies that in a procedure invocation the parameter supplied to a variable parameter must be a variable. Any change made in the variable parameter in the procedure will affect the corresponding variable used in the procedure invocation.

As an illustration, consider the procedure in *FIGURE 8.5*. This procedure swaps or interchanges the values contained in two integer variables.

Suppose that M and N were integer variables of a program, containing the values 19 and 34, respectively. If the statement SwapIntegers(M, N) was executed, then after the procedure call M would have the value 34 and N would have the value 19. This occurs because during the procedure call I is another name for the variable M and J is another name for the variable N. This process is illustrated in *FIGURE 8.6*.

A short program which illustrates the difference between value and variable parameters is given in *FIGURE 8.7*, which also contains the output of the program. The two procedures in the program differ only in

| **Value Parameter Passing** | **FIGURE 8.4** |

```
 |
 |

VAR
    M : Integer;

 |
 |
 |

PROCEDURE P(I : Integer);
```

```
 |
 |
 |


 |

P(M)

 |
 |
```

FIGURE 8.5

```
PROCEDURE SwapIntegers(VAR I, J : Integer);

{  This procedure interchanges the values that I and J
   contain.  }

VAR
   Temp : Integer;   { Temporary storage }

BEGIN { SwapIntegers }
   Temp := I;
   I := J;
   J := Temp
END;  { SwapIntegers }
```

FIGURE 8.6

Variable Parameter Passing

Before the procedure call SwapIntegers(M, N)

19	34
M	N

At the start of the procedure invocation

19	34
M I	N J

At the end of the procedure invocation

34	19
M I	N J

After the procedure invocation

34	19
M	N

name and type of parameter. The first procedure uses a value parameter, the second a variable parameter. When the program is run, the first output statement prints the original value of M. M is then passed to the procedure AddTenValue. In this procedure, N is a new variable which is initially 7. N is changed to 17 (by adding 10), and the procedure terminates. The program resumes and prints the value of M, which is still 7. The procedure AddTenVariable is then invoked. Because N is a variable parameter, it becomes a new name for M and has the value 7. In the

FIGURE 8.7

```
PROGRAM ParameterExample(Output);

{ Program to illustrate the difference between value and
  variable parameters.

      Author :        John Riley
      Date :          January 1, 1986
      File name :     CH8EX2.PAS
}

VAR
     M : Integer;

PROCEDURE AddTenValue(N : Integer);

BEGIN { AddOneValue }
  N := N + 10
END;  { AddOneValue }

PROCEDURE AddTenVariable(VAR N : Integer);

BEGIN { AddTenVariable }
  N := N + 10
END;  { AddTenVariable }

BEGIN { ParameterExample }
  M := 7;
  Writeln('M is ', M);
  AddTenValue(M);
  Writeln('M is ', M);
  AddTenVariable(M);
  Writeln('M is ', M)
END.  { ParameterExample }


Output:

M is 7
M is 7
M is 17
```

procedure, 10 is added to N, and so N, and also M, become 17. The procedure ends and the program prints the value of M, which is now 17.

Value parameters may only pass data into a procedure. Variable parameters may pass data to, from, or to and from a procedure. Value parameters are new variables for the procedure's use, whereas variable parameters rename variables of the program.

In the program in *FIGURE 8.7*, the procedure AddTenValue used a value parameter to receive a value for the parameter N. This is an example of a value parameter being used to pass data into a procedure. The procedure AddTenVariable used a variable parameter to pass data in and out of the procedure. The program in *FIGURE 8.8* uses a variable parameter to pass data out of the procedure. The procedure is used to obtain

FIGURE 8.8

```
PROGRAM GetValues(Input, Output);

{ A short program to illustrate the use of a procedure to obtain
  values from the keyboard.

      Author  :      John Riley
      Date :         January 1, 1986
      File name :    CH8EX3.PAS
}

VAR
      M, N : Integer;


PROCEDURE GetInteger(Var Item : Integer);

{ This procedure obtains a value for Item from the keyboard. }

BEGIN { GetInteger }
  Write('Enter an integer >');
  Readln(Item)
END;   { GetInteger }

BEGIN { GetValues }
  GetInteger(M);
  GetInteger(N);
  Writeln('M is ', M, '  N is ', N)
END.   { GetValues }


Output:

Enter an integer >24
Enter an integer >36
M is 24  N is 36
```

integer values from the keyboard. An example of running this program is also included in *FIGURE 8.8*.

Both value and variable parameters may be used in the parameter section of a procedure. An example of using both variable and value parameters is given in the program in *FIGURE 8.9*. *FIGURE 8.9* also includes the output of this program.

In this program, four integer variables, I, J, K, and L, are declared and assigned values. Output statements are placed in the program and in the procedure within the program to indicate values of variables at various stages. The values of I, J, K, and L are displayed before and after each procedure call. Each time the procedure Change is called, the values of its parameters M and N are displayed as the procedure begins and ends.

Within the procedure we see that the values of M and N are affected similarly. However, the change in the parameter N is not reflected in the parameters (J and L) which correspond to N in the procedure call. Changes in M are transmitted to its corresponding parameters (I and K). This should give you an idea of the difference between value and variable parameters.

Here are some definitions which summarize the preceding discussion.

> A *variable parameter* is a formal parameter which refers to the same memory location as its corresponding actual parameter in the subprogram invocation.

DEFINITION

> A *value parameter* is a formal parameter which refers to a new memory location on the subprogram's invocation and which initializes that memory location with the value of the actual parameter.

DEFINITION

Here are some guidelines for using procedures.

Ideally, a procedure is designed to accomplish one task. It should be possible to describe the purpose of a procedure in one sentence. A brief description of the procedure should appear in a comment preceding or following the procedure heading. (Before or after is a matter of preference; however, some such comment is a necessity.) A procedure performs an action, and so the procedure's name should be a verb phrase. Just as the BEGIN and END of a program are commented with the program's name, the BEGIN and END of a procedure are labeled with a comment containing the procedure's name. In fact, one of the purposes of labeling these BEGIN and END pairs is to make it easier to distinguish the statement sections of procedures and the program.

Any variables which are used in the procedure which are not formal parameters should be declared as variables within the procedure. These

FIGURE 8.9

```
PROGRAM SecondParameterExample ( Input, Output );

{  This program illustrates the difference between value and
   variable parameters.

      Author :          John Riley
      Date :            April 15, 1986
      File name :       CH8EX4.PAS
}

VAR
    I, J, K, L : Integer;

PROCEDURE Change(VAR M : Integer; N : Integer);

{ A simple procedure to change the parameters. The values of
  the parameters are printed for purposes of illustration. }

BEGIN { Change }
  Writeln;
  Writeln('M = ', M:2, '   N = ', N:2);
  M := M + 7;
  N := N + 9;
  Writeln('M = ', M:2, '   N = ', N:2);
  Writeln
END; { Change }

BEGIN { SecondParameterExample }
  I := 10;
  J := 20;
  K := 30;
  L := 40;
  Writeln('I = ', I:2, '   J = ', J:2, '   K = ', K:2, '   L = ', L:2);
  Change(I, J);
  Writeln('I = ', I:2, '   J = ', J:2, '   K = ', K:2, '   L = ', L:2);
  Change(K, L);
  Writeln('I = ', I:2, '   J = ', J:2, '   K = ', K:2, '   L = ', L:2)
END. { SecondParameterExample }

Output :

I = 10   J = 20   K = 30   L = 40      (First Writeln of program)

M = 10   N = 20                        (Second Writeln of procedure)
M = 17   N = 29                        (Third Writeln of procedure)

I = 17   J = 20   K = 30   L = 40      (Second Writeln of program)

M = 30   N = 40                        (Second Writeln of procedure)
M = 37   N = 49                        (Third Writeln of procedure)

I = 17   J = 20   K = 37   L = 40      (Third Writeln of program)
```

variables are known as *local variables*. In some sense, formal parameters are also local variables.

Each formal parameter in the procedure heading has an associated type. This type must be given by an identifier. It cannot be constructed within the parameter section. The only predefined types that can be used in a parameter section thus are Boolean, byte (nonstandard), integer, real, and text (which has not been discussed at this point). STRING[ ] and ARRAY OF, as well as any enumerated type or subrange type, may not appear in a parameter section. For example, the following is not allowed.

```
PROCEDURE DoArrayOperation(A : ARRAY[1..10] OF Real);
                                  ^NOT ALLOWED
```

Other types that will be introduced may not occur here either. This does not mean that (for example) an array cannot be passed to a procedure. It means that a type must be declared in the type declaration section of the program and it must be used to declare the actual and formal parameters. For example, if we were storing a name in a string of length 20 and had a procedure Capitalize, we would make the following declarations.

```
CONST
     NameLen = 20;

TYPE
     NameType = STRING[NameLen];

VAR
     Name : NameType;


PROCEDURE Capitalize(VAR N : NameType);


Another approach would be to do the following.

TYPE
     String20 = STRING[20];


VAR
     Name : String20;


PROCEDURE CAPITALIZE(VAR S : String20);

```

This technique is used in the program in *FIGURE 8.10*, where the type to be passed is a string type. In this program, strings are entered and then have any lower-case letters changed to upper case. It is necessary to have defined a string type in order to use this procedure.

FIGURE 8.10

```
PROGRAM CapitalizeWords(Input, Output);

{ A program which reads a word, converts lower case letters to
  upper case and then outputs the word.

     Author :      John Riley
     Date :        January 1, 1986
     File name :   CH8EX5.PAS
}

CONST
     Stop      = '*';    { Ends input }
     StringLen = 20;

TYPE
     Word = STRING[StringLen];

VAR
     WordIn : Word;

PROCEDURE Capitalize(VAR W : Word);

{ This procedure changes the lower case letters in W to upper
  case.  It relies upon there being a constant difference
  between an upper and lower case version of a letter. }

VAR
     ConversionFactor,        { Used to hold difference between
                                upper and lower case          }
     I                : Integer; { Loop index }

BEGIN { Capitalize }
  ConversionFactor := Ord('A') - Ord('a');
  FOR I := 1 TO Length(W) DO
     IF  ('a'  <=  W[I]) AND (W[I] <=  'z')  THEN        { Replace l.c. }
         W[I]   :=  Chr(Ord(W[I])  + ConversionFactor) { letter        }

END; { Capitalize }

BEGIN { CapitalizeWords }
  Writeln('This program converts small letters to capitals.');
  Writeln('Enter words to be converted, one per line.');
  Writeln('Enter ', Stop, ' to end.');
  Write('Enter word >');
  Readln(WordIn);
  WHILE WordIn <> Stop DO
     BEGIN
       Capitalize(WordIn);
       Writeln('Word in capitals >', WordIn);
       Write('Enter word (', Stop,  ' to end) >');
       Readln(WordIn)
     END { WHILE }
END.  { CapitalizeWords }
```

(continued)

```
Output:

This program converts small letters to capitals.
Enter words to be converted, one per line.
Enter * to end.
Enter word >apple
Word in capitals >APPLE
Enter word (* to end) >Pear
Word in capitals >PEAR
Enter word (* to end) >1 banana
Word in capitals >1 BANANA
Enter word (* to end) >*
```

Having to declare types should not be considered an inconvenience. Declaring the types that are used in the program is a good programming practice which helps ensure the correctness of the program.

A value parameter has the advantage that a change made in a value parameter within a procedure does not affect the corresponding actual parameter. This is exactly what one wants when a procedure only uses the actual parameter to initialize a local variable. This means that a formal parameter which is a value parameter can be used without worrying about affecting the program itself. Unfortunately, this is not without cost. Each time a procedure with a value parameter is invoked, a new variable is created and assigned. Thus storage in memory is used, and a copying of the value of the actual parameter takes place. (When the procedure finishes executing, the memory used for the value parameter is reclaimed.) If a program is causing memory problems or is running very slowly, using variable parameters in place of value parameters may help. This should be done reluctantly, because a program becomes less secure if variable parameters are used for the purpose of passing data into a procedure. In this situation the programmer must make certain that the procedure does not inadvertently alter values which are to be the same before and after the procedure's invocation.

Procedures are almost essential in dealing with structured data types such as arrays. By using procedures it is possible to isolate distinct tasks within a program. By doing this, a programmer can concentrate on one task at a time, solving the problem within a procedure. Furthermore, by putting the solution within a procedure it is possible to ensure that the solving of one part of the program does not interfere with another part of the program. In fact, it is possible (and sometimes desirable) to have different programmers work on different procedures of the program and not have their procedures interfere.

The program in *FIGURE 8.11* returns the matrix sum of two matrices the user has entered. (A matrix is a two-dimensional array. The sum of two matrices is obtained by adding their corresponding entries.) The program contains three procedures. Procedure DisplayMatrix prints a ma-

FIGURE 8.11

```
PROGRAM MatrixAdder ( Input, Output );

{  This program adds two matrices.

        Author    : John Riley
        Date      : April 16, 1986
        File name : CH8EX6.PAS
}

{$R+}   { Turn on range checking. }

CONST
    NumOfRows = 4;
    NumOfCols = 3;

TYPE
    RowIndex = 1..NumOfRows;
    ColIndex = 1..NumOfCols;
    Matrix   = ARRAY[RowIndex, ColIndex] OF Integer;

VAR
    In1, In2,              { Two input matrices        }
    Sum      : Matrix; { Matrix sum of In1 and In2 }


PROCEDURE DisplayMatrix(M : Matrix);

{ This procedure outputs the matrix M to the screen. }

VAR
    I : RowIndex;
    J : ColIndex;

BEGIN { DisplayMatrix }
  FOR I := 1 to NumOfRows DO
     BEGIN
       FOR J := 1 to NumOfCols DO
          Write(M[I, J] : 4, ' ');
       Writeln
     END; { FOR I }
  Writeln
END;   { DisplayMatrix }


PROCEDURE GetMatrix(VAR M : Matrix);

{ This procedure obtains the matrix M from the keyboard. }

VAR
    I : RowIndex;
    J : ColIndex;
```

(continued)

```
BEGIN { GetMatrix }
  Writeln('Enter the numbers of the matrix');
  FOR I := 1 to NumOfRows DO
      BEGIN
        Writeln('Row number ', I);
        FOR J := 1 to NumOfCols DO
           BEGIN
             Write('      Entry ', J ,'>');
             Readln(M[I, J])
           END { FOR J }
     END; { FOR I }
  Writeln;
  Writeln('Matrix entered');
  Writeln;
  DisplayMatrix(M)
END;  { GetMatrix }


PROCEDURE AddMatrices(M1, M2 : Matrix; VAR Sum : Matrix);

{ This procedure does a matrix addition putting the sum of M1
  and M2 in Sum. }

VAR
   I : RowIndex;
   J : ColIndex;

BEGIN { AddMatrices }
  FOR I := 1 to NumOfRows DO
     FOR J := 1 to NumOfCols DO
        Sum[I, J] := M1[I, J] + M2[I, J]
END;  { AddMatrices }


BEGIN { MatrixAdder }
  GetMatrix(In1);
  GetMatrix(In2);
  AddMatrices(In1, In2, Sum);
  Writeln;
  Writeln('Matrix sum ');
  Writeln;
  DisplayMatrix(Sum)
END. { MatrixAdder }


Output:

Enter the numbers of the matrix
Row number 1
      Entry 1>1
      Entry 2>2
      Entry 3>3
```

(continued)

```
Row number 2
        Entry 1>4
        Entry 2>5
        Entry 3>6
Row number 3
        Entry 1>7
        Entry 2>8
        Entry 3>9
Row number 4
        Entry 1>10
        Entry 2>11
        Entry 3>12

Matrix entered

     1     2     3
     4     5     6
     7     8     9
    10    11    12


Enter the numbers of the matrix
Row number 1
        Entry 1>10
        Entry 2>20
        Entry 3>30
Row number 2
        Entry 1>40
        Entry 2>50
        Entry 3>60
Row number 3
        Entry 1>70
        Entry 2>80
        Entry 3>90
Row number 4
        Entry 1>100
        Entry 2>110
        Entry 3>120

Matrix entered

    10    20    30
    40    50    60
    70    80    90
   100   110   120


Matrix sum

    11    22    33
    44    55    66
    77    88    99
   110   121   132
```

trix. GetMatrix is a procedure which prompts the user for the entries of a matrix. After the matrix has been entered, GetMatrix uses DisplayMatrix to show the user the values that have been input. The last procedure, AddMatrices, puts the matrix sum of the parameters M1 and M2 in Sum. In this procedure, M1 and M2 should only be used as sources for values and not have their contents changed. The body of the program is rather short. There are only seven statements in the program itself. (The compiler directive {$R+} is not considered a statement.) Each of these statements is a procedure invocation. Three of the procedures called are user defined and the fourth (Writeln) is predefined. This is typical of most programs. The main body of the program consists mostly of procedure statements. This is because a hard problem or task becomes more manageable when it is broken into subproblems or subtasks.

The program in *FIGURE 8.11* illustrates another capability of Pascal. A procedure may invoke another procedure. In *FIGURE 8.11*, the procedure GetMatrix uses the procedure DisplayMatrix to echo the input. One procedure can invoke another procedure under the following circumstances. Procedure A can invoke procedure B if B is declared (or defined) before A (in the program) and B is not contained within another procedure. Procedure A may also invoke procedure B if procedure B is a subprocedure of A. That is, B is defined within the block of A. (Incidentally, not all languages have this capability. This can make programming more difficult.) For example, with the arrangement of the program in *FIGURE 8.11*, DisplayMatrix cannot invoke either GetMatrix or AddMatrices. On the other hand, AddMatrices may invoke both DisplayMatrix and GetMatrix. If DisplayMatrix contained a procedure, that procedure would not be available to GetMatrix, AddMatrices, or the main program. User-defined identifiers generally obey these rules. We will return to this subject later in this chapter.

FIGURE 8.11 also contains a sample run of the program.

8.2 FUNCTIONS

A user-defined *function* obeys many of the same rules as a user-defined procedure. The essential difference between a function and a procedure is that a procedure's purpose is to perform some action whereas a function is used to produce a value which may be used in an expression. For example, we could design either a procedure or a function to compute the cube of a number. Suppose the procedure to do this was named CubeProc and the function was named Cube. Then if X were a real variable which needed to be assigned the cube of 5, we would write either

```
CubeProc(5, X);   { Use a procedure }
```

or

```
X := Cube(5);    { Use a function }
```

This difference is reflected in the differences in the definition and use of functions.

The name of the function used in an expression invokes the function and returns the value of the function. A function designation may appear in an expression any place a variable may appear. The syntax of a function declaration is contained in *FIGURE 8.12*. Function declarations occur in the same place as procedure declarations within a block, and function and procedure declarations may be intermixed. This is indicated by the syntax diagram of a block in *FIGURE 8.2*.

A *function declaration* consists of a function heading followed by a block and a semicolon. The function heading consists of the key word FUNC-TION followed by an identifier which becomes the function's name. These are followed by an optional parameter section which is the same as that of a procedure. The function heading is completed by a colon, a type identifier, and a semicolon. The type identifier at the end of the function heading specifies the type of the value that will be returned by the func-

FIGURE 8.12   Function Declaration

$\longrightarrow$ function-heading $\longrightarrow$ block $\longrightarrow$; $\longrightarrow$

Function heading

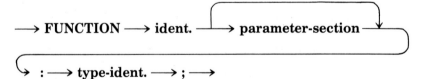

Parameter section

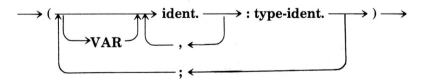

tion and is known as the *result type*. Here is an example of a function heading.

```
FUNCTION Logarithm(N : Integer) : Real;
```

In this example the name of the function is Logarithm. The function has one parameter, N. The result type of the function is Real.

The result type must be Boolean, integer, real, char, a declared enumerated or subrange type, a declared string type, or a declared pointer type (which hasn't been discussed yet). The ability to use a string type for the result type is nonstandard. As in the parameter section, the result type must be given by an identifier which must be among the types just mentioned. For example, STRING[80] would not be permitted here. Declaring String80 = STRING[80] in the type section of the program would enable String80 to be used as the result type for a function.

The identifier which follows the key word FUNCTION in the function heading is used in two places. In the program or subprogram which contains the function declaration, the identifier may be used in an expression to cause the function to return a value (of the result type) to the expression. The identifier must be followed by appropriate actual parameters. The identifier is also used within the block defining the function as a variable which is to contain the value that is to be returned to the expression which invokes the function. Ordinarily, the identifier appears only on the left side of an assignment statement within the function's block.

These concepts are illustrated in the program in *FIGURE 8.13*. This is a simple program which produces a table of integers and their cubes. The function Cube is defined in this program to return the cube of the parameter which is passed to it. Cube is invoked in the output statement. Notice that when it is invoked, an appropriate parameter must be supplied. In this case, this means an integer. Within the block defining the function, Cube is used to hold the value of N * N * N. Within the function, the identifier Cube is used as a variable and does not have any parameters.

With the function Cube defined as in the program and with J and K assumed to be integer variables, we could use Cube as follows.

```
K := 5;
J := Cube(8 * K);
K := 2 * Cube(3 * (4 + J));
J := Cube(9) + 3 * Cube(7);
K := Cube(Cube(2));
IF Cube(J) = 27 THEN
    K := K + 1;
```

In contrast to procedures, which perform actions, functions are used to compute values. To reflect this, the name of a function should be a

FIGURE 8.13

```
PROGRAM TableOfCubes (Output);

{  A program to produce a table of integers and their cubes

      Author    : John Riley
      Date      : April 18, 1986
      File name : CH8EX7.PAS
}

CONST
   NumOfCubes = 15;   { Number of cubes to be printed }

VAR
   I : Integer;        { Loop index }


FUNCTION Cube(N : Integer) : Integer;

{ This function returns the cube of the parameter N.
  Both N and Cube are integers.
}

BEGIN { Cube }
  Cube := N * N * N
END;  { Cube }


BEGIN { TableOfCubes }
  Writeln('Number      Cube');
  FOR I := 1 TO NumOfCubes DO
     Writeln(I : 5, ' ' : 4, Cube(I) : 6);
  Writeln
END. { TableOfCubes }


Output:

Number      Cube
    1         1
    2         8
    3        27
    4        64
    5       125
    6       216
    7       343
    8       512
    9       729
   10      1000
   11      1331
   12      1728
   13      2197
   14      2744
   15      3375
```

FIGURE 8.14

```
PROGRAM MonthlyInterest ( Input, Output );

{  This program provides the user with the future balance of a
   principal amount earning an annual interest rate which is
   compounded monthly for a given number of months.

      Author   : John Riley
      Date     : April 19, 1986
      File name: CH8EX8.PAS
}

CONST
    MonthsInYear = 12;

VAR
    Principal,          { Amount invested                    }
    FutureValue,        { Value of investment at end         }
    Rate,               { Annual interest rate               }
    MonRate             { Monthly rate                       }
                        { Rates in decimal, not percent }
            : Real;
    Months              { Time of investment (months)        }
            : Integer;


FUNCTION Power( Base : Real; Exponent : Integer ) : Real;

{ This function returns the number Base raised to the Power. }

VAR
   I : Integer;       { Loop index }
   Prod : Real;       { Accumulates product }

BEGIN { Power }
  IF Base = 0 THEN
     IF Exponent > 0 THEN
        Power := 0
     ELSE
        BEGIN
          Writeln;
          Writeln('0 cannot be raised to nonpositive power.');
          Writeln('result set to 1');
          Power := 1
        END { ELSE }
  ELSE
     BEGIN
       Prod := 1;
       I := 0;
       WHILE I < Abs( Exponent ) DO
          BEGIN
            I := I + 1;
            Prod := Prod * Base
          END; { WHILE }
```

(continued)

```
            IF Exponent >= 0 THEN
                Power := Prod
            ELSE
                Power := 1=Prod
        END { ELSE }
    END; { Power }


BEGIN { MonthlyInterest }
    Writeln('This program computes the value of an investment');
    Writeln('which earns an annual interest rate, compounded ');
    Writeln('monthly, for a certain number of months.');
    Write('Enter the amount to be invested (0 to quit) >');
    Readln(Principal);
    WHILE Principal <> 0 DO
        BEGIN
            Write('Enter annual rate (as a decimal) >');
            Readln(Rate);
            MonRate := Rate / MonthsInYear;
            Write('Enter number of months invested >');
            Readln(Months);
            FutureValue := Principal * Power(1 + MonRate, Months);
            Writeln('Value will be $', FutureValue : 10 : 2);
            Writeln;
            Write('Enter the amount to be invested (0 to quit) >');
            Readln(Principal)
        END { WHILE }
END. { MonthlyInterest }


Output:

This program computes the value of an investment
which earns an annual interest rate, compounded
monthly, for a certain number of months.
Enter the amount to be invested (0 to quit) >100
Enter annual rate (as a decimal) >.10
Enter number of months invested >18
Value will be $    116.11

Enter the amount to be invested (0 to quit) >900
Enter annual rate (as a decimal) >.18
Enter number of months invested >36
Value will be $   1538.23

Enter the amount to be invested (0 to quit) >0
```

noun phrase indicating what the function computes. A function should not modify the value of any parameter passed to it. This means that value parameters are much more appropriate for functions than variable parameters.

Functions are useful whenever you need to have a value computed and when including the actual computation would obscure the program. The program in *FIGURE 8.13* does not illustrate this very well, because it is very easy to compute the cube of a number. Our next example makes this point more clearly.

The program in *FIGURE 8.14* allows the user to enter an amount to be invested (the principal), the time (in months) it is to be invested, and the annual rate of interest earned on the investment. The program then calculates the value of the investment at the end, taking the compound period to be one month. A sample run of this program follows the program. To do this (as well as many other financial applications) it is necessary to be able to find the result of raising a number to a power. This is done by the function Power of the program.

The function Power of this program has been written rather carefully because it has been used in other programs. (In fact, this is not the original use of this function.) By using the block commands of the editor it is possible to read a portion of code from a file and write a portion to a file. As you might imagine, this can save you some time. Thus it is wise to design functions so that they can be reused.

It is not possible for a base of 0 to be passed to the function Power in this program. (Why?) However, a test for 0 is included so that if this function were used in another program this error would be noticed and an appropriate message would be displayed. (It is not possible to raise 0 to a negative power.)

8.3 SCOPE AND LOCAL AND GLOBAL IDENTIFIERS

Pascal requires that each symbol or identifier that is used in a program be either predefined or defined within the program. Most of the characters which are not letters or digits have special meanings. For example, = is used only for comparisons. Some two-character combinations also have this property. The combination := always denotes the assignment operator. These symbols and combinations can be used only in the way which the language prescribes. A small number of identifiers also have the property that they can have only the meanings given by their definitions within the language. These identifiers are known as *reserved words* and include most of the key words that appear in the syntax diagrams. Pascal also designates another group of identifiers which are predefined but which programmers can redefine if they wish to do so. These are known as *standard identifiers*. The reserved words and standard identifiers of TURBO Pascal are collected in Appendix F. Any identifier which is not a reserved word or a standard identifier must be defined by the programmer within the program.

The meanings of identifiers are defined by the programmer in the declaration section of a block. There may be many different blocks within a program, and each may have a declaration section. The declaration section of a block is used to designate the identifiers that are to be available for use within the block. The declaration section establishes the meanings of identifiers within the block. For example, the following makes I the name of a variable which contains an integer.

```
VAR I : Integer;
```

Every identifier which is not a reserved word or standard identifier must be declared in some block. This defines exactly where the identifier may be used as declared. Where an identifier may be used is called the *scope* of the identifier. The rules which specify exactly what the scope of an identifier is are known as *scope rules* and are the subject of this section.

As an illustration, consider the program outline below.

```
PROGRAM A(Input, Output);

VAR
    I : Integer;

PROCEDURE B;

VAR
    J : Integer;

BEGIN { B }
    { Statements of Procedure B }
END; { B }

BEGIN { A }
    { Statements of Program A }
END.  { A }
```

The variable J may be used in the statements of Procedure B. J may not be used in the statements of Program A. The scope of J is the block of Procedure B. The variable I may be used in the statements of Program A and Procedure B. The scope of I is the blocks of A and B.

DEFINITION

> **The *scope* of an identifier is the set of blocks in which it may be used as defined.**

The Pascal rule for the scope of an identifier is as follows. The scope of an identifier is the block in which it is declared except for blocks within the original block where the identifier is redeclared. To clarify this, consider the program outline in *FIGURE 8.15* and the table in *FIGURE 8.16*.

There are four procedures (subprograms) in the program outline in *FIGURE 8.15*. Procedures P1 and P2 are declared within the block of Prog, and procedures P11 and P12 are nested within procedure P1. That

Scope of Variables

FIGURE 8.15

```
PROGRAM Prog;

VAR
   X, Y, Z : Integer;

PROCEDURE P1;  { Declared in the block of Prog }

VAR
   A, X : Real;

   PROCEDURE P11;  { Declared in the block of P1 }

   VAR

     A, B, Y : Char;

   BEGIN { P11 }
     { Statements of P11: A, B, Y character variables
                          X       real variable
                          Z       integer variable }
   END;  { P11 }

   PROCEDURE P12;  { Declared in the block of P1 }

   VAR
     C, Y : Boolean;

   BEGIN { P12 }
     { Statements of P12: C, Y  Boolean variables
                          A, X  real variables
                          Z     integer variable }
   END;  { P12 }

BEGIN { P1 }
  { Statements of P1: A, X real variables
                      Y, Z integer variables }
END;  { P1 }

PROCEDURE P2; { Declared in the block of Prog }

VAR
   D, X, Y, Z : String[10];


BEGIN { P2 }
  { Statements of P2: D, X, Y, Z string variables }
END;  { P2 }

BEGIN { Prog }
  { Statements of Prog: X, Y, Z integer variables }
END.  { Prog }
```

FIGURE 8.16   Scope of Variables

Program or subprogram	Variables (with types) that may be used	Where declared
Prog	X, Y, Z : Integer	Prog
P1	Y, Z : Integer	Prog
	A, X : Real	P1
P11	Z : Integer	Prog
	X : Real	P1
	A, B, Y : Char	P11
P12	Z : Integer	Prog
	A, X : Real	P1
	C, Y : Boolean	P12
P2	D, X, Y, Z : STRING[10]	P2

is, P11 and P12 are declared within P1. The table in *FIGURE 8.16* indicates which variables are able to be used within each of the procedures and the main program. In the statements of procedure P1, for example, the integer variables Y and Z of the main program may be used as well as the real variables A and X declared in the block defining P1. Notice that when X is used in P1 it refers to the real variable declared within the procedure and not to the integer variable declared in the program. This is an instance of a general rule. When an identifier is used, it refers to its most recent declaration or the nearest block in which it is declared. Within P1 the character variables A, B, and Y of P11, the Boolean variables C and Y of P12, and the string variables D, X, Y, and Z of P2 are not available, because none of these is declared in a block containing P1.

Because procedure P11 is nested within P1 and Prog, any identifiers of P1 and Prog which are not declared within P11 may be used within P11. These are the integer variable Z of Prog and the real variable X of P1. Because A and Y are declared in P11, the variable A of P1 and the variable Y of Prog are not available for use within P11. Within P11 there are two choices for the meaning of X. One of these is the integer variable of Prog and the other is the real variable of P1. How does the compiler decide which X is meant when X is used within P11? It follows the nearest (or innermost or most recent) block rule. In this case the nearest block in which X is declared is the block of P1, and thus when X appears in P11 it means the real variable X of P1. You should study the table in *FIGURE 8.16* and make sure you understand exactly why the variables listed in the middle column occur as they do.

Variables are sometimes classified by where they are declared. Variables declared in the declaration section of the program are called *global variables* and others are called *local variables*. Sometimes these terms are modified to *relatively global* and *relatively local* when a particular procedure is being discussed.

A *global variable* is a variable declared in an outer block.   **DEFINITION**

A *local variable* is a variable declared in a subprogram (procedure or function) block.   **DEFINITION**

Global variables declared in the program exist during the entire time a program is running. Local variables exist only when the subprogram in which they are declared is executing. Each time a subprogram is invoked, the local variables of its defining block are created again. This means that these variables are uninitialized whenever the subprogram is invoked. It also means that local variables cannot be used to retain information from subprogram invocation to subprogram invocation. Local variables should be thought of as auxiliary. Global variables contain information that the entire program must access.

The scope rules we have been discussing apply to all user-defined identifiers, not just to variable identifiers. They pertain to constant, type, procedure, and function definitions. So an identifier may be used to denote a variable in one block, a type in another, and a function in a third. As a rule of thumb, constants and types tend to be declared for an entire program, whereas variables, functions, and procedures are declared at many different levels.

It is important to note that procedures and functions are declared in a block which determines where they may be invoked. Referring to the program of *FIGURE 8.15*, the following procedure calls would be possible. Within the main program Prog, P1 and P2 may be invoked. In the body of P1, the nested procedures P11 and P12 may be invoked as well as the procedure P1 itself. Procedure P11 may include the invocation of itself and P1. Procedure P12 may have calls to P1, P11, and P12. Recall the rule that an identifier may be used if it has been defined. Because the declaration of P12 follows that of P11, P12 is able to invoke P11. The statements of procedure P2 may invoke P1 and P2. Within P2, P11 and P12 are not available, because they are not declared in the same block as P2.

The formal parameters that are declared in a function or procedure heading may be considered to be variables that are to be used in the subprogram. Of course, these variables have the additional task of communicating with the calling program or subprogram. It is not clear from our discussion thus far what the scope of a formal parameter is. The parameter section of a procedure or function heading may be considered to belong to the declaration section of the block defining the subprogram.

FIGURE 8.17

```
PROGRAM Sneaky (Input, Output);

{ This program illustrates how a procedure may change a
  variable's value.  That is, a side effect occurs.

      Author    : John Riley
      Date      : April 22, 1986
      File name : CH8EX9.PAS
}

VAR
   I, J, K : Integer;


PROCEDURE Oops(M : Integer);

VAR
   I : Integer;

BEGIN { Oops }
  Writeln('OOPS');
  FOR I := 1 to M DO
     BEGIN
       J := 2 * I;
        Writeln(I : 3, J : 3)
     END { FOR }
END;   { Oops }


BEGIN  { Sneaky }
  I := 2;
  J := 3;
  K := 4;
  Writeln('I = ', I, '  J = ', J, '  K = ', K);
  Oops(K);
  Writeln('I = ', I, '  J = ', J, '  K = ', K)
END.   { Sneaky }


Output:

I = 2  J = 3  K = 4
OOPS
  1  2
  2  4
  3  6
  4  8
I = 2  J = 8  K = 4
```

Thus the formal parameters may be used within, but not outside, the subprogram.

It is important to understand the scope rules concerning variables so as to avoid what are known as *side effects*. A side effect is the changing of a value of a variable which is not evident from the parameter list. The program in *FIGURE 8.17* contains a side effect. The output of the program shows that the procedure Oops has changed the value of J. A programmer would not expect this, because J was not passed to the procedure. I is not affected, because I is declared to be a local variable within Oops. By examining the procedure heading we would be able to determine that K would be unchanged after the procedure had executed. (Why?) This illustrates the problem of side effects. The cause of a side effect is buried within a procedure, and it may be very difficult to find exactly what statement is causing the side effect. This becomes a very serious problem when a program contains a large number of subprograms any of which could cause the side effect.

8.4   USING PROCEDURES AND FUNCTIONS

In this section we give some guidelines for making good use of procedures and functions. Some techniques for working with procedures and functions are also developed. Some of these ideas have already been introduced in our discussion of subprograms.

When should you use a subprogram? You should use a subprogram whenever you can isolate a task to be done within a program. If you find the body of a program getting very long (more than a page or two), you should be using subprograms. The most important advantage of doing this is that you will never have to keep too much in mind. A subprogram will allow you to focus on one task at a time and suppress details whenever you need to.

A function should be used if the subprogram is to return a value (which can only be one of the following types: Boolean, integer, real, char, enumerated, subrange, string, pointer). If an action is to be carried out, then a procedure should be written.

There are many tasks in programming which arise again and again. For example, the problem of sorting an array into some order occurs frequently. The effort and care of designing procedures and functions that can be used again in other programs will pay off in the long run. You can build a library of subprograms which will aid greatly in writing programs. We will tend to write general-purpose subprograms as procedures and functions.

The conventions of using the extension PRO for files which contain procedures and FUN for the extension of files which contain functions are convenient. For example, the procedure in *FIGURE 8.18* is contained in the file named ARRAYORD.PRO. The editing command which reads a disk file into the file being edited (CTRL/K CTRL/R) is very useful for

FIGURE 8.18

```
PROCEDURE GetArrayInOrder ( VAR A : ArrayType;
                            VAR Size : ArrayRange );

{ This procedure obtains an array A from the keyboard
  putting it into order.  Size returns the actual
  number of elements stored in A.  The types ArrayType,
  ArrayRange, and ArrayElement are defined in the calling
  program.  An insertion sort is used.  The constant Stop
  is used to signal the end of the input.

  Author    : John Riley
  Date      : March 4, 1986
  File name : ARRAYORD.PRO
}

VAR
   Item    : ArrayElement;
   I, Pos  : ArrayRange;


BEGIN { GetArrayInOrder }
  Size := 0;
  Writeln( 'Enter the elements of the array, one per line.');
  Writeln( 'End with ', Stop);
  Write( 'Enter item >' );
  Readln( Item );
  WHILE Item <> Stop DO
     BEGIN
       Pos= 1;
       WHILE ( Pos < Size ) AND ( Item > A[ Pos ] ) DO
          Pos := Pos + 1;
       IF ( Pos = Size ) AND ( Item > A[ Pos ] ) THEN
          BEGIN
             Size := Size + 1;
             A[ Size ] := Item
          END { IF }
       ELSE
          BEGIN
             FOR I := Size DOWNTO Pos DO
                A[ I + 1 ] := A[ I ];
             A[ Pos ] := Item;
             Size := Size + 1
          END; { Else }
       Readln( Item )
     END { While }
END; { GetArrayInOrder }
```

reading a subprogram into a program. When CTRL/K CTRL/R is typed in the editor, a prompt appears asking for the name of the file to be read. When the file name is entered, that file will be placed in the position of the cursor. By using this command it is easy to incorporate previously written subprograms into a program.

Another method of incorporating a file containing a procedure or function into a program is to use the *include directive*. The include directive begins with {$I, followed by the name of the file to be included, and ends with }. This directive must appear on a line by itself. To include the procedure in *FIGURE 8.18*, the compiler directive

```
{$I ARRAYORD.PRO}
```

would appear in the program. This feature of TURBO is available in other implementations of Pascal. An advantage of using the include directive is that it takes up little room in the program file. A disadvantage is that the code for the procedure or function is not visible in the program.

Designing a procedure so that it can be used in a wide variety of programs requires some care. It is wise to document very carefully how the procedure is to be used and what types of variables may be passed to it. By using appropriate names for the types of variables being passed and used in the procedure, you can make inclusion of the procedure fairly easy. This is the place where the ability to rename types and identifiers is very convenient.

In the procedure in *FIGURE 8.18*, the types ArrayType, ArrayElement, and ArrayRange must be defined in the calling program. The constant Stop must also be defined there. These are most conveniently defined in terms of types which have been declared in the main program. We are not assuming anything about the elements of the array other than that they can be read from the keyboard and can be compared (using <). Because the constant Stop must be of a type comparable to values of ArrayElement, Stop may be a character, a string, or a number. For the purposes of the procedure, this does not matter. *FIGURE 8.19* contains a program which has incorporated the procedure of *FIGURE 8.18*.

After developing a procedure such as the one in *FIGURE 8.18*, it is a good idea to test it in a short program. This is the purpose of the program in *FIGURE 8.19*, which puts a list of words in order. The procedure GetArrayInOrder was copied into this program using the editing command discussed above.

Notice that in the program we must define the types used in the procedure GetArrayInOrder. This is done very easily by simply setting the type identifiers of the procedure equal to the type identifiers used by the program.

The body of the program is very short. It consists of invoking the procedure GetArrayInOrder, skipping a line of output, and then printing the list. When the program is run, we find that the list of words is in order,

FIGURE 8.19

```
PROGRAM TestGetArrayInOrder ( Input, Output );

{  This program tests the procedure GetArrayInOrder.  The
   list to be kept in order consists of words.

       Author    : John Riley
       Date      : April 22, 1986
       File name : CH8EX10.PAS
}

{$R+}   { Turn on range checking. }

CONST
   WordLen = 20;
   ListLen = 30;
   Stop    = '!';

TYPE
   Word       = STRING[WordLen];
   Index      = 1..ListLen;
   ListType   = ARRAY[Index] of Word;
   ArrayType    = ListType;          { Three declarations }
   ArrayRange   = 0..ListLen;        { needed for          }
   ArrayElement = Word;              { GetArrayInOrder     }

VAR
   List : ListType;
   Size : 0..ListLen;
   I    : Index;


PROCEDURE GetArrayInOrder ( VAR A : ArrayType;
                            VAR Size : ArrayRange );

{ This procedure obtains an array A from the keyboard
  putting it into order.  Size returns the actual
  number of elements stored in A.  The types ArrayType,
  ArrayRange, and ArrayElement are defined in the calling
  program.  An insertion sort is used.  The constant Stop
  is used to signal the end of the input.

  Written by John Riley
  On March 4, 1986
  File name : ARRAYORD.PRO
}

VAR
   Item    : ArrayElement;
   I, Pos  : ArrayRange;
```

(continued)

```
BEGIN { GetArrayInOrder }
   Size := 0;
   Writeln( 'Enter the elements of the array, one per line.');
   Writeln( 'End with ', Stop);
   Write( 'Enter item >' );
   Readln( Item );
   WHILE Item <> Stop DO
      BEGIN
         Pos := 1;
         WHILE ( Pos < Size ) AND ( Item > A[ Pos ] ) DO
            Pos := Pos + 1;
         IF ( Pos = Size ) AND ( Item > A[ Pos ] ) THEN
            BEGIN
               Size := Size + 1;
               A[ Size ] := Item
            END { IF }
         ELSE
            BEGIN
               FOR I := Size DOWNTO Pos DO
                  A[ I + 1 ] := A[ I ];
               A[ Pos ] := Item;
               Size := Size + 1
            END; { ELSE }
         Write('Enter item >');
         Readln( Item )
      END { WHILE }
END; { GetArrayInOrder }


BEGIN { TestGetArrayInOrder }
   GetArrayInOrder(List, Size);
   Writeln;
   FOR I := 1 TO Size DO
      Writeln(List[I])
END. { TestGetArrayInOrder }
```

Output:

```
Enter the elements of the array, one per line.
End with !
Enter item >BREAD
Enter item >MILK
Enter item >APPLE
Enter item >STEAK
Enter item >PEAR
Enter item >CEREAL
Enter item >!

APPLE
BREAD
CEREAL
MILK
PEAR
STEAK
```

which seems to indicate that the procedure works. This does not prove that the procedure works: no amount of testing can do that. But testing can often point out oversights. More important than testing and correcting is design. Sometimes programmers attempt to construct programs by trial and error, the extreme case of testing and correcting. This is not really programming. Programmers know what their programs are doing and what they are supposed to do.

We conclude this section with another example of how procedures may be used to decompose a problem into smaller problems. An instructor wishes to assign pass or fail marks on the following basis. Any student whose numerical grade is 15 points or more below the class average is to receive a failing grade. All other students pass. The instructor wants a program which takes students' names and numerical grades and produces a list of student names and whether they passed or failed.

To begin solving this problem, we break it into four steps:

1. Get student names and grades

2. Calculate the class average

3. Assign student pass or fail

4. Print the list of student names and pass or fail

We next decide, because we are working with lists, to use three parallel arrays—one for the students' names, one for their grades, and one to record pass or fail. We also notice that we will need to keep track of how many students are in the class. These decisions allow us to add some detail to the outline above.

1. Get student names and grades
   —Return the lists of names and grades and the number of students

2. Calculate the class average
   —Use the list of grades and number of students and produce the class average

3. Assign student pass or fail
   —Use the list of grades and the average and the number of students to record pass or fail for each student

4. Print the list of student names and pass or fail
   —Use the lists of names and pass or fail and the number of students to print student's names and pass or fail

This information is sufficient to write a preliminary version of our program. This program appears in *FIGURE 8.20*. A test for the possibility that no students were entered has been added. The program is complete except for the procedures. In fact, this program will compile and run. Of course, it doesn't do anything when run, but at least we know that what we have written so far is correct. The writing of the subprograms is left as an exercise.

FIGURE 8.20

```
PROGRAM PassOrFail(Input, Output);

{ This program takes lists of student names and numerical grades
  and assigns pass or fail on the following basis.  Students with
  grades 15 or more points below the class average fail. The
  remaining students pass.

      Author :     John Riley
      Date :       April 30, 1986
      File name :  CH8EX11.PAS
}

{$R+}        { Turn on range checking. }

CONST
    MaxSize = 40;     { Maximum size of class }
    NameSize = 20;    { 20 characters for a name }

TYPE
    ClassSize  = 0..MaxSize;
    Names      = STRING[NameSize];
    NameArray  = ARRAY[1..MaxSize] OF Names;
    GradeArray = ARRAY[1..MaxSize] OF Integer;
    CharArray  = ARRAY[1..MaxSize] OF Char;

VAR
    StuName  : NameArray;    { Holds students' names          }
    Grades   : GradeArray;   { Holds students' grades         }
    PassFail : CharArray;    { Holds P (pass) or F (fail)     }
                             { THREE PARALLEL ARRAYS          }
    NumOfStu : ClassSize;    { Number of students in class }
    Ave      : Real;         { Class average                  }


PROCEDURE GetLists(VAR Names : NameArray;
                   VAR Grades : GradeArray;
                   VAR NumEntered : ClassSize);

{ This procedure obtains names and grades from keyboard.
  The number of names and grades entered is recorded. }

BEGIN { GetLists }

END;  { GetLists }


FUNCTION Average(Grades : GradeArray;
                 NumOfGrades : ClassSize) : Real;

{ This function computes the average of the grades in Grades. }

BEGIN { Average }

END; { Average }
```

                                                        (continued)

```
PROCEDURE AssignPOrF(Grades : GradeArray;
                     NumOfGrades : ClassSize;
                     Average : Real;
                     VAR POrF : CharArray);

{  This procedure assigns F or P to the array POrF depending
   upon whether Grades are 15 points below Average or not.
}

BEGIN { AssignPOrF }

END; { AssignPOrF }


PROCEDURE PrintLists(Name : NameArray; POrF : CharArray;
                     NumToPrint : ClassSize);

{ This procedure prints the lists of Name and POrF. }

BEGIN { PrintLists }

END; { PrintLists }


BEGIN { PassOrFail }
  GetLists(StuName, Grades, NumOfStu);
  IF NumOfStu <> 0 THEN
     BEGIN
       Ave := Average(Grades, NumOfStu);
       AssignPOrF(Grades, NumOfStu, Ave, PassFail);
       PrintLists(StuName, PassFail, NumOfStu)
     END  { IF }
  ELSE
     Writeln('No students processed.')
END.  { PassOrFail }
```

8.5 SUMMARY

Using subprograms to develop programs is very important. Pascal has two types of subprograms: procedures and functions. A procedure is used to do some task within the program. A procedure is invoked by using its name (and supplying any necessary parameters) as a statement in the program. A function is used to produce a value. A function is invoked by using the function's name (and supplying values) in an expression.

Parameters serve to pass data between a subprogram and the calling program (or subprogram). There are two ways of passing parameters in Pascal. Value parameters create a new variable within the subprogram whose initial value is given by the calling parameter. A value parameter can be used only to pass a value into a subprogram. A variable parameter is denoted by the key word VAR preceding the parameter in the parameter section. A variable parameter renames the calling parameter, which must be a variable. A variable parameter can be used to receive or transmit (and possibly both) data between the subprogram and the calling program (or subprogram).

Within a subprogram, declarations may be made. Where a variable (or other identifier) is declared determines which subprograms may use the variable. The rules which govern where a declared identifier may be used are known as scope rules.

In the next chapter we develop a larger program. In order for us to do this, subprograms are a necessity. ☐

EXERCISES

1. Explain the output of the program in *FIGURE 8.3* when 0 and 1 are input for Size.

2. Generally speaking, the actual parameter and formal parameter of a procedure or function must be of the same type. When variable parameters are used, this is obviously necessary, because the actual and formal parameters (which are both variables) refer to the same area of memory. However, when a variable parameter is used, the actual parameter may be an expression (of which a variable is a particular case) which passes a value to the formal parameter. In this situation it would make sense to assign an integer value from the actual parameter to a real formal parameter, just as it is possible to assign an integer value to a real variable. Find out if it is possible to pass an integer value to a real variable when a value parameter is used.

3. Give the output of the following program.

```
PROGRAM Ch8Num3(Output);

VAR
     I, J : Integer;

PROCEDURE Change(M : Integer; VAR N : Integer);

BEGIN { Change }
   M := N + 2;
   N := M + 3
END;   { Change }

BEGIN { Ch8Num3 }
   I := 5;
   J := 6;
   Change(I, J);
   Writeln(I, ' ', J);
   Change(J, I);
   Writeln(I, ' ', J)
END. { Ch8Num3 }
```

4. What is the purpose of the following procedure? (That is, what does the procedure do to its parameters?)

```
PROCEDURE OrderIntegers(VAR I, J : Integer);

    PROCEDURE Swap(VAR M, N : Integer);

    VAR
        Temp : Integer;

    BEGIN { Swap }
      Temp := M;
      M := N;
      N := Temp
    END;   { Swap }

BEGIN { OrderIntegers }
  IF J > I THEN
      Swap(I, J)
END;   { OrderIntegers }
```

5. Find the errors in the following program fragments.

a.
```
VAR
        C : Char;

PROCEDURE P(I : Integer);


BEGIN { P }

END;   { P }

BEGIN { Main Program }

  P(C);

END.  { Main Program }
```

b.
```
PROCEDURE ArrayOp(VAR A : ARRAY[1..10] OF Real);

```

c.
```
PROCEDURE P(VAR I : Integer);


BEGIN { P }

END    { P }

BEGIN { Main Program }

  P(7);

END.  { Main Program }
```

d.
```
TYPE
    RealMatrix = ARRAY[1..10, 1..10] OF Real;

VAR
    A, B : RealMatrix;


FUNCTION Inverse(M : RealMatrix) : RealMatrix;


BEGIN { Inverse }

END;   { Inverse }



BEGIN { Main Program }

  B := Inverse(A);

END.   { Main Program }
```

6. Modify the program in *FIGURE 8.14* by adding a function which converts years (possibly with a decimal part) into a whole number (integer) of months. Then, instead of being asked for the number of months, the user enters the number of years. For example, if the user entered 1.25 as the number of years, this would be converted to 15 months, and 15 would be used in calculating the future value. When the value 1.1 is passed to the function you have written, is 13 or 14 returned? To whose advantage (the investor's or the borrower's) does your function work?

7. Modify the program in *FIGURE 8.14* to compute the future value of the investment if the compound period is changed to a day. For financial purposes, a year contains 360 days. The daily interest rate is the annual rate divided by the number of days in a year. The power that is used in compounding is then the number of days. You may have the user enter the number of days of the investment or the number of years of the investment.

8. This exercise finishes the program in *FIGURE 8.20*. For each of the following subprograms you are to write the body of the subprogram (local declarations and statement section) and incorporate the subprogram into the program. Use the subprogram headings of *FIGURE 8.20*. Do each of these individually. When you are finished, you should have a working program.

```
a.    PROCEDURE GetLists
b.    FUNCTION Average
c.    PROCEDURE AssignPOrF
d.    PROCEDURE PrintLists
```

9. Write a Pascal procedure which searches an array (list) for a specified item. The input parameters are the array, the item to be found, and the number of entries in the array which are to be searched. The procedure should return a parameter which is the position of the item if it is in the list and 0 if the item is not in the list. Test your procedure in a program which reads a list of words from the keyboard and then requests items from the keyboard and returns the position of the item in the list.

10. Write a function which takes as input a list (array) and a number of items of the array to be searched (starting with the first element of the array). The function is to return the item in the list which is first in numerical or alphabetical order. Test your program with a list of integers.

11. Write a procedure which has one parameter, a square matrix (a two-dimensional array with the same number of rows and columns), and which interchanges the rows and columns of the matrix. (This is known as finding the transpose of the matrix.) Test your procedure with a four-by-four matrix. Here is an example.

```
Before :   1    2    3    4      After :   1    5    9   13
           5    6    7    8                2    6   10   14
           9   10   11   12                3    7   11   15
          13   14   15   16                4    8   12   16
```

12. Write a program which accepts a list of words and then prints the words in two columns (right justified). For example, if the list of words entered was HISTORY, ENGLISH, GEOGRAPHY, FRENCH, MATHEMATICS, ART, MUSIC, the output would be

```
      HISTORY              ENGLISH
    GEOGRAPHY               FRENCH
  MATHEMATICS                  ART
        MUSIC
```

Your program should use two procedures, one to accept the list of words and the other to output the lists.

13. Modify the program of Exercise 12 so that the columns appear left justified. That is, the output would look like this:

```
HISTORY              ENGLISH
GEOGRAPHY            FRENCH
MATHEMATICS          ART
MUSIC
```

You might want to add a subprocedure to do the left justification.

14. Modify the program of Exercise 12 so that when the list is output in two columns the first half of the list is in the left column and the second half in the right column. If the list of words entered was HIS-

TORY, ENGLISH, GEOGRAPHY, FRENCH, MATHEMATICS, ART, MUSIC, the output would be

```
HISTORY          MATHEMATICS
ENGLISH          ART
GEOGRAPHY        MUSIC
FRENCH
```

15. Use the address functions discussed at the end of Chapter 4 to discover the locations of variables declared within a procedure. Compare these addresses with the addresses of variables declared in the main program. Also compare the addresses of actual and formal parameters that are passed by value and variable.

Up to this point, the programs we have presented have not been too lengthy. In this chapter, a longer program is developed. To do programming of this sort we need adequate control structures (sequencing, looping, selection, and the capability for subprograms); some data types and structures (constants of various sorts, strings, and arrays); and some predefined procedures and functions (particularly input and output). You should know the Pascal forms of these. There are other features of Pascal which would be useful in this discussion and in the program we will be writing. However, in developing a significant program we will review the constructs that have been introduced and show how they may be used in a larger program.

In this chapter we discuss some general considerations in program design. These considerations are aspects of the philosophy of programming known as *structured programming*. We then illustrate them with the actual construction of a program which is longer than those we have dealt with so far. It should be noted that this is not a long program by commercial standards. One definition of a large program is one that has more than 64,000 lines of source code. ❏

CHAPTER 9

PROGRAMMING METHODOLOGY

Case Study I

9.1   TOP-DOWN DESIGN

The phrase "*writing* a computer program" is our nominee for the most accurate description of any activity related to computing. Recall that the purpose of a program is the communication of an algorithm. Writing a program is like writing anything else: it requires planning and design.

If we were attempting to write a lengthy work such as a book, we would begin by outlining the book. This might be done by listing the chapters. We would make a brief note as to what each chapter was to cover. Then we would divide each chapter into a number of sections. At this point we might be able to write a section. In a large work it might be necessary to further divide the sections into subsections. In any case, we would keep breaking the problem of writing the book into smaller and smaller segments until we had segments which were small and concise enough to write easily. This makes the task of writing the book intellectually manageable. It would be impossible to concentrate on an entire book at once.

Similar considerations apply to the construction of programs. It is necessary to break a large programming task into smaller pieces which can be dealt with separately. This is known as *top-down design*. When doing top-down design we break the program into smaller and smaller logical units which can then be tackled independently. We continue this process of stepwise refinement until the pieces are small enough to code.

DEFINITION

> *Top-down design* **is the method of designing a program which proceeds from general to specific program requirements.**

The alternative to top-down design is *bottom-up design*, in which parts of the program are coded in detail and then fitted together. The obvious disadvantage of this method is that it is not easy to predict the exact specifications of each piece without a blueprint of the entire program. If there were standard pieces of program which could be fitted together in a predictable way, a combination of top-down and bottom-up design could be practiced. This is akin to an architect using standard and widely available materials in the design of a building. However, it seems that software is much more difficult to design and that, although standard procedures exist, integrating them is still very much a problem. In our attempt to define general-purpose subprograms, we are providing, for ourselves at least, standard subprograms to use in this fashion. This does not eliminate the need for top-down design, but it sometimes eliminates coding of essentially the same thing over and over again.

There are several advantages to top-down design. It decomposes a program into pieces which may be assigned to different individuals for programming. It delays making decisions about details which may be difficult to amend. At an early stage it is possible to discern the form of the program and make whatever adjustments are necessary. This includes the possibility of having the program requestor review the work to see if the program is functioning along the lines he or she desired.

Large programs must be designed. You must learn to resist the temptation to sit down at a computer or terminal and start coding. Initially this looks as if it will save you time, but in the long run it will cause you to spend more time on your programs. Write down what you are going to do. This is hard work! In particular, it means that at each step of your program you know what that step is doing and the reason for that step. If you can explain to somebody else what your program is doing at each and every step, then you understand your program. This is not as easy as it sounds.

Pascal permits you to document the way in which you have decomposed the programming task. Procedures should be chosen to accomplish the various subtasks of the program. Procedures, in turn, may contain procedures to further divide the problem. We will use procedures to do this in the case studies we present.

9.2 MODULES

Top-down design involves the decomposition of the program into smaller parts. These smaller parts are often referred to as *modules*. Modules are often implemented as subprograms, but the term "module" has connotations that "subprogram" does not. In this section we discuss desirable characteristics of modules. The use of well-designed modules leads to the construction of programs which are more likely to be correct and easier to maintain and modify.

> The *interface* of two components of a computer system is the place where, or means by which, the two components communicate or pass information from one to the other.

DEFINITION

> A *module* is a part of a software system (usually a program or subprogram) which has a specific task and a well-defined interface with the rest of the system.

DEFINITION

Ideally, a module functions as a black box. This has two implications. The user of the module does not need to have any idea of how the module works but must be able to depend on the module to produce the correct output from correct input. On the other hand, the designer or builder of the module knows only what the input is and what the output should be. The designer of the module does not need to know anything else about the use of the module.

To achieve this it is essential that each module have a specific and unambiguous task. This task may be broken into smaller subtasks to be accomplished by submodules. It should be possible to state what a module does in one or two sentences.

It is also necessary to specify exactly what information or data is being passed to the module (input) and what information or data the module is to produce (output or results). This is the module's interface and usually is achieved by using parameters. A module may not have any input or output parameters. A parameter may also be used for both input and output. For example, a sorting module may have as input an array and its length and as output the same array but with its components in order. Finally, the number of parameters of a module should not be too large. A large number of parameters indicates that the module has many tasks and is intellectually cumbersome. If you have ten parameters for a module, you probably have forgotten some others.

Modules are implemented in Pascal by using procedures and functions. The procedure or function heading serves as a specification of the interface. This specification includes not only the parameter list but also the name of the procedure or function and, in the case of the function, the type of the result as well. To make the subprogram a black box, local variables must be used. These are declared in the block which defines the subprogram. These features of Pascal enable us to construct procedures and functions which are modular.

9.3   CASE STUDY I

In this section we illustrate top-down design using modules to actually construct a program. This is not entirely representative of the problems encountered in constructing software. For one thing, the program is being written by one person, not by a team. Also, the program is shorter than a commercial program. However, this program should give you an idea of how programs actually evolve using the principles discussed in Sections 9.1 and 9.2.

An instructor wants a program which will compute the grades of a class. She would like to enter each student's name and scores of three tests and receive the following results. First, a list, in alphabetical order, containing each student's name, three test scores, average of the three test scores, and the letter grade based on the average of the tests. She would also like the high score, low score, and average of each test. She wants to know the number of As, Bs, Cs, Ds, and Fs assigned. Finally, the high, low, and average of the students' averages are to be found.

After thinking about the problem a bit we return to the instructor and ask the following questions. What is the maximum number of students in the class? What should be done about erroneous input? Are the test scores in the range 0 to 100? What average earns an A, a B, etc.? Exactly what is meant by alphabetical order? Some of these questions are answered easily; others require a little more discussion.

The instructor gives us three quick replies. There are no more than 30 students in the class. Test scores should be in the 0 to 100 range. Grades are assigned as follows. Any average from 90 to 100 (inclusive) earns an A, from 80 to 89.99 a B, from 70 to 79.99 a C, from 60 to 69.99 a D, and less than 60 an F.

Our question about alphabetical order perplexes the instructor. We ask whether this means by students' last names and find out that this is what she meant. We then ask if she will be entering the names last name first. Fortunately, she will be.

We point out that it is very easy to input 1000 instead of 100 and that doing so will greatly inflate a grade. For this reason, we and the instructor agree to the following with regard to erroneous data. Any test grade that is not in the 0 to 100 range is to be flagged with a double asterisk (**), and that student's average is not to be computed. Instead of an average and grade, ERROR is to appear. Also, the erroneous test score is not to be used in finding the high, low, and average scores for that test. A student with an error is not to be counted in the over-all averaging process. At this point the instructor makes an additional request. She would like to have a count of the students whose grades were completed and a count of those whose grades could not be completed due to incorrect grades.

At this point we think we have enough information to begin solving the problem. We begin by outlining the program as in *FIGURE 9.1*.

We refine this by listing the subtasks of each of the three parts. This refinement is shown in *FIGURE 9.2*.

We can continue to refine this outline if we wish, but here we think it is worthwhile to begin the actual construction of our program. Our first version of the program is presented in *FIGURE 9.3*. Notice that a one-sentence description of the program appears in the first line of the comment following the heading.

We attempted to compile this program without expecting any problems. After all, the program at this point is very short. The compiler gave us this message:

```
Error 5: ')' expected.   Press <ESC>_
```

| **Program Grader — Compute the Grades of One Class** | **FIGURE 9.1** |

1. Get the names and tests of the students
2. Find each student's grade
3. Do the class summary

FIGURE 9.2   **Program Grader — Compute the Grades of One Class**

1. Get the names and tests of the students
   1. Get the names and tests
   2. Put them in order
2. Find each student's grade
   1. Find the average of the tests
   2. Assign a grade
   3. Print the results
3. Do the class summary
   1. Summarize each test
   2. Total number of letter grades
   3. Summarize the student averages

Inadvertently we put a brace where a parenthesis should have been. (Did you notice this in the program?) The moral of this is that everyone needs to build programs step by step. The corrected program appears in *FIGURE 9.4*.

After we corrected this error we compiled and ran the program again, this time successfully. The output consisted of the three messages contained in the procedures, in the order we expected.

```
GetStudentData called.
DoStudentGrade
SummarizeClass called
```

We will leave these messages in the program for a while. They tell us how the program is running. Whether or not a procedure is invoked becomes obvious. The order in which the procedures are invoked is apparent.

In the process of developing the program it is necessary to supply some statements in a procedure which has not been finished. Such a procedure (or its code) is known as a *stub*. A stub does very little. It simply lets the procedure be invoked so that the rest of the program may be used. If values must be supplied by the stub, they may be assigned directly. For example, if the procedure was supposed to calculate pay, the value 100.00 might be assigned to the appropriate variable.

You may wonder whether doing this little bit is worthwhile. It probably is, because at this point we know that part of the final program is working correctly. If you try to do a large program all at once, chances are that you will have many errors. Trying to correct a large number of errors is very difficult and time-consuming, not to mention frustrating. This is true of both syntax errors and logic errors. Furthermore, by doing it in this way we never have to leave a half-finished version and later try to continue programming it in the middle of the program.

FIGURE 9.3

```
Grader(Input, Output);

{ This program does the grading of one class.  This includes
  assigning a letter grade on the basis of three tests and a
  summary of the class grades.  Erroneous test grades are flagged
  and not included.

     Author     : John Riley
     Date begun : May 3, 1986
     Date done  :
     File name  : CH9EX1.PAS
}

PROCEDURE GetStudentData;

{ This  procedure obtains the class data (names and grades)  and
  puts them in order. }

BEGIN { GetStudentData }
  Writeln('GetStudentData called.')
END;  { GetStudentData }

PROCEDURE DoStudentGrade;

{ This procedure does each student's grade .}

BEGIN { DoStudentGrade }
  Writeln('DoStudentGrade'}
END;  { DoStudentGrade }

PROCEDURE SummarizeClass;

{ This procedure summarizes the results of the class. }

BEGIN { SummarizeClass }
  Writeln('SummarizeClass called')
END;  { SummarizeClass }


BEGIN  { Grader }
  GetStudentData;
  DoStudentGrade;
  SummarizeClass
END.   { Grader }
```

Our next step in working on this program is to start to consider how the procedures are going to communicate with each other. This means figuring out the data each module needs and what data it is supposed to return. It also entails deciding how to represent the data that the program will be manipulating.

FIGURE 9.4

```
PROGRAM Grader(Input, Output);

{ This program does the grading of one class.  This includes
  assigning a letter grade on the basis of three tests and a
  summary of the class grades.  Erroneous test grades are flagged
  and not included.

      Author     : John Riley
      Date begun : May 3, 1986
      Date done  :
      File name  : CH9EX1A.PAS
}

PROCEDURE GetStudentData;

{ This procedure obtains the class data (names and grades) and
  puts them in order. }

BEGIN { GetStudentData }
  Writeln('GetStudentData called.')
END;   { GetStudentData }

PROCEDURE DoStudentGrade;

{ This procedure does each student's grade .}

BEGIN { DoStudentGrade }
  Writeln('DoStudentGrade')
END;   { DoStudentGrade }

PROCEDURE SummarizeClass;

{ This procedure summarizes the results of the class. }

BEGIN { SummarizeClass }
  Writeln('SummarizeClass called')
END;   { SummarizeClass }


BEGIN  { Grader }
  GetStudentData;
  DoStudentGrade;
  SummarizeClass
END.    { Grader }
```

We start by returning to our previous outline and adding what each module needs and supplies. This is given in *FIGURE 9.5*.

After looking at this outline we decide that we need lists for the students' names, test grades, letter grades, and averages. These are naturally done by using parallel arrays. Because there are to be at most 30

FIGURE 9.5

Program Grader —Compute the Grades of One Class

1. Get the names and tests of the student
   —No input to the module
   —Returns the lists of names and test grades
      1. Get the names and tests
      2. Put them in order

2. Find each student's grade
   —Receives the names and test grades
   —Returns the letter grades and averages
      1. Find the average of the tests
      2. Assign a grade
      3. Print the results

3. Do the class summary
   —Receives the test grades, letter grades and averages
   —Returns nothing
      1. Summarize each test
      2. Total number of letter grades
      3. Summarize the student averages

students in the class, this determines the size of the arrays. We now proceed to add these declarations and parameters to the program. The revised program is shown in *FIGURE 9.6*. If you read the program you will notice that the declarations contain a bit more than was mentioned above. For example, a reasonable length (20) was chosen for the size of the students' names. We also decided to store the test grades in a two-dimensional array. The way the indices are given for this array makes it possible to refer to the array of one student's test scores but not the scores on one test for the entire class. Finally we decided the types of letters we will be using in the array of grades. Notice that we have annotated any declaration that might be unclear.

Once again, when we ran the revised program we obtained an error message:

```
Error 36 : Type identifier expected.   Press <ESC>_
```

When we pressed the ESCAPE key the cursor was positioned at the beginning of GradesList in the parameter section of SummarizeClass. Checking the type section of the program, we notice that we have inserted an extra "s" into the identifier GradeList. Correcting this, we obtain a program which compiles and runs. This program is given in *FIGURE 9.7*. At this point we know that the parameters are being passed correctly (in

FIGURE 9.6

```
PROGRAM Grader(Input, Output);

{ This program does the grading of one class.  This includes
  assigning a letter grade on the basis of three tests and a
  summary of the class grades.  Erroneous test grades are flagged
  and not included.

      Author     : John Riley
      Date begun : May 3, 1986
      Date done  :
      File name  : CH9EX2.PAS
}

{$R+}      { Turn on range checking. }

CONST

   MaxClassSize  = 30;
   NameLen       = 20;
   NumOfTests    = 3;

TYPE
   NameType     = STRING[NameLen];
   StuNameList  = ARRAY[1..MaxClassSize] OF NameType;
   StuTests     = ARRAY[1..NumOfTests] OF Integer; { A student's
                                                     test grades }
   TestList     = ARRAY[1..MaxClassSize] OF StuTests;

   Entries      = 'A'..'I';   { A, B, C, D, F legal grades, I is
                                 incomplete, E, G, H unused. }

   GradeList    = ARRAY[1..MaxClassSize] OF Entries;
   AverageList  = ARRAY[1..MaxClassSize] OF Real;

VAR
   Names    : StuNameList; { List of students' names        }
   Tests    : TestList;    { List of students' test scores  }
   Grades   : GradeList;   { List of letter grades          }
   Averages : AverageList; { List of students' averages     }


PROCEDURE GetStudentData(VAR Names : StuNameList;
                         VAR Tests  : TestList);

{ This procedure obtains the class data (names and grades) and
  puts them in order. }

BEGIN { GetStudentData }
  Writeln('GetStudentData called.')
END;   { GetStudentData }


PROCEDURE DoStudentGrade(VAR Names : StuNameList;
                         VAR Tests : TestList;
                         VAR Grades : GradeList;
                         VAR Averages : AverageList);
```

(continued)

```
{ This procedure does each student's grade .}

BEGIN { DoStudentGrade }
  Writeln('DoStudentGrade')
END;  { DoStudentGrade }


PROCEDURE SummarizeClass(VAR Tests : TestList;
                         VAR Grades : GradesList;
                         VAR Averages : AverageList);


{ This procedure summarizes the results of the class. }

BEGIN { SummarizeClass }
  Writeln('SummarizeClass called')
END;  { SummarizeClass }


BEGIN  { Grader }
  GetStudentData(Names, Tests);
  DoStudentGrade(Names, Tests, Grades, Averages);
  SummarizeClass(Tests, Grades, Averages)
END.   { Grader }
```

FIGURE 9.7

```
PROGRAM Grader(Input, Output);

{ This program does the grading of one class.  This includes
  assigning a letter grade on the basis of three tests and a
  summary of the class grades.  Erroneous test grades are flagged
  and not included.

     Author     : John Riley
     Date begun : May 3, 1986
     Date done  :
     File name  : CH9EX2A.PAS
}

{$R+}      { Turn on range checking. }

CONST
   MaxClassSize  = 30;
   NameLen       = 20;
   NumOfTests    = 3;

TYPE
  NameType     = STRING[NameLen];
  StuNameList  = ARRAY[1..MaxClassSize] OF NameType;
  StuTests     = ARRAY[1..NumOfTests] OF Integer; { A student's
                                                    test grades }
```
(continued)

```
TestList     = ARRAY[1..MaxClassSize] OF StuTests;
Entries      = 'A'..'I';   { A, B, C, D, F legal grades, I is
                             incomplete, E, G, H unused. }

GradeList    = ARRAY[1..MaxClassSize] OF Entries;
AverageList  = ARRAY[1..MaxClassSize] OF Real;

VAR
   Names    : StuNameList; { List of students' names        }
   Tests    : TestList;    { List of students' test scores  }
   Grades   : GradeList;   { List of letter grades          }
   Averages : AverageList; { List of students' averages     }



PROCEDURE GetStudentData(VAR Names : StuNameList;
                         VAR Tests : TestList);

{ This procedure obtains the class data (names and grades) and
  puts them in order. }

BEGIN { GetStudentData }
  Writeln('GetStudentData called.')
END;  { GetStudentData }


PROCEDURE DoStudentGrade(VAR Names : StuNameList;
                         VAR Tests : TestList;
                         VAR Grades : GradeList;
                         VAR Averages : AverageList);

{ This procedure does each student's grade .}

BEGIN { DoStudentGrade }
  Writeln('DoStudentGrade')
END;  { DoStudentGrade }


PROCEDURE SummarizeClass(VAR Tests : TestList;
                         VAR Grades : GradeList;
                         VAR Averages : AverageList);

{ This procedure summarizes the results of the class. }

BEGIN { SummarizeClass }
  Writeln('SummarizeClass called')
END;  { SummarizeClass }


BEGIN  { Grader }
  GetStudentData(Names, Tests);
  DoStudentGrade(Names, Tests, Grades, Averages);
  SummarizeClass(Tests, Grades, Averages)
END.   { Grader }
```

the right order, with the right types) and that the procedures are being called in the correct order.

This shows the necessity of having the compiler check our work and then correcting the typographical errors which arise. From now on, only major revisions will be included and not those which are only typographical in nature. You are not to assume that we do not make any mistakes as we proceed. You can assume that we have used the compiler to help detect minor errors.

We continue developing the program by inserting the necessary procedures, one at a time. We start with GetStudentData. Because we already have written a procedure for getting an array in order (the insertion sort), we use it as an outline for the procedure we are working on. As soon as we look at the insertion sort procedure, we realize that another program variable is needed: the number of students entered. This new variable is added to the program and to all the parameter lists as it is needed by all the procedures.

All of the procedures in this program have arrays as parameters. For reasons of efficiency, arrays will be passed as VAR parameters. This means that we must take care not to modify the arrays that are passed when they should not be modified.

The program in *FIGURE 9.8* compiles and runs. When it runs, it accepts the names and grades that we entered and stops properly. But we

FIGURE 9.8

```
PROGRAM Grader(Input, Output);

{ This program does the grading of one class.  This includes
  assigning a letter grade on the basis of three tests and a
  summary of the class grades.  Erroneous test grades are flagged
  and not included.

      Author     : John Riley
      Date begun : May 3, 1986
      Date done  :
      File name  : CH9EX3.PAS
}

{$R+}      { Turn on range checking. }

CONST
   MaxClassSize  = 30;
   NameLen       = 20;
   NumOfTests    = 3;

TYPE
   NameType     = STRING[NameLen];
   StuNameList  = ARRAY[1..MaxClassSize] OF NameType;
   StuTests     = ARRAY[1..NumOfTests] OF Integer; { A student's
                                           test grades }
                                      (continued)
```

```
TestList      = ARRAY[1..MaxClassSize] OF StuTests;
Entries       = 'A'..'I';    { A, B, C, D, F legal grades, I is
                               incomplete, E, G, H unused. }

GradeList     = ARRAY[1..MaxClassSize] OF Entries;
AverageList   = ARRAY[1..MaxClassSize] OF Real;
ClassSizeRange = 0..MaxClassSize;

VAR
  Names    : StuNameList;      { List of students' names      }
  Tests    : TestList;         { List of students' test scores }
  Grades   : GradeList;        { List of letter grades        }
  Averages : AverageList;      { List of students' averages   }
  NumOfStu : ClassSizeRange;   { Number of students in class  }


PROCEDURE GetStudentData(VAR Names : StuNameList;
                         VAR Tests  : TestList;
                         VAR NumOfStu : ClassSizeRange);

{ This procedure obtains the class data (names and grades) and
  puts them in order.  An insertion sort is used.    }

CONST
  Stop = '!';   { Character to signal end of input }


VAR
  NameIn : NameType;   { Name read in  }
  TestIn : StuTests;   { Tests read in }
  I, J,                { Loop indices  }
  Pos    : Integer;    { Holds position for name to be
                         inserted }

BEGIN { GetStudentData }
  Writeln('GetStudentData called.');

  NumOfStu := 0;
  Writeln('Enter a student''s name, followed by his or');
  Writeln('her test grades, names and grades one per line');
  Writeln('End by entering ', Stop, 'for name');
  Write('Enter Student Name >' );
  Readln(NameIn);
  WHILE (NameIn[1] <> Stop) AND (NumOfStu < MaxClassSize) DO
     BEGIN
       FOR J := 1 TO NumOfTests DO
          BEGIN
            Write('Enter test ', J : 1, ' >');
            Readln(TestIn[J])
          END; { FOR }

       Pos := 1;
       WHILE ( Pos < NumOfStu ) AND ( NameIn > Names[Pos] ) DO
                     { Find position of NameIn }
          Pos := Pos + 1;
```

(continued)

```
        IF ( Pos = NumOfStu ) AND ( NameIn > Names[Pos] ) THEN
                    { Insert NameIn and Tests at end of list }
          BEGIN
            NumOfStu := NumOfStu + 1;
            Names[NumOfStu] := NameIn;
            Tests[NumOfStu] := TestIn
          END { IF }
        ELSE    { Insert NameIn and Tests into position }
          BEGIN
            FOR I := NumOfStu DOWNTO Pos DO
              BEGIN    { Shift items out of the way }
                Names[I + 1] := Names[I];
                Tests[I + 1] := Tests[I]
              END; { FOR }
            Names[Pos] := NameIn;
            Tests[Pos] := TestIn;
            NumOfStu := NumOfStu + 1
          END; { ELSE }
        Write('Enter Student Name >');
        Readln(NameIn)
      END   { WHILE }
END;   { GetStudentData }



PROCEDURE DoStudentGrade(VAR Names : StuNameList;
                         VAR Tests : TestList;
                         VAR Grades : GradeList;
                         VAR Averages : AverageList;
                         NumOfStu : ClassSizeRange);

{ This procedure does each student's grade .}

BEGIN { DoStudentGrade }
   Writeln('DoStudentGrade')
END;   { DoStudentGrade }



PROCEDURE SummarizeClass(VAR Tests : TestList;
                         VAR Grades : GradeList;
                         VAR Averages : AverageList;
                         NumOfStu : ClassSizeRange);

{ This procedure summarizes the results of the class. }

BEGIN { SummarizeClass }
   Writeln('SummarizeClass called')
END;   { SummarizeClass }



BEGIN   { Grader }
  GetStudentData(Names, Tests, NumOfStu);
  DoStudentGrade(Names, Tests, Grades, Averages, NumOfStu);
  SummarizeClass(Tests, Grades, Averages, NumOfStu)
END.    { Grader }
```

FIGURE 9.9

```
PROGRAM Grader(Input, Output);

{ This program does the grading of one class.  This includes
  assigning a letter grade on the basis of three tests and a
  summary of the class grades.  Erroneous test grades are flagged
  and not included.

     Author : John Riley
     Date begun : May 3, 1986
     Date done  :
     File name : CH9EX4.PAS
}

{$R+}      { Turn on range checking. }

CONST
   MaxClassSize  = 30;
   NameLen       = 20;
   NumOfTests    = 3;

TYPE
   NameType     = STRING[NameLen];
   StuNameList = ARRAY[1..MaxClassSize] OF NameType;
   StuTests    = ARRAY[1..NumOfTests] OF Integer; { A student's
                                                    test grades }
   TestList    = ARRAY[1..MaxClassSize] OF StuTests;
   Entries     = 'A'..'I';    { A, B, C, D, F legal grades, I is
                                incomplete, E, G, H unused. }
   GradeList   = ARRAY[1..MaxClassSize] OF Entries;
   AverageList = ARRAY[1..MaxClassSize] OF Real;
   ClassSizeRange = 0..MaxClassSize;

VAR
   Names    : StuNameList;      { List of students' names        }
   Tests    : TestList;         { List of students' test scores  }
   Grades   : GradeList;        { List of letter grades          }
   Averages : AverageList;      { List of students' averages     }
   NumOfStu : ClassSizeRange;   { Number of students in class    }


PROCEDURE GetStudentData(VAR Names : StuNameList;
                         VAR Tests  : TestList;
                         VAR NumOfStu : ClassSizeRange);

{ This procedure obtains the class data (names and grades) and
  puts them in order.  An insertion sort is used.  }

CONST
    Stop = '!';  { Character to signal end of input }


VAR
   NameIn : NameType;  { Name read in  }
```

(continued)

```
      TestIn : StuTests;   { Tests read in }
      I, J,                { Loop indices  }
      Pos   : Integer;     { Holds position for name to be
                             inserted }
BEGIN { GetStudentData }
  Writeln('GetStudentData called.');

  NumOfStu := 0;
  Writeln('Enter a student''s name, followed by his or');
  Writeln('her test grades, names and grades one per line');
  Writeln('End by entering ', Stop, 'for name');
  Write('Enter Student Name >' );
  Readln(NameIn);
  WHILE (NameIn[1] <> Stop) AND (NumOfStu < MaxClassSize) DO
      BEGIN
        FOR J := 1 TO NumOfTests DO
            BEGIN
              Write('Enter test ', J : 1, ' >');
              Readln(TestIn[J])
            END; { FOR }
        Pos := 1;
        WHILE ( Pos < NumOfStu ) AND ( NameIn > Names[Pos]  ) DO
                          { Find position of NameIn }
            Pos := Pos + 1;
        IF ( Pos = NumOfStu ) AND ( NameIn > Names[Pos] ) THEN
                          { Insert NameIn and Tests at end of list }
            BEGIN
              NumOfStu := NumOfStu + 1;
              Names[NumOfStu] := NameIn;
              Tests[NumOfStu] := TestIn
            END { IF }
        ELSE          { Insert NameIn and Tests into position }
            BEGIN
              FOR I := NumOfStu DOWNTO Pos DO
                  BEGIN    { Shift items out of the way }
                    Names[I + 1] := Names[I];
                    Tests[I + 1] := Tests[I]
                  END; { FOR }
              Names[Pos] := NameIn;
              Tests[Pos] := TestIn;
              NumOfStu := NumOfStu + 1
            END; { ELSE }
        Write('Enter Student Name >');
        Readln(NameIn)
      END  { WHILE }
END;   { GetStudentData }


PROCEDURE DoStudentGrade(VAR Names : StuNameList;
                         VAR Tests : TestList;
                         VAR Grades : GradeList;
                         VAR Averages : AverageList;
                         NumOfStu : ClassSizeRange);

{ This procedure does each student's grade .}
```

(continued)

```
VAR
     I   : ClassSizeRange; { Loop index }
     J   : 1..NumOfTests; { Loop index }
     Avg : Real;          { Average of tests }
     Gr  : Entries;       { Grade assigned   }


     FUNCTION Average(VAR T : StuTests) : Real;

     { This function returns the average of the tests in T. }

     BEGIN { Average }
       Average := 100.0
     END;  { Average }


     FUNCTION Grade(Ave : Real) : Entries;

     { This function assigns a grade based on the average. }

     BEGIN { Grade }
       Grade := 'A'
     END;  { Grade }


BEGIN { DoStudentGrade }
   Writeln('DoStudentGrade');

   Writeln;
   Writeln('Name     ' : NameLen, '   ', '    Tests   ',
           '        Average   Grade ');
   FOR I := 1 TO NumOfStu DO
      BEGIN
         Write(Names[I], ' ' : NameLen - Length(Names[I]));
         FOR J := 1 TO NumOfTests DO
            Write(Tests[I, J] : 4, '    ');
         Avg := Average(Tests[I]);
         Gr := Grade(Avg);
         Writeln(Avg : 6 : 2, '    ',Gr)
      END; { FOR }
   Writeln
END;  { DoStudentGrade }



PROCEDURE SummarizeClass(VAR Tests : TestList;
                         VAR Grades : GradeList;
                         VAR Averages : AverageList;
                         NumOfStu : ClassSizeRange);

{ This procedure summarizes the results of the class. }

BEGIN { SummarizeClass }
   Writeln('SummarizeClass called')
END;   { SummarizeClass }
```

(continued)

```
BEGIN   { Grader }
  GetStudentData(Names, Tests, NumOfStu);
  DoStudentGrade(Names, Tests, Grades, Averages, NumOfStu);
  SummarizeClass(Tests, Grades, Averages, NumOfStu)
END.    { Grader }


Output:

GetStudentData called.
Enter a student's name, followed by his or
her test grades, names and grades one per line
End by entering ! for name
Enter Student Name >JONES R
Enter test 1 >60
Enter test 2 >70
Enter test 3 >80
Enter Student Name >SMITH K
Enter test 1 >80
Enter test 2 >70
Enter test 3 >90
Enter Student Name >GREEN B
Enter test 1 >80
Enter test 2 >90
Enter test 3 >90
Enter Student Name >BLACK J
Enter test 1 >1000
Enter test 2 >90
Enter test 3 >90
Enter Student Name >!
DoStudentGrade

          Name           Tests            Average  Grade
BLACK  J               1000     90     90   100.00  A
GREEN  B                 80     90     90   100.00  A
JONES  R                 60     70     80   100.00  A
SMITH  K                 80     70     90   100.00  A

SummarizeClass called
```

do not know that the information entered is correct. For this reason, the next thing we add to the program is code in the procedure Do-StudentGrade to output the names and grades we have entered. We also put in two subprocedures to assign the averages and letter grades of the students. To start, these subprocedures contain only a little bit of code to assign some value to the appropriate variable.

After the typographical errors have been corrected, the program in *FIGURE 9.9* runs and shows us that the information we enter is put into order correctly. This means not only that the names are in order but also that the test grades are with the correct student. At this point we also took some time, while the program was small, to get the output nicely aligned. Putting output in readable form is very important. Getting output in the exact format the user wants may require some adjustment of the blank spaces and the field parameters in the write statements.

It should also be noted that at this time we would be able to show the instructor what the output would look like. She might suggest some changes at this point. Being able to show some progress and partial results is valuable when meeting a user's needs.

Furthermore, our choice of making a separate type for the tests of each student enables us to pass the tests of one student as a parameter. This seems natural because it reflects the nature of the data.

Our next step is to add the averaging process to the program. At this point a constant Error is added which, when used as an average, signifies that the average was not computed due to an input error. The exact value of Error is unimportant as long as it is not a value that would arise as an average. At this point we also include a function which checks the test scores to determine if they are in the proper range. This version of the program appears in *FIGURE 9.10*.

FIGURE 9.10

```
PROGRAM Grader(Input, Output);

{ This program does the grading of one class.  This includes
  assigning a letter grade on the basis of three tests and a
  summary of the class grades.  Erroneous test grades are flagged
  and not included.

      Author      : John Riley
      Date begun  : May 3, 1986
      Date done   :
      File name   : CH9EX5.PAS
}

{$R+}      { Turn on range checking. }

CONST
   MaxClassSize = 30;
   NameLen      = 20;
   NumOfTests   = 3;
   Error        = -99;  { Special value indicating bad score }

TYPE
   NameType     = STRING[NameLen];
   StuNameList  = ARRAY[1..MaxClassSize] OF NameType;
   StuTests     = ARRAY[1..NumOfTests] OF Integer; { A student's
                                                     test grades }
   TestList     = ARRAY[1..MaxClassSize] OF StuTests;
   Entries      = 'A'..'I';   { A, B, C, D, F legal grades, I is
                                incomplete, E, G, H unused. }
```

(continued)

```
    GradeList    = ARRAY[1..MaxClassSize] OF Entries;
    AverageList = ARRAY[1..MaxClassSize] OF Real;
    ClassSizeRange = 0..MaxClassSize;

VAR
    Names    : StuNameList;     { List of students' names   }
    Tests    : TestList;        { List of students' test scores }
    Grades   : GradeList;       { List of letter grades      }
    Averages : AverageList;     { List of students' averages  }
    NumOfStu : ClassSizeRange;  { Number of students in class }


PROCEDURE GetStudentData(VAR Names : StuNameList;
                         VAR Tests  : TestList;
                         VAR NumOfStu : ClassSizeRange);

{ This procedure obtains the class data (names and grades) and
  puts them in order.  An insertion sort is used.  }

CONST
     Stop = '!';  { Character to signal end of input }


VAR
    NameIn : NameType; { Name read in  }
    TestIn : StuTests; { Tests read in }
    I, J,              { Loop indices  }
    Pos   : Integer;   { Holds position for name to be
                         inserted }
BEGIN { GetStudentData }
  Writeln('GetStudentData called.');

  NumOfStu := 0;
  Writeln('Enter a student''s name, followed by his or');
  Writeln('her test grades, names and grades one per line');
  Writeln('End by entering ', Stop, 'for name');
  Write('Enter Student Name >' );
  Readln(NameIn);
  WHILE (NameIn[1] <> Stop) AND (NumOfStu < MaxClassSize) DO
      BEGIN
        FOR J := 1 TO NumOfTests DO
           BEGIN
             Write('Enter test ', J : 1, ' >');
             Readln(TestIn[J])
           END; { FOR }

        Pos := 1;
        WHILE ( Pos < NumOfStu ) AND ( NameIn > Names[Pos] ) DO
                            { Find position of NameIn }
           Pos := Pos + 1;
        IF ( Pos = NumOfStu ) AND ( NameIn > Names[Pos] ) THEN
                       { Insert NameIn and Tests at end of list }
```

(continued)

```
            BEGIN
              NumOfStu := NumOfStu + 1;
              Names[NumOfStu] := NameIn;
              Tests[NumOfStu] := TestIn
            END { IF }
         ELSE            { Insert NameIn and Tests into position }
            BEGIN
              FOR I := NumOfStu DOWNTO Pos DO
                 BEGIN  { Shift items out of the way }
                    Names[I + 1] := Names[I];
                    Tests[I + 1] := Tests[I]
                 END; { FOR }
              Names[Pos] := NameIn;
              Tests[Pos] := TestIn;
              NumOfStu := NumOfStu + 1
            END; { ELSE }
         Write('Enter Student Name >');
         Readln(NameIn)
      END   { WHILE }
END;   { GetStudentData }


PROCEDURE DoStudentGrade(VAR Names : StuNameList;
                         VAR Tests : TestList;
                         VAR Grades : GradeList;
                         VAR Averages : AverageList;
                         NumOfStu : ClassSizeRange);

{ This procedure does each student's grade .}

VAR
    I   : ClassSizeRange; { Loop index }
    J   : 1..NumOfTests;  { Loop index }
    Avg : Real;           { Average of tests }
    Gr  : Entries;        { Grade assigned   }


    FUNCTION LegalScore(Test : Integer) : Boolean;

    { This function determines whether the test score is in
      the appropriate range. }

    CONST
        TestMax = 100;
        TestMin = 0;

    BEGIN { LegalScore }
      LegalScore := (TestMin <= Test) and (Test <= TestMax)
    END;   { LegalScore }


FUNCTION Average(VAR T : StuTests) : Real;

{ This function returns the average of the tests in T. }
```

(continued)

```
    VAR

       Sum : Integer;        { Sum of test scores       }
       I   : 1..NumOfTests; { Loop index                }
       OK  : Boolean;        { Indicates no bad scores }

    BEGIN { Average }
      OK := True;
      Sum := 0;
      FOR I := 1 TO NumOfTests DO
          IF LegalScore(T[I]) THEN
              Sum := Sum + T[I]
          ELSE
              OK := False;
      IF OK THEN
          Average := Sum / NumOfTests
      ELSE
          Average := Error
    END;  { Average }




    FUNCTION Grade(Ave : Real) : Entries;

    { This function assigns a grade based on the average. }

    BEGIN { Grade }
      Grade := 'A'
    END;  { Grade }

BEGIN { DoStudentGrade }
   Writeln('DoStudentGrade');

   Writeln;
   Writeln('Name      ' : NameLen, '  ', '     Tests    ',
           '        Average   Grade ');
   FOR I := 1 TO NumOfStu DO
      BEGIN
        Write(Names[I], ' ' : NameLen - Length(Names[I]));
        FOR J := 1 TO NumOfTests DO
           IF LegalScore(Tests[I, J]) THEN
              Write(Tests[I, J] : 4, '   ')
           ELSE
              Write(Tests[I, J] : 4, '** ');
        Avg := Average(Tests[I]);
        Gr := Grade(Avg);
        IF Avg <> Error THEN
           Writeln(Avg : 6 : 2, '    ',Gr)
        ELSE
           Writeln(' ERROR ')
      END; { FOR }
   Writeln
END;  { DoStudentGrade }
```

(continued)

```
PROCEDURE SummarizeClass(VAR Tests : TestList;
                         VAR Grades : GradeList;
                         VAR Averages : AverageList;
                         NumOfStu : ClassSizeRange);

{ This procedure summarizes the results of the class. }

BEGIN { SummarizeClass }
  Writeln('SummarizeClass called')
END;  { SummarizeClass }



BEGIN  { Grader }
  GetStudentData(Names, Tests, NumOfStu);
  DoStudentGrade(Names, Tests, Grades, Averages, NumOfStu);
  SummarizeClass(Tests, Grades, Averages, NumOfStu)
END.    { Grader }
```

Output:

```
GetStudentData called.
Enter a student's name, followed by his or
her test grades, names and grades one per line
End by entering ! for name
Enter Student Name >JONES K
Enter test 1 >100
Enter test 2 >90
Enter test 3 >80
Enter Student Name >SMITH K
Enter test 1 >70
Enter test 2 >70
Enter test 3 >60
Enter Student Name >GREEN M
Enter test 1 >100
Enter test 2 >900
Enter test 3 >80
Enter Student Name >WHITE R
Enter test 1 >60
Enter test 2 >60
Enter test 3 >80
Enter Student Name >!
DoStudentGrade
```

Name		Tests		Average	Grade
GREEN M	100	900**	80	ERROR	
JONES K	100	90	80	90.00	A
SMITH K	70	70	60	66.67	A
WHITE R	60	60	80	66.67	A

```
SummarizeClass called
```

The revision presented in *FIGURE 9.10* compiled and ran correctly on the first try. This can happen if the program is put together in small pieces. This is known as a *clean compile*. It is very difficult to get a clean compile if you attempt to do the entire program at once.

We now feel confident enough to remove the write statements at the beginning of the two procedures GetStudentData and DoStudentGrade. We also code the procedure to assign the letter grade for each student. This version of the program appears in *FIGURE 9.11*.

FIGURE 9.11

```
PROGRAM Grader(Input, Output);

{ This program does the grading of one class.  This includes
  assigning a letter grade on the basis of three tests and a
  summary of the class grades.  Erroneous test grades are flagged
  and not included.

    Author     : John Riley
    Date begun : May 3, 1986
    Date done  :
    File name  : CH9EX6.PAS
}

{$R+}      { Turn on range checking. }

CONST
   MaxClassSize = 30;
   NameLen      = 20;
   NumOfTests   = 3;
   Error        = -99;  { Special value indicating bad score }

TYPE
   NameType     = STRING[NameLen];
   StuNameList  = ARRAY[1..MaxClassSize] OF NameType;
   StuTests     = ARRAY[1..NumOfTests] OF Integer; { A student's
                                            test grades }
   TestList     = ARRAY[1..MaxClassSize] OF StuTests;
   Entries      = 'A'..'I';   { A, B, C, D, F legal grades, I is
                                 incomplete, E, G, H unused. }

   GradeList    = ARRAY[1..MaxClassSize] OF Entries;
   AverageList  = ARRAY[1..MaxClassSize] OF Real;
   ClassSizeRange = 0..MaxClassSize;

VAR
   Names     : StuNameList;      { List of students' names        }
   Tests     : TestList;         { List of students' test scores  }
   Grades    : GradeList;        { List of letter grades          }
   Averages  : AverageList;      { List of students' averages     }
   NumOfStu  : ClassSizeRange;   { Number of students in class    }
```

(continued)

```
PROCEDURE GetStudentData(VAR Names : StuNameList;
                         VAR Tests  : TestList;
                         VAR NumOfStu : ClassSizeRange);

{ This procedure obtains the class data (names and grades) and
  puts them in order.  An insertion sort is used.  }

CONST
     Stop = '!';   { Character to signal end of input }

VAR
   NameIn : NameType;   { Name read in  }
   TestIn : StuTests;   { Tests read in }
   I, J,                { Loop indices  }
   Pos    : Integer;    { Holds position for name to be
                          inserted }

BEGIN { GetStudentData }
  NumOfStu := 0;
  Writeln('Enter a student''s name, followed by his or');
  Writeln('her test grades, names and grades one per line');
  Writeln('End by entering ', Stop, 'for name');
  Write('Enter Student Name >' );
  Readln(NameIn);
  WHILE (NameIn[1] <> Stop) AND (NumOfStu < MaxClassSize) DO
     BEGIN
        FOR J := 1 TO NumOfTests DO
           BEGIN
             Write('Enter test ', J : 1, ' >');
             Readln(TestIn[J])
           END; { FOR }
        Pos := 1;
        WHILE ( Pos < NumOfStu ) AND ( NameIn > Names[Pos] ) DO
                             { Find position of NameIn }
           Pos := Pos + 1;
        IF ( Pos = NumOfStu ) AND ( NameIn > Names[Pos] ) THEN
                        { Insert NameIn and Tests at end of list }
           BEGIN
             NumOfStu := NumOfStu + 1;
             Names[NumOfStu] := NameIn;
             Tests[NumOfStu] := TestIn
           END { IF }
        ELSE    { Insert NameIn and Tests into position }
           BEGIN
             FOR I := NumOfStu DOWNTO Pos DO
                BEGIN                { Shift items out of the way }
                  Names[I + 1] := Names[I];
                  Tests[I + 1] := Tests[I]
                END; { FOR }
             Names[Pos] := NameIn;
             Tests[Pos] := TestIn;
             NumOfStu := NumOfStu + 1
           END; { ELSE }
```

(continued)

```
        Write('Enter Student Name >');
        Readln(NameIn)
     END   { WHILE }
END;   { GetStudentData }



PROCEDURE DoStudentGrade(VAR Names : StuNameList;
                         VAR Tests : TestList;
                         VAR Grades : GradeList;
                         VAR Averages : AverageList;
                         NumOfStu : ClassSizeRange);

{ This procedure does each student's grade .}

VAR
    I   : ClassSizeRange; { Loop index }
    J   : 1..NumOfTests;  { Loop index }
    Avg : Real;           { Average of tests }
    Gr  : Entries;        { Grade assigned   }


    FUNCTION LegalScore(Test : Integer) : Boolean;

    { This function determines whether the test score is in
      the appropriate range. }

    CONST
        TestMax = 100;
        TestMin = 0;

    BEGIN { LegalScore }
      LegalScore := (TestMin <= Test) and (Test <= TestMax)
    END;   { LegalScore }


    FUNCTION Average(VAR T : StuTests) : Real;

    { This function returns the average of the tests in T. }

    VAR
        Sum : Integer;       { Sum of test scores       }
        I   : 1..NumOfTests; { Loop index               }
        OK  : Boolean;       { Indicates no bad scores }

    BEGIN { Average }
      OK := True;
      Sum := 0;
      FOR I := 1 TO NumOfTests DO
         IF LegalScore(T[I]) THEN
            Sum := Sum + T[I]
         ELSE
            OK := False;
```

(continued)

```
            IF OK THEN
                Average := Sum / NumOfTests
            ELSE
                Average := Error
        END;  { Average }


        FUNCTION Grade(Ave : Real) : Entries;

        { This function assigns a grade based on the average.

        CONST
            AMinimum = 90;
            BMinimum = 80;
            CMinimum = 70;
            DMinimum = 60;

        BEGIN { Grade }
          IF Ave = Error THEN
                Grade := 'I'
          ELSE  { Ave is in the appropriate range }
                IF Ave >= AMinimum THEN
                    Grade := 'A'
                ELSE IF Ave >= BMinimum THEN
                    Grade := 'B'
                ELSE IF Ave >= CMinimum THEN
                    Grade := 'C'
                ELSE IF Ave >= DMinimum THEN
                    Grade := 'D'
                ELSE
                    Grade := 'F'
        END;  { Grade }


BEGIN { DoStudentGrade }
    Writeln;
    Writeln('Name     ' : NameLen, '   ,'      Tests   ',
            '         Average  Grade ');
    FOR I := 1 TO NumOfStu DO
        BEGIN
            Write(Names[I], ' ' : NameLen - Length(Names[I]));
            FOR J := 1 TO NumOfTests DO
                IF LegalScore(Tests[I, J]) THEN
                    Write(Tests[I, J] : 4, '   ')
                ELSE
                    Write(Tests[I, J] : 4, '** ');
            Avg := Average(Tests[I]);
            Gr := Grade(Avg);
            IF Avg <> Error THEN
                Writeln(Avg : 6 : 2, '    ',Gr)
            ELSE
                Writeln(' ERROR ')
        END; { FOR }
    Writeln
END;  { DoStudentGrade }
```

                                              (continued)

```
PROCEDURE SummarizeClass(VAR Tests : TestList;
                         VAR Grades : GradeList;
                         VAR Averages : AverageList;
                         NumOfStu : ClassSizeRange);

{ This procedure summarizes the results of the class. }

BEGIN { SummarizeClass }
  Writeln('SummarizeClass called')
End;  { SummarizeClass }


BEGIN  { Grader }
  GetStudentData(Names, Tests, NumOfStu);
  DoStudentGrade(Names, Tests, Grades, Averages, NumOfStu);
  SummarizeClass(Tests, Grades, Averages, NumOfStu)
END.   { Grader }


Output:

Enter a student's name, followed by his or
her test grades, names and grades one per line
End by entering ! for name
Enter Student Name >JONES J
Enter test 1 >100
Enter test 2 >90
Enter test 3 >90
Enter Student Name >SMITH K
Enter test 1 >1000
Enter test 2 >90
Enter test 3 >80
Enter Student Name >GREEN S
Enter test 1 >80
Enter test 2 >70
Enter test 3 >70
Enter Student Name >WHITE L
Enter test 1 >60
Enter test 2 >90
Enter test 3 >70
Enter Student Name >BROWN M
Enter test 1 >60
Enter test 2 >60
Enter test 3 >50
Enter Student Name >!
```

Name		Tests		Average	Grade
BROWN M	60	60	50	56.67	F
GREEN S	80	70	70	73.33	C
JONES J	100	90	90	93.33	A
SMITH K	1000**	90	80	ERROR	
WHITE L	60	90	70	73.33	C

```
SummarizeClass called
```

The program is completed by coding the necessary subprocedures of SummarizeClass. As before, these are implemented one at a time. The finished program is presented in *FIGURE 9.12*.

When we started designing the procedure to do the average of the tests, we noticed that it was necessary to check a test score to see if it was valid. Because we already had coded a function to do this (LegalScore), we decided to move this out of the procedure DoStudentGrade. This was easily accomplished by using the block commands of the editor (CTRL/ KB, CTRL/KK, CTRL/KV, and CTRL/KH). Moving this function was not only a matter of convenience. Using the same function in both procedures contributes to the consistency of the test for legal scores throughout the program. For similar reasons, we changed TestMax and TestMin to be global constants.

The first time the program was run with the procedure Tally-LetterGrades in place, the reported number of each grade was zero. After examining the code in TallyLetterGrades we decided that the problem was elsewhere. Perhaps the grades had not been entered into the array Grades. When we checked the procedure DoStudentGrade we found that Grades (and Averages) had not been filled. (Had you noticed this already?) This was easily corrected. Interestingly, this is where a procedure failed to meet its specifications for input and output (*FIGURE 9.5*).

You should note that in the procedure TallyLetterGrades we have made use of an array which is indexed by the letters to simplify the procedure.

There are other ways of solving this problem. Any good solution would involve the decomposition of the problem into smaller problems. By doing this we never lose control of the program. At all times we can understand what the program is doing. This is very important if you want to know (rather than hope or guess) that a program works.

This program has around 350 lines (counting blank lines and comments). This is not very big and thus we were able to move from our outlines to the code of the program rather quickly. For a larger program we probably would have to spend more time designing the program. Time spent designing the program is always worthwhile. Also, most of the tasks we had to accomplish (sorting, averaging, etc.) were fairly routine. This is typical of programming. No one part is difficult, but getting the parts working together may be tricky.

Another reason that we were able to start coding rather early in the programming process is that we were working in Pascal. Pascal allows us to partially implement routines and has a facility (procedures) for naturally breaking a program into smaller pieces. Many other high-level languages have facilities for doing this.

A powerful editor can be used as a tool for program development as we have done. We consider the TURBO editor to be an example of such an editor. For an editor to be very helpful in developing programs it must easily permit the insertion of new code and the correction of errors. Other tools which may be found in a programming environment are libraries

FIGURE 9.12

```
PROGRAM Grader(Input, Output);

{ This program does the grading of one class.  This includes
  assigning a letter grade on the basis of three tests and a
  summary of the class grades.  Erroneous test grades are flagged
  and not included.

      Author      : John Riley
      Date begun  : May 3, 1986
      Date done   : May 9, 1986
      File name   : CH9EX7.PAS
}

{$R+}       { Turn on range checking. }

CONST
   MaxClassSize = 30;
   NameLen      = 20;
   NumOfTests   = 3;
   Error        = -99;  { Special value indicating bad score }
   TestMax      = 100;
   TestMin      = 0;

TYPE
   NameType     = STRING[NameLen];
   StuNameList  = ARRAY[1..MaxClassSize] OF NameType;
   StuTests     = ARRAY[1..NumOfTests] OF Integer; { A student's
                                                     test grades }
   TestList     = ARRAY[1..MaxClassSize] OF StuTests;
   Entries      = 'A'..'I';   { A, B, C, D, F legal grades, I is
                                incomplete, E, G, H unused. }

   GradeList    = ARRAY[1..MaxClassSize] OF Entries;
   AverageList  = ARRAY[1..MaxClassSize] OF Real;
   ClassSizeRange = 0..MaxClassSize;

VAR
   Names    : StuNameList;    { List of students' names        }
   Tests    : TestList;       { List of students' test scores  }
   Grades   : GradeList;      { List of letter grades          }
   Averages : AverageList;    { List of students' averages     }
   NumOfStu : ClassSizeRange; { Number of students in class    }


FUNCTION LegalScore(Test : Integer) : Boolean;

{ This function determines whether the test score is in
  the appropriate range. }

BEGIN { LegalScore }
  LegalScore := (TestMin <= Test) AND (Test <= TestMax)
END;  { LegalScore }
```

(continued)

```pascal
PROCEDURE GetStudentData(VAR Names : StuNameList;
                         VAR Tests  : TestList;
                         VAR NumOfStu : ClassSizeRange);

{ This procedure obtains the class data (names and grades) and
  puts them in order.  An insertion sort is used.  }

CONST
     Stop = '!';   { Character to signal end of input }

VAR
   NameIn : NameType;   { Name read in  }
   TestIn : StuTests;   { Tests read in }
   I, J,                { Loop indices  }
   Pos    : Integer;    { Holds position for name to be
                          inserted }
BEGIN { GetStudentData }
  NumOfStu := 0;
  Writeln('Enter a student''s name, followed by his or');
  Writeln('her test grades, names and grades one per line');
  Writeln('End by entering ', Stop, 'for name');
  Write('Enter Student Name >' );
  Readln(NameIn);
  WHILE (NameIn[1] <> Stop) AND (NumOfStu < MaxClassSize) DO
     BEGIN
        FOR J := 1 TO NumOfTests DO
           BEGIN
             Write('Enter test ', J : 1, ' >');
             Readln(TestIn[J])
           END; { FOR }
        Pos := 1;
        WHILE ( Pos < NumOfStu ) and ( NameIn > Names[Pos] ) DO
                             { Find position of NameIn }
           Pos := Pos + 1;
        IF ( Pos = NumOfStu ) and ( NameIn > Names[Pos] ) THEN
                        { Insert NameIn and Tests at end of list }
           BEGIN
             NumOfStu := NumOfStu + 1;
             Names[NumOfStu] := NameIn;
             Tests[NumOfStu] := TestIn
           END { IF }
        ELSE              { Insert NameIn and Tests into position }
           BEGIN
             FOR I := NumOfStu DOWNTO Pos DO
                BEGIN     { Shift items out of the way }
                  Names[I + 1] := Names[I];
                  Tests[I + 1] := Tests[I]
                END; { FOR }
             Names[Pos] := NameIn;
             Tests[Pos] := TestIn;
             NumOfStu := NumOfStu + 1
           END; { ELSE }
        Write('Enter Student Name >');
        Readln(NameIn)
     END  { WHILE }
END;  { GetStudentData }
```

(continued)

```
PROCEDURE DoStudentGrade(VAR Names : StuNameList;
                         VAR Tests : TestList;
                         VAR Grades : GradeList;
                         VAR Averages : AverageList;
                         NumOfStu : ClassSizeRange);

{ This procedure does each student's grade .}

VAR
    I   : ClassSizeRange; { Loop index }
    J   : 1..NumOfTests;  { Loop index }
    Avg : Real;           { Average of tests }
    Gr  : Entries;        { Grade assigned    }


    FUNCTION Average(VAR T : StuTests) : Real;

    { This function returns the average of the tests in T. }

    VAR
       Sum : Integer;       { Sum of test scores     }
       I   : 1..NumOfTests; { Loop index             }
       OK  : Boolean;       { Indicates no bad scores }
    BEGIN { Average }
      OK := True;
      Sum := 0;
      FOR I := 1 TO NumOfTests DO
         IF LegalScore(T[I]) THEN
            Sum := Sum + T[I]
         ELSE
            OK := False;
      IF OK THEN
         Average := Sum / NumOfTests
      ELSE
         Average := Error
    END;  { Average }


    FUNCTION Grade(Ave : Real) : Entries;

    { This function assigns a grade based on the average. }

    CONST
       AMinimum = 90;
       BMinimum = 80;
       CMinimum = 70;
       DMinimum = 60;


    BEGIN { Grade }
      IF Ave = Error THEN
         Grade := 'I'
      ELSE  { Ave is in the appropriate range }
         IF Ave >= AMinimum THEN
            Grade := 'A'
```

                                                           (continued)

```
                      ELSE IF Ave >= BMinimum THEN
                         Grade := 'B'
                      ELSE IF Ave >= CMinimum THEN
                         Grade := 'C'
                      ELSE IF Ave >= DMinimum THEN
                         Grade := 'D'
                      ELSE
                         Grade := 'F'
              END;  { Grade }


      BEGIN { DoStudentGrade }
         Writeln;
         Writeln('Name     ' : NameLen, '   ', '     Tests     ',
                  '     Average  Grade ');
         FOR I := 1 TO NumOfStu DO
            BEGIN
               Write(Names[I], ' ' : NameLen - Length(Names[I]));
               FOR J := 1 TO NumOfTests DO
                  IF LegalScore(Tests[I, J]) THEN
                     Write(Tests[I, J] : 4, '   ')
                  ELSE
                     Write(Tests[I, J] : 4, '** ');
               Avg := Average(Tests[I]);
               Averages[I] := Avg;
               Gr := Grade(Avg);
               Grades[I] := Gr;
               IF Avg <> Error THEN
                  Writeln(Avg : 6 : 2, '     ',Gr)
               ELSE
                  Writeln(' ERROR ')
            END; { FOR }
         Writeln
      END; { DoStudentGrade }


      PROCEDURE SummarizeClass(VAR Tests : TestList;
                               VAR Grades : GradeList;
                               VAR Averages : AverageList;
                               NumOfStu : ClassSizeRange);

      { This procedure summarizes the results of the class. }


            PROCEDURE SummarizeTests(VAR Tests : TestList;
                                     NumOfStu : ClassSizeRange);

            { This procedure finds the high, low and average
              for each test. }

            VAR
               I, J,                     { Loop indices        }
               Sum,                      { Sum of test scores }
               High,                     { High test grade     }
               Low,                      { Low test grade      }
               ValidTests : Integer;     { Number of tests     }
               Ave        : Real;        { Average of tests    }
```

(continued)

```
BEGIN { SummarizeTests }
  FOR I := 1 TO NumOfTests DO
     BEGIN
       High := TestMin;
       Low  := TestMax;
       Sum  := 0;
       ValidTests := 0;
       FOR J := 1 TO NumOfStu DO
          IF LegalScore(Tests[J, I]) THEN
             BEGIN
               Sum := Sum + Tests[J, I];
               ValidTests := ValidTests + 1;
               IF Tests[J, I] > High THEN
                  High := Tests[J, I];
               IF Tests[J, I] < Low THEN
                  Low := Tests[J, I]
             END; { IF }
       IF ValidTests > 0 THEN
          BEGIN
            Ave := Sum / ValidTests;
            Writeln('Test ', I, ' Valid Tests : ',
                    ValidTests);
            Writeln('High Grade : ', High,
                    ' Low Grade : ', Low);
            Writeln('Test Average : ', Ave : 6 : 2);
            Writeln
          END { IF }
       ELSE
          BEGIN
            Writeln('No valid scores for test ', I);
            Writeln
          END { ELSE }
     END { FOR }
END;  { SummarizeTests }


PROCEDURE TallyLetterGrades(VAR Grades : GradeList;
                                NumOfStu : ClassSizeRange);

{ This procedure determines the number of each letter
  grade awarded. }

TYPE
   GradeArray = ARRAY[Entries] OF Integer;


VAR
   I           : ClassSizeRange; { Loop index }
   G           : Entries;        { Loop index }
   NumOfGrade : GradeArray; { Holds number of each
                                 grade given }

BEGIN { TallyLetterGrades }
  FOR G := 'A' TO 'I' DO
     NumOfGrade[G] := 0;
```

(continued)

```
      FOR I := 1 TO NumOfStu DO
          NumOfGrade[Grades[I]] := NumOfGrade[Grades[I]] + 1;
      Writeln('Grade   Number Awarded');
      FOR G := 'A' TO 'D' DO
          Writeln('  ', G, '          ', NumOfGrade[G]);
      Writeln('  F        ', NumOfGrade['F']);
      Writeln('  I        ', NumOfGrade['I']);
      Writeln
  END;   { TallyLetterGrades }



  PROCEDURE SummarizeAverage(VAR Averages : AverageList;
                                 NumOfStu : ClassSizeRange);

  { This procedure determines the high, low and average
    for the class. }



  VAR
      I,                          { Loop index        }
      ValidAverages : Integer;    { Number of valid
                                    averages }
      High,                       { High average      }
      Low,                        { Low average       }
      Sum,                        { Sum of averages }
      Ave            : Real;      { Average of averages }


  BEGIN { SummarizeAverage }
    High := TestMin;
    Low  := TestMax;
    Sum  := 0;
    ValidAverages := 0;
    FOR I := 1 TO NumOfStu DO
       IF Averages[I] <> Error THEN
          BEGIN
            Sum := Sum + Averages[I];
            ValidAverages := ValidAverages + 1;
            IF Averages[I] > High THEN
               High := Averages[I];
            IF Averages[I] < Low THEN
               Low := Averages[I]
          END; { IF }
    IF ValidAverages > 0 THEN
       BEGIN
         Ave := Sum / ValidAverages;
         Writeln('High Average : ', High : 6 : 2);
         Writeln('Low Average  : ', Low : 6 : 2);
         Writeln('Average Average : ', Ave : 6 : 2);
       END { IF }
    ELSE
       Writeln('No valid averages');
    Writeln
  END;   { SummarizeAverage }
```

(continued)

```
BEGIN { SummarizeClass }
   SummarizeTests(Tests, NumOfStu);
   TallyLetterGrades(Grades, NumOfStu);
   SummarizeAverage(Averages, NumOfStu)
END;   { SummarizeClass }


BEGIN  { Grader }
   GetStudentData(Names, Tests, NumOfStu);
   DoStudentGrade(Names, Tests, Grades, Averages, NumOfStu);
   SummarizeClass(Tests, Grades, Averages, NumOfStu)
END.   { Grader }
```

Output:

```
Enter a student's name, followed by his or
her test grades, names and grades one per line
End by entering ! for name
Enter Student Name >JONES J
Enter test 1 >100
Enter test 2 >90
Enter test 3 >90
Enter Student Name >SMITH K
Enter test 1 >1000
Enter test 2 >8
Enter test 3 >90
Enter Student Name >GREEN M
Enter test 1 >80
Enter test 2 >90
Enter test 3 >100
Enter Student Name >BROWN L
Enter test 1 >70
Enter test 2 >60
Enter test 3 >700
Enter Student Name >WHITE P
Enter test 1 >80
Enter test 2 >88
Enter test 3 >89
Enter Student Name >BLACK S
Enter test 1 >50
Enter test 2 >62
Enter test 3 >67
Enter Student Name >!
```

Name	Tests			Average	Grade
BLACK S	50	62	67	59.67	F
BROWN L	70	60	700**	ERROR	
GREEN M	80	90	100	90.00	A
JONES J	100	90	90	93.33	A
SMITH K	1000**	8	90	ERROR	
WHITE P	80	88	89	85.67	B

```
Test 1 Valid Tests : 5
High Grade : 100 Low Grade : 50
Test Average :  76.00
```

(continued)

```
Test 2 Valid Tests : 6
High Grade : 90 Low Grade : 8
Test Average :  66.33

Test 3 Valid Tests : 5
High Grade : 100 Low Grade : 67
Test Average :  87.20

Grade   Number Awarded
   A          2
   B          1
   C          0
   D          0
   F          1
   I          2

High Average :  93.33
Low Average  :  59.67
Average Average :  82.17
```

of common routines and debugging facilities. Using the editor and procedures we can develop and use our own library of routines. TURBO does not support a debugging facility. This is not surprising, because debuggers require more computing power than can (at the present time) be found in a microcomputer.

In the development of the grading program we have tried to anticipate changes that might have to be made in the program. The most obvious and likely change would be in the number of tests to be used to compute a student's grade. This is why we have an array of tests instead of three test variables for each student. Three is something of a borderline number in this regard. It is not difficult to handle three distinct variables—e.g., Test1, Test2, and Test3 instead of an array and some coding goes more easily using distinct variables. For example, Average := (Test1 + Test2 + Test3)/3 is easier to code than a loop which sums an array of test scores and then finds the average. This is not the case for a number such as eight. Treating eight test scores as we have just done is at best tedious and prone to error. In either case an array is more adaptable. You should get in the habit of designing your programs to anticipate modifications.

9.4 SUMMARY

Large programs are most successfully developed by proceeding from general program requirements to detailed specifications. This is accomplished by decomposing the task into smaller problems and solving these smaller problems. It may be necessary to break the smaller problems into subproblems as well. This design methodology is known as top-down design.

A module is a piece of a software system which performs one of the tasks of the system. In a program, modules are implemented as subprograms (procedures and functions). A module must be able to pass information to and from other parts of the system. The means of doing this is the interface of the module. Well-designed modules should be self-contained and have interfaces which clearly show the flow of information in and out of the module.

The larger a program is, the more valuable it becomes as an investment in programmer time and energy. For this reason, programs must be planned, designed, and developed very carefully. It also follows that a programmer must try to anticipate changes to the program and make modification of the program as easy as possible.

The features of a programming language ultimately influence the program. In the chapters that follow, other features of Pascal will be discussed. These features give the programmer more choices to make but also enable programs to be written more clearly. ☐

EXERCISES

1. Indicate how the program in the case study would be modified to accommodate the following changes.
   a. The number of tests is now eight.
   b. The minimum averages needed for the various grades are

   A   88

   B   77

   C   66

   D   55

   F   Any legal average below 55

   c. The names of the students with the highest test scores and the highest averages are to be printed.
2. Discuss ways in which an instructor might want the grading program changed and how difficult it would be to incorporate these changes in the program.

   Exercises 3, 4, and 5 are substantial programming tasks. Use the techniques illustrated in the case study to complete these tasks. Try to anticipate changes that might be needed. Document your programs.
3. Write a simple payroll program which accomplishes the following. The input consists of employees' names and payroll data. An employee's name is entered on one line. The next line should contain either the letter H (or h) for an hourly pay rate or the letter S (or s) for a salary. If the employee is paid by the hour (H), the next line consists of the number of hours the employee worked and his or her hourly pay rate

(separated by a space). If the employee is salaried (S), the next line contains the employee's weekly salary. An hourly employee is paid the hourly rate times the hours worked up to 40 hours. Hours in excess of 40 are to be paid at one and one half times the normal rate ("time and a half"). All employees are taxed at a flat rate of 10%. (Recall that this means their tax is 0.1 times their pay.) An employee's take-home (or net) pay is his or her (gross) pay minus the tax. Your program should produce the following: (1) a list of the hourly employees which for each employee contains the hours worked, the pay rate, the (gross) pay, the tax, and the take-home (or net) pay; (2) the total of the (gross) pay and the total of the taxes of the hourly employees; (3) a list of the salaried employees which contains their salaries, taxes, and take-home pay; (4) the totals of the (gross) pay and taxes of the salaried employees; and (5) the totals of all employees' (gross) pay and taxes. Prompt all input. Label and format all output. If an H, h, S, or s is not entered as a code, request the code to be input again. The following errors are to be flagged and the corresponding employee not assigned pay: hours worked which are not in the range from 10 to 80; hourly pay rates not in the range from $3.50 to $50.00; weekly salaries not in the range from $50.00 to $20000.00.

4. Write a program which prints the results of a race among runners. A number between 1 and 100 is to be read from the keyboard which indicates the total number of runners finishing the race. After that, a list of the runners, in the order of their finish, is entered as follows: the name of the runner is entered on one line, and on the next line is a code indicating the runner's sex (M or F for male or female) and the runner's age (separated by a space). Following the list of runners is a list of the times recorded at the finish line in increasing order. Each line in the list consists of two integers representing minutes and seconds (again separated by a space). Each runner has a time. Your program should sort the male and female runners into two lists with their corresponding times and print these lists. Within each list the winner of each age group of ten years (0-10, 11-20, 21-30, . . ., 51-60, and 61 and over) is to be indicated. Finally, a list of all of the age-group winners and their times is to be printed.

5. Write a program which makes the computer function much like a cash register at a supermarket. For each customer, the type of item and price of the item are entered. This is done by entering a one-letter code for the type of item: G (grocery), D (delicatessen), M (meat), N (nonfood), P (produce), or Q (quit) on a line followed by the item's price on a separate line. Nonfood items (code N) are subject to a tax of 6%. The tax is computed on the sum of the taxable items. If Q is entered, a price should not follow, but the total of the taxable items, the total tax on these items, and the complete total should be printed. The user then enters the amount tendered by the customer and is given the change owed. Customers are handled until X (eXit) is entered, at which

time totals for each of the categories (G, D, M, N, P) are produced as well as the total tax and a complete total. No item in the store costs more than $100.00, so check that the amount entered is between $0.01 and $100.00. Also check that only legal characters (G, D, M, N, P, Q, X) are entered. Make your program behave as much like a real cash register as possible.

6. How would you change the program you wrote in Exercise 3 to reflect an increase in the tax rate to 15%? How would you modify the program to make the overtime cutoff point 35 hours? How would you change the program to award all employees a bonus of 10% of their pay?

7. How would you change the program you wrote in Exercise 4 to output the average time of each category? (Recall that times are given in minutes and seconds.)

8. How would you change the program in Exercise 5 to accommodate two new categories, F (frozen foods) and Y (dairY products)?

INTRODUCTION

In this chapter another means of organizing data—i.e., another data type—is introduced. This data type is known as the *record*. Many languages provide a record data type. Records are somewhat like arrays in that they provide a mechanism for grouping related data items together. However, there are significant differences between records and arrays. Both data types are of great utility, and you should become as comfortable with one as with the other. ☐

CHAPTER 10

RECORDS

10.1 RECORD TERMINOLOGY

The record data type is a means of grouping together data items which are of differing data types. For example, by using a record we would be able to group together, as one variable, a student's name, test grades, average, and final grade. Each of the data items within the record may be accessed by name. This is in contrast with arrays, in which the data items must be of the same type and in which the individual items are accessed by an index. The items within a record are called *fields*.

DEFINITION

> **A *record* is a group of related data items (which may be of differing data types) each of which may be referenced by name.**

DEFINITION

> **A *field* of a record is one of the data items within the record.**

FIGURE 10.1 illustrates these concepts. The data in this example is information that might be kept by a college. Notice that the different fields of the record are given names and have different data types.

FIGURE 10.1   Record Example

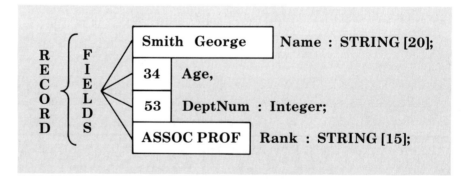

10.2 RECORD TYPES

This section describes how records are declared in Pascal. As with the other user-defined data types of Pascal, a record data type may be used

either to define a new type in the type declaration section or to specify
the type of variables in the variable declaration section. Usually, a record
type is defined in the type declaration section.

The record type declaration consists of the key word RECORD followed
by a list which names the fields of the record and their types and then
the key word END. The list between RECORD and END consists of lists
of identifiers of fields (separated by commas) followed by a colon and the
types of the fields, with items in the list being separated by semicolons.
The syntax diagram of the record type is given in *FIGURE 10.2*.

| **Record Type** | **FIGURE 10.2** |

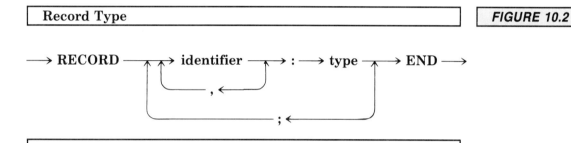

For example, to declare the record type illustrated in *FIGURE 10.1*
we could have the following declaration.

```
TYPE
     FacultyRecord = RECORD
                       Name    : STRING[20];
                       Age,
                       DeptNum : Integer;
                       Rank    : STRING[15]
                     END;   { FacultyRecord }
```

This would serve as a template for faculty records which would contain
a name, an age, a department number, and a rank. Note that the END
of the record declaration is commented. For example, the type above could
be used to declare the variables FacMember and Chair in the variable
section.

```
VAR
     FacMember,
     Chair    : FacultyRecord;
```

Each of these variables could then contain four pieces of information as
depicted in *FIGURE 10.3*.

FIGURE 10.3   Record Variables

| FacMember | | Name : STRING [20]; |
| Age, |
| DeptNum : Integer; |
| Rank : STRING [15] |

| Chair | | Name : STRING [20]; |
| Age, |
| DeptNum : Integer; |
| Rank : STRING [15] |

10.3   ACCESSING RECORDS AND THEIR FIELDS

As with any data type, a means of storing data in and retrieving data from variables of record type is needed. As with most of the data types in Pascal, it is possible to assign the contents of one record variable to another of the same record type. A record variable may only be accessed, not compared. With the declarations of the preceding section, the following assignment statement would be possible.

```
Chair := FacMember
```

This would copy the contents of each of the fields of FacMember into the respective fields of Chair. This answers the question of how to move one record to another but does not provide a means of placing data in the individual fields of the record.

To access an individual field of the record we must use the record variable name and the field name separated by a period. Thus the four fields of FacMember are properly identified by FacMember.Name, FacMember.Age, FacMember.DeptNum, and FacMember.Rank, and the fields of Chair are Chair.Name, Chair.Age, Chair.DeptNum, and Chair.Rank . The individual fields of a record variable may be used in any way that any variable of the type of the field may be. In our example, FacMember.Name and Chair.Name may be considered to be string variables, and FacMember.Age, FacMember.DeptNum, Chair.Age, and Chair.DeptNum may be used as integer variables. With these considerations, the following statements which might occur in a program are valid. (We continue to use the declarations made above. NewYear is a Boolean variable indicating whether the date is January first and used to cause appropriate updating. Answer is a character variable.)

```
Write('Enter faculty member''s name >');
Readln(FacMember.Name);
Write('Enter faculty age >');
Readln(FacMember.Age);
Write('Enter faculty''s department number >');
Readln(FacMember.DeptNum);
Write('Enter faculty rank >');
Readln(FacMember.Rank);


IF NewYear THEN
    FacMember.Age := FacMember.Age + 1;


Write('Is faculty member to be chair? (Y/N) ');
Readln(Answer);
IF (Answer = 'Y') OR (Answer = 'y') THEN
    Chair := FacMember;
Write('Is faculty member to be promoted? (Y/N) ');
Readln(Answer);
IF (Answer = 'Y') OR (Answer = 'y') THEN
    BEGIN
       Write('Enter new rank >');
       Readln(FacMember.Rank)
    END; { IF }
```

No restrictions on the types that may be used for the fields of a record have been stated. This is because there are none—with the exception that you must, of course, stay within the limits of the computer's memory. This means that not only simple types (both predefined and user defined) may be used as fields but also structured types such as arrays and even records themselves. In the program developed in Chapter 9, we might have grouped all the information about one student (Student) in a record (StuRec) using the following declarations.

```
CONST
     NumOfTests = 3;
     NameLen    = 20;

TYPE
     TestArray = ARRAY[1..NumOfTests] OF Integer;
     Entries   = 'A'..'I';
     StuRec    = RECORD
                      Name  : STRING[NameLen];
                      Tests : TestArray;
                      Ave   : Real;
                      Grade : Entries
                  END; { StuRec }

VAR
     Student : StuRec;
```

Accessing the student's name, average, and grade would be done as before (Student.Name, Student.Ave, and Student.Grade). What about the student's tests? Most likely we would want to be able to access these one by one (say to do the student's average). If Pascal is consistent, then Student.Tests would refer to an array, and this indeed would be the case. But if Student.Tests were an array, then indexing the array would enable us to use the components of the array. Thus Student.Tests[1], Student.Tests[2], and Student.Tests[3] would be the components (of type integer) desired. It is also possible to use an expression (usually a variable) as an index. To find the sum of the test grades we would write a program segment like the following. Sum and I are integer variables.

```
Sum := 0;
FOR I := 1 TO NumOfTests DO
    Sum := Sum + Student.Tests[I];
```

Records, as well as arrays, can occur as fields of records. These are known as *nested records*. The fields within nested records are accessed by using the record's name, a period, the nested record's name, another period, and the field name. For example, we could modify the student record above to include a first name, middle initial, and last name as follows.

```
TYPE

    StuRec = RECORD
                Name  : RECORD
                            First   : STRING[10];
                            MidInit : Char;
                            Last    : STRING[20]
                        END; { Name }
                Tests : TestArray;
                Ave   : Real;
                Grade : Entries
            END; { StuRec }


VAR
    Student : StuRec;
```

With these declarations, the parts of the student's name would be known as Student.Name.First, Student.Name.MidInit, and Student.Name.Last. As you can imagine, organizing the student's name in this way would give us greater flexibility in designing the format of the report.

Most likely we would have separated the record declaration of the name in the above from the student record declaration.

```
TYPE

    NameRec = RECORD
                    First   : STRING[10];
                    MidInit : Char;
                    Last    : STRING[20]
                END; { NameRec }
    StuRec  = RECORD
                    Name  : NameRec;
                    Tests : TestArray;
                    Ave   : Real;
                    Grade : Entries
                END; { StuRec }
```

This would enable us to declare other variables to be of the same type (NameRec) as the field Name within StuRec. This is convenient because the new variables would then be assignment compatible with the field of the record. Furthermore, any changes made to NameRec would be reflected in all these variables. For example, a change in the maximum length of the last name is easily accommodated.

Record declarations can be used to ensure consistency in our programs and to guarantee that variables denoting items of the same sort are compatible. For example, the format for dates and addresses could be specified as below.

```
TYPE
    DateRec    = RECORD
                    Month : 1..12;
                    Day   : 1..31;
                    Year  : Integer
                END;   { DateRec }
    AddressRec = RECORD
                    Street : STRING[30];
                    City   : STRING[15];
                    State  : STRING[2];
                    Zip    : STRING[5]
                END; { AddressRec }
```

This would enable us to declare types and variables for a company in a uniform manner, as we see in the following program fragment.

```
    { Continuing the type declaration section }

    EmployeeRec = RECORD
                    Name       : STRING[30];
                    BirthDate,
                    HireDate   : DateRec;
                    Salary     : Real;
                    Address    : AddressRec
                END; { EmployeeRec }
```

```
        PartNum     = 1..MaxInt;              { Parts identified by
                                                positive numbers }
        SupplierRec = RECORD
                      Name    : STRING[30];
                      Parts   : ARRAY[1..100]     { Parts this co. }
                                OF PartNum;       { supplies }
                      Address : AddressRec
                      END; { SupplierRec }


VAR
      Today :        DateRec;
      NewEmployee : EmployeeRec;


Writeln('Enter today''s date');
Write('Month (1 - 12) >');
Readln(Today.Month);
Write('Day >');
Readln(Today.Day);
Write('Year >');
Readln(Today.Year);


Writeln('Enter name >');
Readln(NewEmployee.Name);
NewEmployee.HireDate := Today;
Writeln('Enter birth date');
Write('Month (1 - 12) >');
Readln(NewEmployee.BirthDate.Month);
Write('Day >');
Readln(NewEmployee.BirthDate.Day);
Write('Year >');
Readln(NewEmployee.BirthDate.Year);
```

Actually it is unlikely that we would encounter records for both employees and suppliers in the same program. One is a concern of the personnel department, the other of the department in charge of inventory. However, because the same record structures are used for both (e.g., addresses), we would not confuse ourselves when we moved from one program to another. Using the same record declarations also makes it possible to develop procedures which can be used in many places. A statement which makes programming with records easier is discussed next.

10.4   THE WITH STATEMENT

You may have noticed in the discussion above that a disadvantage of using records is that rather cumbersome names for the fields of the records arise. This was especially true when nested records such as NewEmployee.BirthDate.Month were being used. Identifying a field of a record in this way is known as giving its *completely qualified name*. In many situations, using the completely qualified names for the fields of the record involves repeating the record's name several times. This is at best inconvenient, and at worst a potential source of error. Pascal provides a means of qualifying the fields of a record using the *with statement*.

The with statement consists of the key word WITH followed by a list of record variables (separated by commas) followed by the key word DO and a statement. The statement will frequently be a compound statement. The syntax diagram of the with statement is given in *FIGURE 10.4*. The effect of the with statement is that in the statement following the key word DO, fields within records named in the list after WITH may have the record name or names omitted.

As a first example of the use of the with statement, consider the example at the beginning of this chapter, for which the declarations are reproduced below.

```
TYPE
    FacultyRecord = RECORD
                        Name : STRING[20];
                        Age,
                        DeptNum : Integer;
                        Rank : STRING[15]
                    END;   { FacultyRecord }


VAR
    FacMember,
    Chair     : FacRec;
```

Using the with statement we would write the code to fill FacMember as follows. Contrast this with the equivalent code in Section 10.2.

```
WITH FacMember DO
   BEGIN
     Write('Enter faculty member''s name >');
     Readln(Name);
     Write('Enter faculty age >');
     Readln(Age);
     Write('Enter faculty''s department number >');
     Readln(DeptNum);
     Write('Enter faculty rank >');
     Readln(Rank)
   END; { WITH }
```

In this segment, Name means FacMember.Name and Age means FacMember.Age, and so forth.

In order for the computer to correctly use a variable, the variable must not be ambiguously identified. Ambiguity can arise when using the with

FIGURE 10.4 | With Statement

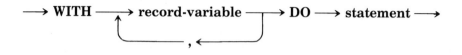

statement if two of the record variables named in the with statement have fields with the same identifier. For example, if both FacMember and Chair appeared in the same with statement, the identifiers Name, Age, DeptNum, and Rank would be ambiguous. This problem is resolved by using the last record variable in the with statement to qualify the field identifier. Thus this statement assigns 57 to the field DeptNum of Chair, not FacMember.

```
WITH FacMember, Chair DO
     DeptNum := 57;
```

FIGURE 10.5 |

```
PROCEDURE GetDate(VAR D : DateRec);

{ This procedure obtains the month, day and year for D where
  D is a variable of the type   DateRec = RECORD
                                            Month : 1..12;
                                            Day   : 1..31;
                                            Year  : Integer
                                          END;   DateRec


        Author    : John Riley
        Date      : May 14, 1986
        File name : GETDATE.PRO
}

BEGIN { GetDate }
   WITH D DO
      BEGIN
        Write('Enter month (1 -12) >');
        Readln(Month);
        Write('Enter day >');
        Readln(Day);
        Write('Enter year >');
        Readln(Year)
      END { WITH }
END;   { GetDate }
```

In fact, in the preceding with statement the fields of FacMember must be specified in full, because any unqualified field name is resolved by using Chair. For a detailed explanation of this, see [Co]. Refrain from doing this altogether.

The with statement can be used to write procedures for accomplishing some standard tasks. We had the following declaration for a record for a date.

```
TYPE
    DateRec = RECORD
                  Month : 1..12;
                  Day   : 1..31;
                  Year  : Integer
              END;  { DateRec }
```

FIGURE 10.5 gives a procedure which obtains the information for this record from the keyboard. A program which tests this procedure is presented in *FIGURE 10.6*.

With the declarations of Section 10.3, we could invoke this procedure to accomplish some of the input tasks of that section. Notice that we are able to pass a field (NewEmployee.BirthDate) which is a record to the procedure GetDate.

```
Writeln('Enter today''s date');
GetDate(Today);

Writeln('Enter name >');
Readln(NewEmployee.Name);
NewEmployee.HireDate := Today;
Writeln('Enter birth date');
GetDate(NewEmployee.BirthDate);
```

FIGURE 10.6

```
PROGRAM TestGetDate(Input, Output);

{ This program tests the procedure GetDate.


    Author    : John Riley
    Date      : May 14, 1986
    File name : CH10EX1.PAS
}
```

(continued)

```
TYPE
   DateRec = RECORD
                  Month : 1..12;
                  Day   : 1..31;
                  Year  : Integer
              END;  { DateRec }

VAR
   Date : DateRec;


PROCEDURE GetDate(Var D : DateRec);

{ This procedure obtains the month, day and year for D where
  D is a variable of the type  DateRec = RECORD
                                             Month : 1..12;
                                             Day   : 1..31;
                                             Year  : Integer
                                         END;   DateRec

      Author     : John Riley
      Date       : May 14, 1986
      File name  : GETDATE.PRO
}

BEGIN { GetDate }
  WITH D DO
     BEGIN
       Write('Enter month (1 -12) >');
       Readln(Month);
       Write('Enter day >');
       Readln(Day);
       Write('Enter year >');
       Readln(Year)
     END { WITH }
END;  { GetDate }



BEGIN  { TestGetDate }
  GetDate(Date);
  Writeln;
  WITH Date DO
     Writeln(Month : 1, '/', Day : 1, '/', Year)
END.   { TestGetDate }


Output:

Enter month (1 -12) >3
Enter day >14
Enter year >1986

3/14/1986
```

10.5 ARRAYS OF RECORDS

Just as an array may be one of the fields within a record, a record type may be the component type of an array. This is very convenient when a list of items is needed and each item has several pieces of information (of differing types) associated with it. This eliminates the need for parallel arrays, because one array may be used for all the information.

As an illustration, consider the runners in a road race. Associated with each runner would be several items of information: name, race number, age, sex, place, and time (minutes and seconds). We might expect that there would be about 200 entrants. To handle this data we could make these declarations.

```
CONST
    NumOfRunners = 200;

TYPE
    RunnerRec = RECORD
                    Name  : STRING[30];
                    Age   : Integer;
                    Sex   : Char;  { M = Male, F = Female }
                    Place : 1..NumOfRunners;
                    Time  : RECORD
                                Min : Integer; { Minutes }
                                Sec : Real       { Seconds }
                            END   { Time }
                END; { RunnerRec }
    RaceArray = ARRAY[1..NumOfRunners] OF RunnerRec;


VAR
    Race : RaceArray;
```

This would make Race an array of 200 (NumOfRunners) components, each of which would be a record. The first component of this array is Race[1]. The fields of this component would be Race[1].Name, Race[1].Age, Race[1].Sex, Race[1].Place, and Race[1].Time. The last field has two subfields which would be identified by Race[1].Time.Min and Race[1].Time.Sec. A program segment used to print a message for each runner follows. (I is an integer variable.) Notice that we are able to use a subscripted variable in the with statement.

```
FOR I := 1 TO NumOfRunners DO
    WITH Race[I] DO
        BEGIN
            Writeln('Congratulations, ', Name, 'on finishing in ', ):
            Writeln(Place, ' place, in a time of ',
                    Time.Min, ':',Time.Sec)
        END; { WITH }
```

Because many data-processing applications deal with large quantities of data of one format, arrays of records occur frequently.

Records should be used anytime there is a group of related data. In the preceding example, in addition to the information about the runners, it would probably be useful to have a variable for the number of finishers. Because this number would be needed almost anywhere the array of runners is needed, we could include it in a record.

```
VAR
    Race : RECORD
               NumOfFinishers : 1..NumOfRunners;
               Runners         : RaceArray
           END; { Race }
```

Finally, we will see in the next section that it is possible to sort an array of records.

10.6   SORTING REVISITED

Recall that records may not be compared. If an array of records is to be sorted, the basis for ordering the records in the array must be specified. That is, one of the fields of the records in the array must be chosen to determine the order of the records in the array by using the values in that field. This field is known as the *key* or the *key field*. Using the race example of the previous section, we could choose to put the entrants' records in order by name (alphabetically) or by place (numerically). Both orders would have their uses. It is not uncommon to have more than one way to sort the records in an array.

DEFINITION

> The *key* or *key field* of a record is a field which is used to identify the record, usually for use in sorting and searching.

Sorting an array of records requires that a key field be designated and used for comparison. Sorting always involves the interchange of values between variables. In this situation, this means interchanging the values in two records. This is not difficult. We illustrate these concepts with the insertion sort.

This time we have written the insertion sort for an array of records. We are not reading the elements of the array, because it would be too difficult to anticipate exactly what fields might need to be read. A Pascal procedure for this is shown in *FIGURE 10.7*.

The procedure for the insertion sort in *FIGURE 10.7* actually turned out to be simpler than the procedure needed when we were inserting new

FIGURE 10.7

```
PROCEDURE SortArray(VAR A : ArrayType; NumToSort : Integer);

{ This procedure puts the array of records A into order.
  The order is based upon the keyfield.
  NumToSort is the number of elements of A to be sorted.
  The types ArrayType, ArrayRec and KeyFieldType are
  defined in the calling program.  An insertion sort is used.

      Author     : John Riley
      Date       : May 15, 1986
      File name  : SORTARRY.PRO
}

VAR
    Key       : KeyFieldType;  { Key for comparisons     }
    I, J,                      { Loop indices            }
    Pos       : Integer;       { Position for insertion }
    Temp      : ArrayRec;      { Holder for record       }

BEGIN { SortArray }
  FOR I := 1 TO NumToSort DO
    BEGIN
      Key := A[I].KeyField;
      Pos := 1;
      WHILE (A[Pos].KeyField <= Key) AND (Pos < I) DO
          Pos := Pos + 1;
      IF Pos < I THEN { A[I] must be inserted }
        BEGIN
          Temp := A[I];
          FOR J := I DOWNTO Pos + 1 DO
              A[J] := A[J - 1];
          A[Pos] := Temp
        END { IF }
      ELSE { A[I] is in correct position }
    END { FOR}
END; { SortArray }
```

items in the list. This is because if the while loop in the procedure repeats until J = I, then A[I] is in the correct position. The else part of the if-then-else statement is followed by a null statement, which reflects our intent. A[I] is in the correct position, so we do nothing. If another statement were to follow, we would put a semicolon after the else.

As usual, this procedure was tested by using it in a little program. The records used have an integer field and a string field. Within the procedure it was necessary to change KeyField to Int. This is easily done with the find-and-replace command of the editor (CTRL/QA) using the global (G) option. The program is presented in *FIGURE 10.8*.

FIGURE 10.8

```
PROGRAM SortTester ( Input, Output );

{  This program tests the insertion sort for arrays
   procedure.

       Author    : John Riley
       Date      : May 15, 1986
       File name : CH10EX2.PAS
}

{$R+}      { Turn on range checking. }

CONST
   ArraySize = 20;

TYPE
   StringType = STRING[10];
   ArrayRec   = RECORD
                     Int : Integer;
                     Str : StringType;
                  END; { ArrayRec }
   ArrayType  = ARRAY[1..ArraySize] of ArrayRec;
   KeyFieldType = Integer;

VAR
   IntStrArry  : ArrayType;  { Array to be sorted }
   Num         : Integer;    { Number of elements in array }


PROCEDURE GetArray(VAR IntStrArry : ArrayType; VAR Size : Integer);

{ Procedure to obtain entries for the array Arry. }

VAR
   IntIn : Integer;  { Integer read from keyboard }

BEGIN  { GetArray }
   Size := 0;
   Writeln('Enter an integer and a string on separate lines');
   Writeln('Enter 0 for integer to stop ');
   Writeln;
   Write('Enter integer >');
   Readln(IntIn);
   WHILE (IntIn <> 0) AND (Size < ArraySize) DO
      BEGIN
        Size := Size + 1;
        IntStrArry[Size].Int := IntIn;
        Write('Enter string >');
        Readln(IntStrArry[Size].Str);
        Write('Enter integer >');
        Readln(IntIn)
      END { WHILE }
END; { GetArray}
```

(continued)

```
PROCEDURE SortArray(VAR A : ArrayType; NumToSort : Integer );

{ This procedure puts the array of records A into order.
  The order is based upon the keyfield.
  NumToSort is the number of elements of A to be sorted.
  The types ArrayType, ArrayRec and KeyFieldType are
  defined in the calling program.  An insertion sort is used.


    Author    : John Riley
    Date      : May 15, 1986
    File name : SORTARRY.PRO
}

VAR
    Key      : KeyFieldType;  { Key for comparisons    }
    I, J,                     { Loop indices           }
    Pos      : Integer;       { Position for insertion }
    Temp     : ArrayRec;      { Holder for record      }


BEGIN { SortArray }
  FOR I := 1 TO NumToSort DO
    BEGIN
      Key := A[I].Int;
      Pos := 1;
      WHILE (A[Pos].Int <= Key) AND (Pos < I) DO
        Pos := Pos + 1;
      IF Pos < I THEN { A[I] must be inserted }
        BEGIN
          Temp := A[I];
          FOR J := I DOWNTO Pos + 1 DO
            A[J] := A[J - 1];
          A[Pos] := Temp
        END { IF }
      ELSE { A[I] is in correct position }
    END { FOR }
END; { SortArray }


PROCEDURE DisplayArray(IntStrArry : ArrayType; Num : Integer);

{ Procedure to output the contents of the array Arry. }

VAR
   I : Integer;  { Loop index }

BEGIN { DisplayArray }
  Writeln;
  FOR I := 1 to Num DO
    WITH IntStrArry[I] DO
      Writeln(Int : 5, '  ', Str)
END; { DisplayArray }
```

(continued)

```
BEGIN { SortTester }
  GetArray(IntStrArry, Num);
  SortArray(IntStrArry, Num);
  DisplayArray(IntStrArry, Num)
END. { SortTester }


Output:

Enter an integer and a string on separate lines
Enter 0 for integer to stop

Enter integer >54
Enter string >TOM
Enter integer >32
Enter string >SUE
Enter integer >76
Enter string >MARY
Enter integer >29
Enter string >JOE
Enter integer >47
Enter string >HARRY
Enter integer >62
Enter string >MEG
Enter integer >0

    29   JOE
    32   SUE
    47   HARRY
    54   TOM
    62   MEG
    76   MARY
```

One of the main reasons for keeping an array (or any list, for that matter) in order is that it is much easier to find an item in the array (or list). (Think about how useful a telephone directory would be if its names were not in order.) In the next section we will develop a technique of searching an array whose entries are in order (with respect to some key).

10.7 BINARY SEARCHING

In working with an array of records in a program, one task that may be required is finding the record associated with a particular value of the key field. One approach to doing this is simply to search the array until a record with the key is found. This is known as a *linear search*. However, many lists are kept in order by their key field, and this order can be used to make the search go faster.

The search about to be described is known as a *binary search*. The binary search is appropriate only for arrays whose elements are in order by key field. The basic idea is to look at the middle element of the list. If this element contains the value we want, we're done. If it doesn't, the desired entry is in either the part of the list before the middle entry (if the desired entry is before the middle entry) or the part after it (if the desired entry follows the middle entry), and we proceed to search the part of the list indicated by the comparison. We continue this until we find the desired entry or are able to conclude that the entry is not in the list. For example, if we were looking for the number 17 in the list of eleven numbers

```
1    2    5    7    8    9    15   17   20   23   29
---------------------------------------------------
```

we would examine the number in the middle of the list, which is 9. Because 9 is less than 17, we would look at the number in the middle of the portion of the list following (to the right of) 9.

```
1    2    5    7    8    9    15   17   20   23   29
                              ---------------------
```

This number is 20, which is greater than 17, and so we know that the number 17 is in the left half of this portion of the list. The left half contains only the two numbers 15 and 17.

```
1    2    5    7    8    9    15   17   20   23   29
                              -------
```

The middle of a list of two numbers is the "one and a halfth" position. So we either round up (and find the desired number) or round down (and one step later reduce the list to a list of length one which contains the desired element.) We need to do this whenever the list under consideration has an even number of elements. For the sake of definiteness we'll round down.

Before we write an algorithm which does this search, we need to be a little more specific. The basic process entails keeping track of what part of the list is being searched and its middle. To keep track of the part of the list being searched, it is enough to keep track of its left and right ends. Let's use L, R, and M to denote the left end, right end, and middle of the list being searched. We start by putting L and R at the ends of the original list.

```
1    2    5    7    8    9    15   17   20   23   29
↑                                               ↑
L                                               R
```

We then put M in the middle.

```
1    2    5    7    8    9    15   17   20   23   29
↑                        ↑                      ↑
L                        M                      R
```

```
Binary search algorithm

{  Algorithm  to search an array A (whose elements are in
   order) for Item.  Elements 1 through NumToSearch of A
   are searched.  }


Begin binary search

Left  ← 1
Right  ← NumToSearch
Found  ← False
While Not Found
      Mid  ← (Left + Right)/2       { Round off if necessary }
      If Item = A[Mid] Then
            Found  ← True
      Else if A[Mid] < Item Then
            Left  ← Mid + 1
      Else   { A[Mid] > Item }
            Right  ← Mid - 1
EndWhile

End binary search
```

Because the number at M (9) is less than the number desired (17), we move L to the right of M.

1	2	5	7	8	9	15	17	20	23	29
					↑	↑				↑
					M	L				R

Again, M is put in the middle of L and R.

1	2	5	7	8	9	15	17	20	23	29
						↑		↑		↑
						L		M		R

Because the number now at M (20) is greater than the number sought (17), R is placed to the left of M.

1	2	5	7	8	9	15	17	20	23	29
						↑	↑	↑		
						L	R	M		

Moving M this time requires rounding down, so that M and L are the same.

1	2	5	7	8	9	15	17	20	23	29
						↑↑	↑			
						LM	R			

Because the number at M (15) is less than 17, L is moved to the right of M. At this point L and R both point to 17, and adjusting M will make it point to 17 as well. The desired item has been found.

This search is summarized in the algorithm given in *FIGURE 10.9*. The list to be searched is in positions 1 through NumToSearch of an array A. The item to be found is in the variable Item. When the algorithm finishes, Mid contains the position of the desired item within the array.

One problem remains. What if the item to be found is not in the list? If the algorithm is followed for an array which doesn't contain the given item, Left, Right, and Mid will work as before. Eventually, they will all point to the same place. But if the item is not in the array, either Left will be increased by one or Right will be decreased by one. In both cases we will find that Left > Right, so we conclude that the item is not in the list. This condition will be included in the final version of the binary search algorithm.

We are now faced with the problem of describing whether or not the item was found in the list. One way of doing this is to use the Boolean variable Found. Another way is to use the variable Position. Position contains the place of the item within the array if it is in the array. If the item is not in the array we set Position to 0. These modifications are included in the algorithm presented in *FIGURE 10.10*.

FIGURE 10.10

Binary search algorithm

```
{  Algorithm  to search an array A (whose elements are in
   order) for Item.  Elements 1 through NumToSearch of A
   are searched.  If Item is in the array, Position
   indicates its place.  If Item is not in the array,
   Position is set to 0. }

Begin binary search

Left  ←  1
Right  ←  NumToSearch
Found  ←  False
While (Not Found) and (Left <= Right)
      Mid  ←  (Left + Right)/2     { Round off if necessary }
      If Item = A[Mid] Then
            Found  ←  True
      Else if A[Mid] < Item Then
            Left  ←  Mid + 1
      Else   { A[Mid] > Item }
            Right  ←  Mid - 1
EndWhile
If Found Then
      Position  ←  Mid
Else
      Position  ←  0

End binary search
```

The binary search is much faster for large lists than the linear search. However, the list must be ordered for the binary search, whereas a linear search works for an unordered list as well. A procedure implementing the binary search is given in *FIGURE 10.11*. In this procedure the binary search has been modified to use the key field of an array of records.

This procedure is tested by incorporating it in an adaptation of the program in *FIGURE 10.8*. The program used to test this procedure is shown in *FIGURE 10.12*.

FIGURE 10.11

```
PROCEDURE BinarySearch(VAR A : ArrayType; NumToSearch : Integer;
                       Item : KeyFieldType; Var Pos : Integer);

{ This procedure uses a binary search to search the array of
  records A for an entry whose key field is Item.  The first
  NumToSearch components of A are searched.  If Item is found,
  its position is returned in Pos.  If Item is not found Pos is
  set to 0.

        Author    : John Riley
        Date      : May 15, 1986
        File name : BINARYSH.PRO
}

VAR
   Left,              { Left end of subarray being searched  }
   Right,             { Right end of subarray being searched }
   Mid   : Integer; { Middle of subarray }
   Found : Boolean; { Indicates whether Item has been found }


BEGIN { BinarySearch }
   Found := False;
   Left  := 1;
   Right := NumToSearch;
   WHILE (Left <= Right) AND (NOT Found) DO
      BEGIN
         Mid := (Left + Right) DIV 2;
         IF A[Mid].KeyField = Item THEN
            Found := True
         ELSE IF A[Mid].KeyField < Item THEN
            Left := Mid + 1
         ELSE
            Right := Mid - 1
      END; { WHILE }
   IF Found THEN
      Pos := Mid
   ELSE
      Pos := 0
END;   { BinarySearch }
```

FIGURE 10.12

```
PROGRAM SearchTester ( Input, Output );

{  This program tests the binary search for arrays
   procedure.

       Author    : John Riley
       Date      : May 15, 1986
       File name : CH10EX3.PAS
}

{$R+}       { Turn on range checking. }

CONST
   ArraySize = 20;

TYPE
   StringType = STRING[10];
   ArrayRec   = RECORD
                   Int : Integer;
                   Str : StringType;
                END; { ArrayRec }
   ArrayType  = ARRAY[1..ArraySize] OF ArrayRec;
   KeyFieldType = Integer;

VAR
   Arry  : ArrayType;  { Array to be sorted and searched }

   Num   : Integer;    { Number of elements in array }


PROCEDURE GetArray(VAR A:ArrayType; VAR Num : Integer);

{ Procedure to obtain the elements of the array. }

VAR
   IntIn : Integer;  { Integer read in }

BEGIN { GetArray }
  Num := 0;
  Writeln('Enter an integer and a string on separate lines');
  Writeln('Enter 0 for integer to stop ');
  Writeln;
  Write('Enter integer >');
  Readln(IntIn);
  WHILE (IntIn <> 0) AND (Num < ArraySize) DO
     BEGIN
       Num := Num + 1;
       Arry[Num].Int := IntIn;
       Write('Enter string >');
       Readln(Arry[Num].Str);
       Write('Enter integer >');
       Readln(IntIn)
     END { WHILE }
END; { GetArray }
```

(continued)

```
PROCEDURE SortArray(VAR A : ArrayType; NumToSort : Integer );

{ This procedure puts the array of records A into order.
  The order is based upon the keyfield.
  NumToSort is the number of elements of A to be sorted.
  The types ArrayType, ArrayRec and KeyFieldType are
  defined in the calling program.  An insertion sort is used.


      Author    : John Riley
      Date      : May 15, 1986
      File name : SORTARRY.PRO
}

VAR
    Key      : KeyFieldType;  { Key for comparisons     }
    I, J,                     { Loop indices            }
    Pos      : Integer;       { Position for insertion  }
    Temp     : ArrayRec;      { Holder for record       }


BEGIN { SortArray }
  FOR I := 1 TO NumToSort DO
    BEGIN
      Key := A[I].Int;
      Pos := 1;
      WHILE (A[Pos].Int <= Key) AND (Pos < I) DO
        Pos := Pos + 1;
      IF Pos < I THEN { A[I] must be inserted }
        BEGIN
          Temp := A[I];
          FOR J := I DOWNTO Pos + 1 DO
            A[J] := A[J - 1];
          A[Pos] := Temp
        END { IF }
      ELSE { A[I] is in correct position }
    END { FOR }
END; { SortArray }


PROCEDURE FindItems(VAR A : ArrayType; Num : Integer);

{ Procedure to find items requested in the array. }

VAR
   Place,              { Place where item was found using search }
   IntIn : Integer;    { Integer entered from keyboard }


PROCEDURE BinarySearch(VAR A : ArrayType; NumToSearch : Integer;
                   Item : KeyFieldType; VAR Pos : Integer);

{ This procedure uses a binary search to search the array of
  records A for an entry whose key field is Item.  The first
```

(continued)

```
      NumToSearch components of A are searched.  If Item is found,
      its position is returned in Pos.  If Item is not found Pos is
      set to 0.

         Author    : John Riley
         Date      : May 15, 1986
         File name : BINARYSH.PRO
   }


   VAR
      Left,               { Left end of subarray being searched  }
      Right,              { Right end of subarray being searched }
      Mid   : Integer; { Middle of subarray }
      Found : Boolean; { Indicates whether Item has been found }

   BEGIN { BinarySearch }
     Found := False;
     Left  := 1;
     Right := NumToSearch;
     WHILE (Left <= Right) AND (NOT Found) DO
        BEGIN
          Mid := (Left + Right) DIV 2;
          IF A[Mid].Int = Item THEN
             Found := True
          ELSE IF A[Mid].Int < Item THEN
             Left := Mid + 1
          ELSE
             Right := Mid - 1
        END; { WHILE }
     IF Found THEN
        Pos := Mid
     ELSE
        Pos := 0
   END;  { BinarySearch }



   BEGIN { FindItems }
     Writeln('Enter item numbers to be found (0 to stop)');
     Write('Enter number >');
     Readln(IntIn);
     WHILE IntIn <> 0 DO
        BEGIN
          BinarySearch(Arry, Num, IntIn, Place);
          IF Place = 0 THEN
             Writeln(IntIn, ' not found.')
          ELSE
             WITH Arry[Place] DO
                 Writeln('Number : ', Int : 5, '  String : ', Str);
          Write('Enter number >');
          Readln(IntIn)
        END { WHILE }
   END; { FindItems }
```

                                              (continued)

```
BEGIN { SearchTester }
  GetArray(Arry, Num);
  SortArray(Arry, Num);
  Writeln;
  FindItems(Arry, Num)
END. { SearchTester }
```

Output:

```
Enter an integer and a string on separate lines
Enter 0 for integer to stop

Enter integer >56
Enter string >GREEN
Enter integer >43
Enter string >WHITE
Enter integer >88
Enter string >RED
Enter integer >22
Enter string >BLUE
Enter integer >88
Enter string >YELLOW
Enter integer >55
Enter string >ORANGE
Enter integer >0
Enter item numbers to be found (0 to stop)
Enter number >88
Number :    88  String : RED
Enter number >55
Number :    55  String : ORANGE
Enter number >9
9 not found.
Enter number >43
Number :    43  String : WHITE
Enter number >0
```

10.8 SUMMARY

Records are used to group related data items together. These items need not be of the same type. The data items within the record are known as fields. To specify one of the fields of the record, the record's name and the field's name must be given.

The with statement is used when the same record is being used in a number of places. Within the with statement, only the field names of the record need to be used.

One of the fields within the record is sometimes called the key field. The key field is used to identify the record. The key field is also used in sorting an array of records.

An array of records may also be searched for records within the array having a specific value of the key field. If the records of the array are sorted, the binary search is an efficient means of searching. ☐

EXERCISES

1. Write record declarations for the following. You will need to make assumptions about what is being asked. Use whatever auxiliary definitions are appropriate.
   a. The data on a student in college
   b. The data on a part in a factory
   c. The information on a newborn baby at a hospital
   d. The data about a particular course at a college
   e. The information about a house that is for sale
   f. The data for a police record about a stolen car

2. Write the input statements to fill the record variables of the types in Exercise 1. Write statements to output the information in variables of the types of Exercise 1.

3. Try to decide what the output of the following program will be. Run the program and see if you were right. What can you conclude?

```
PROGRAM Ch10Num3(Input, Output);

CONST
   ArraySize = 5;

TYPE
   Rec      = RECORD
                  S : STRING[5];
                  R : Real
              END; { Rec }
   RecArray = ARRAY[1..ArraySize] OF Rec;

VAR
   A : RecArray;
   I : Integer;

BEGIN { Ch10Num3 }
   A[1].S := 'ANT';
   A[1].R := 1.1;
   A[2].S := 'BEAR';
   A[2].R := 2.2;
   A[3].S := 'CAT';
   A[3].R := 3.3;
   I := 1;
   WITH A[I] DO
     BEGIN
       I := I + 1;
       Writeln(S:6, ' ', R:5:1)
     END { WITH }
END.  { Ch10Num3 }
```

4. Find the errors in the following.

a.

```
VAR
    Rec : RECORD
             I1, I2 : Integer;
             R1, R2 : Real
          END; { Rec }


WITH Rec DO
    Writeln(I1 : 5, I2 : 5);
    Writeln(R1 : 6 : 2, R2 : 6 : 2);
```

b.

```
VAR
    Rec1, Rec2 : RECORD
                    I : Integer;
                    R : Real
                 END;

Rec1.I := 1.9;
Rec1.R := 1.8;
Rec2.I := 2;
Rec2.R := 2.1;
IF Rec1 < Rec2 THEN
    Writeln('Rec1 smaller')
ELSE
    Writeln('Rec2 smaller');
```

c.

```
TYPE
    DateRec    = RECORD
                    Mon : 1..12;
                    Day : 1..31;
                    Yr  : Integer
                 END; { DateRec }
    StudentRec = RECORD
                    Name : RECORD
                              First : STRING[10];
                              MidIn : Char;
                              Last  : STRING[15]
                           END { Name }
                    Birth : DatRec;
                    SocSecNum : STRING[9]
                 END; { StudentRec }
```

5. Find out if it is possible to use the same identifier for fields in two different record variables or types.

6. Suppose that ArrayType = Array[1..20] of Integer and IntAry is a variable of type ArrayType. Suppose also that IntAry has values as depicted below.

IntAry

2	4	7	8	12	19	24	29	30	45	49	53	54	60	68	71	79	82	85	88
1	2	3	4	5	6	7	8	9	10	11	12	13	14	15	16	17	18	19	20

Give the output of the writeln statement in the procedure Binary-Search below when it is invoked by BinarySearch(IntAry, 17, 68, P). P is an integer variable.

```
PROCEDURE BinarySearch(VAR A : ArrayType; NumToSearch : Integer;
                       Item : Integer;  VAR Pos : Integer);


VAR
      Left,             { Left end of subarray being searched  }
      Right,            { Right end of subarray being searched }
      Mid   : Integer;  { Middle of subarray }
      Found : Boolean;  { Indicates whether Item has been found }
BEGIN { BinarySearch }
   Found := False;
   Left  := 1;
   Right := NumToSearch;
   WHILE (Left <= Right) AND (NOT Found) DO
      BEGIN
         Mid := (Left + Right) DIV 2;
         Writeln(Left, Mid, Right);
         IF A[Mid] = Item THEN
            Found := True
         ELSE IF A[Mid] < Item THEN
            Left := Mid + 1
         ELSE
            Right := Mid - 1
      END; { WHILE }
   IF Found THEN
      Pos := Mid
   ELSE
      Pos := 0
END;  { BinarySearch }
```

7. Write a program which accepts as input a list of names and addresses and then prints the list in alphabetical order by last name. Use records.

8. Write a program which first accepts as input a list of names and telephone numbers and then accepts names and returns the corresponding phone numbers (if found). If the name is not found, output an appropriate message. Put the list in order and use a binary search.

9. Rewrite the program developed in Chapter 9 using the following type declarations in the main program. (The constants are to remain the same.)

```
TYPE
      NameType = STRING[NameLen];
      Entries  = 'A'..'I';
      StuTests = ARRAY[1..NumOfTests] OF Integer;
      StuRec   = RECORD
                     Name : NameType;
                     Tests : StuTests;
                     Average : Real;
                     Grade   : Entries
                 END; { StuRec }
      StuList  = ARRAY[1..MaxClassSize] OF StuRec;
      ClassRec = RECORD
                     NumOfStu : 0..MaxClassSize;
                     Student  : StuList
                 END; { ClassRec }
```

10. Design a program which keeps statistics about the players on a basketball team. For each player, record the player's name, number, points made, free throw percentage, and shooting percentage. There are at most 15 players on a team. The program should first request the information about the team. Then the user should have two options: to change the information about a player and to list the players' statistics.

   To change a player's statistics, the user enters C in response to a prompt. He or she then enters the player's name. The program should then list the player's statistics and then a series of prompts for the new statistics.

   To list the team's statistics, the user enters L in response to the prompt.

   The user should be able to repeatedly change player statistics and list team statistics. To quit the program, the user enters Q instead of C or L.

11. Write a program which declares a record variable with several fields and then uses the address functions of TURBO (described in Chapter 3, preceding Exercise 11) to print the addresses of the record variable and its fields.

INTRODUCTION

At the heart of many computer programs is file processing. This chapter concerns programming using files. Because the organization of files is dictated by the operating system, exactly how files are handled in a given implementation of a language can differ. In the way in which it handles files, TURBO Pascal is similar (but not identical) to some other Pascal implementations. Entire books have been written about file processing, and this chapter should not be considered to be exhaustive with respect to this topic. ☐

CHAPTER 11

FILES

11.1 FILE CONCEPTS

In this section we discuss the underlying concepts of files and define some of the terms used in file processing. Of course, you began using files as soon as you began working with a computer. For example, in using an editor or a word processor you create and modify files. We are now going to see how a Pascal program can manipulate files.

Basically, a file is a place to store data or information. It differs from memory, which is also a place for storage, in two respects. First, there is a great deal more room for storing information in a file. In principle, there is no limit to the amount of data that may be stored in files. A file also has the property that it is (relatively) permanent. The computer's main memory does not have this property. Main memory is said to be *volatile*, whereas files are *nonvolatile*. The contents of a file may be saved while the computer is off or running another program.

Generally, a file is contained in (or on) some device which is considered to be external to the computer itself. With current technology, storing information in an external file is cheaper than keeping it in the memory of the computer. The trade-off for this reduction in cost is that it is slower and more difficult to access data from a file. A variety of devices (mechanisms used to access files) and media (material on which the file's data is placed) have been used to handle files. Magnetic tape drives, disk and drum drives, card punches and readers, and paper tape punches and readers are examples of file devices. Magnetic tape, disks and drums, punched cards, and paper tape are typical media. Today the principal media are magnetic. However, the technology of external storage may develop devices of a different nature in the near future. For microcomputers, the primary means of storing files is the floppy disk, although more and more microcomputers are being equipped with hard disks. For purposes of illustration, we will assume that files are on floppy disks.

Programmers view a file as another data type which they can use. In some ways a file resembles an array, because both arrays and files can be thought of as lists. Files do have significant differences from arrays that make manipulating them much different.

Many files are limited to only one type of access (storage or retrieval). For example, it may only be possible to add another item to the file at the end of the file.

In addition, data elements of a file can be utilized only one at a time. That is, if the file contains data on Fred, Mary, and Joe, we cannot simultaneously access the data on both Fred and Mary.

These differences make techniques for working with files a little different from those for working with other data structures. Furthermore, because files are organized by the operating system, a program using files must communicate information about the files to the operating system.

> A *file* is a collection of data items of the same type. Each data item is known as a component of the file. Only one component of the file may be accessed (stored or retrieved) at a time.

DEFINITION

> To *read* a component from a file means to retrieve it from the file.

DEFINITION

> To *write* a component to a file means to store it in a file (and replace any previous component).

DEFINITION

Files are often divided into two categories based on how components of the file may be accessed. These categories are *sequential files* and *random-access files*. Sequential files are simpler to handle than random-access files, but are also less flexible. Standard Pascal specifies only sequential files. TURBO Pascal provides mechanisms for random-access files as well. We will work only with sequential files.

> A *sequential file* is a file whose components may only be accessed in order, starting with the first component.

DEFINITION

> A *random-access file* is a file whose components may be accessed in any order.

DEFINITION

For both sequential and random access files, only one component is available at any time. Sequential files may be processed only from beginning to end. A random access file may have its components processed in any order.

Implicit in the discussion above is that there are two ways of regarding files. One is from the point of view of the programmer, who must be concerned with the data structure of files. The other is that there is a physical encoding of the file in (or on) some medium. This means that a sequence of bits (0s and 1s) is recorded in some fashion. Some connection must be made between the two. The connections are usually specified by the programmer with some special statements in the program.

These two ways of viewing files in a program are analogous to giving someone instructions on how to put a set of cards in order and then giving the person sets of cards to actually put in order. In the instructions, you would refer to the first card in the set to be ordered. When the person actually started sorting the cards, he or she would first sort a set of blue cards, then a set of red cards, etc. Then the first card in the set (as specified in the instructions) would refer to the first card in the blue set and then the first card in the red set, and so forth. In a program, programmers must refer to the file to be manipulated, just as instructions for card sorting must refer to the set of cards to be sorted. When the program is actually run, a file to which the program actually refers must be supplied, just as the card sorter, when beginning to follow the card-sorting instructions, must be given an actual set of cards.

A person is smart enough to realize that if you refer to the first card in the set in the sorting instructions and then hand him or her a set of blue cards, the first card in the set refers to the first card in the blue set. When this is done the card sorter has two names for the same set of cards—the set to be sorted (what it is called in the instructions) and the set of blue cards (the actual set of cards to be sorted). A similar correspondence must be made in programming with files. We will need a name for the file being manipulated by the program and one for the actual file. In addition, some way of specifying the correspondence between the two must be provided. This means (just as above) that there will be two names for the same file (what it is called in the program and what it is called by the operating system). When programming (writing instructions for the computer), programmers refer only to the file to be manipulated.

In Pascal, the files that a program manipulates are declared in the variable declaration section. When an actual file is needed, it is connected to the file of the program by a special statement. At this time, the operating system names for the actual files to be used are supplied.

DEFINITION

> A *logical* or *program file* is the file that is used within the program.

DEFINITION

> A *physical file* is the physical encoding of the collection of data on some medium. A device for reading or writing the medium is necessary.

In the special statements making the connection, two files are named. One identifier is given which specifies the name of the file as it is used throughout the program—i.e., the program file name. The program file name is the name given the file in the variable declaration section. The other name identifies the physical file that is to be associated with the program file when the program is executed. This name must conform to the operating-system specifications for a file name. (Refer to Section 2.2 for more information on operating-system file names.) These statements cause the operating system and language implementation to make a connection between the program file and the physical file. After these statements have been executed, the program refers only to the program file. Then, whenever the program file needs to access a component of the file, the physical file named in these statements is used. This is known as *opening* a file.

> To *open* a file means to establish a connection between a physical file and the program. Opening a file allows the components of the file to be accessed.

DEFINITION

> To *close* a file means to sever the connection between a physical file and the program. Closing a file prevents the components of the file from further access.

DEFINITION

The data from a file is not placed directly in the memory locations to be manipulated. Instead, a portion of memory known as the *file buffer* is used to temporarily store the data before it is actually needed. This enables the computer to anticipate the reading of a file. Similarly, data to be written to a file is placed in the file buffer before actually being written to the file. Fortunately, all of this is done by the operating system and is not an immediate concern of the programmer.

> A *file buffer* is a portion of memory for storing the input from or output to a file.

DEFINITION

A schematic illustration depicting these ideas is presented in *FIGURE 11.1*. Using the file name of the physical file, the operating system transmits data to the floppy disk drive to position the read/write head of the drive over the portion of the floppy disk which contains the file.

11.2 TURBO FILE COMMANDS

As mentioned above, almost every language has statements which allow the programmer to specify connections between logical and physical files. These statements are correctly thought of as predefined procedures, similar to READ and WRITE. In this section, the basic TURBO Pascal file-handling procedures are given.

A program file, like any other variable, must be declared in the variable declaration section of the program. A program file or file variable is of file type. A file type specifies the type of the components of the file. The syntax of the file type is either the key word TEXT or the key words FILE OF, followed by a type specification. A file of type TEXT is a file

FIGURE 11.1

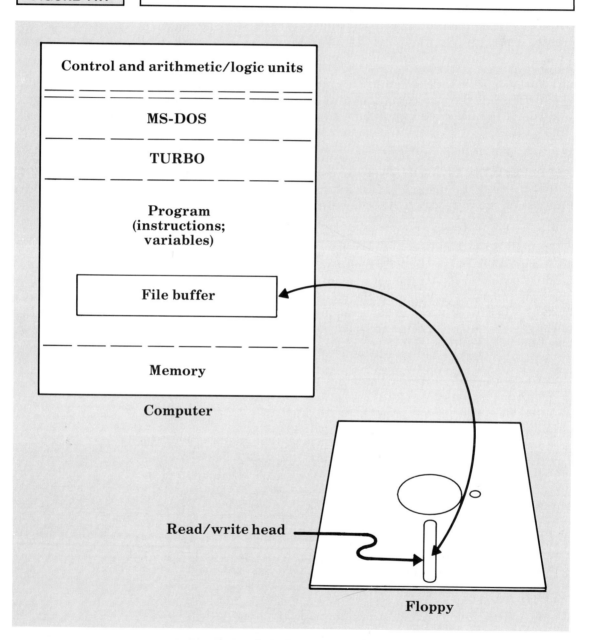

Control and arithmetic/logic units

MS-DOS

TURBO

Program
(instructions;
variables)

File buffer

Memory

Computer

Read/write head

Floppy

of characters. Otherwise, the components' type is given by the type in the declaration. The components' type must not be a file type. Files declared using the key word TEXT are known as *text files*. Files declared otherwise (using FILE OF ..) are known as *binary files*. *FIGURE 11.2* contains the syntax diagram of the file type. We can use this type in declarations in exactly the same way we have used other types. We will discuss the implications of a file being a text file or a binary file later in this chapter. A variable of this type is known as a *file variable* and denotes a program file.

File Type

FIGURE 11.2

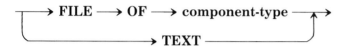

Throughout the following discussion it is assumed that FileVar is a variable that has been declared to be of file type. That is, something like

```
VAR
      FileVar : FILE OF ComponentType;
```

or

```
VAR
      FileVar : Text;
```

appears in the program.

The TURBO Pascal statement for specifying the physical file that is to be associated with a file variable is the *assign statement*. The assign statement consists of the procedure name ASSIGN followed by two parameters enclosed in parentheses. The first parameter is a file variable which denotes a program file. The second parameter is a string or string variable containing the name of the physical file to be associated with the file variable. Here is an example of this statement.

```
Assign(FileVar, 'PROG.DAT');
```

The effect of this statement would be that any time FileVar was used in the program the action specified would use the file named PROG.DAT . If FileName were a string variable, the following two statements would accomplish the same thing.

```
FileName := 'PROG.DAT';
Assign(FileVar, FileName);
```

Here are two examples of assign statements that would be seen at the beginning of a program.

```
Assign(InFile, 'DATA.IN');
Assign(OutFile, 'DATA.OUT');
```

The first statement associates the physical file named DATA.IN with the program file InFile, and the second associates DATA.OUT with OutFile.

The files named by the second parameter are usually on the disk in the logged or default drive, and the drive need not be given. The drive for the disk which is to contain the files may be specified in the second parameter of the assign statement.

```
Assign(FileVar, 'B:PROG.DAT');
```

This associates FileVar with the file on drive B named PROG.DAT.

It is an error to use the assign statement with a file variable which has already been assigned to a physical file.

The assign statement is not standard. The exact means of associating a program file with a physical file varies considerably from implementation to implementation, largely depending on the environment of the implementation. Very few implementations of Pascal adhere precisely to standard Pascal on this point.

After a physical file has been assigned to a program file using the assign statement, the file may be opened. This is done with either the reset statement or the rewrite statement. Both of these statements are standard Pascal.

To open a file for input (or for random-access input and output), the *reset statement* is used. The reset procedure has only one parameter, a file variable. To open FileVar with reset, we would code

```
Reset(FileVar);
```

The physical file associated with FileVar (by the assign statement) must exist when this statement is executed. If the file associated with FileVar does not exist, a run-time error will occur and cause the program to terminate. After the reset statement is executed, the file is ready for reading, starting with the first component of the file.

To open a file for output in TURBO Pascal, the *rewrite statement* is used. The rewrite procedure has one parameter, a file variable. To open FileVar using the rewrite procedure, we would code

```
Rewrite(FileVar)
```

This opens the physical file associated with FileVar for output, starting with the first component of the file. If the physical file associated with FileVar exists when the rewrite statement is executed, its contents will be lost.

After a program has finished with a file, the file should be closed using the *close statement*. The close procedure has one parameter, a file variable. An example follows.

```
Close(FileVar)
```

The close statement severs the connection between the program file and the physical file. If you do not use the close statement with an output file, you may lose the contents of the output file. You should get in the habit of closing all files used at the end of the program. The close statement is nonstandard.

TURBO Pascal provides two standard procedures for accessing components of files. For input, the *read procedure* is used. For output, the *write procedure* is used. For text files, variations on these are permitted: *readln* and *writeln*. We have been using these already for input and output. The general forms are discussed next.

To input values from a file, the read procedure is used. The read procedure has two or more parameters. The first parameter is a file variable. The remaining parameters are variables whose type is identical to the component type of the file variable. If V1, . . ., Vn are variables of the type of the components of FileVar, we would write

```
Read(FileVar, V1, V2, ..., Vn);
```

The effect of this statement would to be to obtain the next n values from the physical file associated with FileVar and place them in V1, . . ., Vn (respectively). In practice, files which are not text files are read one component at a time. The file variable which is used in the read statement must be an input file—that is, a file opened using the reset statement.

Output to files is done using the write statement. The write statement has two or more parameters. The first parameter is a file variable. The remaining parameters are variables of the same type as the components of the file variable. For example, we would code (using the variables above)

```
Write(FileVar, V1, V2, ..., Vn);
```

The effect of this statement would be to put the n values currently in the variables V1, ..., Vn in the next n components of the file associated with FileVar. FileVar usually is an output file (opened using the rewrite statement), but it is possible to write to a file which is being used for random access.

It is possible to tell when the end of a file has been reached by using the *end-of-file function*, EOF. EOF is a Boolean-valued function which has one parameter, a file variable. EOF is normally used for input files to detect when the reading of the file is complete. EOF is True when the last component of the file has been read. Otherwise, EOF is False. A typical use of the EOF function is illustrated below.

```
Assign(FileVar,'PROG.DAT');
Reset(FileVar);
WHILE NOT EOF(FileVar) DO
    BEGIN
       Read(FileVar, V);

          { Process the data in V }

    END;   { WHILE }
Close(FileVar);
```

This example shows a program file (FileVar) being associated with a physical file (PROG.DAT). The file is then opened [Reset(FileVar)]. A value is read from FileVar into V, and then this value is processed. This cycle repeats until all the values in the file have been read. Note that it is not necessary to read before the loop is executed. If the file is empty— i.e., has zero components—the loop will not be executed at all.

Frequently, two files are used in a program. One contains the input for the program and the other is used to hold the output of the program. As a simple example, the input file might hold records containing an employee's name, hourly pay rate, and hours worked. The output file might consist of records containing the names and weekly pay. Each component of the input file is to be processed to produce a component of the output file. If appropriate declarations have been made, the following segment of code will appear in the program. (EMPWK5.12 is the file containing employee work for the week ending 5/12. PAY5.12 is the file containing the payroll information for the week ending 5/12. EmpInfo and EmpPay are record variables.)

```
Assign(EmpInfoFile,  'EMPWK5.12');
Reset(EmpInfoFile);
Assign(EmpPayFile,  'PAY5.12');
Rewrite(EmpPayFile);
WHILE NOT EOF(EmpInfoFile) DO
    BEGIN
       Read(EmpInfoFile, EmpInfo);
       EmpPay.Name := EmpInfo.Name;
       EmpPay.Wages := EmpInfo.Hrs * EmpInfo.Rate;
       Write(EmpPayFile, EmpPay)
    END;   { WHILE }
Close(EmpInfoFile);
Close(EmpPayFile);
```

Standard Pascal requires that the program heading contain the names of the program files used in the program. These are to be listed between the parentheses following the program name. As an example, we would have

```
PROGRAM Example (Input, Output, FileVar);
```

The files Input and Output are standard files referring to the keyboard and screen. TURBO Pascal makes these files and the entire heading optional. However, it is a good idea to include the program heading and the files that are to be used, because this makes it easier to transport a program to another implementation of Pascal. It also documents the files that are being used. Because files serve as the means by which the program communicates with its environment, files serve the same role for programs as parameters serve for procedures.

A file variable may be passed to a procedure, but only as a variable parameter. Within the procedure it must be used correctly. For example, an output file may not be used for input within a procedure.

We have seen that there are two types of files, text files and binary files. Because working with these two types differs somewhat, they are treated separately in the next two sections.

11.3 TEXT FILES

The simplest type of file to work with is a text file. This section discusses text files and serves as an introduction to the use of files in general. One limitation of text files is that they may not be used as random-access files. They must be processed sequentially. Furthermore, text files are input only or output only.

A text file is a file whose component type is character (Char). Here, character is taken in the widest possible sense. Any of the ASCII characters may appear in a text file. So not only may digits (0 to 9) and letters (A to Z and a to z) appear in a text file but also punctuation and other symbols (. ' " < > ( ) + = : ; etc.). Text files also contain control characters signifying the end of a line and other printing characteristics. The files containing your programs are text files. In fact, any file created with an editor is a text file. Because a text file contains printable characters, it is possible to view the file on the screen of the computer or to print the file using a printer. What this really means is that the sequence of 0s and 1s in the file when grouped into bytes (groups of eight) are interpreted as characters which are then able to be displayed. Data which is stored in binary files is not capable of being displayed.

A *text file* is a file of characters in which the end-of-line marker has special significance. The end-of-line marker serves to organize the characters in the file into lines.

DEFINITION

A file variable is declared to be a text file by using the predefined type TEXT. The declaration below is an example of such a declaration.

```
VAR
    InFile,
    OutFile : Text;
```

All of the file-handling procedures described in Section 11.2 may be used with text files. In addition, the special character denoting the end of a line extends the input and output procedures and enables a special function to be defined.

If FileVar is a file variable of type Text, then the end-of-line function EOLn is defined on FileVar. EOLn is a Boolean-valued function. EOLn(FileVar) is True if the next character to be read is the end-of-line marker or if EOF(FileVar) is true. Otherwise EOLn(FileVar) is False. EOLn is a standard Pascal function which is very useful for handling character input in the absence of string-handling procedures. Because TURBO Pascal has the ability to read string variables, EOLn will not be needed.

The procedures read and write have two alternatives for text files. These are readln and writeln. Both readln and writeln manipulate the end-of-line marker. Readln causes the next input to come from a new line and writeln causes the next output to start on a new line. Readln and writeln also have the option of using only one parameter, the file variable. The syntax diagrams of these are given in *FIGURE 11.3*. If the file variable is omitted in a read or readln statement, the standard file Input is used. Input refers to characters read from the keyboard. If the file variable is omitted from the write or writeln statement, the standard file Output is used. In this situation, output appears on the video screen.

The characters in a text file may be read into character or string variables, of course. However, a sequence of characters representing a number (real or integer) may be read into a real or integer variable. Similarly, numerical values may be written in a text file being used for output. This means that the numerical value of a variable is transformed to a string of characters representing that value. We will give the exact rules governing the input and output of text files after some examples. Briefly, variables of the types character, string, integer, and real may be input from and output to text files. It is possible to use expressions instead of variables in output statements. It is also possible to use Boolean expressions in output statements. A Boolean expression causes the output to be either TRUE or FALSE. A program fragment illustrates these possibilities.

```
VAR
    InFile,
    OutFile     : Text;
    B           : Boolean;
```

Text File Input and Output		**FIGURE 11.3**

Input statement

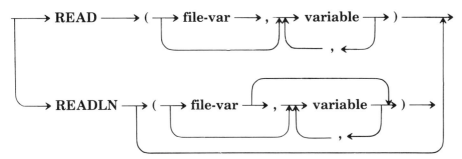

Output statement

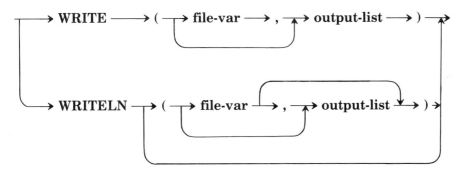

Output list

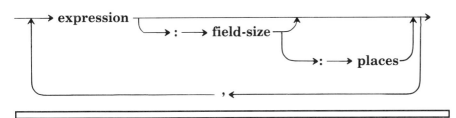

```
        C          : Char;
        I, J       : Integer;
        R          : Real;
        S1, S2     : STRING[5];


BEGIN
  Assign(InFile, 'DATA.IN');
  Reset(InFile);
  Assign(OutFile, 'DATA.OUT');
  Rewrite(OutFile);
```

```
Read(InFile, I, J);
Readln(InFile, C, S1, S2);
Read(InFile, I);
Readln(InFile);
Read(InFile, C);
R := I + J / 2;
S2 := 'OUT';
B := (I = J);
Write(OutFile, 'I = J is ', B : 6);
Writeln(OutFile);
Writeln(OutFile, R : 8 : 2);
Write(OutFile, S1, S2);
Writeln(OutFile, I, J : 7);



Close(InFile);
Close(OutFile);
```

In this fragment the physical files DATA.IN and DATA.OUT are assigned to the text files InFile and OutFile, which are opened for input and output. If the physical input file DATA.IN has the correct data, the sequence of read and readln statements proceeds in this way. The first Read statement obtains values for the integer variables I and J. The Readln next fills the character variable C and the strings S1 and S2. The next Read inputs a value for I using a new line, because the previous input was a Readln. The statement Readln(InFile) causes the next input, Read(InFile, C), to obtain a value for C from a new line. Following the assignment statements is a sequence of output statements. All output is placed in the physical file DATA.OUT. The first output statement writes the string 'I = J is ' and TRUE or FALSE (in a field six spaces wide). The following Writeln causes a new line to be started for the next output. The next line writes the value of R on a line with two decimal places. This value is written using a total of eight spaces. The next two lines (Write followed by Writeln) put the strings S1 and S2 and the integers I and J on one line. The value of J is written in a field of width seven. Finally the files are closed.

The preceding example illustrates the different forms that input and output statements may take for text files. A complete program is given in *FIGURE 11.4*. This program prompts the user for the name of a file to be used for input and then the name of a file to be used for output. The input file named should have been created (probably using an editor)

FIGURE 11.4

```
PROGRAM FileExample ( Input, Output, InFile, OutFile );

{  This is a simple program to illustrate the use of files.
   The output file consists of double the input.
```

(continued)

```
        Author     : John Riley
        Date       : February 12, 1986
        File name  : CH11EX1.PAS
}

VAR
   ItemIn,
   ItemOut  : Integer;
   InFile,
   OutFile  : Text;


PROCEDURE InputOpen(VAR InFil : Text);

{ This procedure opens a file for input.  The file designator is
  obtained from the keyboard. }

VAR
   FileName : STRING[20];   { Holds the name of the input file. }

BEGIN   { InputOpen }
  Write('Enter the input file name >' );
  Readln(FileName);
  Assign(InFil, FileName);
  Reset(InFil)
END;   { InputOpen }


PROCEDURE OutputOpen(VAR Out : Text);

{ This procedure opens a file for output.  The file designator is
  obtained from the keyboard. }

VAR
   FileName : STRING[20];   { Holds the name of the output file. }

BEGIN   { OutputOpen }
  Write( 'Enter the output file name >' );
  Readln( FileName );
  Assign( Out, FileName );
  Rewrite( Out )
END;   { OutputOpen }


BEGIN { FileExample }
  InputOpen( InFile );
  OutputOpen( OutFile );
  WHILE NOT EOF( InFile ) DO
     BEGIN
        Readln(InFile, ItemIn);
        ItemOut := 2 * ItemIn;
        Writeln(OutFile, ItemOut)
     END;   { WHILE }
  Close( InFile );
  Close( OutFile )
END. { FileExample }
```

and should contain integers (one per line). After the program is run, the output file named will contain integers that are double the integers in the input file.

Suppose that we had created an input file named IN.DAT with the following contents.

```
12
23
32
21
```

We would be able to use this file for the input to our program. If we wanted the output in the file OUT.DAT we could run the program and give this name in response to the prompt. This would occur as follows.

```
Enter the input file name >IN.DAT
Enter the output file name >OUT.DAT
```

This would be all that would appear on the screen when the program was run. One of the disk drives (the default drive) would be active during the program's execution. After the program was finished we would be able to view the contents of OUT.DAT either with the editor or with any operating system command which prints or displays a file. The contents of OUT.DAT would be

```
24
46
64
42
```

We could then use this file for the input for the next run of our program. We named the output file OUTOUT.DAT. This is what would appear on the screen.

```
Enter the input file name >OUT.DAT
Enter the output file name >OUTOUT.DAT
```

After the program was run, OUTOUT.DAT would contain

```
48
92
128
84
```

The computer does not "see" these files as a sequence of numbers, each on a separate line. From the computer's point of view each file consists of a sequence of characters. Among these characters are nonprinting or control characters. For example, the special character denoting the end of a line is included. We will use ⟨RET⟩ to denote RETURN or end of line.

There is also a special character which denotes the (logical) end of the file, which we will denote by ⟨EOF⟩ (for end of file). This end-of-file marker is automatically inserted by the computer (either when the editor is exited or when the close statement is executed). So, for example, the contents of IN.DAT is the following sequence of characters.

```
12<RET>23<RET>32<RET>21<EOF>
```

It must be emphasized that the 12 in the file is a two-character sequence (consisting of a '1' and a '2'). If this is to be used as an integer by the computer it must be translated into the internal (binary) form for the number 12.

It is possible to insert an extra RETURN before the end of the file so that the file's contents may be

```
12<RET>23<RET>32<RET>21<RET><EOF>
```

If you find that the last line of input of a text file has been used more than once, you probably have inserted extra RETURNs (which are not visible). Correct this by going to the end of the file in the editor and using the delete key to eliminate the extra RETURNs.

We now give the exact rules governing the input of data from text files using read and readln. In other words, we are giving precisely what happens when statements such as

```
Read(FileVar, V1, V2, ..., Vn)
```

```
Readln(FileVar, V1, V2, ..., Vn)
```

and

```
Readln(FileVar)
```

are executed. FileVar denotes a text file variable which has been opened for input, and V1, V2, ..., Vn are variables of type integer, real, character, or string. The rules are as follows:

○ If variables are present in the statement, the computer attempts to obtain values for all the variables. If more than one line of data is needed to fill the list of variables, more than one line of data will be read.

○ The data for any one variable must come from one line. Thus, if there are fewer characters than the maximum length of a string variable, the string variable is only partially filled by the characters on one line and its length is adjusted.

○ When the end of an input file is reached, any additional attempts to read from the file will cause string variables to have length zero. Character variables will be undefined. Integer and real variables will retain their previous values.

○ The data for numeric (integer and real) variables must conform to the form of a constant of the corresponding type and be separated from other data by one or more blank spaces, tabs, or returns. The characters are interpreted to yield a numeric value for the variable.

○ The next read or readln statement following a Readln (where variables may or may not be present) uses input data found following the next end-of-line character in the input file. That is, the next input uses a new line.

To illustrate the rules above, we will give a fragment of code which shows how a sequence of characters from a file would be read to produce a value for an integer. That is, the code emulates Read(F, I), where F is a text file variable which has been opened for input and I is an integer variable. This code is found in *FIGURE 11.5*. You should be able to understand this code. Most of the code serves to check that the character being read conforms to the form of an integer.

The main loop used to build the value for the integer I rests on two observations. The first is that if another digit (character between 0 and 9) is read, the preceding sequence of integers needs to be multiplied by 10. The second is that the value of a digit read into C is given by Ord(C) − Ord('0'). For example, if C is '6' then Ord(C) − Ord('0') is 54 − 48 (from the ASCII table) or 6.

Write and writeln cause the values of the expressions that appear as parameters to be output. In addition, writeln causes the output of the next write or writeln to be printed on a new line.

Each item in the output list of a write or writeln statement may be followed by parameters which dictate the format of the output. The following list of rules specifies these formats. Recall that an output item may be a Boolean, integer, real, character, or string expression. Output is said to be right-adjusted in a field when the rightmost character of the output is in the rightmost position of the field. The left of the field is padded with blanks. Suppose that FldWd (field width) and DecPl (decimal places) are integer expressions to serve as parameters for output. Let B be a Boolean, I an integer, R a real, C a character, and S a string expression. Then the following formats are possible.

B	The word TRUE or FALSE is output.
B : FldWd	TRUE or FALSE is output right-adjusted in a field FldWd characters wide.
I	The value of I is output. No spaces surround the value.

FIGURE 11.5

Reading an Integer From a Text File

```
{ Code to show how an integer is read from a text file.
  That is, this is essentially Read(F, I).  F is assumed
  to be have been opened for input. }

VAR
   I :   Integer;           { Integer being read                }
   F :   Text;              { File being read, already open     }
   C :   Char;              { Character read from file          }
   S :   (Plus, Minus);     { Indicates whether I is positive
                                  or negative }

BEGIN    { Read(F, I) }
  IF NOT EOF(F) THEN     { Skip blanks, tabs, returns }
     REPEAT
        Read(F, C)
     UNTIL EOF(F) OR ( (C <> ' ')      { blank }   AND
                       (C <> Chr(9))  { tab }      AND
                       (C <> Chr(13)) { return } ) ;
  IF Not EOF(F) THEN   { Attempt to fill I }
     IF (C = '+') OR (C = '-') OR
        (('0' <= C) AND (C <= '9')) THEN   { C is O. K. }
        BEGIN
           S := Plus;
           IF (C = '+') OR (C = '-') THEN
              BEGIN
                 IF C = '-' THEN
                    S := Minus;
                 Read(F, C)
              END; { IF }
           I := 0;
           WHILE ('0' <= C) AND (C <= '9') DO
              BEGIN { Build I }
                 I := 10 * I + (Ord(C) - Ord('0'));
                 Read(F, C)
              END;   { WHILE }
           IF (C <> ' ')      { blank }   OR
              (C <> Chr(9))  { tab }      OR
              (C <> Chr(13)) { return } OR
              (C <> Chr(26)) { EOF }
              THEN
                 Writeln (' ** ERROR **')
           IF S = Minus THEN
              I := -I
        END { IF }
     ELSE
        Write(' ** ERROR **')
END; { Read(F, I) }
```

I : FldWd	The value of I is output right-adjusted in a field FldWd characters wide.
R	The value of R in scientific format is output in a field 18 characters wide, starting with either two blank spaces or a blank space and a minus sign.
R : FldWd	The value of R in scientific format is output right-adjusted in a field FldWd characters wide.
R : FldWd : DecPl	The value of R is output in decimal notation in a field FldWd characters wide, with DecPl to the right of the decimal point. DecPl must be between 0 and 24.
C	The character value of C is output.
C : FldWd	The character value of C is output right-adjusted in a field FldWd characters wide.
S	The string value of S is output. Null characters are not output. Arrays of characters may be output.
S : FldWd	The string value of S is output right-adjusted in a field FldWd characters wide.

In the beginning of this chapter it was mentioned that the procedures read, readln, write, and writeln require one parameter that denotes a file variable. You may have wondered about this, because previous to this chapter we have used these without specifying files. There are two files always defined for input and output. These are Input and Output, defined for both standard Pascal and TURBO Pascal. Read(V1, V2, ..., Vn) is equivalent to Read(Input, V1, V2, ..., Vn). Write(V1, V2, ..., Vn) is equivalent to Write(Output, V1, V2, ..., Vn). In standard Pascal, the physical devices associated with these files are left undefined. TURBO assigns the keyboard to the file Input and the video screen to the file Output. This is done automatically. As a general rule, Input and Output should not be used in an assign, reset, or rewrite statement. EOF and EOLn without a file variable refer to Input.

Write and writeln with Output as a file variable (either explicitly or by default) work in much the same way as write and writeln do with any other file variable. The only difference is that output with a write statement is directed to the screen and not to a disk file. This makes the output transient in nature. Such output is sometimes called "soft copy." "Hard copy" is printed matter.

The standard file Input works differently from other text files used for input. This is because the input from the keyboard may be edited (using the delete key). One difference is that read and readln will not continue to input beyond the end of a line. In some sense the end of each line of the input is treated as the end of the file. This makes using the end-of-file function (EOF) with Input somewhat difficult.

The end-of-file character is entered from the keyboard as CTRL/Z (the control key held down and then Z typed). This may be used to signal EOF(Input) if when entering numeric data the user types a space after the number entered and before the return. If strings are being input, the number of characters entered must equal or exceed the maximum length of the string variable or else EOF(Input) will be True. If these rules are not followed, EOF(Input) will be True when you don't expect it to be. Each read and readln sets EOF(Input) to False before the input is actually read. Avoid using EOF(Input) and instead use some other means signaling the end of input if it is not terribly inconvenient to do so.

Although text files are easy to work with, they may store only a limited number of types (integer, real, character, string) of values. The next section concerns another type of file which overcomes this limitation.

11.4 BINARY FILES

This section discusses files which are not text files. Such files are called *binary files*. Binary files have a number of advantages over text files. The one disadvantage of binary files is that they may not be printed or viewed using an editor. The data in a binary file is stored in binary form and can only be utilized by the computer.

In Section 11.2 we mentioned that one way of declaring a file was to use the key words FILE OF followed by some component type, as indicated by the syntax diagram in *FIGURE 11.6*. An example of this would be

```
VAR
    IntFile : FILE OF Integer;
```

This declares IntFile to be a file of integers. This is not the same as a text file whose characters happen to represent integers. In IntFile the sequence of bits that represent an integer value will be the same sequence that is used internally by the computer. This means that the computer can read this file directly and hence more quickly, because no conversions need to be made. There is no need for the processing done in the manner of *FIGURE 11.5*.

| Binary File Type | FIGURE 11.6 |

$\longrightarrow$ **FILE** $\longrightarrow$ **OF** $\longrightarrow$ **component-type** $\longrightarrow$

A second advantage of binary files is that they store data more densely. For example, the integer 1234 requires two bytes in a binary file, but when represented in a text file as a sequence of characters '1', '2', '3', '4' it requires four bytes for the four characters as well as extra bytes for blank spaces. This difference is illustrated in *FIGURE 11.7* for storing the integers 123 and 4567. In this case we see that storage in a binary file takes half the bytes that it takes in a text file. It is usually the case that data can be stored more compactly in a binary file than in a text file.

Input to and output from a binary file may only be done using variables of the same type as the component type of the file. In TURBO Pascal, the procedures for input and output are read and write. Their syntax is given in *FIGURE 11.8*. Note that readln and writeln are not permitted for binary files.

For files which are not being used as random-access files, read and write work sequentially. That is, the next data item read is the next item in sequence in the file, and similarly the next item written will be written at the end of the file. The file variable used in either read or write must have been associated with a physical file using the assign statement and then named either in a reset statement (for input) or a rewrite statement (for output).

As a simple example of the use of binary files, the program in *FIGURE 11.9* uses binary files to do the same thing that was done with text files in Section 11.3. That is, the program takes its input from a file of integers and produces a file of integers which are double those of the input file. The program that does this is a simple modification of the program in

---

FIGURE 11.7   **Storing Integers in Text and Binary Files**

Text file

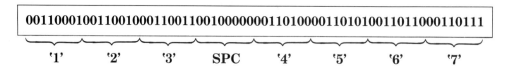

'1'   '2'   '3'   SPC   '4'   '5'   '6'   '7'

Binary file

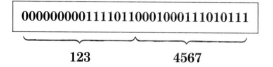

123   4567

Binary File Input/Output | FIGURE 11.8

$$\longrightarrow \text{READ} \longrightarrow (\longrightarrow \text{file-variable} \longrightarrow , \longrightarrow \text{variable} \longrightarrow) \longrightarrow$$

$$\longrightarrow \text{WRITE} \longrightarrow (\longrightarrow \text{file-variable} \longrightarrow , \longrightarrow \text{variable} \longrightarrow) \longrightarrow$$

FIGURE 11.9

```pascal
PROGRAM BinaryFileExample (Input, Output, InFile, OutFile);

{  This is a simple program to illustrate the use of binary
   files.  The output file consists of double the input.

      Author    : John Riley
      Date      : May 21, 1986
      File name : CH11EX2.PAS
}

TYPE
   IntegerFile = FILE OF Integer;

VAR
   ItemIn,
   ItemOut  : Integer;
   InFile,
   OutFile  : IntegerFile;


PROCEDURE InputOpen(VAR InFil : IntegerFile);

{ This procedure opens a file for input.  The file designator is
  obtained from the keyboard. }

VAR
   FileName : STRING[20];   { Holds name of input file. }

BEGIN  { InputOpen }
  Write('Enter the input file name >');
  Readln(FileName);
  Assign(InFil, FileName);
  Reset(InFil)
END;  { InputOpen }


PROCEDURE OutputOpen(VAR Out : IntegerFile);
```

(continued)

```
{ This procedure opens a file for output.  The file designator is
  obtained from the keyboard. }

VAR
    FileName : STRING[20];   { Holds name of output file. }

BEGIN   { OutputOpen }
  Write('Enter the output file name >');
  Readln(FileName);
  Assign(Out, FileName);
  Rewrite(Out)
END;   { OutputOpen }


BEGIN { BinaryFileExample }
  InputOpen(InFile);
  OutputOpen(OutFile);
  WHILE NOT EOF(InFile) DO
     BEGIN
        Read(InFile, ItemIn);
        ItemOut := 2 * ItemIn;
        Write( OutFile, ItemOut)
     END;   { WHILE }
  Close(InFile);
  Close(OutFile)
END. { BinaryFileExample }
```

FIGURE 11.4. (In fact, the program in *FIGURE 11.9* is a copy of the program in *FIGURE 11.4* which has been suitably altered using an editor.)

In response to the prompt requesting an input file, the file name of a file of integers must be given. How is such a file to be created ? An editor cannot be used, because an editor produces a text file. We must write a program which creates a file of integers. This program (*FIGURE 11.10*) simply reads an integer from the keyboard and writes it in a file of integers. (Because any integer may be input to the file, EOF(Input) is used.)

Similarly, a program is needed to view the contents of a file of integers. A program designed to do this is given in *FIGURE 11.11*.

We would use these programs in the following way. First we would run CreateIntegerFile. A session to create a file named INTEGER.IN containing 1 through 5 would appear as follows. ([RET] denotes the return key.)

```
Enter the output file name >INTEGER.IN[RET]
Enter an integer, followed by a blank. (RETURN to stop) >1 [RET]
Enter an integer, followed by a blank. (RETURN to stop) >2 [RET]
Enter an integer, followed by a blank. (RETURN to stop) >3 [RET]
Enter an integer, followed by a blank. (RETURN to stop) >4 [RET]
Enter an integer, followed by a blank. (RETURN to stop) >5 [RET]
Enter an integer, followed by a blank. (RETURN to stop) >[RET]
```

FIGURE 11.10

```
PROGRAM CreateIntegerFile(Input, Output, IntFile);

{ This is a simple program which creates a file of integers,
  the integers being entered from the keyboard.

    Author :     John Riley
    Date :       May 21, 1986
    File name : CH11EX3.PAS
}

TYPE
   IntegerFile = FILE OF Integer;

VAR
   Item : Integer;          { Read from keyboard and put in file }
   IntFile : IntegerFile;   { File to be created }


PROCEDURE OutputOpen(VAR Out : IntegerFile);

{ This procedure opens a file for output.  The file designator is
  obtained from the keyboard. }

VAR
   FileName : STRING[20];   { Holds input file name }

BEGIN   { OutputOpen }
  Write('Enter the output file name >');
  Readln(FileName);
  Assign(Out, FileName);
  Rewrite(Out)
END;   { OutputOpen }


BEGIN{ CreateIntegerFile }
  OutputOpen(IntFile);
  REPEAT
    Write('Enter an integer, followed by a blank. ');
    Write('(RETURN to stop) >');
    Readln(Item);
    IF NOT EOF(Input) THEN
        Write(IntFile, Item)
  UNTIL EOF(Input);
  Close(IntFile)
END.   { CreateIntegerFile }
```

FIGURE 11.11

```pascal
PROGRAM ViewIntegerFile(Input, Output, IntFile);

{   This program prints the contents of a file of integers on the
    screen.

        Author :      John Riley
        Date :        May 21, 1986
        File name :   CH11EX4.PAS
}


TYPE
    IntegerFile = File of Integer;


VAR
    Item : Integer;          { Item read from file and printed }
    IntFile : IntegerFile;   { File to be displayed }



PROCEDURE InputOpen(Var InFil : IntegerFile);

{ This procedure opens a file for input.  The file designator is
  obtained from the keyboard. }

VAR
    FileName : STRING[20];

BEGIN   { InputOpen }
  Write('Enter the input file name >');
  Readln(FileName);
  Assign(InFil, FileName);
  Reset(InFil)
END;   { InputOpen }


BEGIN   { ViewIntegerFile }
  InputOpen(IntFile);
  WHILE NOT EOF(IntFile) DO
     BEGIN
        Read(IntFile, Item);
        Writeln(Item)
     END; { WHILE }
  Close(IntFile)
END. { ViewIntegerFile }
```

After creating INTEGER.IN we may wish to view its contents. To do this we run ViewIntegerFile, supplying INTEGER.IN as the input file name. Here is what we would see.

```
Enter the input file name >INTEGER.IN
1
2
3
4
5
```

This seems to indicate that the programs CreateIntegerFile and ViewIntegerFile are working correctly. It is now possible to use the program BinaryFileExample because we can create an input file for it. We next run the program BinaryFileExample, supplying INTEGER.IN as an input file and naming the output file INTEGER.OUT as follows.

```
Enter the input file name >INTEGER.IN
Enter the output file name >INTEGER.OUT
```

After the program finishes running, we view the output file INTE-GER.OUT using ViewIntegerFile.

```
Enter the input file name >INTEGER.OUT
2
4
6
8
10
```

In practice, the component type of a binary file is most often a record. Typically, a record from an input file is updated and then placed in an output file of the same type. As an example of this, a very simple student record might consist of the student's name, class standing (freshman, sophomore, junior, senior), and average or QPA. A file containing a record for each student would then be used to hold this information about the student body. At the end of a semester, this information would need to be updated. Here are some fragments of the program which would do this.

```
TYPE
   StudentRec =   RECORD
                     Name  : STRING[20];
                     Class : STRING[2];   { FR, SO, JR, SR }
                     QPA   : Real
                  END; { StudentRec }
   StudentFile = FILE OF StudentRec;
```

```
VAR
    OldStuFile,
    NewStuFile : StudentFile;
    Student    : StudentRec;
    FileName   : STRING[20];


    Write('Enter old student file name >');
    Readln(FileName);
    Assign(OldStuFile, FileName);
    Reset(OldStuFile);
    Write('Enter new student file name >');
    Readln(FileName);
    Assign(NewStuFile, FileName);
    Rewrite(NewStuFile);


    WHILE NOT EOF(OldStuFile) DO
        BEGIN


            Read(OldStuFile, Student);


            WITH Student DO
                BEGIN
                    Writeln('Student : ', Name);
                    Writeln('Present class : ', Class);
                    Write('Enter new class >');
                    Readln(Class);
                    Write('Enter new QPA >');
                    Readln(QPA)
                END;   { WITH }


            Write(NewStuFile, Student);


        END;   { WHILE }


    Close(OldStuFile);
    Close(NewStuFile);
```

When the program begins, the user is prompted for the names of the input and output files. Records are then read from the input file. Each record is updated appropriately and then written in the output file. This process continues until the entire input file has been read. At the end of the next semester, the file created by this semester's run would be used as input. The process of reading an input file and creating an output file is a standard data-processing application.

11.5   AN EXAMPLE

To illustrate how files are used in programs, let us write a simple payroll application. A weekly payroll for hourly workers is to be produced. A file consists of records, each of which contains an employee's name, an hourly pay rate, and the amount earned to date in the current year. A program uses this data and how many hours were worked in the current week, entered from the keyboard, to produce the payroll. The output is to consist of another file containing records like those of the original file with the year-to-date earnings updated and also to print in a text file the amount earned this week and the year-to-date earnings for each employee. Pay is computed at time and a half for hours over 40.

Before the program is started we need to write a program to create a master file. Of course, the year-to-date earnings recorded initially are 0. This program appears in *FIGURE 11.12*. A sample of what happens when it is used also appears in *FIGURE 11.12*.

FIGURE 11.12

```
PROGRAM CreateFirstFile(Input, Output, EmployeeFile);

{      Program to create a file containing data for hourly
       employees.

       Author :       John Riley
       Date :         May 12, 1986
       File name :    CH11EX5.PAS
}

CONST
   NameLen = 30;
   Stop    = '!';

TYPE
   NameType    = STRING[NameLen];
   EmployeeRec = RECORD
                    Name      : NameType;
                    Rate,                    { Hourly pay rate }
                    YrToDate : Real        { Year to date earnings }
                 END;   { EmpRec }
   EmpFileType = FILE OF EmployeeRec;

VAR
   NameIn        : NameType;       { Name read in }
   EmpInfo       : EmployeeRec; { Record of employee data }
   EmployeeFile : EmpFileType;
```

(continued)

```
PROCEDURE OutputOpen(VAR Out : EmpFileType);

{ This procedure opens a file for output.  The file designator is
  obtained from the keyboard. }

VAR
   FileName : STRING[20];  { Holds input file name }

BEGIN  { OutputOpen }
  Write('Enter the output file name >');
  Readln(FileName);
  Assign(Out, FileName);
  Rewrite(Out)
END;  { OutputOpen }


BEGIN { CreateFirstFile }
  OutputOpen(EmployeeFile);
  Writeln;
  Writeln('Enter employee data as requested.  Use ', Stop);
  Writeln('for employee name to end');
  Writeln;
  Write('Enter name >');
  Readln(NameIn);
  EmpInfo.YrToDate := 0.0;
  WHILE NameIn <> Stop DO
     WITH EmpInfo DO
        BEGIN
          Name := NameIn;
          Write('Enter hourly rate >');
          Readln(Rate);
          Write(EmployeeFile, EmpInfo);
          Write('Enter name (', Stop, ' to end) >');
          Readln(NameIn)
        END;  { WITH }
  Close(EmployeeFile)
END. { CreateFirstFile }


Output:

Enter the output file name >EMPJAN1.DAT
Enter employee data as requested.  Use !
for employee name to end

Enter name >JONES, J
Enter hourly rate > 3.75
Enter name (! to end) >SMITH, K
Enter hourly rate > 5.45
Enter name (! to end) >ROBERTS, P
Enter hourly rate > 4.50
Enter name (! to end) >!
```

The main program, which appears in *FIGURE 11.13*, consists of opening the appropriate files, reading data from the file containing the employee information, calculating the pay and year to-date earnings, and then outputting the information in the appropriate files.

For its first run, the main program uses the file created by the preceding program (EMPJAN1.DAT) to create two files, EMPJAN8.DAT and JAN8.PAY. The first of these (EMPJAN8.DAT) serves as the input file for the next run of the payroll program, which creates two more files, EMPJAN15.DAT and JAN15.PAY. The files JAN8.PAY and JAN15.PAY contain the payroll information. The data files EMPJAN1.DAT, EMPJAN8.DAT, and EMPJAN15.DAT cannot be viewed. What the user of the payroll program would see is the outputs in *FIGURE 11.13* as well as the contents of the two pay files, JAN8.PAY and JAN15.PAY. Incidentally, it is important to adopt a consistent and meaningful naming scheme for the files used in this manner. We have done this, as you probably have observed.

FIGURE 11.13

```
PROGRAM Payroll(Input, Output, OldEmpFile, NewEmpFile, PayFile);

{    A program to do a simple payroll, keeping track of year to
     date earnings, pay rate in files.

     Author :       John Riley
     Date :         May 12, 1986
     File name :    CH11EX6.PAS
}

CONST
   NameLen       = 30;
   OTHours       = 40;      { Cut off for overtime hours }
   OTBonusFactor = 1.5;     { Multiplier for overtime bonus }

TYPE
   NameType     = STRING[NameLen];
   EmployeeRec  = RECORD
                     Name     : NameType;
                     Rate,                    { Hourly pay rate }
                     YrToDate : Real          { Year to date earnings }
                  END;  { EmpRec }
   EmpFileType  = FILE OF EmployeeRec;

VAR
   Hrs,                       { Hours worked this week }
   Pay          : Real;       { Pay this week }
   EmpInfo      : EmployeeRec; { Record of employee data }
   OldEmpFile,
   NewEmpFile   : EmpFileType;
   PayFile      : Text;
```

(continued)

```
PROCEDURE InputOpen(Var InFil : EmpFileType);

{ This procedure opens a file for input.  The file designator is
  obtained from the keyboard. }

VAR
   FileName : STRING[20];

BEGIN  { InputOpen }
  Write('Enter the file name of last week''s data >');
  Readln(FileName);
  Assign(InFil, FileName);
  Reset(InFil)
END;  { InputOpen }


PROCEDURE OutputOpen(VAR Out : EmpFileType);

{ This procedure opens a file for output.  The file designator is
  obtained from the keyboard. }

VAR
   FileName : STRING[20];  { Holds input file name }

BEGIN  { OutputOpen }
  Write('Enter the file name for week''s data >');
  Readln(FileName);
  Assign(Out, FileName);
  Rewrite(Out)
END;  { OutputOpen }


PROCEDURE TextOutputOpen(VAR Out : Text);

{ This procedure opens a text file for output.  The file designator
  is obtained from the keyboard. }

VAR
   FileName : STRING[20];  { Holds input file name }

BEGIN  { OutputOpen }
  Write('Enter the file name for the payroll data >');
  Readln(FileName);
  Assign(Out, FileName);
  Rewrite(Out)
END;  { OutputOpen }


BEGIN { Payroll }
  InputOpen(OldEmpFile);
  OutputOpen(NewEmpFile);
  TextOutputOpen(PayFile);
  Writeln(PayFile, 'Employee Name':NameLen, '   ', 'Week':12,
                    'Year':12);
```

(continued)

```
   Writeln(PayFile);
   WHILE NOT EOF(OldEmpFile) DO
      BEGIN
         Read(OldEmpFile, EmpInfo);
         WITH EmpInfo DO
            BEGIN
               Writeln('Employee name : ', Name);
               Write('Enter hours worked >');
               Readln(Hrs);
               IF Hrs > OTHours THEN
                  Pay := (Hrs - OTHours) * OTBonusFactor * Rate +
                          OTHours * Rate
               ELSE
                  Pay := Hrs * Rate;
               YrToDate := YrToDate + Pay;
               Writeln(PayFile, Name:NameLen, '  ', '$', Pay:12:2,
                          YrToDate:12:2)
            END; { WITH }
         Write(NewEmpFile, EmpInfo)
      END; { WHILE }
   Close(OldEmpFile);
   Close(NewEmpFile);
   Close(PayFile)
END.  { Payroll }


Output of first run:

Enter the file name of last week's data >EMPJAN1.DAT
Enter the file name for week's data >EMPJAN8.DAT
Enter the file name for the payroll data >JAN8.PAY
Employee name : JONES, J
Enter hours worked >  35
Employee name : SMITH, K
Enter hours worked >  45
Employee name : ROBERTS, P
Enter hours worked >  30


Contents of JAN8.PAY:

             Employee Name           Week         Year

                   JONES, J   $      131.25       131.25
                   SMITH, K   $      258.87       258.87
                   ROBERTS, P $      135.00       135.00


Output of second run:

Enter the file name of last week's data >EMPJAN8.DAT
Enter the file name for week's data >EMPJAN15.DAT
Enter the file name for the payroll data >JAN15.PAY
Employee name : JONES, J
```

(continued)

```
Enter hours worked >   42
Employee name : SMITH, K
Enter hours worked >   38
Employee name : ROBERTS, P
Enter hours worked >   39


Contents of JAN15.PAY:

                  Employee Name          Week          Year

                       JONES, J  $     161.25        292.50
                       SMITH, K  $     207.10        465.97
                     ROBERTS, P  $     175.50        310.50
```

The way this program works is a simple example of the way files are usually used. In particular, the output file created by one run of the program is used as the input file for the next run of the program.

11.6 SUMMARY

Files are used whenever there are large amounts of data to be stored or there is a need for permanent storage of data.

The assign statement is used to link a program file with a physical file. The reset statement opens a file for input, the rewrite statement opens files for output. The close statement closes files at the end of the program. The read statement inputs from a file, the write statement outputs to a file. The end-of-file function (EOF) is used to detect the end of a file.

There are two types of Pascal files, binary files and text files. Text files may be created by an editor and viewed on a video display or printed using a printer. Binary files store data in its internal format. Binary files may not be displayed.

It is possible to view the data structures we have discussed as the process of combining groups of simpler objects to form more and more complex objects. This is depicted in *FIGURE 11.14*. This book concen-

FIGURE 11.14   **Organizing Data**

$$\text{Bit} \rightarrow \text{Byte} \rightarrow \left\{ \begin{array}{l} \textbf{Integer} \\ \textbf{Real} \\ \textbf{String} \end{array} \right\} \rightarrow \textbf{Record} \rightarrow \textbf{File} \rightarrow \textbf{Data base}$$

trates on working with objects in the middle of this diagram. Assembly language tends to deal with objects at the left of the diagram. Data-base systems are concerned with groups of related files. Almost all programming involves the use of files. In Chapter 13, files are used extensively.

❑

EXERCISES

1. Find the errors in the following program fragments.

a.
```
VAR
     I, J : Integer;
     F    : Text;


     Assign(F, 'IN.DAT');   { Assume IN.DAT exists }
     Reset(F);
     Writeln(F, I, J);    { Assume I and J are initialized }

```

b.
```
VAR
     I, J : Integer;
     F    : Text;


     Assign(F, 'OUT.DAT');
     Rewrite(F);
     Writeln(F, I, J);    { Assume I and J are initialized }
     Write(F);

```

c.
```
VAR
     I, J : Integer;
     IntF : FILE OF Integer;


     Assign(IntF, 'INTEGER.OUT');
     I := 2;
     J := 5;
     Write(IntF, I, J);

```

d.
```
VAR
     I : Integer;
     J : Real;
     F : FILE OF Integer;

```

```
Assign(F, 'INTEGER.IN');    { Assume INTEGER.IN exists }
Reset(F);
Read(F, J);
```

e.
```
TYPE
    IntegerFile : FILE OF Integer;
VAR
    IntF : IntegerFile;

PROCEDURE P(F : IntegerFile);

BEGIN { P }
END; { P }

BEGIN { Main }

  P(IntF);

END. { Main }
```

2. In the discussion concerning output to text files, the action taken when the field specified by the field-width parameter is smaller than the value is not specified. For example, what is the output of the following?

```
I := 1234;
Writeln(F, I : 2);
```

I is an integer and F is an output text file variable. Find out what happens in the situations when the output expression is an integer, a real, and a string.

3. In *FIGURE 11.5* we gave a segment of code for reading characters from a text file and forming a value in an integer variable. Write a segment of code which reads a sequence of characters from an input text file into a real variable. (This is not an easy exercise.)

4. This exercise is designed to give you some feel for how EOF(Input) works. Enter and run the following program.

```
PROGRAM EndOfFileDemo (Input, Output);

{  This is a simple program to demonstrate how EOF(Input)
   behaves.
```

```
        Author :    John Riley
        Date :      May 20, 1986
        File name : CH11NUM4.PAS
}

VAR
  I : Integer;    { Integer to read }
  S : STRING[5]; { String to read   }

BEGIN { EndOfFileDemo }
  REPEAT
    Writeln;
    Writeln('EOF(Input) = ', EOF(Input));
    Writeln('Enter an integer, followed by blank. ');
    Write('CTRL/Z or RETURN to stop >');
    Readln(I);
    Writeln(I)
  UNTIL EOF(Input);
  Writeln;
  REPEAT
    Writeln;
    Writeln('EOF(Input) = ', EOF(Input));
    Writeln('Enter five letters, followed by blank. ');
    Write('CTRL/Z or RETURN to stop >');
    Readln(S);
    Writeln(S)
   UNTIL EOF(Input)
  END. { EndOfFileDemo }
```

All input, including CTRL/Z, must be followed by [RETURN]. Try inputting various things in response to the prompts. For example, find out what happens if an integer is entered without a blank afterward. Find out what happens if only [RETURN] is entered. Continue to run this program until you understand the way EOF(Input) works.

5. Write a Pascal program which creates a text file containing a table of the first 20 integers and their squares, cubes, and fourth powers.

6. Create a program which reads the file created in the previous exercise and prints its information in a table on the screen.

7. Write a program which eliminates the underscores (ASCII character 95) from a text file. The program should create a new text file which does not have the underscore character.

8. Write a program which reads from a text file and produces a new text file which has the old file's contents with lower-case letters converted to upper case. Use the TURBO Pascal function UpCase which has one argument, a character, and returns the upper-case version of the character if one exists. If the character does not have an upper-case version, UpCase returns the character.

9. Write a Pascal program which reads a text file containing infor-

mation about hourly employees and writes their weekly pay in another text file. The input text file contains on one line an employee's name and on the next line the number of hours worked and hourly pay (separated by a blank space). Each line of the output text file should contain an employee's name and weekly pay appropriately formatted. To run this program you will need to use the editor to create the input file.

10. Write a Pascal program which repeatedly reads two integers from a binary file of integers and places their sum in a binary file of integers. Assume that the input file contains an even number of integers. Use the programs in *FIGURES 11.9* and *11.10* to create binary files and view binary files.

11. Modify the program of Exercise 10 so that it works correctly if there is an odd number of integers in the file. If there is an odd number of integers in the file, the last integer is ignored.

12. Why are two different procedures needed to open output files in the program in *FIGURE 11.13*?

13. Write a program which will display the information in the employee data files (e.g., EMPJAN1.DAT) created by the programs in *FIGURES 11.12* and *11.13*.

14. Write two Pascal programs to work with binary files of records concerning cars. The first program is to create the binary file from information from the keyboard. The second is to write the information from such a file to the screen. Each record is to contain the following data about a car: serial number, manufacturer, style, and color.

INTRODUCTION

This chapter discusses the last of the stuctured data types, *sets*. In some sense, "structured" is something of a misnomer, because sets are not structured in the rigid way in which arrays, records, and files are structured. Sets are not used as often as these other types. However, sets are very useful in some contexts. It should be noted that the set type is not found in many other languages. ❏

CHAPTER 12

SETS

12.1 SET CONSTANTS, TYPES, AND VARIABLES

The notion of a set in Pascal is derived from the mathematical construct known as a set. A set is a group or aggregation of objects. When a set is implemented in a computer language, restrictions must be placed on the objects that may occur in the set. For example, a set in mathematics can have infinitely many elements, but a set in a computer language must be finite.

DEFINITION

> A *set* is a collection of values taken from some base type. The base type must be an ordinal type.

DEFINITION

> An *element* of a set is one of the values that occur in the set.

In Pascal a set constant is given by enclosing the values that are in the set in brackets ([ ]). The values may be listed individually (separated by commas) or by giving the first and last elements of a range (separated by two periods) or by a combination of these means. The values that occur in the set must all be of the same ordinal type. The order in which the values are listed is insignificant. A value may appear in the set only once. Any duplication in the list is ignored by the computer (but might confuse a reader). The syntax diagram for a set constant is given in *FIGURE 12.1*.

Here are some examples of set constants. (Assume that J and K are integer variables.)

```
['a', 'e', 'i', 'o', 'u']        Set of 5 characters
['A' .. 'Z']                     Set of 26 characters
[10, 12, 4, 6, 8, 0]             Set of 6 integers
[1..10, 15, 21..30]              Set of 21 integers
[2, 4, 2, 4]                     Set of 2 integers
[2 + 3, J * K]                   Set of 1 or 2 elements
                                 (depending on the
                                 values of J and K)
```

FIGURE 12.1	Set Constant

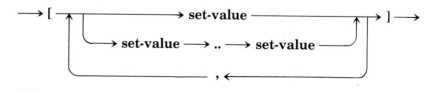

If an enumerated type has been defined, the constants of that type may be used as the values of a set. For example, if we have

```
TYPE
    Colors = (White, Red, Orange, Yellow, Green, Blue,
              Purple, Black);
```

then the following are valid set constants.

```
[White, Black]
[Red .. Purple]
[Red, White, Blue]
```

The maximum number of elements that may occur in a set is implementation dependent. TURBO Pascal allows up to 256 elements to be in a set.

For sets constructed from a given (ordinal) type, two sets are of particular interest. The first is the set containing all the values of the base type. This set is known as the *universal set*. The second is the set with no values, which is called the *empty set* or *null set*. The empty set is a set which can be considered to be of any base type, because its elements (there are none) can be considered to be among the constants of any type.

The *universal set* is the set of all values of a base type.   *DEFINITION*

The *empty set* is the set with no elements.   *DEFINITION*

The empty set is denoted by [ ]. For the type Colors defined above, the universal set is [White, Red, Orange, Yellow, Green, Blue, Purple, Black].

It is possible to form a set type using an ordinal type and then declare variables to be of that set type. Such variables are set valued. The set type is declared using the key words SET OF followed by the base type. The base type must be an ordinal type. In TURBO Pascal the base type must have no more than 256 constants. The syntax diagram for this is presented in *FIGURE 12.2*. This diagram indicates that the base type of the set may be given as a subrange type or enumerated type directly in the definition of the set type.

Using the set type declaration, we can declare variables to be of set type as in the following example.

```
TYPE
    Colors   = (White, Red, Orange, Yellow, Green, Blue,
                Purple, Black);
    ColorSet = SET OF Colors;
    SkillSet = SET OF (Welding, Painting, Electrical);
```

| FIGURE 12.2 | Set Type |

Set type

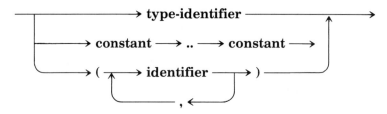

Base type

```
VAR
   Hues,
   Primaries       : ColorSet;
   EmployeeSkills : SkillSet;
   IntSet1,
   IntSet2,         : SET OF 0..100;
   CharSet1,
   CharSet2         : SET OF Char;
```

Once set variables have been declared, they may be used in assignment statements. Using the declarations above (and assuming that J is an integer variable and Ch is a character variable), the following assignment statements are possible.

```
Hues := [Orange, Green, Purple];
Primaries := [Red, Yellow, Blue];
EmployeeSkills := [Welding, Painting];
J := 20;
IntSet1 := [J, 1, 3, 5 .. 13];
IntSet2 := IntSet1;
Ch := 'A';
CharSet1 := ['B', Chr(70), Ch];
CharSet2 := CharSet1;
CharSet1 := [];
```

In the next section we introduce set expressions, which also may be used on the right side of an assignment statement. These are useful in building new sets from old sets.

12.2   SET OPERATIONS

Just as it is possible to combine numeric values to form expressions producing numerical values, it is possible to combine sets to produce other sets. These combinations are known as *set expressions*. The operations used to make set expressions form a type of set arithmetic. Indeed, the symbols used for these operations are the symbols of arithmetic. We start by defining the ways in which sets may be combined.

We can form a set from two sets in several different ways. We can consider the set formed using all the elements in the two sets. Another possibility is the set of all the elements that the two sets have in common. A third set is formed from all the elements which are in one set but not in the other. These new sets are known as the *union, intersection*, and *difference*, respectively.

> The *union* of the sets A and B is the set of elements which occur in either A or B.

DEFINITION

> The *intersection* of the sets A and B is the set of elements which occur in both A and B.

DEFINITION

> The *difference* of the sets A and B is the set of elements which occur in A but not in B.

DEFINITION

In Pascal the union of sets A and B is denoted by A + B. The intersection of A and B is denoted by A * B. The difference of A and B is denoted by A − B. When two sets are combined with one of these operators they must be of the same type. This means that, for example, it is not possible to form the union of a set of integers and a set of characters. The operators *, +, and − have the same priority or rules of precedence as in ordinary arithmetic. The intersection operator has higher priority than the union and difference operators, which are of equal priority. When operators of equal priority occur, the evaluation proceeds from left to right. Parentheses may be used to change the order of evaluation of expressions. In practice, complex set expressions rarely arise.

Here are some set expressions and their values.

Expression	Value
[1, 2, 3, 4] + [2, 4, 6, 8]	[1, 2, 3, 4, 6, 8]
[1, 2, 3, 4] * [2, 4, 6, 8]	[2, 4]
[1, 2, 3, 4] − [2, 4, 6, 8]	[1, 3]
['A'..'Z'] + ['A', 'E', 'I', 'O']	['A'..'Z']
['A'..'Z'] * ['A', 'E', 'I', 'O']	['A', 'E', 'I', 'O']
['A'..'Z'] − ['A', 'E', 'I', 'O']	['B'..'D', 'F'..'H', 'J'..'N', 'P'..'Z']
['A'..'Z'] + ['a'..'z']	['A'..'Z', 'a'..'z']
['A'..'Z'] * ['a'..'z']	[ ]
['A'..'Z'] − ['a'..'z']	['A'..'Z']

The sets used in set expressions may be set variables. The expressions may be used on the right side of assignment statements. Here is a program fragment which uses expressions in assignment statements.

```
VAR
    J           : Integer;
    IntSet1,
    IntSet2,
    IntSet3     : SET OF 0..100;
    Ch          : Char;
    Alphabet,
    Consonants,
    Vowels      : SET OF Char;

IntSet1 := [0..100];
IntSet2 := [];
FOR J := 0 TO 50 DO
    IntSet2  :=  IntSet2 + [2 * J];   { IntSet2 contains
                                         even numbers
                                         between 0 and 100 }
IntSet3 := IntSet1 − IntSet2;       { IntSet3 contains
                                       odd numbers }
Vowels := ['A', 'E', 'I', 'O', 'U', 'Y'];
Alphabet := ['A'..'Z'];
Ch := 'Y';
Consonants := Alphabet − Vowels + [Ch];
```

The for loop in the program fragment above illustrates one way of filling a set variable. Initialize the set variable to the empty set and then use a loop and the union operator to add elements to the set. Similarly, the variable Alphabet could have been filled as follows.

```
Alphabet := [];
FOR Ch := 'A' TO 'Z' DO
    Alphabet := Alphabet + [Ch];
```

Of course, this is unnecessary, as the assignment Alphabet : = ['A'..'Z'] shows.

Note that the symbols $+$, $-$, and $*$ now have more than one meaning. They may denote either a set operation or an arithmetic operation. Such symbols are said to be *overloaded*. An overloaded symbol's meaning must be determined by its context. The vast majority of occurrences of these symbols are in the arithmetic context. However, you should be aware of their other meanings.

12.3   SET COMPARISONS

It is possible to make comparisons of sets to reveal whether two sets are equal or one set contains the other. The exact meanings of "equal" and "contains" need to be made precise.

Two sets are equal if every element of one is an element of the other. If two sets are not equal, they are unequal.

One set is contained in another if all of its elements are in the other set. The contained set is called a *subset* of the containing set. Infrequently the larger set is called a *superset* of the smaller. The smaller set is said to be included in the larger.

A set A is a *subset* of a set B if every element of A is an element of B.

DEFINITION

There are four comparison operators for sets in Pascal. Each requires two operands which are sets with the same base type. Each returns a Boolean value.

The equality operator for sets uses the equals sign (=). The expression A = B has the value True if every element of A is an element of B and every element of B is an element of A. Otherwise, A = B has the value False. The inequality operator is denoted by $<>$. A $<>$ B has the value NOT(A = B). That is, A $<>$ B is True if there is an element in A which is not in B, or vice versa.

There are two operators for testing inclusion, denoted by $<=$ and $>=$. A $<=$ B ("A is a subset of B" or "A is included in B" or "A is contained in B") has the value True if every element of A is an element of B. If there is an element of A which is not an element of B, then A $<=$ B has the value False. A $>=$ B ("A contains B") has the value True if every element of B is an element of A and has the value False otherwise.

It should be noted that the empty set is a subset of every set. All of the elements of the empty set (there are none) occur in any other set. Thus if A is any set, both of the expressions ([ ] $<=$ A) and (A $>=$ [ ]) have the value True.

Comparisons between sets using the operators described above may be used in Boolean-valued expressions formed using Not, And, Or, and parentheses. Experience shows that elaborate expressions involving set comparisons arise very rarely.

Here are some examples of set comparisons and their values.

Comparison	Value
[1, 2, 3] = [1, 3, 2]	True (the order of elements does not matter)
[1, 2, 3] = [1, 2, 3, 4]	False (4 is not in the set on the left)
[1, 2, 3] <> [1, 2]	True
[2, 4] <= [1..10]	True
[1, 3] <= [3..10]	False (1 is not in the set on the right)
[1..20] >= [5..15]	True

The final operator involving sets allows us to determine whether or not a set has a specific value among its elements. This is known as *testing for set membership*. This operator is denoted by the key word IN. If A is a set and X is an expression of the type of the elements of A, then the Boolean-valued expression X IN A has the value True if the value of X occurs among the elements of A. If the value of X is not among the values in the set A, then X IN A has the value False. For X IN A to be defined, X must be of the same type as the elements of A.

Listed below are some examples of the use of the IN operator. J is an integer variable which has been assigned the value 6, and Ch is a character variable which has been assigned the value 'G'. IntSet is a set of integers which has the value [2, 4, 6, 8, 10], and ChSet is a set of characters with the value ['A', 'E', 'I', 'O', 'U', 'a', 'e', 'i', 'o', 'u'].

Expression	Value
1 IN [0..10]	True
2 IN [1, 3, 5]	False
J IN [10..20]	False
7 IN IntSet	False
J IN IntSet	True
2 * J IN IntSet	False
'a' IN ['0'..'9', 'A'..'Z']	False
'A' IN ['0'..'9', 'A', 'B', 'C']	True
Ch IN ['0'..'z']	True
'b' IN ChSet	False
Ch IN ChSet	False
Ch IN ChSet * ['A'..'Z']	False
Ch IN ChSet + ['A'..'Z']	True

12.4   USING SETS

There are a small number of ways in which sets are very useful. Two ways of using sets are demonstrated in this section.

A simple use of sets is to check that a constant is in a certain range. Checks of this sort occur with great regularity in data processing. Set constants can be used to do this checking quite naturally. For example, in Chapter 11 we needed to check whether a character variable C was a plus or minus sign or a digit. We wrote this as

```
IF (C = '+') OR (C = '-') OR
   (('0' <= C) AND (C <= '9')) THEN
```

This is much more easily expressed as

```
IF C IN ['+', '-', '0'..'9'] THEN
```

These two fragments do exactly the same thing, but the second is far simpler and more easily understood. It is also much less prone to error.

Integer values may also be checked using set constants. To check that the integer variable Grade is in the appropriate range (0 to 100) before processing, we would write

```
IF Grade IN [0..100] THEN  { Grade is OK }
   BEGIN { Processing the grade }
```

Whenever a collection of values is needed, a set is appropriate. For example, a person may speak one or more languages. To keep track of the languages spoken, we could make the following declarations.

```
TYPE
   Languages  = (English, French, Spanish, Italian,
                 German, Russian, Chinese, Japanese,
                 Hindi);
   LanguageSet = SET OF Languages;

VAR
   LanguagesSpoken = LanguageSet;
```

A small problem occurs here. Because the constants of Languages are user defined, they may not be input or output. This makes it difficult to fill the set LanguagesSpoken with the appropriate entries. This obstacle may be overcome by devising a string-valued function which has values corresponding to the constants. Assuming that the type String20 has been declared to be STRING[20], a function that does this appears in *FIGURE*

12.3. The declarations above are utilized. The length 20 was chosen so that longer languages could be added easily.

The function in *FIGURE 12.3* illustrates a general technique for making a correspondence from user-defined constants to strings.

Using the function in *FIGURE 12.3*, the set LanguagesSpoken may be filled in the following manner. Assume that L is declared to be a variable of type Languages and Answer is of type character.

```
LanguagesSpoken := [];
FOR L := English TO Hindi DO
    BEGIN
        Write('Do you speak ', LangStr(L), ' ? (Y/N) >');
        Readln(Answer);
        IF Answer in ['Y', 'y'] THEN
            LanguagesSpoken := LanguagesSpoken + [L]
    END; { FOR }
```

If we were concerned with an organization which had international dealings such as a trading corporation or a diplomatic corps, the languages spoken by the employees or members would be kept in their personnel records. If the information on all personnel was to be stored in an array, we might have declarations as follows. (The last three variable declarations are for use later on.)

FIGURE 12.3

```
FUNCTION LangStr(L : Languages) : String20;

{ This function yields a string corresponding to the
  language L.
}

BEGIN { LangStr }
  CASE L OF
     English  : LangStr := 'English';
     French   : LangStr := 'French';
     Spanish  : LangStr := 'Spanish';
     Italian  : LangStr := 'Italian';
     German   : LangStr := 'German';
     Russian  : LangStr := 'Russian';
     Chinese  : LangStr := 'Chinese';
     Japanese : LangStr := 'Japanese';
     Hindi    : LangStr := 'Hindi'
  END { Case }
END;  { LangStr }
```

```
CONST
    NumOfEmp = 200;


TYPE
    Languages   = (English, French, Spanish, Italian, German,
                    Russian, Chinese, Japanese, Hindi);
    LanguageSet = SET OF Languages;
    EmpRec      = RECORD
                      Name : STRING[25];
                          { Other employee data }


                      LangSpoken : LanguageSet
                    END; { EmpRec }
    EmpArry     = ARRAY[1..NumOfEmp] OF EmpRec;


VAR
    EmpList : EmpArry;
    OrgLang : LanguageSet;
    L       : Languages;       { Loop index }
    I       : Integer;         { Loop index }
```

By using these declarations, a number of problems could be handled
quite easily. For example, the following code finds which languages are
spoken by the employees in the organization. (The declarations above and
the function in *FIGURE 12.3* are assumed.)

```
OrgLang := [];
FOR I := 1 TO NumOfEmp DO
    WITH EmpList[I] DO
        OrgLang := OrgLang + LangSpoken;
Writeln('Languages spoken by employees');
FOR L := English TO Hindi DO
    IF L IN OrgLang THEN
        Writeln(LangStr(L));
```

It would also be possible to output those employees speaking a given
combination of languages. The program fragment below prints the names
of those employees speaking English, Russian, and Chinese.

```
Writeln('Employees speaking English, Russian and Chinese');
FOR I := 1 TO NumOfEmp DO
    WITH EmpList[I] DO
        IF LangSpoken >= [English, Russian, Chinese] THEN
            Writeln(Name);
```

The preceding program fragment works correctly even in the case that no employees speak all three languages. Unfortunately, in this situation the line "Employees speaking English, Russian and Chinese" will be printed with nothing else. This is unsatisfactory, because the user will not be sure whether there is an error in the program or there are no such employees. By using a Boolean variable, None, we are able to correct this deficiency.

```
Writeln('Employees speaking English, Russian and Chinese');
None := True;
FOR I := 1 TO NumOfEmp DO
    WITH EmpList[I] DO
        IF LangSpoken >= [English, Russian, Chinese] THEN
            BEGIN
                Writeln(Name);
                None := False
            END; { IF }
IF None THEN
    Writeln('None');
```

In this section, some ideas on how sets may be used were presented. The examples dealing with languages should convey some idea of the power of this data type. Getting used to working with sets takes some time. You should start using them for checking ranges and then work into more complex applications.

12.5 SUMMARY

A set serves to record a collection of values of some ordinal type. Values may be added or deleted from a set. Sets may be combined using the union (+), intersection (*), and difference (−) operators. Sets may be compared using the usual comparison operators (= <> <= >=). By using IN, it is possible to test whether a given value occurs in a set.

Sets are very useful for checking whether a value is in a particular range. They may also be used to record information which may have zero, one, or more values.

Sets are the last of the structured data types. One of the problems that a programmer faces is determining which data type is appropriate for a given problem. This topic is considered in the next chapter. ❑

EXERCISES

1. Assume that the following declarations and assignments have been made.

```
TYPE
    EnType  = (A1, A2, A3, A4, B1, B2, B3, B4);
    SetType = SET OF EnType;

VAR
    J             : Integer;
    Ch            : Char;
    E1, E2        : EnType;
    S1, S2, S3 : SetType;



    J  := 4;
    Ch := 'X';
    E1 := A1;
    E2 := B4;
    S1 := [A1..A4];
    S2 := [B1..B4];
    S3 := [A1, A3, B1, B3];
```

Give the value and the type of each of the following expressions.

```
[J, 2 * J, 4 + J]
[J] + [1, 3, 5]
J in ([2, 4, 6] * [1..10])
['A', 'b', 'C', 'd'] * ['A'..'Z']
Ch in ['a'..'z']
S1 + S2
S1 * S3
S2 - S1
S1 <= S3
(S1 + S2) >= S3
E1 in S1
E1 in S2
E2 in (S2 + S3)
E2 in (S2 * S3)
```

2. Find the errors in the following program fragments.

a.
```
VAR
    X : Real;



    X := 4.0;
    IF X IN [1.0, 2.0, 3.0] THEN
        Writeln('OK');
```

b.

```
VAR
    J : Integer;


    Readln(J);
    IF J IN ['0'..'9'] THEN
        Writeln(J, 'is a digit.');
```

c.

```
VAR
    J : Integer;
    S : SET OF Integer;


    J := 1;
    S := [0];
    WHILE S <> [] DO
        BEGIN
            S := S - [J];
            J := J + 1
        END;   { WHILE }
```

d.

```
VAR
    I      : Integer;
    IntSet : SET OF Integer;
    ChSet  : SET OF Char;


    IntSet := [0, 1, 2, 3, 5, 7];
    ChSet  := ['1'..'9'];
    FOR I := 0 TO 10 DO
        IF I IN (IntSet * ChSet) THEN
            Writeln(I);
```

3. Use sets to do the following.
   a. Write a Boolean-valued function which has one integer parameter
      and which is True whenever the integer is a multiple of 7 between
      1 and 100.
   b. Suppose that SetType has been defined to be a set type using some
      base type. Two sets S1 and S2 of SetType are said to be *disjoint* if
      they have no elements in common. That is, no element of S1 is in
      S2, and vice versa. Write a Boolean-valued function which has two
      parameters of SetType and which has the value True whenever the
      two actual parameters are disjoint sets.
   c. Suppose that the following declarations have been made.

```
TYPE
    Days   = (Sun, Mon, Tue, Wed, Thu, Fri, Sat);
    DaySet = SET OF Days;
```

Write an integer-valued function which has as input a set S of type DaySet which returns the number of Days actually in DaySet. Thus the function's value is always between 0 and 7. For example, if the function is named NumOfDaysIn, then NumOfDaysIn([Sun, Mon, Tue]) is 3.

d. Suppose that DaysWorked is a set variable of type DaySet, as defined in c. Write a procedure which queries a user as to the days he or she worked and then fills DaysWorked with the corresponding constants from Days.

4. An employment firm which places computer programmers needs a program which matches a programmer with a job based on the programming languages the programmer knows. The languages that a programmer may know are Ada, Algol, BASIC, COBOL, C, FORTRAN, Lisp, Pascal, and PL1. (These are just a few of the languages in use today.) Write a program which consists of two phases. In the first phase, a list of programmers and the computer languages they each know is to be input. The list of languages may be input by asking appropriate Yes/No questions (as in the program fragment in Section 12.4). In the second phase of the program, a potential employer is asked for the languages his or her programmers use (again using Yes/No questions), and a list of candidates who know these languages is printed. If none of the potential programmers knows a particular combination of languages, an appropriate message indicating this should be printed. Use sets to do this program.

5. Write a program which is used to maintain a list of baseball players and the positions they play. The possible positions are Pitcher, Catcher, FirstBase, SecondBase, ShortStop, ThirdBase, LeftField, CenterField, and RightField. In the first part of the program, the user is to enter a player's name and then be asked which positions the player is able to play. A special character entered for the name ends the input. Use an array of records, with each record consisting of a name and set of positions. There are no more than 20 players on a team. In the second phase of the program, the user is prompted for combinations of positions desired and is given a list of players who play the positions. At the end of each query, the user is asked whether he or she wishes to continue.

6. The sieve of Eratosthenes (circa 230 B.C.) is a method for finding the prime numbers in some range. The idea is to start with a list of integers beginning with 2. Then all the multiples of 2 are deleted. The next number in the list (3) is also prime. All the multiples of 3 are then removed from the list. At each step, the next number left is prime

(because it has been eliminated as a multiple of some smaller prime). All of its multiples are deleted from the list. This process continues until only prime numbers are left in the list.

Use sets to emulate the sieve of Eratosthenes and produce a listing of the primes between 2 and 100. Hints: Start with the set of integers between 2 and 100 and remove elements. A number A is a multiple of a number B if A MOD B is 0.

In Chapter 9, some aspects of program design were discussed. These were illustrated with a case study. In this chapter we examine another facet of the programming process and also do another case study to show that this facet of programming indeed arises. The present chapter also serves as a review of the topics introduced in the preceding chapters. In particular, it shows how the data types of Pascal are used in a program. ❑

CHAPTER 13

PROGRAMMING METHODOLOGY

Case Study II

13.1 DATA STRUCTURES AND ALGORITHMS

A program may be considered to have two aspects. One of these is the "what" of the program—that is, the objects (necessarily abstract) manipulated by the program. These are known as the *data structures* or *data objects* of the program. The data structures used by the program represent objects of the "real" world. For example, the assignment EmployeePay := 123.45 represents the fact that an employee is to be paid $123.45. It is not the same thing as the employee being handed $123.45. It is in this sense that the objects manipulated by the program are abstract.

The other aspect of a program is the "how" of the program—that is, the manipulations of the program on the objects of the program. The word we have used for this aspect is *algorithm*. One part of an algorithm may be computational. EmployeePay := HoursWorked * HourlyRate would be an example of a computation. Another part of an algorithm is the specification of which steps are needed to accomplish a given task, such as the logic needed to compute overtime pay.

In all but the simplest of programs, these aspects are intimately related. The data structure being used influences the design of the algorithm and the possible algorithms influence the data structures chosen for the program. For certain programming tasks, the algorithms are somewhat more important, whereas for others the data structures involved dominate the design process. It is impossible to ignore either aspect of the programming process.

In Chapter 9, the discussion of programming methodology centered around the problem of controlling the complexity of the program and describing the necessary actions to be taken. This may be considered to be related to the development of an algorithm for the program. The data-structures aspect of the program was not very much in evidence. At this point, a sufficient variety of types of data objects causes us to pause before choosing which are to be used in a program.

The data types that may be used to construct the data structures of a program include the simple types [Boolean, character, integer, real, and user-defined (enumerated) types] as well as the types which are built using these simple types (strings, arrays, records, files, and sets). These data types may be combined in a large number of ways. Just as different control statements may be used to achieve the same end, different combinations of data types may be used to represent the objects of a program. What is needed is a set of guidelines for choosing among these types. The list of rules which follows is intended to help the programmer decide which data types are appropriate for the programming task under consideration and how these are normally used. These rules are not meant to be absolute. At a given stage of a program's development it may become apparent that the data structure chosen is not the best one. In this situation, it may be best to start anew.

The use of constants and enumerated types can improve a program significantly. Both constants and enumerated types tend to make the data structures and flow of control more evident. For example, if the declaration

```
VAR
    HoursWorked : ARRAY[1..7] OF Real; { Hours worked each day }
```

is made, it is not clear which element of the array represents the hours worked on Sunday and needs to be treated separately. A comment such as { 1 = Mon .. 7 = Sun } helps but is likely to be forgotten. In contrast, the declarations

```
TYPE
    DaysOfWeek = (Mon, Tue, Wed, Thu, Fri, Sat, Sun);

VAR
    HoursWorked : ARRAY[DaysOfWeek] OF Real;
```

make it obvious which element of the array represents the hours worked on Sunday.

Arrays are appropriate for collections of data objects which are all of the same type. Generally, the component type of an array is one of the simple types or a string or a record. Do not forget that the size of an array is limited by the memory of the machine. A declaration ARRAY[1..100, 1..100] OF STRING[20] will probably cause problems. Arrays of more than two dimensions are very difficult to handle mentally and should be used with great caution. Finally, the contents of an array are lost when the program stops (either normally or abnormally). In other words, an array is not suitable for storing data between runs of the program.

A record is suitable for aggregating a group of data objects of differing types which are logically related. One way to think of this is that a record contains the information which might be found about something on a sheet of paper or a card in a file cabinet. The usual types for fields of a record are the simple types, strings, arrays, and records. Set types sometimes occur among the fields of a record. The number of fields in a record should not be excessive. Managing the information to be held in a record can be difficult, because a large number of fields may be needed to hold all the information desired. The use of subrecords and arrays can help keep the record under control. For example, we can modify

```
TYPE
    StuRec = RECORD
                 FirstName : STRING[10];
                 MidInit   : Char;
                 LastName  : STRING[15];
                 Test1,
                 Test2,
                 Test3,
                 Test4,
                 Test5,
                 Test6     : Integer;
                 Ave       : Real
             END; { StuRec }
```

to be more manageable as

```
CONST
   NumOfTests = 6;

TYPE
   NameRec = RECORD
                 First   : STRING[10];
                 MidInit : Char;
                 Last    : STRING[15]
              END; { NameRec }
   StuRec  = RECORD
                 Name : NameRec;
                 Test : ARRAY[1..NumOfTests] OF Integer;
                 Ave  : Real
              END; { StuRec }
```

The latter format has other advantages. For example, changing the number of tests is not difficult. Like an array, the contents of a record are lost when a program is completed. This makes a record inappropriate for storing data between runs of a program.

Files are used when a large amount of data is being manipulated or when data is to be saved when the program has finished running. The components of a file are all of the same type. This type is usually a simple type (most frequently character) or a record type. The special file type Text is used to create files which may be used to generate hard copy or to contain data which may be read by humans. Binary files are used to store data which is used only by a program. A binary file may not be directly read by a human. Thus if a program uses a binary file for input, the binary file must have been created by another program. If a binary file's contents are to be examined, a program to read and display it must be written.

A file of records is similar to a folder (or file) of pieces of paper or cards. Each piece of paper or card has been laid out in the same format to contain data about objects of some class. Files are used frequently in data processing, and you should get used to working with them.

A set is appropriate whenever the number of values that an object may take varies. For example, a machinist may be qualified to operate any number of different machines. This is modeled by declaring

```
TYPE
   Machines     = (Lathe, Mill, Borer, Saw, DrillPress);
   MachineSet   = SET OF Machines;
   MachinistRec = RECORD
                     |
                     |
                     Operates : MachineSet;
                     |
                  END; { MachinistRec }

VAR
   Apprentice,
   Expert       : MachinistRec;
```

and then making assignments like

```
Apprentice.Operates := [];       { That's why he or she  is
                                   an apprentice. }

Expert.Operates := [Lathe, Mill, Borer, Saw, DrillPress];
                             {    That's   what   makes
                                 an   expert }
```

The values that may appear in a set must be of some ordinal type. Sets may also be used in a program to check that an expression has a value in an appropriate range.

These guidelines concerning data types, along with the discussion in Chapter 9, are meant to help in the design and implementation of "good" programs. The criteria for a good program are that it works and can be seen to work. A program "works" if it accomplishes the task for which it was designed. A program "can be seen to work" if it is possible for a person (who knows the programming language) to read the program, understand its operation, and verify that it accomplishes its task. Incidentally, unless a program can be seen to work it is not known whether it will work. All that one can conclude from testing is either that the program does not work or that it *seems* to work. However, appropriate test data can help you understand why a program does not work. In order for a program to be seen to work, it must be carefully designed and written. Each statement in a program must have a purpose, and it is incumbent on the programmer to know this purpose and to code the statement so that it achieves its purpose. Of course, the statements must work together correctly to accomplish the programming task. Appropriate stylistic conventions aid in making the program more readable and aid in making it possible to see that the program works. However, they are not a substitute for sound design. Considering that modern technological societies use software in critical situations, correctness of programs is of paramount importance.

13.2   CASE STUDY II

Our second case study is an inventory problem. Managing an inventory (a collection of goods or supplies) is very important for many organizations. Keeping too many of a given item on hand is expensive, because storage space and inventory management are costly. On the other hand, running out of a needed item at a crucial moment is also likely to be very expensive. Imagine the cost of shutting down an automobile assembly line because there were no more screws to attach dashboards. The ideal is to keep just enough on hand and no more. In this section we develop a small inventory program.

The manager of a warehouse has decided to keep track of the items stored in the warehouse using a computer. Each item stored in the warehouse is identified by a number. For each item, the manager keeps a description, the number on hand, the minimum number of the item to be kept on hand, and the name and address of the supplier of the item. At the end of each day she wants to enter the numbers and quantities of the items that were shipped and received that day. At the end of each week she wants a list of the items that need to be reordered. For each item in this list, the number on hand, the minimum number, and the supplier's name and address are to be supplied.

The description of the problem given above is, of course, incomplete. Querying the manager reveals the following. An item number can contain letters and punctuation (e.g., a hyphen) but never uses more than 12 characters. (Identification "numbers" frequently aren't numbers: consider a car license plate number.) The description of the item is relatively short; essentially, it is the item's name. Because the quantity of an item shipped is actually counted as it leaves the warehouse, this quantity cannot exceed the number that was on hand.

Because the program will be run once each work day and will need the results of the previous run, we decide to keep the information in a file of records (which is a binary file). Using a binary file will improve the efficiency (speed) of the program, but this is not the basis for our decision to use a binary file. Each record of the file is to contain the information about one item. In order to process this file sequentially, we determine that the items in the file are to be in order according to the items' numbers. On the other hand, it would be inconvenient to have to enter the daily reports in order. So we decide to store them in an array, which we can then put in order if we need to. We also realize that we will need two programs. One program will be needed to create the first inventory file. Because this file is a binary file, it cannot be created using an editor. Another program will be needed to do the updating. This second program is the one that the manager will be using. We see that this second program really has two parts: a daily update, which is done every day; and a weekly summary, which is done only once a week. *FIGURE 13.1* contains a summary of this discussion.

The considerations above are typical. Notice that we need more than one program to accomplish our task. At this stage we have begun to consider the data objects our programs will be manipulating and the decomposition of the programming task into subprograms.

Because the inventory files that are created by these programs are binary files (files of records), it is not possible to view their contents directly (e.g., by using an editor or the system command TYPE). Thus it would be helpful to have a program which permits us to examine the contents of one of the inventory files. We need an inventory file to run the main program, and so we write the program to create an inventory file first. To check this program, we also write the program which displays an inventory file. These programs are given in *FIGURES 13.2* and *13.3*. *FIGURE 13.2* also shows the data being entered into an inventory file (MAY15.INV) which will be used later. Recall that input to and output

FIGURE 13.1

Program CreateInventoryFile

This program is designed to get the information from the keyboard to build the initial inventory file. Its output is a file of records for use as the first input file.

Program Inventory

1.   Daily Update

        This part of the program uses the previous day's inventory file and the day's report to generate a new inventory file which has been updated. Because the items are not input in order, they are stored in an array and sorted.

If end of work week then

2.   Weekly Summary

        This part of the program uses the output file generated by Daily Update to produce a listing of the inventory and the items that need to be ordered.

FIGURE 13.2

```pascal
PROGRAM CreateInventoryFile(Input, Output, InvFile);

{ This program is used to create an inventory file of records.

      Author    : John Riley
      Date      : May 23, 1986
      File name : CH13EX1.PAS
}

CONST
   IDLen       = 12;
   DescripLen  = 20;
   Stop        = '!';

TYPE
   AddressRec =    RECORD
                      Street : STRING[25];
                      City   : STRING[15];
                      State  : STRING[2];
                      Zip    : STRING[5]
                   END;  { AddressRec }
   SupplierRec =   RECORD
                      Name    : STRING[20];
                      Address : AddressRec
                   END;  { SupplierRec }
```

(continued)

```
    ItemRec =        RECORD
                        ID          : STRING[IDLen];
                        Descrip     : STRING[DescripLen];
                        NumOnHand,                  { Number in stock }
                        ReorderNum : Integer;    { Number at which to
                                                    order  more }
                        Supplier    : SupplierRec
                     END;  { ItemRec }
    InventoryFil = FILE OF ItemRec;

VAR
  ItemIn    : ItemRec;
  Inventory : InventoryFil;


PROCEDURE OutputOpen(VAR F : InventoryFil);

{  This procedure obtains a name for the output file and then
   opens it.
}

VAR
     FileName : STRING[15];

BEGIN   { OutputOpen }
  Write('Enter the name of the output file >');
  Readln(FileName);
  Assign(F, FileName);
  Rewrite(F)
END;    { OutputOpen }


BEGIN   { CreateInventoryFile }
  Writeln('This program creates an inventory file. ');
  OutputOpen(Inventory);
  Writeln('Enter items in order, by number.  To stop, enter ');
  Writeln(Stop, ' for the item number.');
  Write('Enter item number >');
  Readln(ItemIn.ID);
  WHILE ItemIn.ID <> Stop DO
     BEGIN
        WITH ItemIn DO
           BEGIN
              Write('Enter item description >');
              Readln(Descrip);
              Write('Enter number on hand >');
              Readln(NumOnHand);
              Write('Enter number at which to reorder >');
              Readln(ReorderNum);
              Writeln('Enter supplier information');
              WITH Supplier, Address DO
                 BEGIN
                    Write('Enter name >');
                    Readln(Name);
```

(continued)

```
                          Write('Enter street address >');
                          Readln(Street);
                          Write('Enter city >');
                          Readln(City);
                          Write('Enter state (two letters) >');
                          Readln(State);
                          Write('Enter zip code >');
                          Readln(Zip)
                        END   { WITH }
                 END;   { WITH }
            Write(Inventory, ItemIn);
            Write('Enter item number >');
            Readln(ItemIn.ID)
        END; { WHILE }
    Close(Inventory)
END.   { CreateInventoryFile }
```

Output:

```
This program creates an inventory file.
Enter the name of the output file >MAY15.INV
Enter items in order, by number.  To stop, enter
! for the item number.
Enter item number >176
Enter item description >3/4 BOLT
Enter number on hand >622
Enter number at which to reorder >200
Enter supplier information
Enter name >BOLTS INC.
Enter street address >22 OAK STREET
Enter city >LEWIS
Enter state (two letters) >NJ
Enter zip code >07111
Enter item number >219
Enter item description >1/2 BOLT
Enter number on hand >534
Enter number at which to reorder >200
Enter supplier information
Enter name >BOLTS INC.
Enter street address >22 OAK STREET
Enter city >LEWIS
Enter state (two letters) >NJ
Enter zip code >07111
Enter item number >276
Enter item description >SIDE PANEL
Enter number on hand >14
Enter number at which to reorder >10
Enter supplier information
Enter name >PENN SHEET METAL
Enter street address >32 MAPLE STREET
Enter city >ORANGE
Enter state (two letters) >PA
Enter zip code >18922
Enter item number >!
```

FIGURE 13.3

```pascal
PROGRAM ReadInventoryFile(Input, Output, InvFile);
{ This program is used to read an inventory file of records.

     Author    : John Riley
     Date      : May 23, 1986
     File name : CH13EX2.PAS
}

CONST
   IDLen      = 12;
   DescripLen = 20;

TYPE
   AddressRec =    RECORD
                      Street : STRING[25];
                      City   : STRING[15];
                      State  : STRING[2];
                      Zip    : STRING[5]
                   END;   { AddressRec }
   SupplierRec =   RECORD
                      Name    : STRING[20];
                      Address : AddressRec
                   END;   { SupplierRec }
   ItemRec     =   RECORD
                      ID         : STRING[IDLen];
                      Descrip    : STRING[DescripLen];
                      NumOnHand,                  { Number in stock }
                      ReorderNum : Integer;   { Number at which to
                                                 order  more }
                      Supplier   : SupplierRec
                   END;   { ItemRec }
   InventoryFil = FILE OF ItemRec;

VAR
   ItemIn    : ItemRec;
   Inventory : InventoryFil;


PROCEDURE InputOpen(VAR F : InventoryFil);

{  This procedure obtains a name for the input file and then
   opens it.
}

VAR
   FileName : STRING[15];

BEGIN  { InputOpen }
  Write('Enter the name of the input file >');
  Readln(FileName);
  Assign(F, FileName);
  Reset(F)
END;    { InputOpen }
```

(continued)

```
BEGIN  { ReadInventoryFile }
  InputOpen(Inventory);
  Writeln('Contents of the file ');
  Writeln;
  Writeln('Item No.' : IDLen, ' Description' : DescripLen,
          ' On Hand  Min   Supplier');
  WHILE NOT EOF(Inventory) DO
     BEGIN
       Read(Inventory, ItemIn);
       WITH ItemIn DO
          Writeln(ID : IDLen, Descrip : DescripLen,
                  NumOnHand : 6, ReorderNum : 8, '    ',
                  Supplier.Name)
     END; { WHILE }
  Close(Inventory)
END.  { ReadInventoryFile }
```

from binary files must be done using the procedures read and write with variables whose type is the same as the type of the components of the file. Incidentally, it is no coincidence that the declaration sections of these two programs are similar. One has been copied from the other using the editor. This is a useful technique. It not only saves us typing time but also ensures that the file descriptions are identical.

In the second program we decide to output only the supplier's name, because it would be too cumbersome to put the address on one line. We choose to make the lengths of the item numbers and descriptions constants, because we know that these might change and will be used elsewhere in the programs. It is not clear that 20 characters will be enough for the descriptions of the items in the inventory. We feel a little more comfortable about not documenting the lengths used in the address field. When to use a constant is a subjective matter. For example, using two letters as the abbreviation for a state name is standard and is not likely to change. When in doubt, use a constant.

The next step is to start working on the main program. Our first version of this program is presented in *FIGURE 13.4* and obviously does very little other than put in a program the information in *FIGURE 13.1*.

This first version of the program runs without any errors.

It would be possible to work on either of the procedures DailyUpdate or WeeklySummary. We choose to develop DailyUpdate. This procedure seems to consist of two pieces: getting the day's data and using this data to create an updated file. When we begin to create these subprocedures we find that we need the declarations used to form the inventory files. Using the editor, we copy the types from the program CreateInventoryFile. While we are doing this we notice the procedure InputOpen, and we copy this as well because we think it will be useful. We also copy OutputOpen for the same reason. The resulting program (which has been run) is given in *FIGURE 13.5*.

FIGURE 13.4

```
PROGRAM Inventory(Input, Output, OldInvFile, NewInvFile);

{ This program maintains an inventory for a warehouse. It has
    two main parts : a daily update and a weekly summary.

        Author        : John Riley
        Date begun     : May 24, 1986
        Date finished :
        File name      : CH13EX3.PAS
}

VAR
    Answer : Char;


PROCEDURE DailyUpdate;

{ This procedure does the daily updating of the inventory  files.

}

BEGIN { DailyUpdate }
  Writeln('Updating not implemented')
END;   { DailyUpdate }


PROCEDURE WeeklySummary;

{ This procedure produces a report of items needing to be
  ordered.
}

BEGIN   { WeeklySummary }
  Writeln('Summary not implemented')
END;    { WeeklySummary }


BEGIN   { Inventory }
  DailyUpdate;
  Write('Do you want end of week report? (Y/N) >');
  Readln(Answer);
  IF Answer IN ['Y', 'y'] THEN
     WeeklySummary
END.    { Inventory }
```

The next step is to implement the procedures needed to accomplish GetDaysData. In order to use the daily date with the inventory file, which is in order, the data must be in order (by ID). Two familiar routines are needed: one to enter the data, and the other to put it in order. We also include a procedure to write the array of data so that we can check our

FIGURE 13.5

```
PROGRAM Inventory(Input, Output, OldInvFile, NewInvFile);

{  This program maintains an inventory for a warehouse.  It  has
   two main parts : a daily update and a weekly summary.
      Author        : John Riley
      Date begun     : May 24, 1986
      Date finished :
      File name     : CH13EX4.PAS
}


CONST
   IDLen      = 12;
   DescripLen = 20;

TYPE
   AddressRec =    RECORD
                      Street : STRING[25];
                      City   : STRING[15];
                      State  : STRING[2];
                      Zip    : STRING[5]
                   END;  { AddressRec }
   SupplierRec =   RECORD
                      Name    : STRING[20];
                      Address : AddressRec
                   END;  { SupplierRec }
   ItemRec     =   RECORD
                      ID         : STRING[IDLen];
                      Descrip    : STRING[DescripLen];
                      NumOnHand,               { Number in stock }
                      ReorderNum : Integer;   { Number at which to
                                                 order  more }
                      Supplier   : SupplierRec
                   END;  { ItemRec }
   InventoryFil = FILE OF ItemRec;

VAR
   Answer : Char;


PROCEDURE InputOpen(VAR F : InventoryFil);

{  Procedure to obtain a name for the input file and open it. }

VAR
   FileName : STRING[15];

BEGIN  { InputOpen }
  Write('Enter the name of the input file >');
  Readln(FileName);
  Assign(F, FileName);
  Reset(F)
END;   { InputOpen }
```

(continued)

```pascal
PROCEDURE OutputOpen(VAR F : InventoryFil);

{ Procedure to obtain a name for the output file and open it. }

VAR
   FileName : STRING[15];

BEGIN   { OutputOpen }
  Write('Enter the name of the output file >');
  Readln(FileName);
  Assign(F, FileName);
  Rewrite(F)
END;    { OutputOpen }



PROCEDURE DailyUpdate;

{ Procedure to do the daily updating of the inventory files. }

CONST
   DailyMax = 100;   { Maximum number of items for a day }

TYPE
   ItemInfo = RECORD
                 ID     : STRING[IDLen];
                 Action : Char;         { S = Ship
                                          R = Receive }
                 Num    : Integer       { Number shipped
                                          or received }
              END;   { ItemInfo }
   ItemArry = ARRAY[1..DailyMax] OF ItemInfo;

VAR
   DailyData : ItemArry;   { Data about all items shipped,
                             received today }
   NumOfItems : Integer;   { Number of items shipped or
                             received }



PROCEDURE GetDaysData(VAR DailyData : ItemArry;
                      VAR NumOfItems : Integer);

{ Procedure to get the daily information from the keyboard.
  The information is stored in an array.   }

BEGIN { GetDaysData }
  Writeln('GetDaysData not implemented')
END;   { GetDaysData }



PROCEDURE UpdateInventoryFile(VAR DailyData : ItemArry;
                              NumOfItems : Integer);
```

(continued)

```
BEGIN { UpdateInventoryFile }
  Writeln('UpdateInventoryFile not implemented')
END;  { UpdateInventoryFile }


BEGIN { DailyUpdate }
  GetDaysData(DailyData, NumOfItems);
  UpdateInventoryFile(DailyData, NumOfItems)
END;  { DailyUpdate }


PROCEDURE WeeklySummary;

{ Procedure to produce a report of items needing to be ordered. }

BEGIN  { WeeklySummary }
  Writeln('Summary not implemented')
END;   { WeeklySummary }


BEGIN  { Inventory }
  DailyUpdate;
  Write('Do you want end of week report? (Y/N) >');
  Readln(Answer);
  IF Answer IN ['Y', 'y'] THEN
     WeeklySummary
END.   { Inventory }
```

work. When the program is finished we can remove this procedure or
leave it as a comment. The resulting program is given in *FIGURE 13.6*.

When the program in *FIGURE 13.6* is run for the first time, our decision to include a procedure to write the array pays off. Even though we
are very comfortable with the sorting routine and know that it is correct,
it does not work. The error is quickly found (we typed J + 1 instead of
J − 1). The error has been corrected in the program in *FIGURE 13.6*.
However, this points out the need to constantly check one's work. Incidentally, the order used in ordering the array is the order of strings in
which '12' precedes '2' (for the same reason 'ANT' precedes 'B').

We next do the procedure which creates a new inventory file using the
old inventory file and the ordered array of daily data. The basic idea of
this procedure is to get an item from the array of daily changes and then
get items from the input file. If an item from the file does not match the
item from the array, it is written immediately. Eventually, an item from
the input file will match the item from the array. Before it is output, the
NumOnHand field is updated and then the item is output. Another item
is read from the array, and the process repeats until all the elements in
the array have been used to update the file. After all of the elements in
the array have been used, the remaining elements in the input file are
written.

FIGURE 13.6

```
PROGRAM Inventory(Input, Output, OldInvFile, NewInvFile);

{  This program maintains an inventory for a warehouse.  It  has
   two main parts : a daily update and a weekly summary.

      Author        : John Riley
      Date begun    : May 24, 1986
      Date finished :
      File name     : CH13EX5.PAS
}

Const
   IDLen      = 12;
   DescripLen = 20;

TYPE
   AddressRec =    RECORD
                      Street : STRING[25];
                      City   : STRING[15];
                      State  : STRING[2];
                      Zip    : STRING[5]
                   END;  { AddressRec }
   SupplierRec =   RECORD
                       Name    : STRING[20];
                       Address : AddressRec
                   END;  { SupplierRec }
   ItemRec =       RECORD
                      ID          : STRING[IDLen];
                      Descrip     : STRING[DescripLen];
                      NumOnHand,                  { Number in stock }
                      ReorderNum : Integer;   { Number at which to
                                                  order  more }
                      Supplier   : SupplierRec
                   END;  { ItemRec }
   InventoryFil = FILE OF ItemRec;

VAR
   Answer : Char;


PROCEDURE InputOpen(VAR F : InventoryFil);

{  Procedure to obtain a name for the input file and open it. }

VAR
   FileName : STRING[15];

BEGIN  { InputOpen }
  Write('Enter the name of the input file >');
  Readln(FileName);
  Assign(F, FileName);
  Reset(F)
END;    { InputOpen }
```

(continued)

```
PROCEDURE OutputOpen(VAR F : InventoryFil);

{  Procedure to obtain a name for the output file and open it. }

VAR
    FileName : STRING[15];

BEGIN  { OutputOpen }
  Write('Enter the name of the output file >');
  Readln(FileName);
  Assign(F, FileName);
  Rewrite(F)
END;    { OutputOpen }


PROCEDURE DailyUpdate;

{ Procedure to do the daily updating of the inventory files. }

CONST
    DailyMax = 100;  { Maximum number of items for a day }

TYPE
    ItemInfo = RECORD
                  ID     : STRING[IDLen];
                  Action : Char;          { S = Ship
                                            R = Receive }
                  Num    : Integer        { Number shipped
                                            or received }
               END;  { ItemInfo }
    ItemArry = ARRAY[1..DailyMax] OF ItemInfo;

VAR
    DailyData  : ItemArry;  { Data about all items shipped,
                              received today }
    NumOfItems : Integer;   { Number of items shipped or
                              received }


PROCEDURE GetDaysData(VAR DailyData : ItemArry;
                      VAR NumOfItems : Integer);

{ Procedure to get the daily information from the keyboard.
  The information is stored in an array. }


PROCEDURE  FillArray(VAR DailyData : ItemArry;
                     VAR NumOfItems : Integer);
{  This procedure obtains the information on the day's
   transactions from the keyboard.
}

CONST
    Stop = '!';
```

(continued)

```
VAR
    ItemIn : ItemInfo;

BEGIN { FillArray }
  NumOfItems := 0;
  Writeln('Enter the day''s actions.  Enter ', Stop, ' for ');
  Writeln('item ID to end input');
  Write('Enter item ID >');
  Readln(ItemIn.ID);
  WHILE ItemIn.ID[1] <> Stop DO
     BEGIN
        WITH ItemIn DO
           BEGIN
             Write('Shipped or received ? (S/R) >');
             Readln(Action);
             Write('Number shipped or received >');
             Readln(Num)
           END; { WITH }
        NumOfItems := NumOfItems + 1;
        DailyData[NumOfItems] := ItemIn;
        Write('Enter item ID >');
        Readln(ItemIn.ID)
     END  { WHILE }
END;  { FillArray }


PROCEDURE PutInOrder(VAR DailyData : ItemArry;
                         NumOfItems : Integer);
{ This procedure puts the array DailyData in order by ID.
  An insertion sort is used.
}

VAR
    Temp : ItemInfo;        { Holder for a record      }
    Key  : STRING[IDLen];   { Key for comparisons      }
    I, J,                   { Loop indices             }
    Pos  : Integer;         { Position for insertion   }

BEGIN { PutInOrder }
  FOR I := 1 TO NumOfItems DO
     BEGIN
        Key := DailyData[I].ID;
        Pos := 1;
        WHILE (DailyData[Pos].ID <= Key) AND (Pos < I) DO
           Pos := Pos + 1;
        IF Pos < I THEN { Shift entries and insert }
           BEGIN
              Temp := DailyData[I];
              FOR J := I DOWNTO Pos + 1 DO
                 DailyData[J] := DailyData[J - 1];
              DailyData[Pos] := Temp
           END { IF }
        ELSE  { DailyData[I] is in correct position }
     END { FOR }
END;  { PutInOrder }
```

(continued)

```pascal
PROCEDURE WriteArray(VAR DailyData : ItemArry;
                         NumOfItems : Integer);

{ This procedure outputs the contents of the array DailyData.
  It is meant to be used to check the procedures.
}

VAR
   I : Integer;  { Loop Index }

BEGIN { WriteArray }
   Writeln('Item ID' : IDLen, ' Action Number');
   FOR I := 1 TO NumOfItems DO
      WITH DailyData[I] DO
         Writeln(ID : IDLen, '     ', Action, '     ', Num)
END; { WriteArray }


BEGIN { GetDaysData }
  FillArray(DailyData, NumOfItems);
  WriteArray(DailyData, NumOfItems);   { Output array to check }
  PutInOrder(DailyData, NumOfItems);
  WriteArray(DailyData, NumOfItems)
END;   { GetDaysData }


PROCEDURE UpdateInventoryFile(VAR DailyData : ItemArry;
                                  NumOfItems : Integer);

BEGIN { UpdateInventoryFile }
  Writeln('UpdateInventoryFile not implemented')
END;   { UpdateInventoryFile }


BEGIN { DailyUpdate }
  GetDaysData(DailyData, NumOfItems);
  UpdateInventoryFile(DailyData, NumOfItems)
END;   { DailyUpdate }


PROCEDURE WeeklySummary;

{ Procedure to produce a report of items needing to be ordered. }

BEGIN  { WeeklySummary }
  Writeln('Summary not implemented')
End;   { WeeklySummary }

BEGIN  { Inventory }
  DailyUpdate;
  Write('Do you want end of week report? (Y/N) >');
  Readln(Answer);
  IF Answer IN ['Y', 'y'] THEN
     WeeklySummary
END.   { Inventory }
```

To test this we create a file using the program CreateInventoryFile (*FIGURE 13.2*) and then run the program which appears in *FIGURE 13.7*. We check that the new file has been correctly produced by the program Inventory using ReadInventoryFile. We also check that the output file from one run of the program can be used in the next run. Because we do not feel that it is necessary to output the array of daily data, we enclose the statements that do this in braces to make them into a comment. Notice that we do not eliminate these statements altogether. They may be useful in debugging at some later date. By placing them in a comment, we can easily put them back into the program by removing the braces.

At this point, the only procedure that needs to be implemented is the weekly summary. To do the weekly summary we need the file that has

FIGURE 13.7

```
PROGRAM Inventory(Input, Output, OldInvFile, NewInvFile);

{  This program maintains an inventory for a warehouse.   It   has
   two main parts : a daily update and a weekly summary.

       Author          : John Riley
       Date begun      : May 24, 1986
       Date finished   :
       File name       : CH13EX6.PAS
}

CONST
    IDLen      = 12;
    DescripLen = 20;

TYPE
    AddressRec =    RECORD
                        Street : STRING[25];
                        City   : STRING[15];
                        State  : STRING[2];
                        Zip    : STRING[5]
                    END;  { AddressRec }
    SupplierRec =   RECORD
                        Name    : STRING[20];
                        Address : AddressRec
                    END;  { SupplierRec }
    ItemRec =       RECORD
                        ID            : STRING[IDLen];
                        Descrip       : STRING[DescripLen];
                        NumOnHand,                { Number in stock }
                        ReorderNum : Integer;     { Number at which to
                                                    order   more }
                        Supplier    : SupplierRec
                    END;   { ItemRec }
    InventoryFil = FILE OF ItemRec;
```

(continued)

```
BEGIN { PutInOrder }
  FOR I := 1 TO NumOfItems DO
     BEGIN
       Key := DailyData[I].ID;
       Pos := 1;
       WHILE (DailyData[Pos].ID <= Key) AND (Pos < I) DO
          Pos := Pos + 1;
       IF Pos < I THEN { Shift entries and insert }
          BEGIN
            Temp := DailyData[I];
            FOR J := I DOWNTO Pos + 1 DO
               DailyData[J] := DailyData[J - 1];
            DailyData[Pos] := Temp
          END { IF }
       ELSE   { DailyData[I] is in correct position }
     END { FOR }
END;  { PutInOrder }


PROCEDURE WriteArray(VAR DailyData : ItemArry;
                     NumOfItems : Integer);

{ This procedure outputs the contents of the array DailyData.
  It is meant to be used to check the procedures.
}

VAR
   I : Integer;  { Loop index }

BEGIN { WriteArray }
   Writeln('Item ID' : IDLen, ' Action Number');
   FOR I := 1 TO NumOfItems DO
      WITH DailyData[I] DO
         Writeln(ID : IDLen, '     ', Action, '     ', Num)
END; { WriteArray }


BEGIN { GetDaysData }
  FillArray(DailyData, NumOfItems);
{  WriteArray(DailyData, NumOfItems);   Output array to check }
  PutInOrder(DailyData, NumOfItems);
{  WriteArray(DailyData, NumOfItems)    }
END;  { GetDaysData }


PROCEDURE UpdateInventoryFile(VAR DailyData : ItemArry;
                             NumOfItems : Integer);

{ This procedure uses the data in the array DailyData and the
  file OldInvFile to produce a new file, NewInvFile.  Both the
  array and the file must be in order by ID.
}
```

(continued)

```
VAR
    OldInvFile,
    NewInvFile : InventoryFil;
    Item       : ItemRec;
    I          : Integer;
BEGIN { UpdateInventoryFile }
    InputOpen(OldInvFile);
    OutputOpen(NewInvFile);
    I := 1;
    WHILE (NOT EOF(OldInvFile)) AND (I <= NumOfItems) DO
        BEGIN
            Read(OldInvFile, Item);
            WHILE Item.ID < DailyData[I].ID DO
                BEGIN
                    Write(NewInvFile, Item);
                    Read(OldInvFile, Item)
                END; { WHILE }
            IF DailyData[I].Action IN ['S', 's'] THEN
                Item.NumOnHand := Item.NumOnHand - DailyData[I].Num
            ELSE
                Item.NumOnHand := Item.NumOnHand + DailyData[I].Num;
            Write(NewInvFile, Item);
            I := I + 1
        END; { WHILE }
    WHILE NOT EOF(OldInvFile) DO
        BEGIN
            Read(OldInvFile, Item);
            Write(NewInvFile, Item)
        END; { WHILE }
    Close(OldInvFile);
    Close(NewInvFile)
END;   { UpdateInventoryFile }

BEGIN { DailyUpdate }
    GetDaysData(DailyData, NumOfItems);
    UpdateInventoryFile(DailyData, NumOfItems)
END;   { DailyUpdate }


PROCEDURE WeeklySummary;

{ Procedure to produce a report of items needing to be ordered. }

BEGIN  { WeeklySummary }
    Writeln('Summary not implemented')
END;   { WeeklySummary }

BEGIN  { Inventory }
    DailyUpdate;
    Write('Do you want end of week report? (Y/N) >');
    Readln(Answer);
    IF Answer IN ['Y', 'y'] THEN
        WeeklySummary
END.   { Inventory }
```

just been created (NewInvFile). Because this file has been closed in the procedure DailyUpdate, we need to open it again, this time as an input file. To do this we need the name of the file that was entered for New-InvFile. This is taken care of by simply passing the appropriate name through the procedures OutputOpen, DailyUpdate, UpdateInventory-File, and WeeklySummary.

After NewInvFile has been opened to produce the weekly report, all we have to do is go through it, item by item, and find the items for which the number on hand is at or below the reorder point. The output from this procedure must go in a text file so that it can be printed. The revised program is presented in *FIGURE 13.8*. A run of the program, along with the contents of the weekly report file (WEEKLY.REP), is included.

The program in *FIGURE 13.8* meets the user's specifications. However, it is far from satisfactory because there is no provision for errors made in the input. Anticipating mistakes in input and handling them is a major task. A program might have 50% of its code devoted to error handling. We next give an example of some error-detecting code that could be added to the program in *FIGURE 13.8*.

In the procedure FillArray, there is no check that the action being read is an R or an S. We could change the lines

```
Write('Shipped or received ? (S/R) >');
Readln(Action);
```

to

```
Write('Shipped or received ? (S/R) >');
Readln(Action);
WHILE NOT (Action IN ['R', 'r', 'S', 's'] DO
   BEGIN
      Writeln('Action must be S or R');
      Write('Shipped or received ? (S/R) >');
      Readln(Action)
   END; { WHILE }
```

FIGURE 13.8

```
PROGRAM Inventory(Input, Output, OldInvFile, NewInvFile,
                  WeeklyReport);

{  This program maintains an inventory for a warehouse.  It  has
   two main parts : a daily update and a weekly summary.

      Author         : John Riley
      Date begun     : May 24, 1986
      Date finished  : May 27, 1986
      File name      : CH13EX7.PAS
}
```

(continued)

```
CONST
   IDLen      = 12;
   DescripLen = 20;


TYPE
   AddressRec =   RECORD
                     Street : STRING[25];
                     City   : STRING[15];
                     State  : STRING[2];
                     Zip    : STRING[5]
                  END;  { AddressRec }
   SupplierRec =  Record
                     Name    : STRING[20];
                     Address : AddressRec
                  END;  { SupplierRec }
   ItemRec =      RECORD
                     ID          : STRING[IDLen];
                     Descrip     : STRING[DescripLen];
                     NumOnHand,                  { Number in stock }
                     ReorderNum : Integer;   { Number at which to
                                               order  more }
                     Supplier   : SupplierRec
                  END;  { ItemRec }
   InventoryFil = FILE OF ItemRec;
   FileNameType = STRING[15];


VAR
   Answer        : Char;
   NewInvFileName : FileNameType;


PROCEDURE InputOpen(VAR F : InventoryFil);

{ Procedure to obtain a name for the input file and open it. }

VAR
   FileName : FileNameType;

BEGIN  { InputOpen }
  Write('Enter the name of the input file >');
  Readln(FileName);
  Assign(F, FileName);
  Reset(F)
END;   { InputOpen }


PROCEDURE OutputOpen(VAR F : InventoryFil;
                     VAR FileName : FileNameType);

{ Procedure to obtain a name for the output file and open it. }

BEGIN  { OutputOpen }
  Write('Enter the name of the output file >');
  Readln(FileName);
```

(continued)

```
   Assign(F, FileName);
   Rewrite(F)
END;    { OutputOpen }


PROCEDURE DailyUpdate(VAR NewInvFileName : FileNameType);

{ Procedure to do the daily updating of the inventory files. }

CONST
   DailyMax = 100;   { Maximum number of items for a day }

TYPE
   ItemInfo = RECORD
                   ID     : STRING[IDLen];
                   Action : Char;            { S = Ship
                                               R = Receive }
                   Num    : Integer          { Number shipped
                                               or received }
              END;   { ItemInfo }
   ItemArry = ARRAY[1..DailyMax] OF ItemInfo;

VAR
   DailyData : ItemArry;   { Data about all items shipped,
                             received today }
   NumOfItems : Integer;   { Number of items shipped or
                             received }


PROCEDURE GetDaysData(VAR DailyData : ItemArry;
                      VAR NumOfItems : Integer);

{ Procedure to get the daily information from the keyboard.
  The information is stored in an array. }


PROCEDURE  FillArray(VAR DailyData : ItemArry;
                     VAR NumOfItems : Integer);

{   This procedure obtains the information on the day's
    transactions from the keyboard.
}

CONST
   Stop = '!';

VAR
   ItemIn : ItemInfo;

BEGIN { FillArray }
  NumOfItems := 0;
  Writeln('Enter the day''s actions.  Enter ', Stop, ' for ');
  Writeln('item ID to end input');
  Write('Enter item ID >');
  Readln(ItemIn.ID);
```

(continued)

```
            WHILE ItemIn.ID[1] <> Stop DO
               BEGIN
                  WITH ItemIn DO
                     BEGIN
                        Write('Shipped or received ? (S/R) >');
                        Readln(Action);
                        Write('Number shipped or received >');
                        Readln(Num)
                     END; { WITH }
                  NumOfItems := NumOfItems + 1;
                  DailyData[NumOfItems] := ItemIn;
                  Write('Enter item ID >');
                  Readln(ItemIn.ID)
               END  { WHILE }
      END;  { FillArray }


      PROCEDURE PutInOrder(VAR DailyData : ItemArry;
                               NumOfItems : Integer);

      { This procedure puts the array DailyData in order by ID.
        An insertion sort is used.
      }


      VAR
         Temp : ItemInfo;       { Holder for a record     }
         Key  : STRING[IDLen];  { Key for comparisons     }
         I, J,                  { Loop indices            }
         Pos  : Integer;        { Position for insertion  }

      BEGIN { PutInOrder }
         FOR I := 1 TO NumOfItems DO
            BEGIN
               Key := DailyData[I].ID;
               Pos := 1;
               WHILE (DailyData[Pos].ID <= Key) AND (Pos < I) DO
                  Pos := Pos + 1;
               IF Pos < I THEN { Shift entries and insert }
                  BEGIN
                     Temp := DailyData[I];
                     FOR J := I DOWNTO Pos + 1 DO
                        DailyData[J] := DailyData[J - 1];
                     DailyData[Pos] := Temp
                  END { IF }
               ELSE  { DailyData[I] is in correct position }
            END { FOR }
      END;  { PutInOrder }


      PROCEDURE WriteArray(VAR DailyData : ItemArry;
                               NumOfItems : Integer);

      { This procedure outputs the contents of the array DailyData.
        It is meant to be used to check the procedures.
      }
```

(continued)

```
VAR
   I : Integer;  { Loop index }

BEGIN { WriteArray }
   Writeln('Item ID' : IDLen, ' Action Number');
   FOR I := 1 TO NumOfItems DO
      WITH DailyData[I] DO
         Writeln(ID : IDLen, '     ', Action, '     ', Num)
END; { WriteArray }


BEGIN { GetDaysData }
  FillArray(DailyData, NumOfItems);
{ WriteArray(DailyData, NumOfItems);    Output array to check }
  PutInOrder(DailyData, NumOfItems);
{ WriteArray(DailyData, NumOfItems)     }
END;  { GetDaysData }


PROCEDURE UpdateInventoryFile(VAR DailyData : ItemArry;
                                  NumOfItems : Integer;
                                  VAR NewInvFileName : FileNameType);

{ This procedure uses the data in the array DailyData and the
  file OldInvFile to produce a new file, NewInvFile.  Both the
  array and the file must be in order by ID.
}

VAR
   OldInvFile,
   NewInvFile : InventoryFil;
   Item       : ItemRec;
   I          : Integer;


BEGIN { UpdateInventoryFile }
   InputOpen(OldInvFile);
   OutputOpen(NewInvFile, NewInvFileName);
   I := 1;
   WHILE (NOT EOF(OldInvFile)) AND (I <= NumOfItems) DO
      BEGIN
        Read(OldInvFile, Item);
        WHILE Item.ID < DailyData[I].ID DO
           BEGIN
             Write(NewInvFile, Item);
             Read(OldInvFile, Item)
           END; { WHILE }
        IF DailyData[I].Action IN ['S', 's'] THEN
           Item.NumOnHand := Item.NumOnHand - DailyData[I].Num
        ELSE
           Item.NumOnHand := Item.NumOnHand + DailyData[I].Num;
        Write(NewInvFile, Item);
        I := I + 1
      END; { WHILE }
```

(continued)

```
      WHILE NOT EOF(OldInvFile) DO
          BEGIN
             Read(OldInvFile, Item);
             Write(NewInvFile, Item)
          END; { WHILE }
      Close(OldInvFile);
      Close(NewInvFile)
   END;  { UpdateInventoryFile }


   BEGIN { DailyUpdate }
     GetDaysData(DailyData, NumOfItems);
     UpdateInventoryFile(DailyData, NumOfItems, NewInvFileName)
   END;  { DailyUpdate }


   PROCEDURE WeeklySummary(NewInvFileName : FileNameType);

   { Procedure to produce a report of items needing to be ordered. }

   VAR
      WeeklyReport : Text;
      NewInvFile   : InventoryFil;
      Item         : ItemRec;
      EmptyReorder : Boolean;   { Indicates whether no items are
                                  to be reordered }

   BEGIN  { WeeklySummary }
     Assign(NewInvFile, NewInvFileName);
     Reset(NewInvFile);
     Assign(WeeklyReport, 'WEEKLY.REP');
     Rewrite(WeeklyReport);
     Writeln(WeeklyReport, '      ITEMS TO ORDER');
     Writeln(WeeklyReport, 'Item No.        Description ');
     Writeln(WeeklyReport, 'On Hand        Reorder Number');
     Writeln(WeeklyReport, 'Supplier Name and Address');
     Writeln(WeeklyReport);
     EmptyReorder := True;
     WHILE NOT EOF(NewInvFile) DO
         BEGIN
            Read(NewInvFile, Item);
            WITH Item DO
               IF NumOnHand <= ReorderNum THEN
                   BEGIN
                     EmptyReorder := False;
                     Writeln(WeeklyReport, ID :  IDLen,
                             Descrip : DescripLen);
                     Writeln(WeeklyReport, NumOnHand : 6, '    ',
                             ReorderNum);
                     WITH Supplier DO
                        BEGIN
                           Writeln(WeeklyReport, Name);
                           Writeln(WeeklyReport, Address.Street);
```

(continued)

```
                    Writeln(WeeklyReport, Address.City, ' ',
                            Address.State, ' ', Address.Zip)
                    END; { WITH }
                  Writeln(WeeklyReport)
                END  { IF }
        END;  { WHILE }
        IF EmptyReorder THEN
            Writeln('No items to reorder');
        Close(NewInvFile);
        Close(WeeklyReport)
END;   { WeeklySummary }



BEGIN  { Inventory }
  DailyUpdate(NewInvFileName);
  Write('Do you want end of week report? (Y/N) >');
  Readln(Answer);
  IF Answer IN ['Y', 'y'] THEN
      WeeklySummary(NewInvFileName)
END.   { Inventory }



Output:

Enter the day's actions.  Enter ! for
item ID to end input
Enter item ID >219
Shipped or received ? (S/R) >S
Number shipped or received >300
Enter item ID >176
Shipped or received ? (S/R) >S
Number shipped or received >500
Enter item ID >276
Shipped or received ? (S/R) >R
Number shipped or received >3
Enter item ID >!
Enter the name of the input file >MAY15.INV
Enter the name of the output file >MAY22.INV
Do you want end of week report? (Y/N) >Y



Weekly report (WEEKLY.REP):

     ITEMS TO ORDER
Item No.         Description
On Hand          Reorder Number
Supplier Name and Address


        176              3/4 BOLT
    122    200
BOLTS INC.
22 OAK STREET
LEWIS NJ 07111
```

Actually any entry other than S or s is treated as an R, and the program runs to completion. However, if the user has entered a Q it is unclear what he or she really meant and it would be better to find out. This is what the revised code is intended to do.

A second, more serious, problem is that of having an ID number entered which is not actually in the list of items in the inventory file. It would be possible to determine what the program does in this situation, but what we would like is to have the program do something reasonable. On the other hand, the ID number cannot readily be checked when it is input. This is a consequence of having the inventory information stored on a file. (Data structures influence algorithms.) One solution to this problem is to print all the incorrect ID numbers so that the user knows which input was not used. We would amend these lines of the procedure UpdateInventoryFile

```
IF DailyData[I].Action IN ['S', 's'] THEN
    Item.NumOnHand := Item.NumOnHand - DailyData[I].Num
ELSE
    Item.NumOnHand := Item.NumOnHand + DailyData[I].Num;
Write(NewInvFile, Item);
I := I + 1
```

to be the following:

```
IF Item.ID = DailyData[I].ID THEN
    BEGIN
        IF DailyData[I].Action in ['S', 's'] THEN
            Item.NumOn and := Item.NumOnHand - DailyData[I].Num
        ELSE
            Item.NumOnHand := Item.NumOnHand + DailyData[I].Num;
        Write(NewInvFile, Item)
    END { IF }
ELSE
    Writeln('ERROR - ID : ', DailyData[I].ID,
            ' not found.');
I := I + 1
```

We have sent the error message to the screen so that it would be immediately noticed. If the user had merely made an error in entering the data, it would be possible to rerun the program using the newly made inventory file and only the corrected entries as input. On the other hand, the error in the ID number may have been made on a form submitted to the person entering the data, in which case a corrected entry would probably take some time to obtain and be made with the next day's data.

13.3 SUMMARY

There are many other programs which would meet the manager's needs. Any solution would encompass at least 100 to 200 lines of code. In fact, the program we have presented would need much improvement before it could be considered usable. However, you should notice that we have used most of the control statements and data structures that were discussed in preceding chapters. This is typical for programs. No program is "an array program" or "a record program." Real programs use many different features of a language.

In the next chapter, another means of organizing and maintaining a list is covered, along with another data type provided by Pascal. ❏

EXERCISES

1. In the beginning of the chapter it was stated that a programmer has some responsibility for ensuring that his or her program is correct. What would be the consequences of reversing the shipped and received codes (in the procedure FillArray)—i.e., what would happen if we had mistakenly coded and released the following incorrect lines?

```
IF DailyData[I].Action IN ['S', 's'] THEN
    Item.NumOnHand := Item.NumOnHand + DailyData[I].Num
ELSE
    Item.NumOnHand := Item.NumOnHand - DailyData[I].Num;
```

Notice that the error is "minor" (a plus sign and a minus sign were interchanged). By "consequences" we mean what would happen to the manager, the warehouse, and the company if reordering were done on the basis of reports generated with the incorrect lines above. What would be an appropriate penalty (if any) for the programmer? Would it make a difference if the mistake had been made on purpose?

This sort of problem extends to other programs. Name some places where incorrect software could cause loss of life. What are the programmer's responsibilities in this situation? What would be an appropriate or just penalty for the person producing incorrect software causing a fatality?

The next five exercises concern the program developed in this chapter. Refer to the program in *FIGURE 13.8*.

2. It is asserted that any action entered other than S or s is treated as an R. Why?

3. It is possible for the same item to be shipped and received in the same day (or to be shipped more than once). What does the program do if the same item ID is used more than once? Does the program run correctly in this situation?

4. Name some errors which the program developed in this chapter should detect. Pretend that you are not responsible for actually writing the code to do this checking.

5. Can you think of any additions to the program which would improve or enhance it? Again, you are not to worry about how difficult it would be to make these additions.

6. Without actually attempting to code them, try to explain how difficult (or easy) it would be to implement the changes suggested in Exercises 4 and 5. Indicate features of the program which make the changes difficult or easy.

7. An airline maintains a list of flights. Each flight has an associated list of passengers. The passenger lists for all the flights are updated at the end of each day. The flights are numbered using positive integers. The information for each flight includes a flight number, a date, a time of departure, a departure city, and a destination city as well as a passenger list. All flights have a maximum of 200 passengers. This information is kept in a file. Each day, a list of passengers and their flights are entered using the keyboard. No more than 100 passengers (and flights) are entered at the end of the day. Write programs to do the following. (1) Create the list of flights, including the flight number, date, time of departure, and departure and destination cities. You may assume that this information is entered in order by flight number. (2) Print the information about one flight whose number is entered via the keyboard. This program should print the flight number, date and time of departure, cities, number of passengers currently booked, and names of passengers. (3) Accept a list of passengers and their flight numbers and add these to the file. This list is not in order.

   Suggestions: Store each flight's information in a record similar to the following (which is purposefully left incomplete).

```
FlightRec = RECORD
              Num : Integer;
              Date : DateRec;
              DepTime : TimeRec;
              DepCity,                        { Departure city }
              Destination : STRING[ ? ];  { Destination }
              NumOfPass : Integer;
              Passengers : ARRAY[1..200] OF NameRec
            END; { FlightRec }
```

   The information about all flights should be stored in a file of records of this sort. The first program mentioned is used to build this file from keyboard input. (No passengers will be entered at this time.)

   To do the second program it will be necessary to linearly search the file of flight records to find the flight number entered. This is similar to searching an array for an entry. Output a message if the flight is not found.

   The third program (to update the file of flights) is similar to the main program of case study II. Before updating the file, put the passenger list in order by flight number.

8. At the end of a semester, the registrar of a college needs to have grades assigned to each student enrolled at the college. Each student takes a number of courses and receives a grade in each course. Students are identified by their social security numbers. For each class a teacher

teaches, the registrar supplies a list of student names and social security numbers. The teacher assigns each student a letter grade. This
information is given to the registrar's office where for each class the
course title is input and then the list of student social security numbers
and grades. This list is to be used to add the course title and grade to
the record of each student enrolled in the course. A student may take
from one to seven courses. Any letter of the alphabet may be a legal
grade.

Write programs to (1) create the file of student records (data—name
and social security number—is input in order by social security number); (2) update the file of student records using the information from
one class; and (3) output each student's name, courses, and grades in
a text file (which may then be used to print a report).

Suggestions: Store the information about each student in a record
similar to the following (which is incomplete).

```
StudentRec = RECORD
                IDNum : STRING[9]; { Social Security Num }
                Name  : NameRec;
                NumOfCourses : 0..MaxNumOfCourses;
                Course : ARRAY[1..MaxNumOfCourses] OF
                            RECORD
                                Name  : STRING[ ? ];
                                Grade : Char
                            END
             END; { StudentRec }
```

The first program should create a file of these records.

Sort the class list by social security number and then update the
file. Each time a class is entered, a new file of records should be created.

9. Write a program which maintains a card catalog for a library. At the
end of each week, a librarian enters data concerning books that have
been added to and deleted from the library's collection. A file contains
records of the following sort to hold the information on the books in
the library.

```
BookRec = RECORD
             CallNum : STRING[10];   { Call number }
             Author  : NameRec;      { NameRec holds first, last
                                       and middle initial }
             Year    : Integer;      { Copyright year }
             PubCo   : STRING[30]    { Publishing company }
          END;  { BookRec }
```

The records are kept in order by call number. A book is deleted by
entering D in response to a prompt and then providing its call number.
A book is added to the collection by entering A in response to a prompt
and then supplying the information for the book's record. The additions
and deletions may not be in order. You will also need a program to

create the original file and will probably need a program to display the files your programs create.

10. Write a program to maintain a college transcript of a student. At the end of each semester, a new file is to be created which contains course information added to the previous work done. In addition, the semester's grade point average and over-all grade point average are to be output. The first step in doing this is to decide what information is to be recorded about each course taken. At a minimum, the course name, department, and credit hours, as well as grade received, should be stored. Other data might include the semester in which the course is taken and the professor's name. Add any other information you would keep. You will need to write another program to create the initial file (or have the main program contain a special section to be run the first time). Use your program and see how well you like it. After you have used it a while, try making some improvements.

INTRODUCTION

In this chapter, the data type *pointer* and an elementary data structure, the *linked list*, are discussed. Both are used in programming.

The idea of linking together the elements of a list is used in many ways to manage a list which must be flexible.

Pointers are a very flexible data type. Pointers can be used to build many data structures. In this chapter, they are used to implement linked lists. ☐

CHAPTER 14

LINKED LISTS
AND POINTERS

14.1   LINKED LISTS

Many of the tasks for which a programmer must write programs involve lists. Arrays (of one dimension) are well suited for holding a list but have a significant drawback. Many of the lists that are manipulated by programs need to be kept in order. Furthermore, it frequently is necessary to be able to insert and delete items from the list. If the list is kept in an array, inserting an item into its correct position within the array will require that all the items that follow it be shifted down one slot in the array. For example, if DICK is added to the list BOB, CAROL, ERIC, FAY, HANK, JOE, KAY which is stored in an array, the last five entries must be moved down one slot in the array. This process is depicted in *FIGURE 14.1*.

Similarly, deleting an item from a list necessitates moving the items below the deleted item up one space. For long lists, this movement of items can be quite time-consuming.

Another drawback of the array is its fixed size. At times the list will be rather short and not need all the space of the array. Some space will be wasted. Even more of a problem is that the size of an array limits the size of the list that may be stored.

An alternative way of organizing an ordered list is needed. It should

---

FIGURE 14.1 | **Insertion Into an Ordered Array**

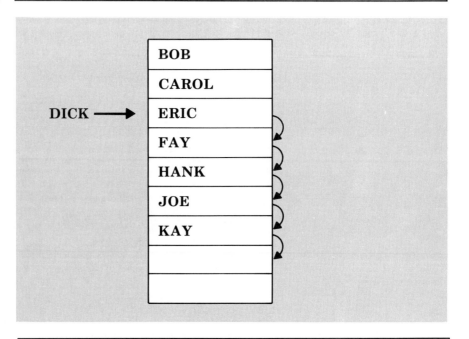

Insertion Into a Linked List

FIGURE 14.4

Before insertion

3

Start

	Item	Next
1	HANK	6
2	FAY	1
3	BOB	7
4	KAY	0
5	ERIC	2
6	JOE	4
7	CAROL	5
8		
9		
10		

After insertion

3

Start

	Item	Next
1	HANK	6
2	FAY	1
3	BOB	7
4	KAY	0
5	ERIC	2
6	JOE	4
7	CAROL	8
8	DICK	5
9		
10		

that 0 indicates the end of the list. If we keep the free space in a linked list, then whenever we use one of the spaces from the free-space list we must update the free-space list. In *FIGURE 14.6* we give an algorithm which adds an item to the linked list and updates the free-space list. The three lines InsertPos ⟵ Free, L[InsertPos].Item ⟵ ItemToInsert, and Free ⟵ L[Free].Next serve to get a free node for the insertion and update the free-space linked list.

The algorithm for inserting an item in a linked list is somewhat unwieldy due to the necessity of checking for three special cases. Two of the cases involve putting the new item at the beginning of the list. This can happen if the list is empty or if the item to be inserted precedes all the items currently in the list. This possibility can be eliminated by placing

FIGURE 14.5

Linked Free-Space List

	3		9
	Start		**Free**

	Item	Next
1	HANK	6
2	FAY	1
3	BOB	7
4	KAY	0
5	ERIC	2
6	JOE	4
7	CAROL	8
8	DICK	5
9		10
10		0

FIGURE 14.6

Algorithm to Add an Item to a Linked List

```
{ Assume the linked list is L with components Item and Next and
  L is indexed by integers.  }

Begin Add Item to Linked List

Get ItemToInsert
InsertPos ← Free
L[InsertPos].Item ← ItemToInsert
Free ← L[Free].Next
```

(continued)

```
If (Start = 0)   { List is empty }
   or (ItemToInsert < L[Start].Item) Then
                                         {ItemToInsert is first }
      L[InsertPos].Next ← Start
      Start ← InsertPos

Else
      After ← Start
      While (ItemToInsert > L[After].Item) and
            (L[After].Next <> 0)    { Move down list }
          Before ← After
          After ← L[After].Next
      End While
      If L[After].Item >= ItemToInsert Then
          L[Before].Next ← InsertPos
          L[InsertPos].Next ← After

      Else         { While loop was exited because end of list }
                   { was reached. ItemToInsert is put at end.  }
          L[After].Next ← InsertPos
          L[InsertPos].Next ← 0
      End If Then Else

End Add Item to Linked List
```

a dummy node at the beginning of the list whose data item precedes all the items in the list. For example, if the items in the list are words, the first node could contain 'A'. Safer yet would be the string consisting of a space, because the space character precedes all the printable characters (using the ASCII ordering.) Because this makes the algorithm much simpler, we will use this technique throughout this chapter. The algorithm appears in *FIGURE 14.7*.

| **Algorithm to Add an Item to a Linked List With Header Node** | **FIGURE 14.7** |

```
{ Assume the linked list is L with components Item and Next and
  L is indexed by integers.

  L always has a dummy node which precedes all others.    }

Begin Add Item to Linked List

Get ItemToInsert
InsertPos ← Free
L[InsertPos].Item ← ItemToInsert
Free ← L[Free].Next
After ← Start     { Points to dummy node }
```

(continued)

```
While (ItemToInsert > L[After].Item) and
      (L[After].Next <> 0)    { Move down list }
   Before ← After
   After  ← L[After].Next
End While
If L[After].Item >= ItemToInsert Then
   L[Before].Next ← InsertPos
   L[InsertPos].Next ← After

Else     { While loop was exited because end of list }
         { was reached. ItemToInsert is put at end   }
   L[After].Next ← InsertPos
   L[InsertPos].Next ← 0
End If Then Else

End Add Item to Linked List
```

Another special case that must be handled is when the item to be inserted is at the end of the list. When this occurs, the while loop in the algorithm is exited because the condition (L[After].Next <> 0) becomes False. However, when this happens it is not known whether the other part of the condition (ItemToInsert > L[After].Item) is True or False. This means that a test to see exactly where the new item is to be inserted must be done.

When an item is deleted from a linked list, the links of the linked list must be rearranged to omit the deleted entry and add its space to the free-space linked list. Usually the released space is added to the beginning of the free-space list. The result of deleting the entry ERIC from the linked list depicted in *FIGURE 14.5* is given in *FIGURE 14.8*. (A dummy node containing A has been added.)

Throughout this section we have been depicting linked lists as arrays with components which are records having two fields. Using Pascal, these would be declared along the following lines.

```
CONST
   ListSize = 10;  { or whatever }

TYPE
   NodeRec =  RECORD
                  Item : STRING[15];
                  Next : 0..ListSize
              END; { NodeRec }
   ListType = ARRAY[1..ListSize] OF NodeRec;

VAR
   L    : ListType;
   Start,
   Free : 0..ListSize;
```

| Deletion From Linked List | FIGURE 14.8 |

Before deletion

1		**10**	
Start		**Free**	

	Item	Next
1	A	4
2	HANK	7
3	FAY	2
4	BOB	8
5	KAY	0
6	ERIC	3
7	JOE	5
8	CAROL	9
9	DICK	6
10		0

After deletion

1		**6**	
Start		**Free**	

	Item	Next
1	A	4
2	HANK	7
3	FAY	2
4	BOB	8
5	KAY	0
6		10
7	JOE	5
8	CAROL	9
9	DICK	3
10		0

The rest of this chapter is devoted to introducing a data type which is able to directly specify the next item in a list. This will enable us to implement linked lists without using arrays.

14.2 POINTERS

The last of the Pascal data types to be discussed is the *pointer*. In the previous section we used variables to specify the next item in an array. Another way of stating this is to say that we were describing where an item was to be found—that is, we were giving its address (in terms of an index). A pointer is a variable which gives (directly) the address of a variable. An address of a memory location is usually an integer, and we will use integers as addresses in our examples. The ability to specify a location in memory enables us to implement linked lists and other data structures more directly than we did in the preceding section.

> A *pointer* is the address of a variable.

> A *pointer variable* is a variable which contains the address of a variable.

Because a pointer describes (or points to) where a variable is, we will often use arrows to depict pointers.

As with the other types in Pascal, we may declare pointer types in the type declaration section or specify a variable to be of the pointer type in the variable declaration section. In either case, the type of variable to which the pointer may point must be given. The pointer type is declared using an up arrow or circumflex followed by a type identifier. We will use the circumflex (^). The type identifier in the declaration specifies the type of variable to which the pointer may point. A syntax diagram for the pointer type is given in *FIGURE 14.9*.

If P is declared to be a pointer variable which may point to a variable of type T, then (upon allocation of memory) P contains the address of a location storing a value of type T. Of course, we frequently would need to be able to use this variable. The notation P^ specifies the variable to which P points. P^ may be used in the same ways that any other variable of type T may be used.

For example, let us suppose that two pointers to real variables have been declared:

```
|
VAR
    RPtr1,
    RPtr2  :  ^Real;
|
```

and that space has been associated with each of them. For example, RPtr1 might contain the address 14 and RPtr2 might contain the address 16.

FIGURE 14.9

Pointer Type

$\longrightarrow$ ^ $\longrightarrow$ **type-ident.** $\longrightarrow$

Because RPtr1 and RPtr2 have been declared to point to real variables, this means that real numbers may be stored at these two locations. Then we could think of memory being organized as in *FIGURE 14.10*. Then RPtr1ˆ denotes the real variable located at address 14 and RPtr2ˆ denotes the real variable at address 16. These real variables may be used as any other real variables are. So the statements

```
RPtr1^  := 7.2;
RPtr2^  := RPtr1^  + 4.3;
```

store the values 7.2 and 11.5 in the integer variables at locations 14 and 16. The effects of these statements are included in *FIGURE 14.10*.

It is possible to assign the value of one pointer variable to another pointer variable of the same type, as in

```
RPtr1 := RPtr2;
```

The effect of this is to copy the address contained in RPtr2 (16) into RPtr1.

Pointers and Memory | *FIGURE 14.10*

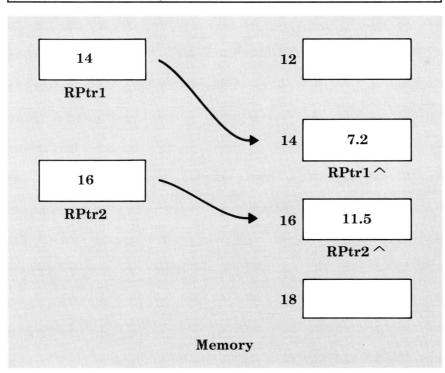

Memory

This means that both RPtr1 and RPtr2 point to location 16 in memory. *FIGURE 14.11* contains a diagram of memory after this assignment. A consequence of doing this is that we have lost track of location 14 and hence the value it contains. Because it is possible to lose values in this way, much care must be exercised when using pointers.

Except for the special value NIL (which is discussed below), Standard Pascal does not permit a value to be directly assigned to a pointer variable. TURBO Pascal provides a mechanism by which a pointer variable may be assigned a value. This feature of TURBO should be used with extreme caution. We have never found it necessary to directly assign an address to a pointer variable.

If the assignment

```
RPtr1^ := 23.1;
```

is made, the real number 23.1 will be stored in the location whose address is contained in RPtr1, which is 16. Because RPtr2 also points to location 16, after this statement is executed the number stored in RPtr2^ will also be 23.1. This is another way in which pointers require careful use. Chang-

---

FIGURE 14.11 | **Effect of RPtr1 := RPtr2;**

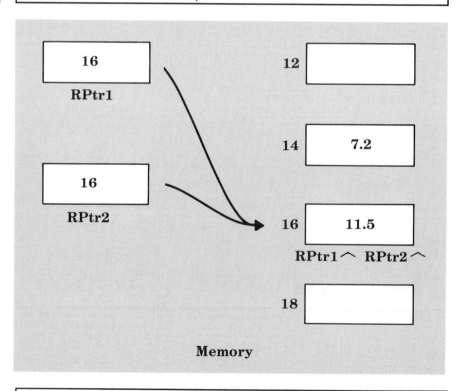

Memory

ing the value of the variable to which one pointer points may change the value of another pointer variable.

In a number of situations we need to be able to indicate that a pointer does not point to anything. The predefined, standard pointer constant NIL allows the programmer to do this. NIL may be assigned to any pointer variable (regardless of the type of variable to which it points). The value NIL indicates that the pointer is not pointing to any location. It would be possible to assign NIL to RPtr2:

```
RPtr2 := NIL;
```

This is akin to having a 0 in the next field in the examples of Section 14.1. The effect of this statement (and the assignment RPtr1^ := 23.1) in terms of our memory diagram is shown in *FIGURE 14.12*.

A pointer variable does not point to any location when it is declared. Like other variables in Pascal, pointer variables are uninitialized when the program begins running. Unlike other variables, assigning values to pointer variables affects the way in which memory is being allocated. A

Effect of RPtr2 := NIL;   **FIGURE 14.12**

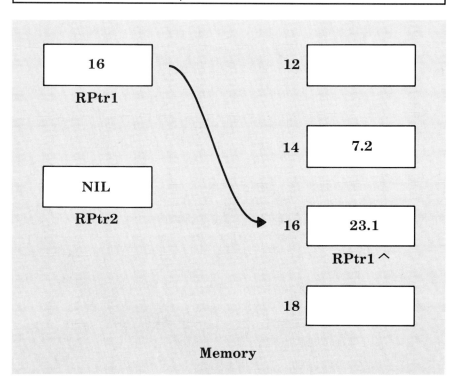

Memory

special procedure NEW is used to assign a value to a pointer and thus allocate storage.

Suppose that P is a pointer variable which will point to a variable of type T—e.g.,

```
VAR
    P :  ^T;
```

Then the statement

```
New(P);
```

creates a new variable of type T and sets P to point at that new variable. The diagram in *FIGURE 14.13* illustrates this. In this diagram, P has been set to point to the memory location 12, which is a variable of type T and is accessed using P^.

Unless New(P) has been executed or P has been assigned a value from another pointer variable, P^ does not exist. After New(P) is executed, P^ is a variable of type T. P^ would be uninitialized at this point.

It is possible to use New(P) when P is already pointing to a location. In this situation the previous location may be lost.

It is possible to deallocate or release the memory to which a pointer is pointing. This is done using the predefined, standard procedure Dis-

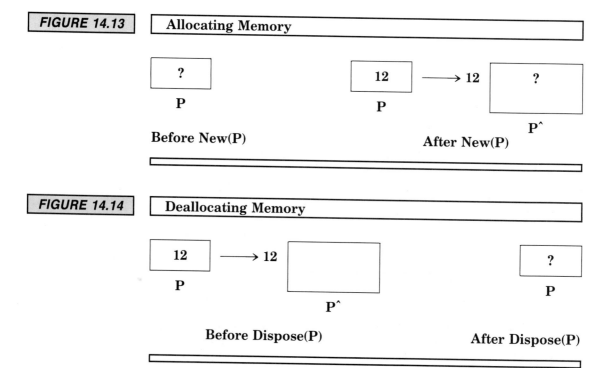

FIGURE 14.13   **Allocating Memory**

P   ?

Before New(P)

P   12 ⟶ 12   P^   ?

After New(P)

FIGURE 14.14   **Deallocating Memory**

P   12 ⟶ 12   P^

Before Dispose(P)

P   ?

After Dispose(P)

pose. If P is a pointer variable, Dispose(P) releases the space in memory
to which P is currently pointing. After Dispose(P) is executed, P is undefined and P^ does not exist. *FIGURE 14.14* depicts this process.

Being undefined is not the same as having the value NIL. By assigning
NIL to a pointer we indicate that the pointer is not pointing to anything.
If the pointer's value is undefined it is not possible to use it in any mean-
ingful way.

With the pointer variables RPtr1 and RPtr2, a typical segment of program would involve the allocation of space, its use, and then its release
in the following manner.

```
New(RPtr1);        { Allocate some space }
New(RPtr2);

                   { Do some processing using RPtr1^ and RPtr2^ }

Dispose(RPtr1);    { Release (deallocate) space }
Dispose(RPtr2);
```

Pointer variables are distinct from the other types of variables we have
discussed in that pointer variables allow the programmer some control
of how memory is used. Furthermore, pointer variables are said to be
dynamic variables because space for them is allocated while the program
is running. In contrast, static variables have their storage space allocated
before the statements of the program are executed.

> **A *static variable* is a variable whose memory allocation is de-
> termined when a program is compiled. Space for the variable
> is allotted before the statements of the program are executed.**

DEFINITION

> **A *dynamic variable* is a variable whose storage allocation is
> determined during program execution. Space for the variable
> is allotted when some statement of the program is executed.**

DEFINITION

It is possible to compare pointer variables. Two comparison operators
are provided for pointer variables: equals (=) and not equals (<>). If
P1 and P2 are pointer variables of the same type, then P1 = P2 is True
whenever P1 and P2 point to the same location in memory; otherwise the
expression is False. The expression P1 <> P2 is True whenever P1 and
P2 point to different locations in memory and is False otherwise. Finally,
it is possible to use either operator to compare a pointer with the value
NIL. This enables us to test whether or not a pointer is actually pointing
at a location.

As before, let RPtr1 and RPtr2 be pointer variables to reals:

```
VAR
    RPtr1,
    RPtr2 : ^Real;
```

Then the following program fragment illustrates the use of these comparison operators.

```
IF RPtr1 = Nil THEN
    Writeln('RPtr1 is not pointing to anything.');
IF RPtr1 = RPtr2 THEN
    Writeln('RPtr1 and RPtr2 point to the same location.');
IF RPtr1^ = RPtr2^ THEN
    BEGIN
        Writeln('RPtr1 and RPtr2 point to locations');
        Writeln('containing the same values.')
    END; { IF }
```

There is an important distinction between the comparisons made in the second and third if statements in the fragment above. In the second if statement, two pointer variables are being compared. The condition in this statement is True if the pointer variables point to the same place or, in other words, the pointer variables contain the same address. In the third if statement, two real variables are being compared to determine whether the reals stored in them are the same. These real variables are in the locations pointed to by RPtr1 and RPtr2.

For any pointer variable P, it is important to keep the distinction between P and P^ clearly in mind. P is the address or location of a variable; P points to the variable. P^ is the variable to which P points.

There is a further distinction between the pointer type and other types. Ordinarily, Pascal demands that an identifier be declared (or be predefined) before it is used. An exception to this is made for pointer types. A pointer type may be declared using a type identifier which has not yet been declared. This is necessary whenever dynamic data structures are being built using records which contain fields which are pointers to a record of the same type. For example, to implement a linked list we might have

```
TYPE
    ListPtr  = ^ListNode;
    ListNode = RECORD
                    Item :         ;  { Whatever }
                    Next : ListPtr
               END;  { ListNode }


VAR
    List : ListPtr;
```

With these declarations, List is a pointer variable which may point to a record. This record is identified by List^. List^ has two fields. List^.Item denotes the first field (which is of whatever type we have declared it to be). The second field is denoted by List^.Next. It is a pointer variable which may point to another record of the type ListNode. Thus (after space has been allocated), it makes sense to refer to List^.Next^, which is a record variable, List^.Next^.Item (of whatever type), and List^.Next^.Next, which is a pointer variable. These variables may be used in whatever contexts are appropriate. For example, the following assignment is legal (and useful).

```
List := List^.Next;
```

In addition, it would be possible to allocate space for the pointer variable List^.Next by using the New procedure, as in

```
New(List^.Next)
```

Some of these features of pointers will be used in the program developed in the next section.

In fact, it is possible to have more than one pointer within a record, as in the following example.

```
TYPE
   DequePtr  = ^DequeNode;
   DequeNode = RECORD
                    Data :                ; { Whatever }
                    Before,
                    After  : DequePtr
               END;  { DequeNode }

VAR
   Deque : DequePtr;
```

After space has been allocated for the variable Deque, we may refer to Deque^ (a record variable), Deque^.Data, and Deque^.Before and Deque^.After (two pointer variables).

As we have seen, there are some difficulties and dangers in using pointers. For example, the sequence of statements

```
P1^ := Info;
P1  := P2;
```

(where P1 and P2 are pointer variables) loses Info unless P1 and P2 happen to point to the same location. In fact, pointers are not used just to allocate and deallocate variables (as was done with RPtr1 and RPtr2). Pointers allow the programmer to build dynamic data structures. In the next section, pointers are used to implement a linked list.

14.3   LINKED LISTS USING POINTERS

As an example of the use of pointers, we implement a linked list using pointers in this section. A linked list may also be implemented by using an array of records. There are other data structures which may be implemented using arrays or pointers, but it is often the case that pointers are easier.

It has been our experience that it is very difficult to work with pointers unless we draw suitable diagrams, particularly at the beginning. For example, we will be working with a linked list of words and make the following declarations.

```
TYPE
   WordType = STRING[WordLen];
   ListPtr  = ^ListNode;
   ListNode = RECORD
                 Word : WordType;
                 Next : ListPtr
              END;  { ListNode }


VAR
   List : ListPtr;  { Points to the first word in list }
```

Each ListNode would have two fields, the second being a pointer. We would depict one ListNode as follows.

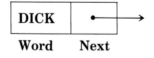

Word   **Next**

This depicts the string 'DICK' being stored in the Word field and the Next field pointing to some other node. Frequently we will not label the fields (Word and Next). If the Next field is NIL we will indicate this by placing the numeral 0 in the Next field. With these conventions, a list of four words ('BOB', 'DICK', 'ERIC', 'HANK') would be depicted as follows.

List

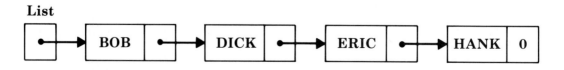

Now suppose that we wanted to add a node containing 'FAY' to this list so that the words in the list would still be in alphabetical order. What we want is the picture below, in which the pointers have been arranged to keep the words in order.

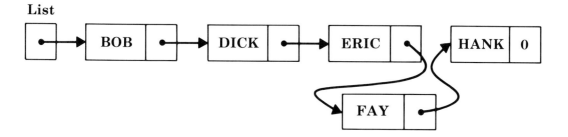

To achieve this we need a new node in which we store 'FAY'. We also need to change the pointer of the node containing 'ERIC' to point to this new node and the pointer of the new node (containing 'FAY') to point to the node containing 'HANK'. If we had three pointer variables, Before, After, and Temp, pointing as in this diagram

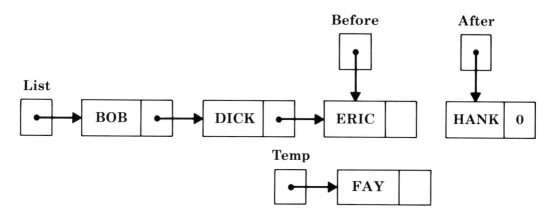

our task would not be difficult. In fact, if Before and After are pointing as in this diagram, the following code creates the new node and links it properly.

```
New(Temp);                { Create a new node }
Temp^.Word := 'FAY';      { Put 'FAY' in the word field of the
                            new node }
Before^.Next := Temp;     { Make the pointer of the node before
                            the new node point to the new node }
Temp^.Next := After;      { Make the pointer of the new node point
                            to the node after it }
```

All that remains is to determine how to get Before and After pointing to the proper nodes in the list. We notice that the word contained in After^.Word should be the first word in the list after 'FAY'. Furthermore, we want Before to point to the node preceding the node pointed to by After. This means that Before^.Next equals After (both pointers point to the same node). To find where 'FAY' is to be put in the list, we follow the links down the list until we find the correct spot. Of course, we must be careful to watch for the end of the list. The end of the list is marked by a pointer equal to NIL. The next program fragment does this.

```
After := List;
WHILE (After^.Word <= 'FAY') AND (After^.Next <> NIL) DO
   BEGIN
      Before := After;
      After := After^.Next
   END; { WHILE }
```

This fragment will find the correct place for 'FAY' in the list if it does not come first or last in the list. 'FAY' will be the first word in the list if the list is empty (signified by List equaling NIL) or if 'FAY' precedes the first word in the list which is List^.Word. This problem could be solved by testing for these special cases and then taking care of the situation when 'FAY' is first in the list. An easier solution is to put a dummy node first which contains a value preceding all others. Then the while loop will always be executed once.

Unfortunately, if the loop terminates because the end of the list has been encountered (signaled by After^.Next being equal to Nil), we don't know whether After^.Word precedes or follows 'FAY'. If After^.Word precedes 'FAY', then the node containing 'FAY' should become the last node in the linked list following the node pointed to by After. The lines below do just that.

```
After^.Next := Temp;   { Link Temp to the end of the list }
Temp^.Next := NIL;     { Mark the end of the list         }
```

Otherwise, the nodes can be connected as previously described. You should draw the diagrams associated with these special cases to make sure you understand how they work.

All of these ideas are incorporated in the program presented in *FIGURE 14.15*.

The program in *FIGURE 14.15* is a program which maintains a list of words in alphabetical order. It is an example of a menu-driven program. The user is presented with a menu of actions he or she can use and then enters his or her choice. Menu-driven programs are a convenient means of providing a user with a variety of options.

FIGURE 14.15

```
PROGRAM Lister (Input, Output);

{  This program maintains a linked list of words.  The
   words are kept in alphabetic order.  The linked list
   is implemented using pointers.  The list has a dummy
   first node containing a value which precedes all
   other values.   The program is menu driven.

      Author     : John Riley
      Date       : May 29, 1986
      Revised    : January 3, 1987
      File name  : CH14EX1.PAS
}

CONST
   WordLen = 15;

TYPE
   WordType = STRING[WordLen];
   ListPtr  = ^ListNode;
   ListNode = RECORD
                  Word : WordType;
                  Next : ListPtr
              END;   { ListNode }

VAR
   Com  : Char;      { Command from keyboard }
   List : ListPtr;   { Points to the first word in list }



PROCEDURE Initialize(VAR L : ListPtr);

{ This procedure initializes the list by setting up a dummy
  containing the blank, which precedes all strings. }

CONST
   Blank = ' ';

BEGIN { Initialize }
   New(L);
   L^.Word := Blank;
   L^.Next := NIL
END;   { Initialize }



PROCEDURE GetCommand(VAR Com : Char);

{ This procedure obtains a commmand (consisting of one
  character) from the keyboard.
}
```

(continued)

```
BEGIN { GetCommand }
  Writeln;
  Write('Enter a command (M for menu of commands) >');
  Readln(Com);
  Writeln
END;  { GetCommand }


PROCEDURE PrintMenu ;

{ This procedure prints the menu of possible commands. }

BEGIN { PrintMenu }
  Writeln;
  Writeln('Available commands (a command is a letter)');
  Writeln;
  Writeln('Add words to list          : A');
  Writeln('Delete words from list     : D');
  Writeln('Print words in list        : P');
  Writeln('Print this menu            : M');
  Writeln('Quit the program           : Q');
  Writeln
END;  { PrintMenu }


PROCEDURE InsertItems(VAR List : ListPtr);

{ This procedure adds words to the list. }

CONST
   Stop = '*';  { End of input }

VAR
   WordIn : WordType;


PROCEDURE InsertOneItem(VAR List : ListPtr; Word : WordType)

{ This procedure adds one word to the list.}

VAR
  Temp,                { Holds the item being inserted }
  Before,              { Node before inserted item     }
  After   : ListPtr;   { Node after inserted item      }

BEGIN { InsertOneItem }
  New(Temp);
  Temp^.Word := Word;
  After := List;
  WHILE (Word >= After^.Word) AND  { Find place in list }
        (After^.Next <> NIL) DO
     BEGIN                            { Move down list one node
       Before := After;
       After := After^.Next
     END; { WHILE }
```

(continued)

```
   IF WordIn < After^.Word THEN      { Word is within list }
       BEGIN                         { Insert Word }
         Before^.Next := Temp;
         Temp^.Next := After
       END { IF }
     ELSE                            { Word is at end of list,
                                        After is last node }
       BEGIN                         { Put Word at end of list }
         After^.Next := Temp;
         Temp^.Next := NIL
       END { ELSE }
END;   { InsertOneItem }


BEGIN  { InsertItems }
  Writeln;
  Writeln('To add a word to the list enter the word.  To stop');
  Writeln('enter ', Stop, ' .');
  Write('Enter word >');
  Readln(WordIn);
  WHILE WordIn[1] <> Stop DO
      BEGIN
        InsertOneItem(List, WordIn);
        Write('Enter word >');
        Readln(WordIn)
      END; { WHILE }
  Writeln;
  Writeln
END;    { InsertItems }


PROCEDURE DeleteItems(VAR List : ListPtr);

{ This procedure removes items from the list. }

CONST
   Stop = '*';

VAR
   WordOut : WordType;  { Word to be deleted }


PROCEDURE DeleteOneItem(VAR List : ListPtr; Word : WordType);

{ This procedure deletes one word from the list. }

VAR
  Before,                { Node before node to be deleted   }
  NodeOut : ListPtr;     { Node to be deleted                }
  Found   : Boolean;     { Indicates whether Word was found }


BEGIN  { DeleteOneItem }
  Found := False;
  Before := List;
```

(continued)

```
      WHILE (NOT Found) AND (Before^.Next <> NIL) DO
         IF Before^.Next^.Word = Word THEN   { Delete a word }
            BEGIN
               Found := True;
               NodeOut := Before^.Next;
               Before^.Next := Before^.Next^.Next;
               Dispose(NodeOut)
            END { IF }
         ELSE
            Before := Before^.Next;
      IF NOT Found THEN
         Writeln(Word, ' was not in list.')
   END;    { DeleteOneItem }

BEGIN   { DeleteItems }
   Writeln;
   Writeln('To remove a word from the list enter the word.  To ');
   Writeln('stop, enter ', Stop, ' .');
   Write('Enter word >');
   Readln(WordOut);
   WHILE (WordOut[1] <> Stop) AND (List^.Next<> NIL) DO
      BEGIN
         DeleteOneItem(List, WordOut);
         Write('Enter word >');
         Readln(WordOut)
      END; { WHILE }
   IF List^.Next = NIL THEN
      Writeln('List is empty');
   Writeln;
   Writeln
END;    { DeleteItems }

PROCEDURE PrintList(List : ListPtr);

{ This procedure prints the words in the list. }

VAR
   Ptr : ListPtr;   { Pointer used to move down the list }

BEGIN { PrintList }
   Writeln;
   IF List^.Next = NIL THEN
      Writeln('List is empty')
   ELSE
      BEGIN
         Writeln('Current list of words');
         Writeln
      END;   { ELSE }
   Ptr := List^.Next;
   WHILE Ptr <> NIL DO
      BEGIN
         Writeln(Ptr^.Word);
         Ptr := Ptr^.Next
      END; { WHILE }
   Writeln
END;    { PrintList }
```

(continued)

```
BEGIN { Lister }
   Initialize(List);
   Writeln('This program maintains a list of words in');
   Writeln('alphabetic order.  The following menu gives');
   Writeln('the possible commands.');
   PrintMenu;
   REPEAT
      GetCommand(Com);
      CASE Com OF
          'A', 'a' : InsertItems(List);
          'D', 'd' : DeleteItems(List);
          'M', 'm' : PrintMenu;
          'P', 'p' : PrintList(List);
          'Q', 'q' : ; { Quit }
      ELSE
          Writeln('Illegal command')
      END { CASE }
   UNTIL Com IN ['Q', 'q'];
   Writeln;
   Writeln('Exiting program')
END. { Lister }
```

Output:

```
This program maintains a list of words in
alphabetic order.  The following menu gives
the possible commands.

Available commands (a command is a letter)

Add words to list          : A
Delete words from list      : D
Print words in list         : P
Print this menu             : M
Quit the program            : Q

Enter a command (M for menu of commands) >A

To add a word to the list enter the word.  To stop
enter * .
Enter word >APPLE
Enter word >PEAR
Enter word >BANANA
Enter word >ORANGE
Enter word >GRAPE
Enter word >*

Enter a command (M for menu of commands) >P

Current list of words
APPLE
BANANA
GRAPE
ORANGE
PEAR
```

(continued)

```
Enter a command (M for menu of commands) >D


To remove a word from the list enter the word.  To
stop, enter * .
Enter word >PEAR
Enter word >GRAPE
Enter word >PLUM
PLUM was not in list.
Enter word >*


Enter a command (M for menu of commands) >P


Current list of words
APPLE
BANANA
ORANGE

Enter a command (M for menu of commands) >Q


Exiting program
```

The options provided by the program Lister are to add words to the list, delete words from the list, print the list of words, and quit the program. Each of these actions is invoked by a single-letter command. Single-letter commands have the advantage of being easily programmed and, more importantly, are generally a convenience for the user. Unfortunately, it is easy for the user to forget the commands. For this reason it is also possible for the user to request a menu of the commands. Additionally, the menu is printed at the beginning of the program. This helps make the program "user friendly."

To maintain the list of words, the program uses a linked list which is implemented using pointers. The process of adding a word to the linked list that we discussed above is found in the subprocedure InsertOneItem. Notice that InsertOneItem is called by the procedure InsertItems, which repeatedly requests words from the user for insertion. This isolates the task of inserting a word from the task of prompting the user and obtaining his or her input.

The procedure to delete items is implemented similarly and also uses a subprocedure for the main task of deleting one item. You should use diagrams to help you understand how this procedure actually maintains the list.

Finally, we must note that the program was developed in pieces. One procedure at a time was written, tested, and corrected. The program was not written all at once.

14.4 SUMMARY

A linked list provides a way of keeping a list of items in order and allows items to be efficiently added to or deleted from a list. A linked list is maintained by recording the position of the next item in the linked list.

Pointers allow the programmer to access memory in a controlled fashion. Space for a pointer to point to is allocated by the procedure New and deallocated by the procedure Dispose. The special value NIL is used to indicate that a pointer is not pointing to anything.

Pointers may be used to build very useful data structures. To manipulate these data structures recursive techniques are often used. Recursion is the subject of the next chapter. ❑

EXERCISES

1. Fill in the links in the diagrams below so that the words in the list are linked in alphabetical order. Link the free-space list as well.

Start

Free

	Word	Link
1	HELP	
2	GOOD	
3		
4	NICE	
5	BAD	
6	PEOPLE	
7		
8		
9	HELLO	
10	JUNK	

2. Consider the following linked list.

Start
1

Free
10

	Word	Link
1	**APPLE**	6
2	**PEAR**	0
3	**ORANGE**	8
4		7
5	**GRAPE**	9
6	**BANANA**	5
7		0
8	**PEACH**	2
9	**LEMON**	3
10		4

Adjust the links in the linked list to show how it would appear after the following words are added or deleted as indicated. (The linked list is to be maintained so that the words are in alphabetical order. 0 indicates the end of the list.)

```
Add      PLUM
Delete   APPLE
Delete   ORANGE
Add      LIME
Delete   PEAR
Add      BERRY
```

3. Devise an algorithm for deleting items from a linked list. This should be similar to the algorithm given in *FIGURE 14.6* for adding an item to a linked list. Compare your algorithm with the procedure DeleteOneItem in the program in *FIGURE 14.15*.

4. Are the local variables declared within a procedure dynamic or static variables? Why?

5. Find the errors in the following program fragments.

```
a. |
   VAR
        IntPtr : ^Integer;
   |
   IntPtr := 23;
   |
```

b.
```
VAR
    IntPtr1, IntPtr2 : ^Integer;


New(IntPtr1^);
IntPtr1^ := 7
IntPtr2 := ^IntPtr1;
```

c.
```
TYPE
    Pointer  : ^Node;
    Node     = RECORD
                     Num : Integer;
                     Ptr : Pointer
                 END;


VAR
    P. P1 : Pointer;



New(P);
P^ := NIL;
```

d.
```
TYPE
    Pointer  : ^Node;
    Node     = RECORD
                     Num : Integer;
                     Ptr : Pointer
                 END;

VAR
    P, P1 : Pointer;


New(P);
P^.Num := 10;
New(P^.Ptr);
P^.Ptr^.Num := 20;
P^.Ptr^.Ptr := P;
P1 := P;
WHILE P1 <> NIL DO
    BEGIN
       Writeln(P1^.Num);
       P1 := P1^.Ptr
    END; { WHILE }
```

6. Write a Pascal program to do the same thing as the program Lister (*FIGURE 14.15*) except that the program is to implement the linked list using an array of records.

7. Write a program which uses a linked list to maintain a list of names and telephone numbers. The linked list is to be implemented using pointers. The list is to be kept in alphabetical order by name. The user of the program should have the options of adding a name and number to the list, deleting a name (and the number) from the list, printing the entire list, and requesting the number of a name. Also provide help and information to the user.

8. Write a menu-driven program which maintains a list of students and their grade point averages. The list is to be in order by decreasing average—that is, the student with the highest average is to be listed first. The program should allow the user to add items, delete items, and view the list.

9. Write a program which maintains a list of words and prints them in the reverse of the order in which they were entered. The user is to be able to add words to the list, view the list (in reverse order), or quit. To do this, use a linked list and always add a word to the beginning of the list.

10. Write a program which uses a linked list to keep track of cities visited. The user may either add another city to the list or view the list of cities already visited (or quit). The list of cities is to be printed in the order entered. This means that each new city is added to the end of the list. It may be useful to keep pointers to both the beginning and the end of the list.

11. A minor problem with the insertion algorithm and procedure for linked lists occurs when the loop terminates at the end of the list. To accommodate this problem, a separate test is needed to determine whether the item is to be inserted before or after the last item. A technique for eliminating this problem is to add a dummy node at the end of the list whose value always exceeds the other values in the list.

    Using this idea, rewrite the linked list program of *FIGURE 14.15*. Hint: The last possible string of printable characters consists of tildes. The tilde is ASCII character 126.

12. Use the address functions described in Chapter 3 (before Exercise 11) to output the addresses of some integer pointer variables and the integer variables to which they point. Do the output both before and after a sequence of statements which allocate space (New) and deallocate space (Dispose).

INTRODUCTION

This chapter is an introduction to *recursion*. Recursion is a powerful programming technique. When used properly, recursive procedures and functions can greatly simplify problem solving and increase program clarity. Recursive programming entails some effort, and so this chapter may seem a little difficult at first. A lengthy discussion of recursion is contained in [Ro]. ◻

CHAPTER 15

RECURSION

15.1   RECURSIVE PROCEDURES AND FUNCTIONS

In the discussion of scope in Chapter 8, we commented that it is possible for a procedure or function to invoke itself. Such a procedure or function is said to be recursive. Recursive subprograms afford the programmer great power in solving problems.

DEFINITION

> A *recursive subprogram* is a subprogram which (directly or indirectly) invokes itself.

Of course, if a subprogram calls itself, it must contain its own name within the statement section of the subprogram. If the subprogram is a procedure, this means that the procedure will be invoked within its own body. If the subprogram is a function, the function is used in an expression within itself. If the subprogram is invoked by itself, the possibility exists that it may be invoked again. In other words, it is possible for a subprogram to have called itself repeatedly. This implies that there must be a point at which the subprogram stops calling itself. This is the key to designing recursive subprograms and solving problems recursively.

A problem may have a recursive solution when two conditions exist. First, there must be a simplest case (or cases) of the problem which can be solved explicitly. Second, the nonsimple cases of the problem must be solvable by breaking the problem into a slightly simpler version of the same problem, and repeatedly doing this must lead to one of the explicit solutions. Thus a recursive solution frequently is an algorithm which is of the form shown in *FIGURE 15.1*.

Some rather difficult problems may be solved in this manner. (The classic example is the Towers of Hanoi problem, which may be found in

FIGURE 15.1   **Recursive Algorithm**

```
Begin   { Recursive algorithm outline }

If CaseToBeSolved is simple Then

     Solve it explicitly

Else             { CaseToBeSolved is not simple }

     Phrase the CaseToBeSolved in terms of a simpler case
     and use the recursive algorithm to solve the simpler
     case.

EndIfThenElse

End   { Recursive algorithm outline }
```

[Ro] and many other places. Because it is so widely known, indeed over-worked, we do not present it here.) There are also a number of mathematical definitions which are recursive. Because these are easier, our first example will be one of these.

The program in *FIGURE 15.2* contains a recursive function which computes the factorial of an integer. (The factorial of a positive integer is the

FIGURE 15.2

```
PROGRAM FactorialTable ( Output );

{  This program prints a short list of numbers and their
   factorials using a recursive function.

       Author    : John Riley
       Date      : April 23, 1986
       File name : CH15EX1.PAS
}

CONST
   NumInList = 7;

VAR
   I : Integer;

FUNCTION Factorial(N : Integer) : Integer;

BEGIN   { Factorial }
  IF N = 0 THEN
     Factorial := 1
  ELSE
     Factorial := N * Factorial(N - 1)
END;    { Factorial }

BEGIN { FactorialTable }
  Writeln;
  Writeln('Number   Factorial');
  FOR I := 1 TO NumInList DO
     Writeln(I : 4, ' ' : 8, Factorial(I) : 5);
  Writeln
END. { FactorialTable }

Output:

Number    Factorial
   1              1
   2              2
   3              6
   4             24
   5            120
   6            720
   7           5040
```

product of the integers 1 through the number itself. The factorial of N is denoted N! For example, 4! = 4 × 3 × 2 × 1 = 24. Zero factorial is defined to be one.) The statement Factorial := N * Factorial(N − 1) causes Factorial to be invoked with N − 1. Eventually, Factorial is called with 0 and the process of repeatedly invoking Factorial ends. At this point the successive values of Factorial [Factorial(0), Factorial(1), Factorial(2), ...] are returned to Factorial, and the function terminates.

A trace of the pattern of calls and returns that occurs when Factorial(5) is invoked is given in *FIGURE 15.3*. The indentation indicates that the calls are nested. It should be apparent that the computer (including the Pascal system) keeps track of the various invocations of Factorial. Fortunately, this is done automatically and need not concern the programmer.

Two notes should be made about recursive subprograms using TURBO running under CP/M. If you use a recursive subprogram you must use the compiler directive {$A −}. Furthermore, a local variable must not be passed to a recursive procedure as a VAR parameter.

As with loop constructions, care must be exercised to ensure that a recursive subprogram terminates at some point. This is done when N = 0 in the function Factorial.

As another illustration of how recursion works, consider the program in *FIGURE 15.4*, which outputs the characters entered in reverse order. The basic idea is, if the character currently being read is not a period

---

FIGURE 15.3   **Invoking Factorial(5)**

```
Factorial(5) := 5 * Factorial(4)
                          { Calls Factorial(4) }
        Factorial(4) := 4 * Factorial(3)
                                { Calls Factorial(3) }
            Factorial(3) := 3 * Factorial(2)
                                    { Calls Factorial(2) }
                Factorial(2) := 2 * Factorial(1)
                                        { Calls Factorial(1) }
                    Factorial(1) := 1 * Factorial(0)
                                            { Calls Factorial(0) }
                        Factorial(0) := 1
                                            { 1 is returned }
                    Factorial(1) := 1 * 1
                                        { 1 is returned }
                Factorial(2) := 2 * 1
                                    { 2 is returned }
            Factorial(3) := 3 * 2
                                { 6 is returned }
        Factorial(4) := 4 * 6
                            { 24 is returned }
Factorial(5) := 5 * 24
                    { 120 is returned }
```

| | **FIGURE 15.4**

```
PROGRAM Reverser(Input, Output);

{  A  program  to  reverse the  characters  in  a  sequence.  A
recursive procedure is used.

      Author :         John Riley
      Date :           May 14, 1986
      File name :      CH15EX2.PAS
}


PROCEDURE GetAndWriteChar;

{  A recursive procedure which gets characters from the keyboard
   and outputs them in reverse order.
}

CONST
   Period = '.';

VAR
   CharIn : Char;  { Character read from the keyboard }

BEGIN { GetAndWriteChar }
  Readln(CharIn);
  IF CharIn <> Period THEN
     GetAndWriteChar;
  Write(CharIn)
END; { GetAndWriteChar }

BEGIN { Reverser }
  Writeln;
  Writeln('Enter characters, one per line');
  Writeln('End with a period');
  Writeln;
  GetAndWriteChar;
  Writeln
END.  { Reverser }



Output :

Enter characters, one per line
End with a period

a
b
c
d
.
dcba
```

(the terminating character), to keep going and get another character. Upon returning to the procedure, the character is to be printed.

The use of a recursive procedure makes this program quite short and readable. Also notice that there is only one variable (CharIn) in the entire program. The computer saves different versions of this variable (and its values). In the next two sections, two more examples of recursive procedures are given.

15.2   THE BINARY SEARCH REVISITED

In Chapter 10, the binary search algorithm was developed. This is an algorithm for searching for the position of a given item in an array that is in order. The basic idea of the algorithm is to determine in which half of the array the item is located and then search this part of the array. This is done until either the item is found or it is possible to conclude that the item does not occur in the array.

The binary search can be expressed quite naturally as a recursive algorithm. Basically, the part of the array to be searched is halved until the part being examined is of length one. To do this we use two variables, Left and Right, which mark the left and right ends of the part of the array being searched. When Left equals Right, either the item has been found or it is not in the array. To start, Left is set to 1 and Right is set to the number of elements of the array to be searched. An algorithm expressing this is presented in *FIGURE 15.5*.

FIGURE 15.5 | **Recursive Binary Search**

```
{  An algorithm to search an array A whose elements are in order
   using a recursive binary search.

     Input parameters:

           A        the array being searched
           Left     the left position (beginning) of the part
                    of A being searched
           Right    the right position (end) of the part of A
                    being searched
           Item     the item to be found

     Output parameter:

           Pos      the position of Item in A or 0 if Item is not
                    in A

   The algorithm starts with Left equal to 1 and Right equal to
   the number of elements of A to be searched.
}
```

(continued)

```
Begin { BinarySearch }

Mid ← (Left + Right)/2                          {Truncate if
                                                 necessary }
If (A[Mid] = Item) or (Left = Right) Then       { Done }
    If A[Mid] = Item Then                       { Item found }
        Pos ← Mid
    Else                                        { Item not found }
        Pos ← 0
    End If Then Else
Else                                            { Continue search }
    If A[Mid] < Item Then                       { Search right half }
        BinarySearch(A, Mid + 1, Right, Item, Pos)
    Else                                        { Search left half }
        BinarySearch(A, Left, Mid - 1, Item, Pos)
    End If Then Else
End If Then Else

End { BinarySearch }
```

The recursive binary search is implemented as a procedure which is given in *FIGURE 15.6*. ArrayType and ItemType must be defined in the calling program (or subprogram). It is assumed that ItemType is an ordered type. ArrayType is an array type made from components of type ItemType and indexed by a range of integers. If ItemType were a record type and A were ordered by a key field, then the key field would need to be used for comparisons in the binary search.

FIGURE 15.6

```
PROCEDURE BinarySearch(VAR A : ArrayType;  { Array to search   }
                           Left,           { Left,             }
                           Right : Integer; { Right ends of A   }
                                             to search         }
                           Item  : ItemType; { To be found      }
                           VAR Pos : Integer { Records place of
                                             Item in A, 0 if not
                                             in A   }         );

{ Procedure to do a recursive binary search. }

VAR
    Mid : Integer;

BEGIN { BinarySearch }
  Mid := (Left + Right) DIV 2;
  IF (A[Mid] = Item) OR (Left >= Right) THEN   { Done }
    IF A[Mid] = Item THEN                      { Item found }
        Pos := Mid
```

(continued)

```
      ELSE                                      { Item not found }
          Pos := 0
    ELSE                                        { Continue search }
      BEGIN
        IF A[Mid] < Item THEN                   { Search right half }
          BinarySearch(A, Mid + 1, Right, Item, Pos)
        ELSE                                    { Search left half  }
          BinarySearch(A, Left, Mid - 1, Item, Pos)
      END { ELSE }
END;   { BinarySearch }
```

Searching and sorting are two problems which occur frequently. Some algorithms for doing a search or a sort are most naturally expressed recursively. Others, such as the binary search algorithm, can be expressed both recursively and nonrecursively. Frequently, the nature of the data structure dictates the type of algorithm used. In the next section, a recursive procedure is used in working with a linked list.

15.3   LINKED LISTS REVISITED

At the end of Chapter 14 we developed a program for maintaining a linked list. In this section we use a recursive procedure to output the list in reverse order.

The procedure used to print the list in reverse order is similar to the procedure of Section 15.1 used to print letters in reverse order. For each node, if there is a next node the procedure is invoked with the next node. Upon return, the information at the node is printed.

The program that does this is given in *FIGURE 15.7*. (The delete procedure in the original program has been omitted to save space.)

FIGURE 15.7

```
PROGRAM Lister (Input, Output);

{   This program maintains a linked list of words.  The
    words are kept in alphabetic order.  The linked list
    is implemented using pointers.  The list has a dummy
    first node containing a value which precedes all
    other values.  The program is menu driven.

        Author    : John Riley
        Date      : May 29, 1986
        Revised   : January 3, 1987
        File name : CH15EX3.PAS
}
```

(continued)

```
CONST
   WordLen = 15;

TYPE
   WordType = String[WordLen];
   ListPtr  = ^ListNode;
   ListNode = RECORD
                 Word : WordType;
                 Next : ListPtr
              END;   { ListNode }

VAR
   Com  : Char;       { Command from keyboard }
   List : ListPtr;    { Points to the first word in list }

PROCEDURE Initialize(VAR L : ListPtr);

{ This procedure initializes the list by setting up a dummy
  containing the blank, which precedes all strings. }
CONST
   Blank = ' ';
BEGIN { Initialize }
  New(L);
  L^.Word := Blank;
  L^.Next := NIL
END;   { Initialize }


PROCEDURE GetCommand(VAR Com : Char);

{ This procedure obtains a command (consisting of one
  character) from the keyboard.
}
BEGIN { GetCommand }
  Writeln;
  Write('Enter a command (M for menu of commands) >');
  Readln(Com);
  Writeln
END;   { GetCommand }


PROCEDURE PrintMenu ;

{ This procedure prints the menu of possible commands. }

BEGIN { PrintMenu }
  Writeln;
  Writeln('Available commands (a command is a letter)');
  Writeln;
  Writeln('Add words to list                : A');
  Writeln('Print words in list              : P');
  Writeln('Print words in reverse order : R');
  Writeln('Print this menu                  : M');
  Writeln('Quit the program             : Q');
  Writeln
END;   { PrintMenu }
```

(continued)

```
PROCEDURE InsertItems(VAR List : ListPtr);

{ This procedure adds words to the list. }

CONST
   Stop = '*';   { END of input }
VAR
   WordIn : WordType;


PROCEDURE InsertOneItem(VAR List : ListPtr; Word : WordType);

{ This procedure adds one word to the list.}

VAR
   Temp,                 { Holds the item being inserted }
   Before,               { Node before inserted item      }
   After   : ListPtr;    { Node after inserted item       }

BEGIN { InsertOneItem }
  New(Temp);
  Temp^.Word := Word;
  After := List;
  WHILE (Word >= After^.Word) AND   { Find place in list }
        (After^.Next <> NIL) DO
     BEGIN { Move down list one node }
        Before := After;
        After := After^.Next
     END; { WHILE }
  IF WordIn < After^.Word THEN   { Word is within list }
       BEGIN   { Insert Word }
         Before^.Next := Temp;
         Temp^.Next := After
       END { IF }
  ELSE            { Word is at end of list, After is last node }
       BEGIN  { Put Word at end of list }
         After^.Next := Temp;
         Temp^.Next := NIL
       END { ELSE }
END;  { InsertOneItem }


BEGIN  { InsertItems }
  Writeln;
  Writeln('To add a word to the list enter the word.  To stop');
  Writeln('enter ', Stop, ' .');
  Write('Enter word >');
  Readln(WordIn);
  WHILE WordIn[1] <> Stop DO
     BEGIN
       InsertOneItem(List, WordIn);
       Write('Enter word >');
       Readln(WordIn)
     END; { WHILE }
  Writeln;
  Writeln
END;   { InsertItems }
```

(continued)

```
PROCEDURE PrintList(List : ListPtr);

{ This procedure prints the words in the list. }
VAR
   Ptr : ListPtr;  { Pointer used to move down the list }

BEGIN { PrintList }
  Writeln;
  IF List^.Next = NIL THEN
     Writeln('List is empty')
  ELSE
     BEGIN
       Writeln('Current list of words');
       Writeln
     END;  { ELSE }
  Ptr := List^.Next;
  WHILE Ptr <> NIL DO
     BEGIN
       Writeln(Ptr^.Word);
       Ptr := Ptr^.Next
     END;
  Writeln
END;  { PrintList }

PROCEDURE PrintInReverse(L : ListPtr);

{  A recursive procedure to print the list in reverse order. }

BEGIN  { PrintInReverse }
  IF L^.Next <> NIL THEN
     PrintInReverse(L^.Next);
  Writeln(L^.Word)
END;    { PrintInReverse }

BEGIN { Lister }
   Initialize(List);
   Writeln('This program maintains a list of words in');
   Writeln('alphabetic order.  The following menu gives');
   Writeln('the possible commands.');
   PrintMenu;
   REPEAT
      GetCommand(Com);
      CASE Com OF
          'A', 'a' : InsertItems(List);
          'M', 'm' : PrintMenu;
          'P', 'p' : PrintList(List);
          'R', 'r' : PrintInReverse(List^.Next);
          'Q', 'q' : ; { Quit }
      ELSE
          Writeln('Illegal command')
      END { CASE }
   UNTIL Com IN ['Q', 'q'];
   Writeln;
   Writeln('Exiting program')
END. { Lister }
```

(continued)

```
Output:

This program maintains a list of words in
alphabetic order.  The following menu gives
the possible commands.

Available commands (a command is a letter)

Add words to list          : A
Print words in list         : P
Print words in reverse order : R
Print this menu             : M
Quit the program            : Q


Enter a command (M for menu of commands) >A

To add a word to the list enter the word.  To stop
enter * .
Enter word >PEAR
Enter word >ORANGE
Enter word >APPLE
Enter word >GRAPE
Enter word >*


Enter a command (M for menu of commands) >P


Current list of words

APPLE
GRAPE
ORANGE
PEAR


Enter a command (M for menu of commands) >R

PEAR
ORANGE
GRAPE
APPLE

Enter a command (M for menu of commands) >A


To add a word to the list enter the word.  To stop
enter * .
Enter word >BANANA
Enter word >LEMON
Enter word >*


Enter a command (M for menu of commands) >P
```

(continued)

```
Current list of words

APPLE
BANANA
GRAPE
LEMON
ORANGE
PEAR


Enter a command (M for menu of commands) >R

PEAR
ORANGE
LEMON
GRAPE
BANANA
APPLE

Enter a command (M for menu of commands) >Q


Exiting program
```

15.4 FORWARD PROCEDURES AND FUNCTIONS

When a procedure or function is invoked in a program it is assumed that the procedure's or function's definition has been given, in the sense that the definition precedes the invocation in the text of the program. This is a rule which simplifies the task of the implementor of the language. It also helps people who read programs. Any time a subprogram is used, the reader knows that its definition should have already occurred. However, on rare occasions, it is necessary for each of two subprograms to refer to the other. Because only one can occur first, this would be impossible to achieve with normal Pascal declarations. *Forward procedures and functions* allow us to write procedures and functions which call one another.

A forward procedure or function has its body and heading in different places. The complete heading appears first followed by the key word FORWARD followed by a semicolon. This informs the compiler (and the reader) that the body of the subprogram is located further on in the program. The body of the subprogram is preceded by the key word PROCEDURE or FUNCTION (as appropriate), the subprogram's identifier, and a semicolon. The parameter list does not occur here. An outline of this for two procedures, First and Second, which call each other would be as follows (assume that variables have been declared appropriately).

```
PROCEDURE First(I : Integer; X : Real); FORWARD;

PROCEDURE Second(C : Char);

    { Body of Second }

First(M, R);    { Invocation of First }

END;   { Second }


PROCEDURE First;

    { Body of First }

Second(Ch);    { Invocation of Second }


END;   { First }
```

Functions may be followed by FORWARD in a similar manner. FOR-WARD is known as a *directive*. You may have noticed that forward subprograms may be mutually recursive. In fact, they must be used with care to avoid infinite recursion.

Syntax diagrams which include the possibility of a forward directive are given in *FIGURE 15.8*. In the diagrams for the procedure declaration and the function declaration, the second line indicates the usual form of the declaration, which does not involve the forward directive. If the forward directive is used, the subprogram's body must be declared elsewhere in the program.

| **FIGURE 15.8** | **Procedure Declaration** |

Procedure declaration

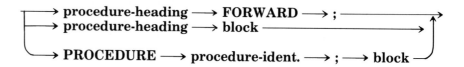

Procedure heading

$\rightarrow$ **PROCEDURE** $\rightarrow$ **ident.** $\rightarrow$ ($\rightarrow$ **parameter-list** $\rightarrow$) $\rightarrow$; $\rightarrow$

(continued)

Function declaration

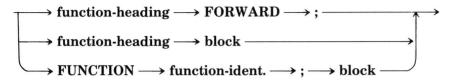

Function heading

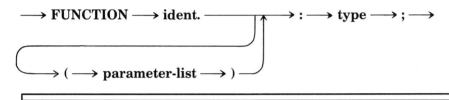

To illustrate the use of forward procedures, a program for a simple guessing game is given. The user thinks of a number between 1 and 100 and the program determines the number by making guesses and being informed whether the guess was too high or too low. The program is presented in *FIGURE 15.9*.

Forward procedures enable the programmer to construct more complex flows of control. Although it may be useful to do this, there is the danger of being confusing.

FIGURE 15.9

```pascal
PROGRAM GuessTheNumber(Input, Output);

{    Program to play a simple guessing game to illustrate the
     use of forward procedures.

          Author    : John Riley
          Date      : June 11, 1986
          File name : CH15EX4.PAS
}

VAR
   Answer : Char;


PROCEDURE Guess(PreviousLow, ThisGuess,
                PreviousHigh : Integer); FORWARD;
```

(continued)

```
PROCEDURE TooHigh(Low : Integer; VAR G, NewHigh : Integer);

{    This procedure forms a new guess when the guess was too
     high. }

BEGIN { TooHigh }
  NewHigh := G;
  G := (Low + NewHigh) DIV 2;
  Guess(Low, G, NewHigh)
END;  { TooHigh }


PROCEDURE TooLow(VAR NewLow, G : Integer; High : Integer);

{    This procedure forms a new guess when the guess was too
     low. }

BEGIN { TooLow }
  NewLow := G;
  G := (NewLow + High) DIV 2;
  Guess(NewLow, G, High)
END; { TooLow }


PROCEDURE Guess;

{ This procedure makes the guess. }

VAR
   Answer : Char;

BEGIN { Guess }
  Writeln('Is the number ', ThisGuess : 2, ' ? (Y/N)');
  Readln(Answer);
  IF Answer IN ['Y', 'y'] THEN
     Writeln('GOTCHA')
  ELSE
     BEGIN
       Writeln('Shucks, am I too high? (Y/N)');
       Readln(Answer);
       IF Answer IN ['Y', 'y'] THEN
          TooHigh(PreviousLow, ThisGuess, PreviousHigh)
       ELSE
          TooLow(PreviousLow, ThisGuess, PreviousHigh)
     END { ELSE }
END;  { Guess }


BEGIN { GuessTheNumber }
  Writeln;
  Writeln('Think of a number between one and a hundred and');
  Writeln('I will try to guess it.');
  Writeln('Press RETURN when you are ready');
  Readln;
  Guess(0, 50, 101)
END.  { GuessTheNumber }
```

15.5 SUMMARY

Recursion is a powerful programming technique. This chapter has introduced recursive procedures and functions. A recursive program works by having a simple case explicitly solved and all other cases reduced to simpler cases.

Forward procedures and functions enable the programmer to program two subprograms which may be invoked from each other.

Recursive and forward subprograms must be used with care, because they can cause program logic to be complicated. ❑

EXERCISES

1. What would happen if Factorial(− 1) (*FIGURE 15.2*) were invoked?

2. Like many subprograms, Factorial may be written recursively or non-recursively. In the text it is written recursively. Write it nonrecursively.

3. The Fibonacci numbers are defined as follows. The zeroth and first Fibonacci numbers are both 1. Successive Fibonacci numbers are defined to be the sum of the preceding two Fibonacci numbers. For example, the second Fibonacci number is 2 (the sum of 1 and 1) and the third is 3 (2 plus 1). Write a recursive function to produce the Nth Fibonacci number and use it in a program to produce a table of the first 15 Fibonacci numbers.

4. Write the procedure PrintList (*FIGURE 15.7*) recursively.

5. Write a program which tests whether characters (input one per line) are the same forward and backward. Such a sequence is known as a palindrome. For example,

```
A
B
D
B
B
D
B
A

A palindrome!

A
B
C
C
A
B

Not a palindrome.
```

Your program should start checking for duplication when two letters are entered that are the same. In the examples above, this occurs at the middle two Bs and Cs. A recursive procedure will help.

6. What is the output of the following program?

```
PROGRAM Chapter15Number6(Input, Output);

{
     Author        : John Riley
     Date          : June 12, 1986
     File name     : CH15NUM6.PAS
}


PROCEDURE One(N : Integer); FORWARD;


PROCEDURE Two(N : Integer);

BEGIN { Two }
   IF  N > 0 THEN
      BEGIN
        Writeln('Up and');
        One(N - 1)
      END { IF }
END; { Two }


PROCEDURE One;

BEGIN { One }
    IF  N > 0 THEN
        BEGIN
          Writeln('Down and');
          Two(N - 1)
        END { IF }
END;   { One }


BEGIN { Chapter15Number6 }
   Writeln;
   One(4);
   Writeln('Out')
END.   { Chapter15Number6 }
```

APPENDICES

| Operating-System Commands (MS-DOS and CP/M) |

The following is a list of operations that you can do when you are at the operating-system level. (This is signified by the prompt A> or B> .)

The list is organized by function, not by command. This means that you will find "Printing a file" rather than "PRINT" or "PIP."

If no notation appears after a command, the command works for both MS-DOS and CP/M. (PC-DOS is like MS-DOS. CP/M-86 is like CP/M.) The file-naming conventions are the same for both systems and are described in Chapter 2. The words "file," "source-file," "destination-file," etc., denote file designators. A "source-drive" or "destination-drive" means A: or B:. A command line must be followed by RETURN. When some commands are executed, they will be followed by instructions which you will need to follow.

Because there are many versions of both MS-DOS and CP/M, these commands may not exactly match the version of the system you are using. Beware of variations. When in doubt, consult the manual for your system.

○ Changing the default (logged) disk drive
  d: [d denotes the letter of the new disk drive]

○ Copying a disk

  DISKCOPY source-drive destination-drive [MS-DOS]
  COPY   [CP/M]

○ Copying a file

  COPY source-file destination-file   [MS-DOS]
  PIP destination-file = source-file   [CP/M]

○ Deleting or erasing a file

  DEL file   [MS-DOS]
  ERA file   [CP/M]

○ Finding out which files are on a disk (directory)

  DIR
  DIR d: [d denotes letter of drive]

○ Printing a file (using the printer)

  PRINT file   [MS-DOS]
  PIP LST: = file [CP/M]

○ Readying (formatting) a disk

  FORMAT drive   [MS-DOS]
  COPY   [CP/M]

○ Readying a disk which will boot the system

  FORMAT drive /S [MS-DOS]
  SYSGEN   [CP/M]

○ Renaming a file

  REN oldfilename newfilename   [MS-DOS]
  REN newfilename = oldfilename   [CP/M]

○ Running a program

Type the file name (without the extension). The file must contain an executable program and have the extension .COM (CP/M-86 .CMD).

○ Viewing a file (on the video screen)

TYPE file

TURBO Commands

This appendix contains a summary of the TURBO commands which are useful in doing the sorts of programs that are described in this book. These commands may be invoked whenever the main TURBO menu is available. Note that the TURBO prompt is >. If the prompt appears without the menu, pressing RETURN or the space bar will cause the menu to reappear. The program that is being developed is contained in the work file. The default extension is PAS. That is, if no file extension is specified, .PAS is assumed.

Some of the available commands are not discussed.

More is presented here than you will typically need. In particular, you might want to skip the O command (compiler options).

L—Change Logged drive. A prompt for the new drive will be printed. (Do this whenever the disk in the logged drive is changed.)

W—Change Work file. A prompt will request the new work file name.

E—Edit the work file. The TURBO editor will be invoked to edit the work file. (See Appendix C for editing commands.)

C—Compile the work file. The program in the work file will be compiled. The compiled version will be either in memory (the usual case) or in a file with the extension .COM.

R—Run the program. If the source program in the work file has been compiled into an object program (either in memory or in a file), the compiled program will be run. If the program has not been compiled, compilation will take place before the program is run.

S—Save the work file. The current work file is saved in a disk file.

D—Do a Directory. A prompt "Dir mask" will appear. Entering a drive designator will cause a directory of the disk in the drive to appear. (Pressing RETURN will do a directory of the logged drive.)

Q—Quit. Exit TURBO and return to the operating-system level.

O—Change the compiler Option. Normally, the compiled version of the program in the work file (the object program) is placed in memory. This may be changed so that the object program is placed in a file. When O is entered in response to the TURBO prompt, a menu will appear. This menu is depicted below.

```
compile  →  Memory
            Com-file
            cHn-file

command line Parameter:

Find run-time error   Quit
```

To cause the compiled program to be placed in a file, type C. Another menu will appear. (It differs among operating systems.) It may be ignored. "compile →" will now be pointing to "Com-file." Type Q (to quit) and the TURBO prompt will appear. Typing C (or R) will now cause the object program to be placed into a file with extension .COM (.CMD in CP/M-86). Typing O and then M will cause the compiled version of the program to be placed in memory.

Editing Commands (TURBO)

This appendix contains a list of the editing commands of the TURBO editor. Throughout we express these as a combination of pressing the control key (CTRL) and one or two letters. For example, CTRL/D means press the control key and D. CTRL/KD means press the CTRL key with K and then D. It is quite possible that the computer you are using has other means of doing the same thing. In particular, it may be possible to use arrow keys to move the cursor. IBM PC keys for editing are listed below the CTRL commands. It will take some time before you know all of these. Don't try to learn them all at once. Use a few until you become comfortable with them, and then learn a few more.

1. Commands for Moving the Cursor

To edit a file it is necessary to be able to position the cursor where changes (insertions or deletions) are to be made. The following commands are for moving the cursor, the smaller moves first.

Move cursor one character to the right	CTRL/D Left Arrow
Move cursor one character to the left	CTRL/S Right Arrow
Move cursor up one line (in the same column)	CTRL/E Up Arrow
Move cursor down one line (in the same column)	CTRL/X Down Arrow
Move cursor one word to the right (a word starts and ends at blank space or any of the following: < > , ; . ( ) [ ] ^ ' * + − / $)	CTRL/F CTRL/R. Arrow
Move cursor one word to the left (word is defined as above)	CTRL/A CTRL/L. Arrow
Move cursor up one page (some fixed number of lines, about one screen)	CTRL/R PgUp
Move cursor down one page (some fixed number of lines, about one screen)	CTRL/C PgDn
Move cursor to right end of current line (defined by last character entered)	CTRL/QD End
Move cursor to left end of current line (column 1)	CTRL/QS Home
Move cursor to top of page (moves cursor to the top of the screen)	CTRL/QE CTRL/Home
Move cursor to bottom of page (moves cursor to the bottom of the screen)	CTRL/QX CTRL/End

Move cursor to beginning of the file (moves cursor to line 1)	CTRL/QR CTRL/PgUp
Move cursor to end of the file (moves cursor to the last line of the file)	CTRL/QC CTRL/PgDn
Move cursor to beginning of block (moves cursor to position identified by CTRL/KB, see below)	CTRL/QB
Move cursor to end of block (moves cursor to position identified by CTRL/KK)	CTRL/QK
Move cursor to previous position (restores cursor to position before command was issued)	CTRL/QP

2. Commands for Insertion and Deletion

The commands for deletion allow you to remove a part of the file you no longer want. The insertion commands enable new text to be entered.

Delete character to left of cursor (erases character immediately to left of cursor, remaining characters on line are shifted to the left)	CTRL/− Del
Delete character above cursor (erases character directly above cursor, remaining characters on line are shifted to the left)	CTRL/G
Delete word to the right (characters starting at cursor and to the next space (or < > , ; . ( ) [ ] ^ ' * + − / $) to the right are erased, rest of line is shifted left)	CTRL/T
Delete current line (erases the line in which the cursor is positioned, remaining lines are moved up)	CTRL/Y
Delete right end of current line (erases characters from cursor position to right end of line)	CTRL/QY
Open line (a blank line is inserted to the right of the cursor)	CTRL/N
Switch between Insert mode and Overwrite mode (normally typing characters inserts characters, moving the rest of the file to the right and down the page; Insert mode. In Overwrite mode the characters are replaced by the characters being typed. Typing CTRL/V switches back and forth between the two modes.)	CTRL/V Ins

3. Block Commands

It is often convenient to designate a portion of the file for special treatment. For example, you might want to move a number of lines from one place in the file to another. A section of the file which has been designated for this sort of treatment is known as a block. All block commands are of the form CTRL/Kx where x denotes a specific letter.

Mark block beginning (typing CTRL/KB defines the place in the file where the block begins to be the cursor position)   CTRL/KB

Mark block end (causes the end of the block to be the cursor position; the block will be in half intensity; to turn off the half intensity put the block begin and end at the same place)   CTRL/KK

Mark single word as a block (causes the word at cursor position to be defined as a block, replacing the CTRL/KB, CTRL/KK sequence)   CTRL/KT

Copy block (copies the block to the position of the cursor; the original block is unaffected, so this results in two copies of the block)   CTRL/KC

Move block (moves the block from its location to the position of the cursor)   CTRL/KV

Delete block (erases the entire block, use with care)   CTRL/KY

Read block from file (a prompt requesting a file name is issued, the file entered is read into the file being edited at the position of the cursor, the file becomes a block)   CTRL/KR

Write block to file (a prompt requesting a file name is issued and the block becomes the file; i.e., if the file named exists, it is overwritten)   CTRL/KW

Display/hide block (makes current block reverse video or half tone (toggle on/off))   CTRL/KH

4. Miscellaneous Commands

End edit (return to the TURBO system, the work file is in memory)   CTRL/KD

Switch Indent feature on and off (Normally the TURBO editor starts a new line beneath the beginning of the previous line, this command turns this feature on and off, the current status is reported in the status line)   CTRL/QI

Find [finds the string entered in response to the prompt, options include nothing (find next occurrence of string), B (search backwards for the string), G (search global or entire file), n (find nTH occurrence of string from current cursor position, n any integer), U (ignore the difference be-   CTRL/QF tween upper- and lower-case letters), W (search for whole words only, ignore matches which are within other words), combinations of options are permitted]

Find and replace [finds the specified search string and replaces it with the specified substitution, options are nothing, B (search and replace backwards), G (global or entire file search and replace), n (n = integer, find and replace nTH occurrence of search string), N (normally you are asked whether you want the string replaced or not (Y/N), this turns off this feature), U (ignore difference between capital and lowercase letters), W (search and replace whole word only), combinations of options are permitted]   CTRL/QA

Scroll one line up [moves the text of the file up one line on the screen, the top line disappears and another line (if any) appears on the bottom]   CTRL/Z

Scroll one line down [moves the text of the file down one line on the screen, the bottom line disappears and another line (if any) appears on the top]   CTRL/W

Abort operation (this stops any command when given as input to a prompt, e.g., CTRL/KR or CTRL/QA)   CTRL/U

Enter a control character (typing CTRL/P followed by a control character places the control character into the text)   CTRL/P

| Differences Between TURBO and Standard Pascal |

TURBO Pascal includes almost all the features of standard Pascal. In this section we mention the few standard features that TURBO does not provide. You may encounter these other features elsewhere, and you should not be totally unacquainted with these terms. Generally, the omitted features are compensated for in some way. The compensating features are indicated. Of course, TURBO (like almost any implementation) provides a number of additional features. With the exception of strings and string procedures and functions, we have dealt with standard Pascal. TURBO has a large number of other features which cannot be covered in this book.

Several of the omitted standard procedures are related to input and output. Standard Pascal has two procedures, Get and Put, which are used with a file variable to control the file buffer. Get is an input operation and Put is an output operation. The versions of Read and Write that TURBO provides (which are also standard) eliminate the need for Get and Put. The other output procedure which is not provided by TURBO is the Page procedure. Page is used to start a new page.

If the printer you are using recognizes form feeds, it is possible to cause it to start a new page. The form feed character is ASCII character 12 (FF or CTRL/L). If this character is embedded in a text file, when the text file is printed the form feed character will cause the paper to advance to the next page. If F is a text file variable which is opened for output, then the statement Writeln(F, Chr(12)) will put a form feed character in the file. It is also possible to put form feeds in program files by typing CTRL/P CTRL/L. This is handy if you want each procedure of your program to be printed on a new page.

Standard Pascal also allows the programmer to specify that a structured variable is to be stored to conserve memory space (at the expense of execution speed). This is done by preceding the type definition by the reserved word PACKED, as in

```
TYPE
    SmallArray = PACKED ARRAY[1..10] OF Integer;
    PackedString = PACKED ARRAY[1..20] OF Char;
```

TURBO permits PACKED to appear in a declaration. However, the appearance of PACKED has no effect. On the other hand, allowing PACKED does enhance portability. In particular, standard Pascal uses packed arrays of characters for strings (but without the flexibility of the string type of TURBO). Standard Pascal also provides two procedures, PACK and UNPACK, for conversions between packed data types and unpacked data types. TURBO does not provide these, because they are not needed.

A minor limitation of TURBO is that a variant record cannot be used with pointers and the procedure New.

Standard Pascal allows functions and procedures to be parameters to functions and procedures. This is convenient if, for example, the maximum values of a number of different functions are to be found. By passing the different functions to a subprogram which finds the maximum of the passed function, we would need to code an algorithm for finding the maximum once. As you might expect, this feature of Pascal has caused some problems. TURBO does not provide for function and procedure parameters.

Outside of the variations we have mentioned in the previous chapters, these are the only parts of standard Pascal that TURBO Pascal does not include.

| Syntax Diagrams for TURBO Pascal | APPENDIX E |

This appendix contains syntax diagrams for the elements of TURBO Pascal which are covered in this book. They include most parts of elements which are standard. These syntax diagrams are not in the normal style of syntax diagrams for Pascal. We have attempted to make them as helpful as possible by being a little more explicit than is usually done.

Words in the syntax diagrams which are capitalized are elements of the language itself. Words within the syntax diagrams which are not capitalized are usually defined by another syntax diagram. A few terms which are not defined in the syntax diagrams are defined following the diagrams.

The abbreviation "ident." stands for "identifier" and usually is used with another word, as in "type-ident.", which means an identifier denoting a type. When "identifier" appears without a prefix in a syntax diagram, this denotes that the actual identifier used at this point is defined at this point. For example, in the constant declarations, when an identifier is used, that identifier is now a "constant-ident.", which means that it may be used wherever constant-ident. appears. The suffix "-type" denotes that a type must be used and that the type indicated serves in the role designated. For example, "base-type" means that a type must be supplied for the structure and that type is known as the base type of the structure.

Syntax diagrams do not express the entire syntax of the language. For example, a syntax diagram does not indicate that an identifier may be used only once in a declaration section.

Notes have been added wherever they would be helpful. The meaning of "nonstandard" is that TURBO has this feature but standard Pascal does not.

Identifier

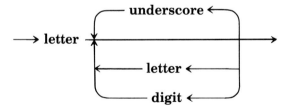

NOTE: *The underscore is nonstandard.*

Integer

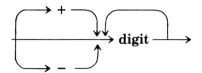

Digit

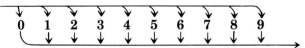

Real

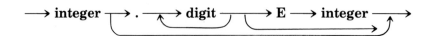

Boolean constant

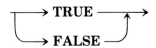

String

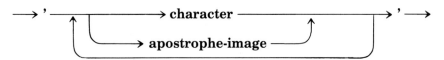

Apostrophe image

Program

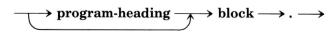

NOTE: *Standard Pascal requires a program heading.*

Program heading

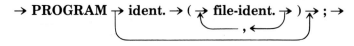

Block

⟶ declaration-section ⟶ statement-section ⟶

Declaration section

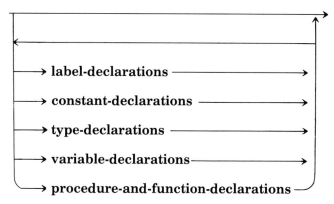

NOTE: *Standard Pascal requires that label, constant, type, and variable declarations precede (in that order) procedure and function declarations.*

Label declarations

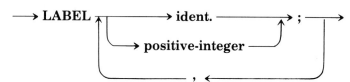

NOTE: *Standard Pascal permits only numbers (1- to 4-digit unsigned integers) for labels.*

Constant declarations

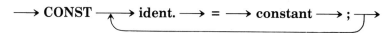

Constant

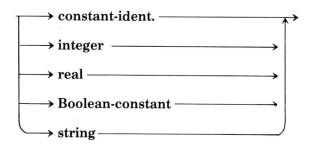

Type declarations

→ TYPE ⟶ ident. ⟶ = ⟶ type ⟶ ; ⟶

Type

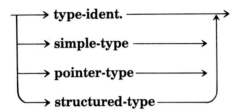

Simple type

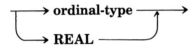

Ordinal type

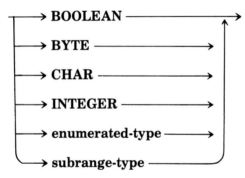

NOTE: *Byte is nonstandard.*

Enumerated type

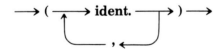

Subrange type

⟶ constant ⟶ .. ⟶ constant ⟶

NOTE: *Constants must be of an ordinal type, and the first constant must precede the second.*

Pointer type

⟶ ˆ ⟶ type-ident. ⟶

Structured type

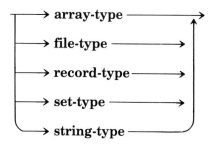

NOTE: *String-type is nonstandard.*

Array type

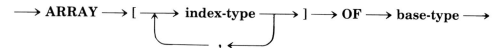

Index-type

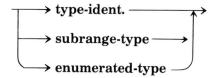

File type

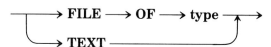

NOTE: *Component type must not be a file type (or include a file type).*

Record type

⟶ RECORD ⟶ field-list ⟶ END ⟶

Field list

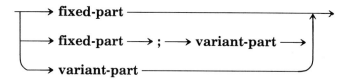

Fixed part

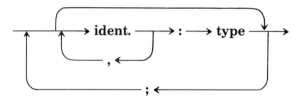

Variant part

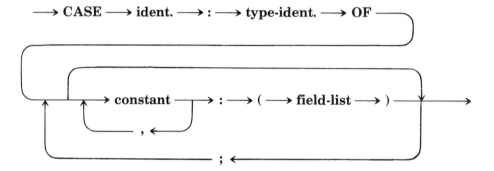

Set type

$$\longrightarrow SET \longrightarrow OF \longrightarrow \text{set-base-type} \longrightarrow$$

Set base type

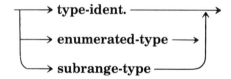

String type

$$\longrightarrow STRING \longrightarrow [\longrightarrow \text{integer-constant} \longrightarrow] \longrightarrow$$

NOTE: *Nonstandard. Integer constant must denote a positive integer.*

Variable declarations

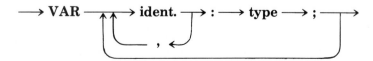

Procedure and function declarations

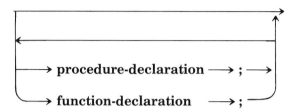

Procedure declaration

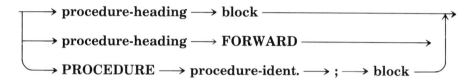

Procedure heading

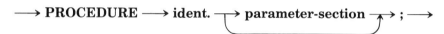

Parameter section

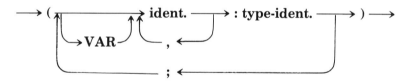

Function declaration

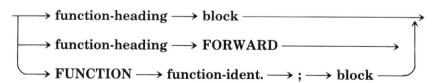

Function heading

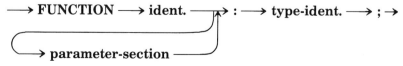

NOTE: *The type of a function must be simple, string, or pointer.*

Statement section

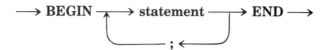

Statement

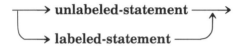

Unlabeled statement

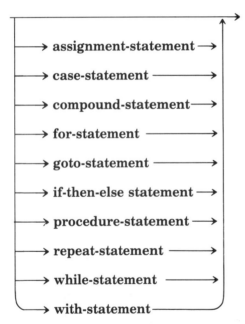

NOTE: *The first line represents the empty or null statement.*

Assignment statement

$\longrightarrow$ variable $\longrightarrow$:= $\longrightarrow$ expression $\longrightarrow$

NOTE: *The variable and expression must be compatible. Within the body defining a function, the variable may be the name of the function.*

Variable

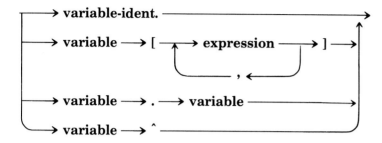

Arithmetic expression

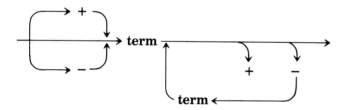

Term

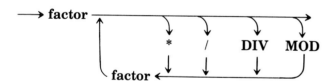

Factor

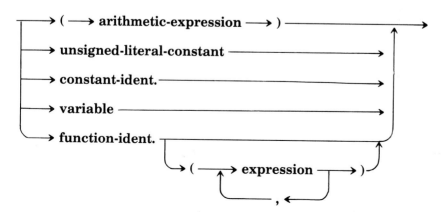

Unsigned literal constant

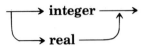

NOTE: *The constant must not begin with a plus or minus sign.*

Boolean expression

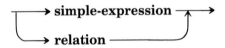

Simple expression

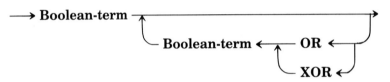

NOTE: *XOR is nonstandard.*

Boolean term

Boolean factor

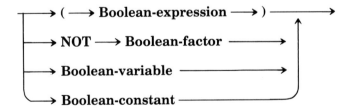

Relation

⟶ expression ⟶ relational-operator ⟶ expression ⟶

NOTE: *The expressions must be comparable.*

Relational operator

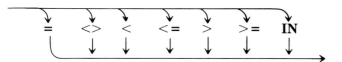

Set constant

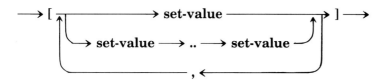

Case statement

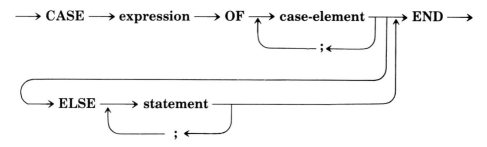

Case element

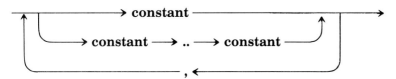

Case list

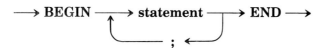

NOTE: *A subrange here is nonstandard.*

Compound statement

→ BEGIN ——→ statement ——→ END →

For statement

$\longrightarrow$ **FOR** $\longrightarrow$ **variable** $\longrightarrow$ **:=** $\longrightarrow$ **expression** $\longrightarrow$ **TO** / **DOWNTO**

$\longrightarrow$ **expression** $\longrightarrow$ **DO** $\longrightarrow$ **statement** $\longrightarrow$

NOTE: *Variables and expressions must be of ordinal type.*

Goto statement

$\longrightarrow$ **GOTO** $\longrightarrow$ **label-ident.** $\longrightarrow$

If-then-else statement

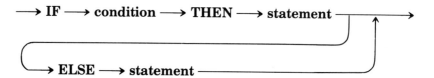

$\longrightarrow$ **IF** $\longrightarrow$ **condition** $\longrightarrow$ **THEN** $\longrightarrow$ **statement** $\longrightarrow$

$\longrightarrow$ **ELSE** $\longrightarrow$ **statement** $\longrightarrow$

Procedure statement

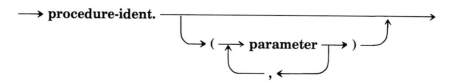

$\longrightarrow$ **procedure-ident.** $\longrightarrow$

($\longrightarrow$ parameter $\longrightarrow$) ,

Repeat-until statement

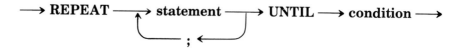

$\longrightarrow$ **REPEAT** $\longrightarrow$ **statement** $\longrightarrow$ **UNTIL** $\longrightarrow$ **condition** $\longrightarrow$
;

While statement

$\longrightarrow$ **WHILE** $\longrightarrow$ **condition** $\longrightarrow$ **DO** $\longrightarrow$ **statement** $\longrightarrow$

With statement

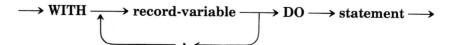

$\longrightarrow$ **WITH** $\longrightarrow$ **record-variable** $\longrightarrow$ **DO** $\longrightarrow$ **statement** $\longrightarrow$
,

Labeled statement

$\longrightarrow$ label-ident. $\longrightarrow$: $\longrightarrow$ unlabeled-statement $\longrightarrow$

Input statement

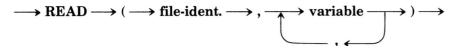

NOTE: *This is really a procedure statement. The type of the variable must be the component type of the file.*

Output statement

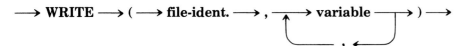

NOTE: *This is really a procedure statement. The type of the variable must be the component type of the file.*

Text file input

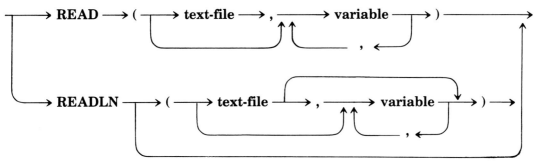

NOTE: *This is really a procedure statement. The variable must be an integer, real, character, or string variable.*

Text file output

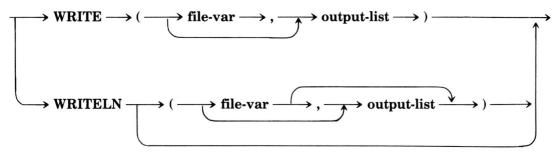

NOTE: *This is really a procedure statement.*

Output list

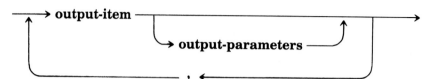

Output item

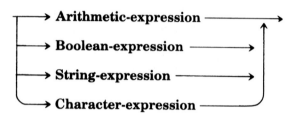

Output parameters

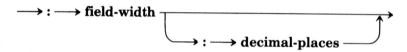

Field width

$\longrightarrow$ **integer-expression** $\longrightarrow$

Decimal places

$\longrightarrow$ **integer-expression** $\longrightarrow$

NOTE: *The integer expression for field width and decimal places must not be negative.*

Here are the meanings of some of the terms used in the above diagrams and notes.

Character: Implementation-defined character set (ASCII characters).

Comparable: Declared to be of the same or equivalent type or a subrange of the same or equivalent type, which cannot be array, file, or record type.

Compatible: Declared to be of the same or equivalent type or subrange of the same or equivalent type.

Condition: Boolean expression.

Parameter: Expression or variable. A variable must be used when call by reference is used.

APPENDIX F

Reserved Words and Standard Identifiers

Reserved Words

ABSOLUTE*	EXTERNAL*	NIL	SHL*
AND	FILE	NOT	SHR*
ARRAY	FOR	OF	STRING
BEGIN	FORWARD	OR	THEN
CASE	FUNCTION	OVERLAY*	TO
CONST	GOTO	PACKED	TYPE
DIV	IF	PROCEDURE	UNTIL
DO	IN	PROGRAM	VAR
DOWNTO	INLINE*	RECORD	WHILE
ELSE	LABEL	REPEAT	WITH
END	MOD	SET	XOR*

* Nonstandard Pascal (TURBO)

[Standard Pascal also includes the standard identifiers Get, Pack, Page, Put, Unpack.]

[When TURBO runs under MS-DOS or CP/M-86, the following are also standard identifiers: CSeg, DSeg, MemW, Ofs, PortW, Seg, SSeg.

When TURBO runs under CP/M, the following are also standard identifiers: Bios, BiosHL, Bdos, BdosHL, RecurPtr, StackPtr.]

Standard Identifiers

Abs	DelLine*	Kbd*	Real
Addr*	Delay*	KeyPressed*	Release*
Arctan	Dispose	Length*	Rename*
Assign*	Delete*	Ln	Reset
Aux*	EOF	Lo*	Rewrite
AuxInPtr*	EOLn	Lst*	Round
AuxOutPtr*	Erase*	LstOutPtr*	Seek*
BlockRead*	Execute*	Mark*	Sin
BlockWrite*	Exp	MaxAvail*	SizeOf*
Boolean	False	MaxInt	Sqr
BufLen*	FilePos*	Mem*	Sqrt
Byte*	FileSize*	MemAvail*	Str*
Chain*	FillChar*	Move*	Succ
Char	Flush*	New	Swap*
Chr	Frac*	NormVideo*	Text
Close*	FreeMem*	Odd	Trm*
ClrEOL*	GetMem*	Ord	True
ClrScr*	GoToXY*	Output	Trunc
Con*	HeapPtr*	Pi*	UpCase*
ConInPtr*	Hi*	Port*	Usr*
ConOutPtr*	HighVideo*	Pos*	UsrInPtr*
Concat*	IOResult*	Pred	UsrOutPtr*
ConstPtr*	Input	Ptr*	Val*
Copy	InsLine*	Random*	Write
Cos	Insert*	Randomize*	Writeln
CrtExit*	Int*	Read	
CrtInit*	Integer	Readln	

* Nonstandard Pascal (TURBO)

[Standard Pascal also includes the standard identifiers Get, Pack, Page, Put, Unpack.]

[When TURBO runs under MS-DOS or CP/M-86, the following are also standard identifiers: CSeg, DSeg, MemW, Ofs, PortW, Seg, SSeg.

   When TURBO runs under CP/M, the following are also standard identifiers: Bios, BiosHL, Bdos, BdosHL, RecurPtr, StackPtr.]

APPENDIX G | ASCII Table

This appendix presents a table of ASCII values where the numbers under Dec are the decimal numbers of the character and those under Hex the hexadecimal. The characters preceded by ˆ are control characters—i.e., a combination of the CTRL key and the character. The standard abbreviations for the meanings of the control characters are given.

ASCII Table															
Dec	Hex	Char	Use	Dec	Hex	Char	Dec	Hex	Char	Dec	Hex	Char
0	00	ˆ@	NUL	32	20	SPC	64	40	@	96	60	`
1	01	ˆA	SOH	33	21	!	65	41	A	97	61	a
2	02	ˆB	STX	34	22	"	66	42	B	98	62	b
3	03	ˆC	ETX	35	23	#	67	43	C	99	63	c
4	04	ˆD	EOT	36	24	$	68	44	D	100	64	d
5	05	ˆE	ENQ	37	25	%	69	45	E	101	65	e
6	06	ˆF	ACK	38	26	&	70	46	F	102	66	f
7	07	ˆG	BEL	39	27	'	71	47	G	103	67	g
8	08	ˆH	BS	40	28	(	72	48	H	104	68	h
9	09	ˆI	HT	41	29	)	73	49	I	105	69	i
10	0A	ˆJ	LF	42	2A	*	74	4A	J	106	6A	j
11	0B	ˆK	VT	43	2B	+	75	4B	K	107	6B	k
12	0C	ˆL	FF	44	2C	,	76	4C	L	108	6C	l
13	0D	ˆM	CR	45	2D	–	77	4D	M	109	6D	m
14	0E	ˆN	SO	46	2E	.	78	4E	N	110	6E	n
15	0F	ˆO	SI	47	2F	/	79	4F	O	111	6F	o
16	10	ˆP	DLE	48	30	0	80	50	P	112	70	p
17	11	ˆQ	DC1	49	31	1	81	51	Q	113	71	q
18	12	ˆR	DC2	50	32	2	82	52	R	114	72	r
19	13	ˆS	DC3	51	33	3	83	53	S	115	73	s
20	14	ˆT	DC4	52	34	4	84	54	T	116	74	t
21	15	ˆU	NAK	53	35	5	85	55	U	117	75	u
22	16	ˆV	SYN	54	36	6	86	56	V	118	76	v
23	17	ˆW	ETB	55	37	7	87	57	W	119	77	w
24	18	ˆX	CAN	56	38	8	88	58	X	120	78	x
25	19	ˆY	EM	57	39	9	89	59	Y	121	79	y
26	1A	ˆZ	SUB	58	3A	:	90	5A	Z	122	7A	z
27	1B	ˆ[	ESC	59	3B	;	91	5B	[	123	7B	{
28	1C	ˆ\	FS	60	3C	<	92	5C	\	124	7C	|
29	1D	ˆ]	GS	61	3D	=	93	5D	]	125	7D	}
30	1E	ˆˆ	RS	62	3E	>	94	5E	ˆ	126	7E	~
31	1F	ˆ_	US	63	3F	?	95	5F	_	127	7F	DEL

The following table contains some useful control characters. The number is the decimal value from the table above.

0	Null	10	Line Feed	26	End Of File
7	Bell	12	Form Feed	32	Space
8	Backspace	13	Carriage Return	127	Delete
9	Tab				

This appendix contains some guidelines to help you improve your programs. There are two sections. The first contains some programming adages which are worth keeping in mind as you program. The second section consists of a set of stylistic conventions (matters of form) for use in writing programs.

These guidelines are meant to assist you in writing correct, clear, and understandable Pascal programs. On rare occasions, it may be necessary to break a rule. Do so only when there is a good reason.

The rules are in no particular order.

1. Programming Adages

○ Resist the urge to code. Effort spent on design will save time later on.

○ Understand the programming task. Make the program reflect the steps needed to accomplish the task.

○ Document the program. This means providing useful and helpful information to the reader of the program.

○ Avoid tricky code. If code is tricky, it probably needs to be rewritten and possibly redesigned.

○ Do not worry about speed or program "efficiency." Correct programs are much better than fast ones which may be incorrect.

○ The statement section of a program, procedure, or function should not exceed one page (about 50 or 60 lines) in length. Any statement section longer than this should be rewritten using subprograms.

○ Know the purpose of a statement. Each statement in a program has a reason for its inclusion, and the programmer should know what this reason is.

○ Initialize variables. Never use a variable for which a value has not been supplied.

○ Don't nest structures deeply. Deeply nested structures indicate complexity that has gotten out of control.

○ If a procedure or function has ten arguments, an argument has probably been forgotten. Keep the number of parameters small.

○ If a user is to supply data, prompt the input, giving the form of the data needed and how to terminate the input.

○ Label all output that is to be used by people. Make the labels accurate and informative.

○ Declare types rather than using long type definitions in the variable declarations. For example, the first sample below is preferable to the second.

```
1. CONST
       SmallListSize = 10;
   TYPE
       SmallList = ARRAY[1..SmallListSize] OF Integer;

   VAR
       Grades : SmallList;
2. VAR
       Grades : ARRAY[1..10] OF Integer;
```

○ Avoid comparing reals for equality. Although the assignment $X :=$ 0.1 will make $X = 0.1$ True, the assignment $X := 10.0 * 0.01$ may not.

○ Use comments to clarify. Never comment the obvious. For example,

```
IF Node^.Next = NIL THEN   { End of the list }
   BEGIN     { Add the new node to the end of the list }
     ¦
```

is helpful, but

```
I := 0;  { Set I to 0 }
```

is worthless.

○ Use parentheses to clarify the meaning of an expression, particularly to clarify the order of evaluation of quantities within the expression.

○ Use mnemonic names for identifiers. Do not use identifiers which may easily be confused—e.g., XXXX and XXXXX. Be careful with 0 (zero) and O (oh) as well as 1 (one) and l (el).

○ All variables in a subprogram should be parameters or local variables.

○ Names of procedures should be verbs or verb phrases conveying the action the procedure performs.

○ Names of functions should be nouns or noun phrases conveying the meaning of the quantity returned.

2. Stylistic Conventions

○ Be consistent in style. If you adopt one way of doing something in a program, do it the same way throughout the program. This is very important.

○ Identifiers should start with a capital letter and be followed by small letters, except that words that are within the identifier should be capitalized—e.g., YardsToGo. In general, identifiers should be mnemonic. It is acceptable to use I, i, J, and j for integer loop indices and C or c for character loop indices. TURBO permits the underscore

(_) to appear in an identifier. It may be used between the words comprising an identifier, as in Yards_To_Go.

○ Adopt a consistent manner of writing reserved words and standard identifiers. Acceptable conventions are to capitalize all letters, to make all letters lower case, or to capitalize only the first letter.

○ Every program should have a program heading (the key word PRO-GRAM followed by the program identifier, followed by the files used). Following this there should be a comment containing a brief description of the program. Also in this comment should be the following information: the date written, the author, any references, and the file name for the program. This comprises a major comment at the beginning of the program. It should be preceded and followed by a blank line.

○ Every procedure and function declaration should include a comment describing what the subprogram does. This should precede or follow the procedure or function heading. A blank line should precede and follow the comment.

○ Every procedure and function should be preceded and followed by two blank lines.

○ Major blocks of comments (one line or more) should be separated from their surroundings by a blank line before and after the comment.

○ The identifiers in a declaration should be aligned on the left, the following = or : should be aligned, and the comments (if any) should be aligned. For example,

```
VAR
    I,                        { Loop index }
    DayOfMonth : Integer;     { Current day of month }
    Balance    : Real;        { Bank account balance }
```

○ A comma or a semicolon should always be followed by a space. The relational operators =, <>, <=, >=, <, >; the binary arithmetic operators +, −, *, /, DIV, MOD; the Boolean operators NOT, AND, OR; the assignment operator :=; and the : and = of declarations should be preceded and followed by a blank.

○ Comment delimiters [{ } or (* *)] should be preceded and followed by a blank.

○ A comment which is on the same line as part of the program should be to the right side of the page.

○ The BEGIN and END of a program, procedure, or function should be labeled with the appropriate identifier in a comment. (Main is an acceptable alternative for the program identifier.) For example,

```
PROGRAM Grades(Input, Output);        PROGRAM Grades(Input, Output);

BEGIN   { Grades }                    BEGIN { Main }


END.   { Grades }                     END.   { Main }
```

○ Indentation consists of two to five spaces per level.

○ The statements between a BEGIN and END should be aligned and indented. The statements following an END should be aligned with the appropriate statements before the BEGIN.

○ Indent the line following an IF, ELSE, WHILE, REPEAT, CASE, WITH, or FOR.

○ Annotate the END associated with a control structure with an in-line comment.

Here are two examples of formats which are acceptable (others are possible).

```
statement;                            statement;
IF condition THEN                     IF condition THEN BEGIN
   BEGIN                                  statement;
      statement;

                                      END   { IF }
   END   { IF }                       ELSE BEGIN
ELSE                                     statement;
   BEGIN
      statement;
                                      END; { ELSE }
   END; { ELSE }                      statement;
statement;
```

○ If the list of an input or output statement does not fit on one line, put the first word of the next line under the column following the left parentheses of the I/O statement. For example,

```
Readln(Departure, Destination, Date, DepartureTime, ArrivalTime,
       NumberInParty, AirLine, FlightNumber);
```

○ If a condition does not fit on one line, continue on the following line starting under the beginning of the condition (not the key word of the statement). For example,

```
   WHILE ((Today IN LegalHolidays) OR
          (Today IN [Saturday, Sunday])) DO
      BEGIN
```

○ If the expression to the right of the assignment operator (:=) does not fit on one line, continue it beneath the beginning of the expression in the line above. For example,

```
TodaysEarnings := TotalEarnedToDate -
                  TotalEarnedToYesterday -
                  TaxesToday;
```

○ The use of "white space" (blank spaces and lines) is advised. In particular, a section of code within a statement sequence which has a specific purpose but is too small to be a procedure may be preceded and followed by a blank line.

Variant Records

There are times when one record format does not exactly fit all the items in a class. For example, the records for the pitchers on a baseball team are likely to be different from the records for the rest of the team members. For a pitcher it might be desirable to keep his number of innings pitched, earned-run average, strikeouts, and walks. The other team members' records should include home runs and runs batted in. Pascal has a record mechanism which enables the programmer to do this. This mechanism is called the *variant record*.

The records we have used so far have had only fixed parts. It is possible to follow the fixed part of a record with a variant part. (It is possible for the fixed part to be empty and thus have a record with only a variant part.) The fixed part of a record consists of field names and types. The variant part of a record somewhat resembles the case statement. The variant part of a record includes a tag field which is used to select which of the variant fields are to be used, much as the variable of a case statement is used to select a statement to execute. Using variant records, we might declare a record type for a baseball player in this manner.

```
TYPE
    Positions = (P,          { Pitcher       }
                 C,          { Catcher       }
                 FirstB,     { First base    }
                 SecondB,    { Second base   }
                 SS,         { Shortstop     }
                 ThirdB,     { Third base    }
                 LeftF       { Left field    }
                 CenterF,    { Center field  }
                 RightF);    { Right field   }

    PlayerRec = RECORD
                    Name    : STRING[30];
                    Number,
                    Errors : Integer;
                    BatAvg : Real;
                    CASE Position : Positions OF
                        P : (InningsPitched,
                             ERA             : Real;
                             StrikeOuts,
                             Walks           : Integer);

                        C, FirstB, SecondB, SS, ThirdB, LeftF,
                        CenterF, RightF :
                                        (Singles,
                                         Doubles,
                                         Triples,
                                         HomeRuns,
                                         RBI      : Integer)
                END;  { PlayerRec }
```

```
VAR
    PlayerStats : PlayerRec;
```

The fixed part of PlayerRec consists of the fields Name, Number, Errors, and BatAvg, which may be used as usual. The remainder of PlayerRec (starting with Case) is the variant part. Position is the tag field of this variant part. It names another field of the record. Thus we may refer to PlayerStats.Position, which is a variable of type Positions. If Player-Stats.Position is P (for pitcher), we may refer to Player-Stats.InningsPitched and PlayerStats.ERA (both real variables) and to PlayerStats.StrikeOuts and PlayerStats.Walks (both denoting integer variables). It would be an error to use PlayerStats.Singles. If Player-Stats.Position is not P (i.e., was one of the other positions), then the fields for Singles, Doubles, etc., are available for use.

For example, to output some of the information in PlayerStats, we might code

```
WITH PlayerStats DO
    BEGIN
        Writeln(Name);
        CASE Position OF
            P : BEGIN
                    Writeln('Innings Pitched : ',
                            InningsPitched : 5 : 2, ' ERA : '.
                            ERA : 5 : 2);
                    Writeln('StrikeOuts : ', StrikeOuts : 5,
                            ' Walks : ', Walks)
                END; { P }
            C .. RightF :
                    Writeln('Average : ', BatAvg : 5 : 3,
                            ' RBI : ', RBI : 4)
        END { CASE }
```

When using variant records it is almost always necessary to use the case statement (as above) to properly access the fields within the variant part.

The variant part of a record consists of the key word CASE followed by the tag-field identifier, a colon, the type of the tag field, the key word OF, and a list of constants and fields. Each element of the list of constants and fields consists of a list of constants (separated by commas) followed by a colon and a list of fields and their types, which have the syntax of the fixed part of a record followed by a variant part. This field list is enclosed in parentheses. The field list may be empty. The elements of the list of constants and fields are separated by constants. The complete syntax diagram of a record is given in *FIGURE I.1*.

Notice that a record type consists of the key words RECORD and END surrounding a field list. The field list may contain any combination of a fixed part and a variant part as long as the fixed part precedes the variant part. This includes the possibility that the field list is empty. Because

Record

FIGURE I.1

Record type

$\longrightarrow$ RECORD $\longrightarrow$ field-list $\longrightarrow$ END $\longrightarrow$

Field list

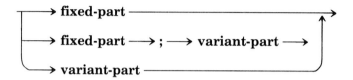

Fixed part

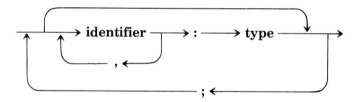

Variant part

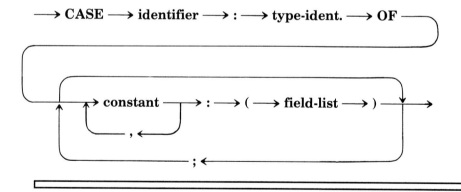

the constants of the variant part of the record are followed by a field list, variant records may be nested. This is rather uncommon. It may also happen that the field list following a constant in the variant part is empty. This is convenient for documenting that certain cases of the tag field have no fields associated with them.

One situation in which an empty field may be useful is in an update operation in which items may be added to or deleted from a list. If an item is to be added to a list, its identification number as well as other information will be needed. On the other hand, an item to be deleted needs only to have its identification number given. Thus, a record declaration for this scenario might be

```
TYPE
   ActionType = (Add, Delete);
   ItemRec    = RECORD
                    ItemNum : Integer;
                    CASE Action : ActionType OF
                        Add    : (NumToAdd : Integer;
                                      Cost    : Real);
                        Delete : ( )
                   END; { ItemRec }
```

It would be possible to build a file of records of this sort which would be useful in updating a master file.

Any time the information about items in a collection may differ (in a limited way), a variant record may be useful. In particular, by using a file of variant records, it is possible to store information about items with differing descriptions. An example of this would be a file of employee records in which some employees were paid using an hourly wage and some were salaried. Then the first type would need the hourly rate and the number of hours worked to be paid. The salaried employees would need only the weekly salary recorded.

Goto Statement

Although it is possible to write any program using the control statements expressing sequence, iteration, and condition, there may be situations in which an alternative form of control is desired. This is achieved by using the *goto statement*. If you have programmed in another language (e.g., BASIC or FORTRAN), you probably used a goto statement. Pascal provides a goto statement.

The form of a goto statement is the key word GOTO followed by a label. A label is an identifier which must be declared in a label declaration section. The label declarations precede the constant declarations in a block. Each label which is declared may precede a statement (in the same block). A colon (:) separates the label from the statement. The effect of the goto statement is to cause control to pass to the statement labeled by the label of the goto statement. The relevant syntax diagrams are presented in *FIGURE J.1*.

The label declaration section consists of the key word LABEL followed by identifiers or numbers, which are separated by commas, followed by a semicolon. The identifiers and numbers in this declaration are then labels for statements. TURBO Pascal permits any legal identifier or unsigned integer to be a label, whereas standard Pascal limits labels to unsigned integers of one to four digits.

FIGURE J.1

Label declaration section

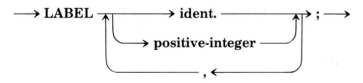

Labeled statement

⟶ label-ident. ⟶ : ⟶ unlabeled-statement ⟶

Goto statement

⟶ GOTO ⟶ label-ident. ⟶

The scope of a label is the block in which it is declared. This implies that a label may appear only in front of a statement which is in that block. Of course, only one statement in the block may have that label. TURBO requires that the label of a goto statement be in the same block as the goto statement itself. Thus, a goto may not be used to exit a procedure or function. This is somewhat more restrictive than standard Pascal.

The following program fragment (which does nothing significant) illustrates the use of labels and the goto statement.

```
LABEL
    Label1, Label2;

CONST
    Hi = 200;
    Lo = 50;


VAR
    I, J : Integer;



        IF I > Hi THEN
            GOTO Label1;


        GOTO Label2;


Label1 : Writeln('Too high');



Label2 : IF J > I THEN
            Writeln(J, ' is too big');
```

After Dijkstra's letter "Goto Statement Considered Harmful" [Di] appeared in the Communications of the A.C.M., some debate about the appropriate use of the goto statement occurred. For a while, structured programming was identified with "goto-less programming." The presence of many goto statements in a program generally indicates the need to redesign the program.

There is one situation that might call for the goto statement. It is known as the *middle exit loop*. It sometimes happens that the natural exit point of a loop occurs in the middle of the loop, as illustrated below. The goto may be used to accomplish this.

```
WHILE Condition DO
    BEGIN

            { First part of loop body }

    IF Done THEN GOTO LoopExit;

            { Second part of loop body }

    END;  { WHILE }
LoopExit :  ;
```

LoopExit labels an empty statement.

We confess that we have never used a goto statement in our own programs. Our preference is to achieve control by using Boolean variables to denote various conditions. For example, we would write the while loop with an exit in the middle as

```
WHILE Condition AND (NOT Done) DO
    BEGIN

            { First part of loop body }

    IF NOT Done THEN
        BEGIN

            { Second part of loop body }

        END { IF }
    END;  { WHILE }
```

Whether this loop has better style and easier readability than one written using the goto statement is an entirely subjective question. One must be very careful with goto statements. They can make your program obscure very easily. Good design will obviate the need for many goto statements.

SOLUTIONS TO
SELECTED
EXERCISES

CHAPTER 1

1. Some examples.

```
THE BOY RAN .
THE GIRL ATE .
HE RAN SLOWLY .
THE GOOD BOY ATE .
THE BIG GIRL RAN .
THE BOY RAN SLOWLY .
THE GOOD GIRL RAN QUICKLY .
THE GOOD, BIG BOY RAN .
THE GOOD, GOOD BOY RAN .
THE BIG GIRL RAN SLOWLY .
```

The minimum number of words in a sentence is two.

3.

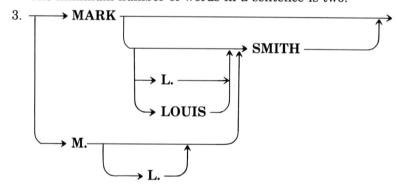

7. Algorithm to produce all two- and three-letter
   sequences made from A, B, C and D

   { Note that a blank for the third letter produces a
   two-letter sequence. }

   For FirstLetter equal to A, B, C, D
       For SecondLetter equal to A, B, C, D
           For ThirdLetter equal to A, B, C, D, blank
               Write FirstLetter, SecondLetter, ThirdLetter
               Start a new line
           End For ThirdLetter
       End For SecondLetter
   End For FirstLetter

CHAPTER 2

3.
    a.   DIR B:
    b.   DEL JUNK.TXT
    c.   TYPE NEW.TXT
    d.   B:

```
    e.    PRINT PROGRAM1.PAS                    [MS-DOS]
          PIP LST: = PROGRAM1.PAS               [CP/M]
    f.    COPY B:OLDFILE.TXT B:NEWFILE.TXT      [MS-DOS]
          PIP B:NEWFILE.TXT = B:OLDFILE.TXT     [CP/M]
    g.    PRINT B:OUTPUT.DAT                    [MS-DOS]
          PIP LST: = B:OUTPUT.DAT               [CP/M]
    h.    REN B:NEW.TXT B:NEWEST.TXT            [MS-DOS]
          REN B:NEWEST.TXT = B:NEW.TXT          [CP/M]
```

4.
```
    a.    DIR *.BAS
    b.    DEL B:*.BAK   [ MS-DOS ]
          ERA B:*.BAK    [ CP/M ]
    c.    DIR PROG????.*
    d.    DEL GARBAGE.*
          ERA GARBAGE.*
```

CHAPTER 3

1. Legal

   Illegal (Apostrophe not allowed.)

   Illegal (Period not allowed.)

   Illegal (Must not start with digit.)

   Legal

   Legal

   Illegal (Colon not allowed.)

2.
```
    a.    VAR        ˘                  { Comma, not semicolon }
               S1,
               S2 : STRING[20];

    b.    VAR                ˘    ˘     { Brackets, not parentheses }
               S1, S2 : STRING[20];

    c.    VAR
               S10,
               S10A : STRING[10];
                 ^                     { Duplicate identifiers }

    d.    |
          |                       ˘    { Missing apostrophe }
          |    Writeln('Enter two strings');

                       ˘                  { Comma, not semicolon }
               Readln(S1, S2);
                        ^                 { Semicolon, not comma }

    e.    |
          |        ˘        { S2 has not been given a value }
          |    Writeln(S1);
```

7.

```
PROGRAM BigInitials(Output);

{    A program to print a set of big initials.

     Author  :
     Date    :
     File name : CH3NUM7.PAS
}

BEGIN { BigInitials }
  Writeln;
  Writeln('********      *********');
  Writeln('*          *   *');
  Writeln('*          *   *');
  Writeln('*          *   *');
  Writeln('*          *   *********');
  Writeln('********      *');
  Writeln('*             *');
  Writeln('*             *');
  Writeln('*             *');
  Writeln('*             *')
END. { BigInitials }
```

CHAPTER 4

3. Numbers in parentheses are correct versions.

Real	Illegal (1.0)	Integer	Real
Character	Illegal (0.22E4)	Illegal (-2345)	Illegal (255E9)
Real	Real	Illegal (0.93E6)	Real
Character	Integer	Illegal (88.0E$+77$)	Real

4.

21.0	Real	2	Integer
600.0	Real	2.4	Real
41.2	Real	21	Integer
3	Integer	Error	Div only for integers
6	Integer	7.0	Real
4	Integer	-0.4	Real
0.6	Real	45	Integer
Error	Square roots of positives only	8.2	Real

5. ```
' 2 dogs'   { Space precedes other characters }
' DOG'
' DOg'
' Many dogs'
'1   dog'   { Digits precede letters }
'1 Dog'
'1 dog'
'DOG'
'DOG '
'DOGGED'
'No dogs'
'a dog'   { Small letters follow capitals }
'dog'
'dogs'
```

6. 
| | |
|---|---|
| True | False |
| True | True |
| True | True |
| False | True |
| False | True |

7.
```
             Hello
789 -- -1234
        789   -1234
789-1234
Twice 789 is 1578
```

8.

a.
```
CONST   ˇ   ˇ   { No comma, missing semicolon }
     OneThousand = 1000 ;
     Message   = 'Help I am trapped' ;
                   ^   ^   { Equals sign,
                                             missing apostrophe }

VAR   ˇ   { Start with letter }
     Skidoo : Integer ;
     Name   : String[20] ;
                     ^   { StringLength not defined }
```

b.
```
CONST
     BigNum   = 100;
     BiggerNum   = 200;
     BiggestNum = 500;
                   ^   { LargeInt undefined }

VAR
     Sum = Integer;
     Average = String[100];
                 ^   ^   { String length positive,
                                  missing semicolon }
```

c.
```
CONST
     HowMany = 30 ;
             ^ ^   { Equals sign, use constant }

VAR
     Sum   : Integer;
     CourseNum : Integer;
     Average,
     Total   : Real;
       ^   { Sum already declared }
```
```

23.
```
I
0.0
1.0
R
R
```

24.
```
(I <= 0) OR (J > 0)
(I < J) AND (J >= 0)
( (I <> J) OR (J <= 0) ) AND (J < 0)
(I <= 100) OR ( (J = 0) OR (J = 100) )
```

CHAPTER 5

1. The program plays a simple guessing game with the user. The user attempts to guess a number and the computer responds with a hint (too high or too low) or tells the user that he or she has guessed correctly.

2.
```
3
5
9
17
33
```

   The loop is executed four times. If I were initially -1, the loop would repeat forever.

3.
```
13
40
20
10
5
16
8
4
2
Done
```

   The program will terminate for any power of 2 as an initial value of I.

4.
```
12 14 17
```

The output would be the same if the values of I and K were interchanged. The statement following K := 14 tests to see whether or not I is less than J.

5.

a.
```
 ¦          ˘         { Missing semicolon }
 I := 0 ;
 WHILE I <= 10 DO
     BEGIN
       Writeln('Enter an integer');
       Readln(J);
       I := I + 1
       ^                  { Prevents infinite loop }
     END; { WHILE }
```

b.
```
 IF X >= 0 THEN                    ˘  { No semicolon }
     Writeln(X, 'is positive')
 ELSE
     Writeln(X, 'is negative');
```

c.
```
 IF X >= 0 THEN
                        { Compound statement needed }
     BEGIN
       Y := Sqrt(X);
       ^                  { Misspelling }
       Z := Sqrt(Y)
     END { IF }
     ^              { Finish compound statement }
 ELSE
                        { Compound statement needed }
     BEGIN
       Y := 0;
       Z := 0
     END; { ELSE }
     ^              { Finish compound statement }
```

CHAPTER 6

1.

a.

Red	Undefined
Yellow	Blue
2	False
1	False
4	False
Orange	False
Blue	True
5	True

b. The comparison is legal, because both variables have the same base type. The value is True.

c. No. The subranges don't overlap, so no values of one fit into the other.

d.

    i.
```
WHILE RainbowColor < Violet DO
                              ^  ( Succ(Violet) is undefined )
```

    ii.
```
    Writeln(RainbowColor);
  ^  ( Illegal statement, enumerated types may not be
      output )
```

2. 71   '+'
   '>'   98
   'J'   'o'
   'Q'   'E'
   'c'

3.
```
False       True
True        False
Undecidable { True if X is not last, but Succ(X) is not
              defined if X is last. }
True
```

4.

  a.
```
          0.00 .. 0.99 : Writeln( ---    { Reals may not be used in
          1.00 .. 1.99 : Writeln( ---      case statement }
          2.00 .. 2.99 : Writeln( ---
          3.00 .. 4.00 : Writeln( ---
```

  b.
```
                                          { 'U' was in two lists }
      'H', 'J' .. 'N', 'P' .. 'T',
      'V' .. 'Z' : Writeln(C, ' is a consonant')
                                            ^
                                      { Missing apostrophe }
```

  c.
```
                   { Colon, not equals sign }
      VAR I, Sum : Integer;

                          { Loop-control variable should not  be
          I := I + 1;     assigned within loop }
```

5.
```
CASE I OF
   1 : Writeln(I, ' is the first number.');
   2 : Writeln(I, ' is the first prime number.');
   3 : Writeln(I, ' is the first odd prime number.');
   4 : Writeln(I, ' is the first even perfect square.')
ELSE
   Writeln(I, ' is not interesting.')
END
```

7. If E2 is the last constant in an enumerated type, Succ(E2) is undefined, so the while loop fails in this instance. The for loop executes correctly.

CHAPTER 7

1.
   a. 2 4 6 8 10 12 14 16
   b. 0 1 2 3 4
   c. A B C D
2.
   a. `List1[I] := List2[4*I];`
   ` ^{ Exceeds ArraySize }`

   b. `List1[1] := Table[1, 1] + 3;`

To make this reasonable, an index must be added after List1, Table should be Table1 (or Table2), and a second index for Table1 should be used.

   c. Addition of arrays is not defined. An index must be used.

   d. `Table1[I, I] := I`
   ` ^ { Last time through loop I exceeds ArraySize }`

   e. `Table1[I, ArraySize - 1] := 2 * I;`
   ` ^ { First time through loop I is 0 }`

   f. `                      ˅ { Or causes infinite loop if K isn't in list }`
   `WHILE Continue AND (I <= ArraySize) DO`
   `                   ^ { Parentheses are needed }`

3. The effect of copying from left to right is to put the character in List[Pos] in the rest of the array List.

CHAPTER 8

1. When Size is set to 1, the parameter N in Procedure DrawASquare becomes 1. The loops forming the top and bottom are executed once, printing one asterisk. The middle loop is not executed at all.

3.
   5 11
   10 11
5.
   a.
   `PROCEDURE P(Ch : Char);`
   `                ^ { Parameter type must match type of`
   `                    argument in procedure call }`

b.
```
TYPE
      RealArray  = ARRAY[1..10] of Real;


PROCEDURE ArrayOp(VAR A : RealArray);
                               ^ { Type definition may not appear
                                   here }
```

c.
```
VAR
      J : Integer;

PROCEDURE P(VAR I : Integer);



BEGIN { Main Program }

  P(J);
      ^ { Argument to a Var parameter must be a variable }
END.   { Main Program }
```

d.
```
FUNCTION Inverse(M : RealMatrix) : Real;
                                   ^     { Function type can't
                                           be structured }

```

The inverse of a matrix is a matrix, so probably what is needed is a procedure which has a parameter to pass the inverse back.

6.
```
FUNCTION ConvertToMonths(Yrs : Real) : Integer;

{ This function converts years to months. }

CONST
      MonthsInYear = 12;

BEGIN { ConvertToMonths }
   ConvertToMonths := Round(MonthsInYear * Yrs)
END;   { ConvertToMonths }
```

Because this function rounds off, for an input of 1.1, ConvertToMonths becomes 13, which is less than 13.2. This would be to the disadvantage of the investor.

9.
```
PROCEDURE Find(VAR List : ListType;  Item : ItemType;
               NumToSearch : Integer;  VAR Pos : Integer);
```

{ This procedure finds the first place Item occurs in List. The first NumToSearch places of List are searched. If the Item is found, Pos is its place; otherwise Pos is set to 0. }

```
VAR
     Found : Boolean;

BEGIN { Find }
  Found := False;
  Pos := 0;
  REPEAT
     Pos := Pos + 1;
     IF List[Pos] = Item THEN
        Found := True
  UNTIL Found OR (Pos >= NumToSearch);
  IF NOT Found THEN
     Pos := 0
END;  { Find }
```

CHAPTER 9

1.
   a. Change NumOfTests to 8 in the constant declaration of the main program.
   b. Change AMinimum, BMinimum, CMinimum, and DMinimum to 88, 77, 66, and 55 in the constant declaration section of the function Grade.
   c. This change is a little more difficult. One way is to declare a few variables which will hold the names of the students with the highest test scores and overall average. These would be filled in the procedure DoStudentGrade.

CHAPTER 10

1.
   a.
```
    CONST
         FirstNameLen = 10;
         LastNameLen  = 20;
         AddressLen   = 15;   { Used for streets and cities }
         DeptLen      = 15;

    TYPE
         NameRec     = RECORD
                           First   : STRING[FirstNameLen];
                           MidInit : Char;
                           Last    : STRING[LastNameLen]
                       END; { NameRec }
         AddressRec = RECORD
                           Street,
                           City  : STRING[AddressLen];
                           State : STRING[2];
                           Zip   : STRING[5]
                       END; { AddressRec }
```

```
                    StudentRec = RECORD
                                  Name          : NameRec;
                                  LocalAddress,
                                  HomeAddress   : AddressRec;
                                  Major         : STRING[DeptLen];
                                  QPA           : Real;
                                  HrsComplete   : Integer;
                                  Year          : 1..5 { 1 = Fr ..
                                                         5 = Grad }
                               END;  { StudentRec }

            VAR
                Stu : StudentRec;

     c.    CONST
                NameLen = 20;

           TYPE
                NameRec    = RECORD
                                  First,
                                  Middle,
                                  Last    : STRING[NameLen]
                               END; { NameRec }
                AddressRec = RECORD
                                  Street,
                                  City   : STRING[AddressLen];
                                  State  : STRING[2];
                                  Zip    : STRING[5]
                               END; { AddressRec }
                BabyRec    = RECORD
                                  Name,
                                  MothersName,
                                  Doctor       : NameRec;
                                  Sex          : (Male, Female);
                                  BirthDate    : RECORD
                                                    Month,
                                                    Day,
                                                    Year : Integer
                                                  END; { BirthDate }

                                  Height       : Real; { In inches }
                                  Weight       : RECORD
                                                    Lbs,
                                                    Oz : Integer;
                                                  END; { Weight }
                                  HomeAddr     : AddressRec
                               END;  { BabyRec }

            VAR
                Baby : BabyRec;

  2.
     a.
            WITH Stu DO
                BEGIN
                    WITH Name DO
```

```
                      BEGIN
                        Writeln('Enter student''s name');
                        Write('First >');
                        Readln(First);
                        Write('Middle Initial >');
                        Readln(MidInit);
                        Write('Last >');
                        Readln(Last)
                      END; { WITH Name }
                    WITH LocalAddress DO
                      BEGIN
                        Writeln('Enter local address >');
                        Write('Street >');
                        Readln(Street);
                        Write('City >');
                        Readln(City);
                        Write('State (2 letter abbrev.) >');
                        Readln(State);
                        Write('ZIP >');
                        Readln(ZIP)
                      END;  { WITH LocalAddress }
                    WITH HomeAddress DO
                      BEGIN
                        Writeln('Enter home address >');
                        Write('Street >');
                        Readln(Street);
                        Write('City >');
                        Readln(City);
                        Write('State (2 letter abbrev.) >');
                        Readln(State);
                        Write('ZIP >');
                        Readln(ZIP)
                      END;  { WITH HomeAddress }
                    Write('Enter major >');
                    Readln(Major);
                    Write('Enter QPA >');
                    Readln(QPA);
                    Write('Enter hours completed >');
                    Readln(HrsComplete);
                    Write('Enter year, 1 (FR) - 5 (GRAD) >');
                    Readln(Year)
                  END; { WITH Stu }

  c.
        WITH BabyRec DO
            BEGIN
              WITH Name DO
                BEGIN
                  Writeln('Enter baby''s name');
                  Write('First >');
                  Readln(First);
                  Write('Middle >');
                  Readln(Middle);
                  Write('Last >');
                  Readln(Last)
                END; { WITH Name }
```

```
WITH MothersName DO
   BEGIN
     Writeln('Enter mother''s name');
     Write('First >');
     Readln(First);
     Write('Middle >');
     Readln(Middle);
     Write('Last >');
     Readln(Last)
   END; { WITH MothersName }
WITH Doctor DO
   BEGIN
     Writeln('Enter doctor''s name');
     Write('First >');
     Readln(First);
     Write('Middle >');
     Readln(Middle);
     Write('Last >');
     Readln(Last)
   END; { WITH Doctor }
Write('Enter sex of baby (M/F) >');
Readln(S);    { Assume S is a character variable }
IF (S = 'M') OR (S = 'm') THEN
   Sex = Male
ELSE
   Sex = Female;
WITH BirthDate DO
   BEGIN
     Writeln('Enter day of birth ');
     Write('Month (1 -12) >');
     Readln(Month);
     Write('Day (1 - 31) >');
     Readln(Day);
     Write('Year >');
     Readln(Year)
   END; { WITH BirthDate }
Write('Enter height >');
Readln(Height);
Writeln('Enter weight');
Write('Pounds >');
Readln(Weight.Lbs);
Write('Ounces >');
Readln(Weight.Oz);
WITH HomeAddr DO
   BEGIN
     Writeln('Enter home address >');
     Write('Street >');
     Readln(Street);
     Write('City >');
     Readln(City);
     Write('State (2 letter abbrev.) >');
     Readln(State);
     Write('ZIP >');
     Readln(ZIP)
  END;  { WITH HomeAddr }
```

4.
   a.
```
WITH Rec DO
   v    { Compound statement is needed to qualify R1  and  R2 }
   BEGIN
     Writeln(I1 : 5, I2 : 5);
     Writeln(R1 : 6 : 2, R2 : 6 : 2)
   END; { WITH }
   ^    { Finish compound statement }
```

   b.
```
Rec1.I := 1.9;
   ^        ^  { Type mismatch, Rec1.I is integer }

   IF Rec1 < Rec2 THEN
            ^  { Records may not be compared }
```

   c.
```
        Last   : STRING[15];
      END; { Name }
         ^   { Semicolon needed }
Birth : DateRec;
           ^  { Missing letter }
```

6. 1   9   17
    10 13 17
    14 15 17

CHAPTER 11

1.
   a.
```
Writeln(F, I, J);
          ^  { F has been opened for input, not output }
```

   b.
```
Writeln(F);
      ^  { Write must have output items }
```

   c.
```
Assign(IntF, 'INTEGER.OUT');
Rewrite(IntF);
          ^  { IntF must be opened for output }
```

   d.
```
Read(F, I);
       ^  { J is real, F is a file of integers }
```

   e.
```
PROCEDURE P(VAR F : IntegerFile);
              ^  { Files must be VAR parameters }
```

CHAPTER 12

1.
[4, 8]	Set of integer
[1, 3, 4, 5]	Set of integer
True	Boolean
['A', 'C']	Set of char
False	Boolean
[A1..B4]	SetType
[A1, A3]	SetType
[B1..B4]	SetType
False	Boolean
True	Boolean
True	Boolean
False	Boolean
True	Boolean
False	Boolean

2.

a.
```
VAR
     X : Integer;
  ¦
  ¦

X := 4;
IF X IN [1, 2, 3] THEN
   Writeln('OK');
  ¦
  ¦
```

Sets must be composed of an ordinal type, not reals.

b.
```
  ¦
IF J IN [0..9] THEN
  ¦        ^   { J is an integer, not a character }
```

c.
```
  ¦            ˇ
WHILE S <= [0 .. 10] DO
   BEGIN
      S := S + [I];
      ¦         ^
```

These changes eliminate an infinite loop.

d.
```
  ¦
IF I IN (IntSet * [1..9]) THEN
  ¦                  ^ { Sets must be of same base type,
                         ChSet base type is character }
```

3.

a.
```
FUNCTION MultipleOf7(N : Integer) : Boolean;

{ Tests whether N is a two digit multiple of 7. }
```

```
        BEGIN { MultipleOf7 }
          MultipleOf7 := (N in [7, 14, 21, 28, 35, 42, 49,
                                 56, 63, 70, 77, 84, 91, 98])
        END; { MultipleOf7 }

   c.   FUNCTION DaysInSet(S : DaySet) : Integer;

        { Function to count the days in S }

        VAR
           Count : Integer;   { Counter }
           D     : Days;      { Loop index }

        BEGIN  { DaysInSet }
          Count := 0;
          FOR D := Sun TO Sat DO
             IF D IN S THEN
                Count := Count + 1;
          DaysInSet := Count
        END;  { DaysInSet }
```

CHAPTER 13

2. If DailyData[I].Action is not 'S' or 's', the else part of an if-then-else statement is executed, which is the action taken for 'R'.

4. Additional errors to be checked.

   Amount shipped is less than number on hand.

   Range checks on number received.

   Check that Item.ID is present in the inventory file.

CHAPTER 14

1.

Start		Word	Link
5	1	HELP	10
Free	2	GOOD	9
3	3		7
	4	NICE	6
	5	BAD	2
	6	PEOPLE	0
	7		8
	8		0
	9	HELLO	1
	10	JUNK	4

4. The local variables of a procedure are dynamic variables. They do not exist until the procedure is invoked when the program is run.

5.

a.
```
IntPtr^ := 23;
         ^  { IntPtr is a pointer variable, IntPtr^ is integer
            variable }
```

b.
```
                v  { New applies only to pointer variables }
New(IntPtr1);

IntPtr2 := IntPtr1;
         ^  { Assignment must be of pointer values }
```

c.
```
   v          { Comma, not period }
P, P1 : Pointer;


P := NIL;
  ^     ( NIL is a pointer value )
```

d. The while loop is an infinite loop because P1 will never be NIL. The effect of the new and assignment statements is depicted below.

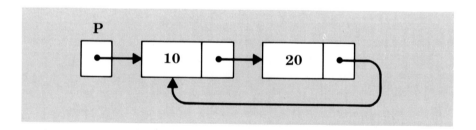

CHAPTER 15

1. Logically, Factorial(-1) causes an infinite recursion. Because memory is used each time a subprogram is called, a run-time error occurs (heap/stack collision).

ANNOTATED BIBLIOGRAPHY AND REFERENCES

[B-J] Bohm, C. and G. Jacopini, *Flow Diagrams, Turing Machines and Languages With Only Two Formation Rules*, Communications of the A. C. M., Vol. 9, No. 5 (May 1966), pp. 366–371.
The paper in which it was proven that the control structures sequence, loop, and decision were adequate for any programming task. Only for the more mathematically inclined.

[Co] Cooper, Doug, *Standard Pascal User Reference Manual*, W. W. Norton and Company, Inc., New York, 1983.
A good reference and explanation for standard Pascal, as defined by the International Standards Organization. Lots of details.

[Di] Dijkstra, E., *Goto Statement Considered Harmful*, Communications of the A.C.M., Vol. 11, No. 3, (March 1968), pp. 147–148.
The shot heard round the computing world. It launched the "goto controversy." Very readable.

[Gr] Graham, Neil, *Introduction to Computer Science*, 2nd Ed., West Publishing Co., St. Paul, MN, 1982.
A good introduction to computer science. Language independent.

[IEEE] *IEEE Standard Pascal Computer Programming Language*, The Institute of Electrical and Electronics Engineers, Inc., New York, 1983.
A technical reference to standard Pascal as defined by the American National Standards Institute. Very technical and suitable only for those already familiar with Pascal.

[J-W] Jensen, Kathleen and Niklaus Wirth, *Pascal User Manual and Report*, 2nd Ed., Springer-Verlag, New York, 1974.
The document from Pascal's creator, giving brief definitions and examples of the language. Still useful.

[Le] Ledgard, H. *The American Pascal Standard With Annotations*, Springer-Verlag, New York, 1984.
An exposition of American Standard Pascal (defined by American National Standards Institute) with some comments. Rather technical.

[L-M] Ledgard, Henry and Michael Marcotty, *The Programming Language Landscape*, Science Research Associates, Inc., Chicago, 1981.
A good and extremely readable book about programming languages. Not too technical, but challenging nonetheless.

[L-N-H] Ledgard, Henry, Paul Nagan and John Hueras, *Pascal With Style Programming Proverbs*, Hayden Book Company, Inc., Rochelle Park, NJ, 1979.
One of the best commentaries on issues of style and use of Pascal.

[Po] Polya, George, *How To Solve It*, 2nd Ed., Princeton University Press, Princeton, NJ, 1973.
A classic book on problem solving. Only mathematical examples, but extremely good advice for problem solving in general and programming in particular.

[R-R] Ralston, Anthony and Edwin D. Reilly, Jr. (eds.), *Encyclopedia of Computer Science and Engineering*, 2nd Ed., Van Nostrand Reinhold Company, Inc., New York, 1983.
Something about everything in computing. Hardware facts have become outdated, but still lots of good information. Highly recommended for filling in gaps and as a starting point for almost anything. Good browsing material.

[Ro] Roberts, Eric S., *Thinking Recursively*. John Wiley & Sons, Inc., New York, 1986.
A detailed look at recursion in its many facets. Uses Pascal. Good supplementary reading for Chapter 15.

[S-B] Schneider, G. M. and S. C. Bruell, *Advanced Programming and Problem Solving With Pascal*, John Wiley & Sons, Inc., New York, 1981.
A nice book on using Pascal with style. In-depth discussion on programming. Not recommended for learning Pascal.

[TP] *TURBO Pascal Reference Manual*, Borland International, Inc., Scotts Valley, CA, 1983.
The reference book for TURBO Pascal. A necessity for anyone using TURBO seriously.

INDEX

Trademarks

Ada	United States Department of Defense
CP/M, CP/M-86	Digital Research Corp., Inc.
MS-DOS, WordStar	Microsoft Corp.
PC-DOS	International Business Machines Corp.
TURBO Pascal	Borland International, Inc.